Animal And Vegetable Physiology
Considered With Reference
To Natural Theology
(Volume I)

Peter Mark Roget

Alpha Editions

This Edition Published in 2021

ISBN: 9789354541353

Design and Setting By
Alpha Editions
www.alphaedis.com
Email – info@alphaedis.com

As per information held with us this book is in Public Domain. This book is a reproduction of an important historical work. Alpha Editions uses the best technology to reproduce historical work in the same manner it was first published to preserve its original nature. Any marks or number seen are left intentionally to preserve its true form.

TO HIS ROYAL HIGHNESS

PRINCE AUGUSTUS FREDERICK,

DUKE OF SUSSEX, K.G.

PRESIDENT OF THE ROYAL SOCIETY,

&c. &c. &c. &c.

THIS TREATISE

IS, WITH PERMISSION, HUMBLY DEDICATED,

AS A TRIBUTE OF PROFOUND RESPECT AND GRATITUDE

FOR THE BENEFITS RESULTING TO

SCIENCE

AND ITS CULTIVATORS,

FROM HIS ILLUSTRIOUS PATRONAGE,

BY HIS DEVOTED, HUMBLE SERVANT,

P. M. ROGET.

PREFACE.

I PROBABLY never should have ventured to engage in the composition and publication of a work like the present, had not that task been assigned me by my nomination as one of the writers of the series of Bridgewater Treatises, and had I not deeply felt the honour done me by that appointment, as well as the importance of the duty which it imposed. The hope, in which I have indulged, that my labours might eventually be useful, has been my chief support in this arduous undertaking; the progress of which has throughout been seriously impeded by the various interruptions incident to my profession, by long protracted anxieties and afflictions, and by the almost overwhelming pressure of domestic calamity.

The object of this treatise is to enforce the

great truths of Natural Theology, by adducing those evidences of the power, wisdom, and goodness of God, which are manifested in the living creation. The scientific knowledge of the phenomena of life, as they are exhibited under the infinitely varied forms of organization, constitutes what is usually termed PHYSIOLOGY, a science of vast and almost boundless extent, since it comprehends within its range all the animal and vegetable beings on the globe. This ample field of inquiry has, of late years, been cultivated with extraordinary diligence and success by the naturalists of every country; and from their collective labours there has now been amassed an immense store of facts, and a rich harvest of valuable discoveries. But in the execution of my task this exuberance of materials was rather a source of difficulty; for it created the necessity of more careful selection and of a more extended plan.

In conformity with the original purpose of the work, which I have all along endeavoured to keep steadfastly in view, I have excluded

PREFACE. ix

from it all those particulars of the natural history both of animals and of plants, and all description of those structures, of which the relation to final causes cannot be distinctly traced; and have admitted only such facts as afford manifest evidences of design. These facts I have studied to arrange in that methodized order, and to unite in those comprehensive generalizations, which not only conduce to their more ready acquisition and retention in the memory, but tend also to enlarge our views of their mutual connexions, and of their subordination to the general plan of creation. My endeavours have been directed to give to the subject that unity of design, and that scientific form, which are generally wanting in books professedly treating of Natural Theology, published prior to the present series; not excepting even the unrivalled and immortal work of Paley. By furnishing those general principles, on which all accurate and extensive knowledge must substantially be founded, I am not without a hope that this compendium may prove a useful introduction to the study of Natural History; the pursuit of which will be found not only to supply inexhaustible sources of intellectual gratification, but also to furnish, to contemplative minds, a rich fountain of religious instruction. To render these benefits generally accessible, I have confined myself to such subjects as are adapted to every class of readers; and, avoiding all unnecessary extension of the field of inquiry, have wholly abstained from entering into historical accounts of the progress of discovery; contenting myself with an exposition of the present state of the science. I have also scrupulously refrained from treading in the paths, which have been prescribed to the other authors of these treatises; and have accordingly omitted all consideration of the hand, the voice, the chemical theory of digestion, the habits and instincts of animals, and the structures of antediluvian races; the extent of the field which remained, and which, with these few exceptions, embraces nearly the whole of the physiology of the two kingdoms of nature,

PREFACE. xi

already affording ample occupation for a single labourer.

The catalogue of authors whose works have furnished me with the principal facts detailed in these volumes, is too long for insertion in this place. I have not encumbered the pages of the work by continual citations of authorities; but have given references to them only when they appeared to be particularly requisite, either as bearing testimony to facts not generally known, or as pointing out sources of more copious information. It may however be proper to mention, that I have more especially availed myself of the ample materials on Comparative Anatomy and Physiology contained in the works of Cuvier, Blumenbach, Carus, Home, Meckel, De Blainville, Latreille, and St. Hilaire, and in the volumes of the Philosophical Transactions, of the Mémoires and Annales du Muséum, and of the Annales des Sciences Naturelles. I should be ungrateful were I not also to acknowledge the instruction I have derived from my attendance on the lectures at the Royal

College of Surgeons, delivered successively, during many years, by the late Sir Everard Home, Sir Astley Cooper, Mr. Lawrence, Mr. Brodie, Mr. Green, and Sir Charles Bell; and also from those of Professor Grant, at the University of London.

I have likewise to return my thanks for the liberal manner in which the Board of Curators of the Hunterian Museum gave me permission to take such drawings of the preparations it contains, as I might want for the illustration of this work; and to Mr. Clift, the conservator, and Mr. Owen, the assistant conservator of the museum, for their obliging assistance on this occasion. Mere verbal description can never convey distinct ideas of the form and structure of parts, unless aided by figures; and these I have accordingly introduced very extensively in the course of the work.*

Being compelled, from the nature of my

---

* All the wood engravings have been executed by Mr. Byfield, and the drawings for them were, for the most part, made by Miss Catlow, whose assistance on this occasion has been most valuable to me.

subject, and in order to avoid tedious and fatiguing circumlocution, to employ many terms of science, I have been careful to explain the meaning of each when first introduced: but as it might frequently happen that, on a subsequent occurrence, their signification may have been forgotten, the reader will generally find in the index, which I have, with this view, made very copious, a reference to the passage where the term is explained.

I beg, in this place, to express my deep sense of the obligation conferred on me by Mr. Davies Gilbert, the late president of the Royal Society, to whose kindness I owe my being appointed to write this treatise.

I also take this opportunity of conveying my best thanks to my friend and colleague, Mr. Children, of the British Museum, for his kind assistance in revising the sheets while the work was printing, and for his many valuable suggestions during its progress through the press.

A catalogue of the wood engravings has been subjoined; and also a tabular view of the classification of animals adopted by Cuvier in his " Regne Animal," with familiar examples of animals included under each division; both of which I conceived might prove useful for purposes of reference. The latter table is reprinted from that which I have given in my " Introductory Lecture on Human and Comparative Physiology," published in 1826, with only such alterations as were required to make it correspond with the second and improved edition of Cuvier's work.

NOTICE.

THE series of Treatises, of which the present is one, is published under the following circumstances:

The RIGHT HONOURABLE and REVEREND FRANCIS HENRY, EARL of BRIDGEWATER, died in the month of February, 1829; and by his last Will and Testament, bearing date the 25th of February, 1825, he directed certain Trustees therein named to invest in the public funds the sum of Eight thousand pounds sterling; this sum, with the accruing dividends thereon, to be held at the disposal of the President, for the time being, of the Royal Society of London, to be paid to the person or persons nominated by him. The Testator further directed, that the person or persons selected by the said President should be appointed to write, print, and publish one thousand copies of a work *On the Power, Wisdom, and Goodness of God, as manifested in the Creation; illustrating such work by all reasonable arguments, as for instance the variety and formation of God's creatures in the animal, vegetable, and mineral kingdoms; the effect of digestion, and thereby of conversion; the construction of the hand of man, and an infinite variety of other arguments; as also by discoveries ancient and modern, in arts, sciences, and the whole extent of literature.* He desired, moreover, that the profits arising from the sale of the works so published should be paid to the authors of the works.

The late President of the Royal Society, Davies Gilbert, Esq. requested the assistance of his Grace the Archbishop of Canterbury and of the Bishop of London, in determining upon the best mode of carrying into effect the intentions of the Testator. Acting with their advice, and with the concurrence of a nobleman immediately connected with the deceased, Mr. Davies Gilbert appointed the following eight gentlemen to write separate Treatises on the different branches of the subject as here stated:

THE REV. THOMAS CHALMERS, D.D.
PROFESSOR OF DIVINITY IN THE UNIVERSITY OF EDINBURGH.

ON THE POWER, WISDOM, AND GOODNESS OF GOD AS MANIFESTED IN THE ADAPTATION OF EXTERNAL NATURE TO THE MORAL AND INTELLECTUAL CONSTITUTION OF MAN.

JOHN KIDD, M.D. F.R.S.
REGIUS PROFESSOR OF MEDICINE IN THE UNIVERSITY OF OXFORD.

ON THE ADAPTATION OF EXTERNAL NATURE TO THE PHYSICAL CONDITION OF MAN.

THE REV. WILLIAM WHEWELL, M.A. F.R.S.
FELLOW OF TRINITY COLLEGE, CAMBRIDGE.

ASTRONOMY AND GENERAL PHYSICS CONSIDERED WITH REFERENCE TO NATURAL THEOLOGY.

SIR CHARLES BELL, K.G.H. F.R.S. L. & E.

THE HAND: ITS MECHANISM AND VITAL ENDOWMENTS AS EVINCING DESIGN.

PETER MARK ROGET, M.D.
FELLOW OF AND SECRETARY TO THE ROYAL SOCIETY.

ON ANIMAL AND VEGETABLE PHYSIOLOGY.

THE REV. WILLIAM BUCKLAND, D. D. F. R. S.
CANON OF CHRIST CHURCH, AND PROFESSOR OF GEOLOGY IN THE UNIVERSITY OF OXFORD.

ON GEOLOGY AND MINERALOGY.

THE REV. WILLIAM KIRBY, M. A. F. R. S.
ON THE HISTORY, HABITS, AND INSTINCTS OF ANIMALS.

WILLIAM PROUT, M. D. F. R. S.
CHEMISTRY, METEOROLOGY, AND THE FUNCTION OF DIGESTION, CONSIDERED WITH REFERENCE TO NATURAL THEOLOGY.

HIS ROYAL HIGHNESS THE DUKE OF SUSSEX, President of the Royal Society, having desired that no unnecessary delay should take place in the publication of the above mentioned treatises, they will appear at short intervals, as they are ready for publication.

CONTENTS

OF THE FIRST VOLUME.

INTRODUCTION.

	Page
CHAPTER I.—FINAL CAUSES	1
II.—THE FUNCTIONS OF LIFE	34

PART I.—THE MECHANICAL FUNCTIONS.

CHAPTER I.—ORGANIC MECHANISM	59
§ 1. Organization in general	59
2. Vegetable Organization	65
3. Developement of Vegetables	82
4. Animal Organization	96
5. Muscular Power	124
CHAPTER II.—THE MECHANICAL FUNCTIONS IN ZOOPHYTES	142
§ 1. General Observations	142
2. Porifera, or Sponges	147
3. Polypifera	161
4. Infusoria	183
5. Acalepha	192
6. Echinodermata	199
CHAPTER III.—MOLLUSCA	213
§ 1. Mollusca in general	213
2. Acephala	217

CONTENTS.

	Page
§ 3. Gasteropoda	227
4. Structure and formation of the Shells of Mollusca	230
5. Pteropoda	257
6. Cephalapoda	258

CHAPTER IV.—ARTICULATA 268
   § 1. Articulated animals in general 268
     2. Annelida 269
     3. Arachnida 282
     4. Crustacea 286

CHAPTER V.—INSECTS 296
   § 1. Aptera 296
     2. Insecta alata 299
     3. Developement of Insects 302
     4. Aquatic Larvæ 309
     5. Terrestrial Larvæ 311
     6. Imago, or perfect Insect 317
     7. Aquatic Insects 335
     8. Progressive motion of Insects on land 338
     9. Flight of Insects 344

CHAPTER VI.—VERTEBRATA 361
   § 1. Vertebrated Animals in general 361
     2. Structure and Composition of the Osseous Fabric 365
     3. Formation and developement of Bone........ 375
     4. Skeleton of the Vertebrata 386

CHAPTER VII.—FISHES 408

CHAPTER VIII.—REPTILIA 435
   § 1. Terrestrial Vertebrata in general 435
     2. Batrachia 436
     3. Ophidia 447
     4. Sauria 457
     5. Chelonia 463

CONTENTS.

	Page
CHAPTER IX.—MAMMALIA	477
§ 1. Mammalia in general	477
2. Cetacea	482
3. Amphibia	487
4. Mammiferous Quadrupeds in general	487
5. Ruminantia	499
6. Solipeda	516
7. Pachydermata	518
8. Rodentia	523
9. Insectivora	525
10. Carnivora	528
11. Quadrumana	532
12. Man	536
CHAPTER X.—VERTEBRATA CAPABLE OF FLYING	545
§ 1. Vertebrata without feathers, formed for flying	545
2. Birds	554

LIST OF ENGRAVINGS.

VOLUME I.

Fig.		Page
1	*Rotifer redivivus*, (from Muller)	62
2	*Vibrio tritici*, (Bauer)	62
3	Simple vegetable cells, (Slack)	67
4	*Fucus vesiculosus*, transverse section, (De Candolle)	67
5	Ditto, longitudinal section, (id.)	67
6	Compressed cells of vegetables, (Slack)	67
7	Hexagonal and elongated cells, (id.)	67
8	Elongated cells, (id.)	67
9	Fibrous cells, (id.)	67
10	Reticulated cells, (id.)	67
12	Junction of cells to form a tube	67
13	Beaded vessels	73
14	Spiral vessels, or Tracheæ	73
15	Annular vessels	73
16	Punctuated vessels	73
17	Transitions of vessels from one class to another	73
18	Woody fibres	73
19	Nervures of a leaf	73
20	Cells composing the cuticle, (De Candolle)	79
21	Stomata magnified, (Amici)	79
22	Arrangement of stomata in cuticle, (De Candolle)	79
23	Roots terminated by spongioles, (id.)	79
24	Cells composing a spongiole, (id.)	79
25	Animal cellular substance	99
26	Blood vessel	103
27	Section of blood vessel, with the valves open	103
28	Ditto, with the valves closed	103
29	Striated surface of the scale of the *Cyprinus alburnus*, (Heisinger)	116

LIST OF ENGRAVINGS.

Fig.		Page
30	Ditto of the *Perca fluviatilis*, (Carus)	116
31	Imbricated arrangement of the scales of fishes (Heisinger)	116
32	Section of the bulbs of hair, magnified	117
33	Quill of *Porcupine*, (F. Cuvier)	121
34	Transverse section of the same, (id.)	121
35	Longitudinal section of the root of ditto, (id.)	121
36	Capsule of bulb of ditto laid open, (id)	121
37	Muscle in a state of relaxation	129
38	The same muscle contracted	129
39	Diagram illustrating the action of oblique muscles	129
40	Semi-penniform muscle	129
41	Penniform muscle	129
42	Complex muscle	129
43	Tendon of muscle	129
44	Trapezius muscle	129
45	Muscular structure of the Ear-drum, (Home)	136
46	Orbicular muscle of the Eye-lids, (Albinus)	136
47	Muscular structure of the Iris, (Home)	136
48	Muscular fibres of a sucking disk	136
49	Longitudinal muscular fibres of a blood-vessel	137
50	Transverse muscular fibres of ditto	137
51	Muscular fibres of the human stomach, (Cooper)	137
52	Muscular fibres of the Heart, (id.)	137
53	Magnified view of a *Sponge*, (Grant)	149
54	Spicula in the texture of a *Sponge*, (id.)	149
55	Gemmule of a *Sponge*, (id.)	149
56	*Lobularia. Alcyonium pelasgica*, (Deterville)	162
57	Detached polype of ditto, (id.)	162
58	*Zoanthus, (Actinia sociata)*, (Ellis)	162
59	*Hydra viridis*, (Trembley)	162
60	*Sertularia pelasgica*, (Deterville)	165
61	*Tubipora musica*, (Ellis)	165
62	Section and polypes of ditto, magnified, (id.)	165
63	*Flustra carbasea*, (id)	165
64	Cells of ditto, magnified, (id.)	165
65	*Corallium rubrum*, (id.)	166
66	Polypes of ditto, magnified, (id.)	166
67	Section of *Gorgonia Briareus*, (id.)	166

xxiv LIST OF ENGRAVINGS.

Fig.		Page
68	*Isis hippuris*, (id.)	166
69	Polype of *Flustra carbasea*, (Grant)	166
70	Tentaculum of ditto, magnified, (id.)	166
71	*Pennatula phosphorea*, (Ellis)	174
72	Magnified view of the polypes of ditto, (id.)	174
73 to 76	Mode of progression of the *Hydra viridis*, (Trembley)	178
77	*Vorticella cyathina*, (Muller)	183
78	*Proteus diffluens*, (id.)	187
79	*Volvox globator*, (id.)	187
80	*Brachionus urceolaris*, (id.)	189
81	*Medusa pulmo*, (Macri)	192
82	*Beroe ovatus*, (Bruguiere)	194
83	*Beroe pileus* (id.)	194
84	*Velella limbosa*, (Guérin)	194
85	*Physalia atlantica* (id.)	194
86	*Actinia rufa*, (original)	198
87	Ditto expanded, (original)	198
88	*Asterias serrulata* (Bruguiere)	199
89	*Asterias regularis*, (id.)	199
90	*Echinus Ananchites ovata*, (id.)	199
91	*Clypeaster rosaceus*, (id.)	199
92	*Ophiura lacertosa*, (id.)	199
93	*Euryale muricatum*, (id.)	199
94	*Pentacrinus europæus*, (Thomson)	199
95	Ambulacra, and feet of *Asterias*, viewed from the under side, (Reaumur)	201
96	Ditto, viewed from the upper side, (id)	201
97	Vesicles appended to the feet of the *Asterias*	201
98	Polygonal pieces composing the test of the *Echinus*	204
99	Structure of a detached piece of ditto	204
100	Spine of the *Cidaris*, (Carus)	204
101	Shell of *Unio batava*, (Goldfuss)	217
102	Adductor muscle of Oyster, (Hunterian Museum)	218
103	Shell of *Pholas candida*, with abductor muscle, (Osler)	220
104	Foot of *Cardium edule*, (Reaumur)	221
105	*Planorbus cornutus* (Cuvier)	227
106	Magnified view of the striæ on the surface of Mother of Pearl, (Herschel)	232

LIST OF ENGRAVINGS.

Fig.		Page
107	Directions of the fibres in the component strata of shells	234
108	Shell of *Achatina zebra*, (De Blainville)	242
109	Longitudinal section of ditto, (id.)	242
110	Shell of *Pterocerus scorpio*, at an early stage of growth, (id.)	246
111	Shell of the same when completely formed, (id.)	246
112	Shell of *Cypræa exanthema* at an early period of growth, (id.)	246
113	Shell of the same animal, when completed, (id.)	246
114	Transverse section of the shell of the *Cypræa exanthema*, (Huterian Museum)	248
115	Shell of *Conus*	248
116	Longitudinal section of the same, (original)	248
117	Transverse section of the same, (Bruguiere)	248
118	Inner surface of the Epiphragma of the *Helix pomatia*, (De Blainville)	253
119	Outer surface of the same, (id.)	253
120	*Clio borealis*, (Cuvier)	258
121	*Sepia loligo*, (De Blainville)	259
122	Suckers of the same (id.)	259
123	Suckers of the *Octopus*, (original)	260
124	Shell of *Spirula australis*, (De Blainville)	265
125	Longitudinal section of the same (id.)	265
126	Shell of *Nautilus pompilius* (id.)	265
127	Longitudinal section of the same (id.)	265
128	*Pontobdella muricata*, (Bruguiere)	271
129	*Nereis*, (id.)	271
130	*Erpobdella vulgaris* (Lam.) *Hirudo hyalina*	271
131	Diagram illustrating the rings and muscles of *Annelida*, (original)	271
132	*Gordius aquaticus*	276
133	*Serpula opercularia*	276
134	*Terebella conchilega*, (De Blainville)	276
135	*Arenicola piscatorum*, or *Lumbricus marinus*	276
136	*Aranea diadema*, (Rœsel)	283
137	Divisions of the limb of a Crustaceous animal	287
138	Mandible and palpus of *Mysis Fabricii*, (Bruguiere)	287

xxvi LIST OF ENGRAVINGS.

Fig.		Page
139 to 141	Feet-jaws belonging to the first, second, and third pairs, (id.)	287
142	True foot, belonging to the first pair, (id.)	287
143	*Julus terrestris*	299
144	Muscles of the trunk of the *Melolontha vulgaris*, (Straus Durckheim)	300
145	Eggs of *Bombyx mori*	305
146	Larva of the same	305
147	Pupa of the same	305
148	Imago of the same	305
148* A	Caterpillar of the *Phalena striaria*, (Hubner)	315
B	The same in a rigid position, (Lyonet)	315
149	*Calosoma Sycophanta*, (Kirby and Spence)	320
150	Analysis of skeleton of the same, (Carus)	321
151	Hind view of the segment of the head in the same, (id.)	321
152	Suckers on the foot of the *Musca vomitoria*, expanded; magnified view, (Bauer)	333
153	Cushions on the foot of the *Cimbex lutea*, magnified, (id.)	333
154	Suckers on the under side of the foot of a male *Dytiscus marginalis*, (id.)	333
155	Cushions and sucker of the *Acridium biguttulum*, Latr. (id.)	333
156	*Dytiscus marginalis*, upper side, (Rœsel)	336
157	Lower side of the same insect, (id.)	336
158	*Notonecta glauca*, (Rœsel)	337
158*	Fore leg of *Gryllotalpa*, (Kidd)	343
159	Wing of *Gryllus nasutus*. Orthoptera	350
160	Wing of *Libellula grandis*. Neuroptera	350
161	Wing of *Ichneumon persuasorius*. Hymenoptera	350
162	Wing of *Tipula oleracea*. Diptera	350
163	Sting of *Anthophora retusa*, (original)	350
164	Separate scales of the wing of *Hesperia Sloanus*, (original)	355
165	Arrangement of the scales in the wing of the same	355
172	Longitudinal section of the thigh-bone to show the cancellated structure, (Cheselden)	373
173	Longitudinal section of the humerus, (id.)	373
174	Ossification of the parietal bone, (id.)	379

LIST OF ENGRAVINGS. xxvii

Fig.		Page
175	Early stage of ossification of the bones of the skull, (Cloquet)	379
176	The same in the adult, showing the sutures	379
177	Dorsal vertebra, human	388
178	Junction of vertebræ forming the spinal column	388
179	Longitudinal section of the same, showing the spinal canal	388
180	Elements of structure of a vertebra, (Carus)	303
181	Skeleton of Hog, (Pander and D'Alton)	402
182	Sternum, clavicle, and scapula; human	402
184	Skeleton of *Cyprinus carpio*, (Bonnaterre)	411
185	Diagram illustrating the progressive motion of Fishes	412
186	Front view of the vertebra of a Cod, (*Gadus morrhua*)	414
187	Side view of the same	414
188	Vertical and longitudinal section of a part of the spinal column in the same	414
189	A similar section, showing the gradation of structure	414
190	Similar section in the *Squalus centrina*, (Carus)	414
191	Bones of the shoulder of the *Lophius piscatorius*, (id.)	422
192	Pectoral fin of the *Raia clavata*, (id.)	422
193	Belt of bones of the shoulder of a Ray, (id.)	423
194	Muscular system of *Cyprinus alburnus*, (id.)	425
195	Air bladder of *Cyprinus carpio*, (Blasius)	429
196	Eggs of the Frog	437
197	Side view of Tadpole magnified, (Rusconi)	437
198	Upper view of the same, (id.)	437
199	Adult Frog	437
200	Skeleton of Frog, (Cheselden)	441
201	Skeleton of the Viper	447
202	Ribs and spine of *Boa constrictor*, (Home)	450
203	Bones of the foot of the same, (Mayer)	448
204	Muscles moving the claw of the same, (id.)	448
205	Rudimental bones of the foot of the *Tortryx scytale*, (id.)	448
206	—— of the *Tortrix corallinus*, (id.)	448
207	—— of the *Anguis fragilis*, (id.)	448
208	—— of the *Amphisbæna alba*, (id.)	448
209	—— of the *Coluber pullutatus*, (id.)	448

Fig.		Page
210	*Chalcides pentadactylus*, (Bonnaterre)	448
211	Under surface of the foot of the *Lacerta gecko*, magnified four times, (Bauer)	461
212	Side view of a longitudinal section of the same, (id.)	461
213	Skeleton of Tortoise, (Carus)	465
214	Section of the thigh bone of the same (id.)	465
215	Hind view of skull of *Testudo mydas*, (id.)	469
216	Bones sustaining the fin of the *Delphinus phocœna*, (Pander and D'Alton)	486
217	Fore part of the Skeleton of an Ox with the *Ligamentum nuchæ*, (original)	502
218	Skeleton of the Stag, (Cheselden)	507
218*A.	Longitudinal section of the horn of an Ox, (original)	515
B.	Ditto, of an Antelope, (original)	515
C.	Extremity of the same, (original)	515
219	Subcutaneous muscles of the Hedge-hog, relaxed, (Carus)	528
220	The same muscles contracted, and drawn over the body, (Cuvier)	528
221	Skeleton of the Lion, (Pander and D'Alton)	530
222	Skeleton of *Draco volans*, (Tiedemann)	550
223	Skeleton of *Vespertilio Molossus*, (Temmink)	551
224	Skeleton of the Swan, (Cheselden)	559
225	Lateral section of the cervical vertebra of the Ostrich, (original)	563
226	Fibrils of the vane of a feather, magnified, (original)	570
227	Edges of the fibres, magnified, (original)	570
228	Feather, showing its structure, (F. Cuvier)	575
229	Capsule, or Matrix of the feather, (id.)	575
230	View of the parts enclosed in the Capsule, when laid open, (id.)	575
231	Section of the stem, while growing, exhibiting the series of conical membranes, (id.)	575
233	Extensor muscles of the foot and toes of a bird, (Borelli)	589
234	Position of a bird in roosting, (id.)	589

VOLUME II.

Fig.		Page
239	Cyclosis, or partial circulation in the cells of the *Caulinia fragilis*, magnified, (Amici)	50
240	The same in the jointed hair of the *Tradescantia virginica*, (Slack)	50
241	Section of the *Hydra vividis*, magnified, (Trembley)	74
242	*Hydra vividis* seizing a worm, (id.)	76
243	The same after swallowing a minnow, (id.)	76
244	A Hydra which has swallowed another of its own species, (id.)	76
245	Compound Hydra, with seven heads, (id.)	76
246	*Veretilla lutea*, showing the communicating vessels of the Polypes, (Quoy et Gaimard)	83
247	Nutrient vessels of the *Tænia solium* (Chiaje)	83
248	*Tænia globosa*, or Hydatid of the Hog, (Goeze)	83
249	Horizontal section of the *Rhizostoma Cuvieri*, Peron, (Eysenhardt)	88
250	*Geronia Hexaphylla*, Peron, *Medusa proboscidalis*, (Forskal)	88
251	Vascular net-work in margin of the disk of the *Rhizostoma Cuvieri*, (Eysenhardt)	88
252	Vertical Section of the *Rhizostoma Cuvieri*, (id.)	89
253	Transverse section of one of the arms of the same, (id.)	89
254	Transverse section of the extremity of a tentaculum of the same, (id.)	89
255	*Leucophra patula*, highly magnified, (Ehrenberg)	96
256	Alimentary canal and cæca of the same, viewed separately, (id.)	66
257	Vertical section of the *Actinia coriacea*, (Spix)	99
258	Digestive organs of the *Asterias*, (Tiedemann)	100
259	Stomachs of the *Nais vermicularis*, (Rœsel)	102
260	Stomachs of the *Hirudo medicinalis*, (original)	103
261	Mouth of the same, showing the three semicircular teeth, (original)	103
262	Tooth of the same, detached, (original)	103

LIST OF ENGRAVINGS.

Fig.		Page
263	*Glossopora tuberculata; Hirudo complanata*, Lin. (Johnson)	104
264	The same seen from the under side, showing the digestive organs, (id.)	104
265	Diagram showing the arrangement and connexions of the organs of the vital functions in Vertebrata, (original)	106
266	Spiral probosces of *Papilio urticæ*, (Griffith)	114
267	Trophi of *Locusta viridissima*, (Goldfuss)	122
268	Filaments composing the rostrum, or proboscis, of the *Cimex nigricornis*, (Savigny)	125
269	Sheath of the proboscis of the same insect, (id.)	125
270	Toothed cartilage of the *Helix pomatia*, (Cuvier)	126
271	Mechanism for projecting and retracting the tongue of the Woodpecker, (original)	132
272	Laminæ of Whalebone descending from the palate of the *Balæna mysticetus*, (Bonnaterre)	137
273	Teeth of the *Delphinus phocœna* (Cloquet)	142
274	Skull of Tiger, (Cuvier)	146
275	Skull of Antelope, (Pander and D'Alton)	147
276	Skull of Rat, (id.)	148
277	Longitudinal section of simple tooth, (Rousseau)	151
278	Surface of the grinding tooth of a Horse, (Home)	151
279	Surface of the grinding tooth of a Sheep, (id.)	151
280	Longitudinal section of the incisor tooth of the Rodentia	151
281	Vertical section of the grinding tooth of the Elephant, (Home)	154
282	Grinding tooth of the African Elephant, (id.)	154
283	Grinding tooth of the Asiatic Elephant, (id.)	154
284	Succession of teeth in the Crocodile, (Carus)	163
285	Venomous fang of the *Coluber naia*, (Smith)	165
286	Transverse section of the same, (id.)	165
287	The same tooth at an earlier period of growth, (id.)	165
288	The same, still less advanced in its growth, (id.)	165
289	Base of the former, (id.)	165
290	Base of the latter, (id.)	165
291	Transverse section of the young fang, about its middle, (id.)	165

LIST OF ENGRAVINGS. xxxi

Fig.		Page
292	A section, similar to the last, of another species of serpent, (id.)	165
293	*Squalus pristis*. B. Under side of its snout, (Latham)	166
294	Interior of the Stomach of a Lobster, (original)	167
295	Gastric teeth of *Bullœa aperta*, (Cuvier)	168
298	Gizzard of the *Swan*, (Home)	169
299	Crop and gizzard of the *Parrot*, (id.)	179
300	Crop of the *Pigeon*, (id.)	179
301	Human stomach, (id.)	182
302	Interior of the stomach of the *African Ostrich*, (id.)	185
303	Gastric glands of the same, (id.)	185
304	Gastric glands of the *American Ostrich*, (id.)	185
305	Longitudinal section of the gastric glands of the *Beaver*, (id.)	185
306	Stomach of Dormouse, (id.)	191
307	Stomach of *Hyrax capensis*, (Cuvier)	191
308	Stomach of *Porcupine*, (id.)	191
309	Stomach of *Kanguroo*, (id)	191
310	Stomach of *Delphinus phocæna*, (id.)	191
311	Cardiac valve of the Horse, (Gurlt)	192
312	The four stomachs of a Sheep, (Carus)	192
313	Inner surface of the honey-comb stomach, (Home)	192
314	Inner surface of the many-plies stomach of an Ox, (id.)	192
315	Interior cellular surface of the second stomach of the Camel, (id.)	192
316	Spiral valve in the intestine of the Shark, (Blasius)	205
317	Digestive organs of the *Mantis religiosa*, (Marcel de Serres)	211
318	—— *Melolontha vulgaris*, (Léon Dufour)	213
319	—— *Cicindela campestris*, (id.)	213
320	Portion of a hepatic vessel of the *Melolontha*, highly magnified, (Straus Durckheim)	214
321	Alimentary canal of the *Acrida aptera*, (original)	214
322	Interior of the gizzard of the same magnified, (original)	214
323	Row of large teeth in the same, still more magnified, (original)	214
324	Profile of one of those teeth still more highly magnified, (original)	214

xxxii   LIST OF ENGRAVINGS.

Fig.		Page
325	Base of the same tooth seen from below, (original)	214
326	Alimentary canal of the Larva of the *Sphinx Ligustri*, (original)	217
327	——— of the Pupa of the same, (original)	217
328	——— of the Imago of the same, (original)	217
329	——— of the *Patella*, (Cuvier)	220
330	Stomachs of the *Pleurobranchus Peronii*, (id.)	220
331	Pyloric appendices in the *Salmon*, (id.)	222
333	Detached Dorsal vessel of *Melolontha vulgaris*, (Straus Durckheim)	237
334	The same with its ligamentous and muscular attachments, (id.)	237
335	Side view of the anterior extremity of the same vessel, (id.)	237
336	Section of the dorsal vessel to show its valves, (id.)	237
337	Circulation in the antenna of the *Semblis viridis*, (Carus)	342
338	Course of circulation in the same insect, (id.)	342
339	Dorsal vessel of the Caterpillar of the *Sphinx ligustri*, side view, (original)	245
340	The same in the Chrysalis, (original)	245
341	The same in the Moth, (original)	245
342	The same viewed from above, (original)	245
343	Magnified lateral view of the anterior extremity of the dorsal vessel, (original)	245
344	Magnified dorsal view of the same, (original)	245
345	Structure of the valves of the dorsal vessel, (original)	245
346	Heart and vessels of the *Aranea domestica* (Treviranus)	249
346*	Circulation in the *Planaria nigra*, (Dugés)	250
347	Course of circulation in the *Erpobdella vulgaris* (Morren)	253
348	Vessels in abdominal surface of the same, (id.)	253
349	Vascular dilatations, or hearts of the *Lumbricus terrestris*, (Morren)	255
350	Cavities and great vessels of the Heart	259
351	The Heart laid open to show its Valves	260
352	Plan of simple circulation	262
353	Plan of double circulation	266
354	Branchial circulation in *Maia Squinado*, (Audouin)	269

LIST OF ENGRAVINGS. xxxiii

Fig.		Page
355	Organs of circulation in the *Loligo sagittata*, (id.)	271
356	Plan of circulation in Fishes	272
357	Plan of circulation in Batrachia	274
359	Plan of double, or warm-blooded circulation	278
360	Heart of the *Dugong*, (Home)	279
361	Valves of the Veins, (Cloquet)	288
366	Heart, branchial artery and gills of a fish, (Blasius)	302
267	Branchial apertures in the *Squalus glaucus*, (Bonnaterre)	302
368	Branchial apertures in the *Petromyzon marinus*, (id.)	302
369	Internal structure of the branchiæ of the same, (Home)	302
370	Stigmata in the abdominal surface of the *Dytiscus marginalis*, (Léon Dufour)	311
371	Stigmata of *Cerambyx heros*, (Fab.) magnified, (id.)	311
372	Longitudinal tracheæ of *Carabus auratus*, (id.)	311
373	Air vesicles and tracheæ of the *Scolia hortorum*, (Fab.) highly magnified, (id.)	311
374	Respiratory apparatus of the *Scorpio europæus*, (Treviranus)	315
375	Internal structure of the lungs of the *Turtle*, (Bojanus)	322
377	Air cells of the *Ostrich*, (Parisian Academicians)	328
378	Lymphatic Absorbents	352
379	Passage of Nerves through a ganglion	359
380	Plexus of nerves	359
381	Varieties of forms of antennæ of Insects, (Goldfuss)	384
382	Vertical and longitudinal section of the right nostril in man	400
383	Vertical transverse section of the same	401
384	Transverse section of the nostril of a *Sheep*, (Harwood)	402
385	Turbinated bones of the *Seal*, (id.)	402
386	Turbinated bones of the *Turkey*, (id.)	405
387	Nerves distributed to the bill of the *Duck*, (id.)	406
388	Nasal cavities of the *Perca fluviatilis*, (Cuvier)	410
389	Nasal cavity of the *Raia batis* or Skate, (Harwood)	410
390	Human ear, (Cloquet)	421
391	Posterior surface of the cavity of the tympanum, (id.)	425
392	Ossicula auditus, or small bones of the tympanum	425
393	The position of the latter in the tympanum	425

LIST OF ENGRAVINGS.

Fig. / Page

394 Magnified view of the labyrinth detached from the surrounding parts, (Breschet) 427
395 Interior structure of the labyrinth, (id.) 428
396 Membranous labyrinth, with its nerves, (id.) 428
397 Cretaceous bodies in the labyrinth of the *Dog*, (id.).. 428
398 Ditto in that of the *Hare*, (id.) 428
399 Organ of hearing in the *Lobster*, (Carus) 435
400 Groove in the sac of the former, (id.) 435
401 Organ of hearing in the *Astacus fluviatilis*, (id.) 435
402 Interior view of the same, (id.) 435
403 Membranous labyrinth of the *Lophius piscatorius*, (id.) 438
404 Organ of hearing in the *Frog*, (Bell) 430
405 Ear of the *Turkey*, (Carus)...................... 430
406 Diagram illustrating one mode of obtaining images of objects, (original)........................... 450
407 Simple Camera Obscura 451
408 Law of the refraction of a ray of light 454
409 Convergence of rays to a focus 455
410 Convergence by a double convex lens 457
411 Spherical aberration........................... 458
412 Variations of focal distance, consequent upon variations of divergence of the incident rays 459
415 Horizontal section of right human eye magnified, (Home) 461
416 Straight and oblique muscles of the eye-ball 464
417 Lacrymal apparatus............................ 467
418 Eye of *Helix pomatia*, (Muller) 481
419 Stemmata of *Caterpillar*, (Marcel de Serres) 484
420 Eye of the *Scorpio tunensis*, (Muller).............. 484
421 Conglomerate eyes of *Julus terrestris*, (Kirby and Spence) 484
422 External magnified view of the compound eye of the *Melolontha vulgaris*, (Straus Durckheim) 487
423 Ditto of that of a *Phalena* 487
424 Section of the compound eye of the *Libellula vulgata*, magnified, (Dugès) 487
425 Highly magnified view of the outer margin of the preceding section, (id.).......................... 488
426 Portion of the section of the eye of the *Melolontha vulgaris*, (Muller) 488

LIST OF ENGRAVINGS.

Fig.		Page
427	Portion of the section of the eye of the *Libellula*, (Dugès)	488
428	Portion of the section of the eye of the *Melolontha vulgaris*, (Straus Durckheim)	488
430	Interior of the eye of the *Perca fluviatilis*, (Cuvier)	488
431	Fibres of the crystalline lens of the *Cod*, (Brewster)	496
432	Denticulated structure of these fibres, (id.)	496
433	Section of the eye of the *Goose*, (Home)	501
434	Nictitating membrane of a Bird, (Petit)	501
435	Muscles of the nictitating membrane, (id.)	501
438	*Talitrus*, (Latreille)	542
439	Nervous system of the *Talitrus*, (Audouin)	543
440	Nervous system of *Cymothoa*, Fab. (id.)	543
441	Nervous system of *Maia squinado*, (id.)	545
442	Nervous system of the Larva of the *Sphinx ligustri*, (Newport)	547
443	Ditto of the Chrysalis of the same, (id.)	547
444	Ditto of the Imago of the same, (id.)	547
445	Nervous system of the *Asterias*, (Tiedemann)	550
446	Ditto of the *Aplysia*, (Cuvier)	550
447	—— of the *Patella*, (id.)	550
448	—— of the *Sepia Octopus*, (id.)	550
449	Brain and spinal marrow of the *Columba turtur*, (id.)	552
450	Transverse section of the spinal marrow of the *Cyprinus carpio*	552
451	Brain and spinal marrow of the *Trigla lyra*, (Arsaky)	552
452	Brain of the *Muræna conger*, (Serres)	552
453	—— *Perca fluviatilis*, (Cuvier)	552
454	—— *Testudo mydas*, (Carus)	552
455	—— *Crocodile*, (id.)	552
456	—— *Lion*, (Serres)	552
457	Lateral view of the brain of the *Perch*, (Cuvier)	552
458	—— of the *Testudo mydas*, (Carus)	552
459	—— of a section of the brain of the *Dove*, (id.)	552
460	—— of the *Lion*	552
461	Vertical section of the human brain, (Monro)	560
462	Progressive changes in the *Monas*	584
463	—— *Vorticella*	584

OUTLINE OF CUVIER'S CLASSIFICATION OF ANIMALS;

WITH EXAMPLES OF ANIMALS BELONGING TO EACH DIVISION.

I. VERTEBRATA.
1. MAMMALIA.

Bimana	Man.
Quadrumana	Monkey, Ape, Lemur.
Cheiroptera	Bat, Colugo.
Insectivora	Hedge-hog, Shrew, Mole.
Plantigrada	Bear, Badger, Glutton.
Digitigrada	Dog, Lion, Cat, Martin, Weasel, Otter.
Amphibia	Seal, Walrus.
Marsupialia	Opossum, Kanguroo, Wombat.
Rodentia	Beaver, Rat, Squirrel, Porcupine, Hare.
Edentata	Sloth, Armadillo, Ant-eater, Pangolin, Ornithorhyncus.
Pachydermata	Elephant, Hog, Rhinoceros, Tapir, Horse.
Ruminantia	Camel, Musk, Deer, Giraffe, Antelope, Goat, Sheep, Ox.
Cetacea	Dolphin, Whale.

2. AVES.

Accipitres	Vulture, Eagle, Owl.
Passeres	Thrush, Swallow, Lark, Crow, Sparrow, Wren.
Scansores	Woodpecker, Cuckoo, Toucan, Parrot.
Gallinæ	Peacock, Pheasant, Grous, Pigeon.
Grallæ	Plover, Stork, Snipe, Ibis, Flamingo.
Palmipedes	Auk, Grebe, Gull, Pelican, Swan, Duck.

3. REPTILIA.

Chelonia	Tortoise, Turtle, Emys.
Sauria	Crocodile, Lizard, Gecko, Chameleon.
Ophidia	Serpents, Boa, Viper.
Batrachia	Frog, Salamander, Newt, Proteus, Siren.

4. PISCES.

Acanthopterygii	Perch, Mackerel, Sword-fish, Mullet.
Malacopterygii	Salmon, Herring, Pike, Carp, Silurus, Cod, Sole, Remora, Eel.
Lophobranchi	Pike-fish, Pegasus.
Plectognathi	Sun-fish, Trunk-fish.
Chondropterygii	Lamprey, Shark, Ray, Sturgeon.

II. MOLLUSCA.

1. Cephalopoda . . Cuttle-fish, Calamary, Nautilus.
2. Pteropoda . . . Clio, Hyalæa.
3. Gasteropoda . . Slug, Snail, Limpet, Whelk.
4. Acephala . . . Oyster, Muscle, Ascidia.
5. Brachiopoda . . Lingula, Terebratula.
6. Cirrhopoda . . Barnacle.

III. ARTICULATA.

1. Annelida.

Tubicola . . . Serpula, Sabella, Amphitrite.
Dorsibranchia . . Nereis, Aphrodite, Lob-worm.
Abranchia . . . Earth-worm, Leech, Nais, Hair-worm.

2. Crustacea.

1. **Malacostraca.**
   Decapoda . . Crab, Lobster, Prawn.
   Stomapoda . . Squill, Phyllosoma.
   Amphipoda . Gammarus, Sand-hopper.
   Læmodipoda . Cyamus.
   Isopoda . . . Wood-louse.
2. Entomostraca . Monoculus.

3. Arachnida.

Pulmonalia . . Spider, Tarantula, Scorpion.
Trachealia . . . Phalangium, Mite.

4. Insecta.

Aptera . . . . Centipede, Podura.
Coleoptera . . . Beetle, Glow-worm.
Orthoptera . . . Grasshopper, Locust.
Hemiptera . . . Fire-fly, Aphis.
Neuroptera . . . Dragon-fly, Ephemera.
Hymenoptera . . Bee, Wasp, Ant.
Lepidoptera . . Butterfly, Moth.
Rhipiptera . . . Xenos, Stylops.
Diptera . . . . Gnat, House-fly.

IV. ZOOPHYTA.

1. Echinodermata . Star-fish, Urchin.
2. Entozoa . . . Fluke, Hydatid, Tape-worm.
3. Acalephæ . . Actinia, Medusa.
4. Polypi . . . Hydra, Coral, Madrepore, Pennatula.
5. Infusoria . . Brachionus, Vibrio, Proteus, Monas.

ANIMAL AND VEGETABLE PHYSIOLOGY.

INTRODUCTION.

Chapter I.

Final Causes.

To investigate the relations which connect Man with his Creator is the noblest exercise of human reason. The Being who bestowed on him this faculty cannot but have intended that he should so exercise it, and that he should acquire, through its means, some insight, however limited, into the order and arrangements of creation; some knowledge, however imperfect, of the divine attributes; and a distinct, though faint, perception of the transcendent glory with which those attributes are encompassed. To Man have been revealed the POWER, the WISDOM, and the GOODNESS of GOD, through the medium of the Book of Nature, in the varied pages of which they are inscribed in indelible characters. On Man has been conferred the high privilege of interpreting these characters, and of deriving from their contemplation those ideas of grandeur and sublimity, and those emotions of admiration and of gratitude, which elevate and refine the soul, and transport it into regions of a purer and more exalted being.

A study which embraces so extensive a range of objects, and which involves questions of such momentous interest to mankind, must necessarily be arduous, and requires for its successful prosecution the strenuous exertions of the human intellect, and the combined labours of different classes of philosophers, during many ages. The magnitude of the task is increased by the very success of those previous efforts: for the difficulties augment as the objects multiply, and the eminence on which the accumulated knowledge of centuries has placed us only discloses a wider horizon, and the prospect of more fertile regions of inquiry; till at length the mind, conscious of the inadequacy of its own powers to the comprehension of even a small part of the system of the universe, is appalled by the overwhelming consideration of the infinity that surrounds us. The reflection continually presents itself that the portion of creation we are here permitted to behold is as nothing when compared with the immensity of space, which, on every side, spreads far beyond the sphere of our vision, and indeed far beyond the powers of human imagination. Of the planetary system, which includes this earth, our knowledge is almost entirely limited to the mathematical laws that regulate the motions of the bodies which compose it, and to the celestial mechanism which patient investigation has at length discovered to be that most admirably calculated to preserve their harmony and maintain their stability. Still less have we the means of penetrating into the remoter regions of the heavens, where the result of our investigations respecting the myriads of luminous bodies they contain amounts to little more than the knowledge of their existence, of their countless numbers, and of the immeasurable distances at which they are dispersed throughout the boundless realms of space.

Measured on the vast scale of the universe, the globe we inhabit appears but as an atom; and yet, within the compass of this atom, what an inexhaustible variety of objects is contained: what an endless diversity of phenomena is presented; what wonderful changes are occurring in rapid and perpetual succession! Throughout the whole series of terrestrial beings, what studied arrangements, what preconcerted adaptations, what multiplied evidences of intention, what signal proofs of beneficent design exist to attract our notice, to excite our curiosity, and to animate our inquiries. Splendid as are the monuments of divine power and wisdom displayed throughout the firmament, in objects fitted by their stupendous magnitude to impress the imagination and overpower us by their awful grandeur, not less impressive, nor less replete with wonder, are the manifestations of those attributes in the minuter portions of nature, which are more on a level with our senses, and more within the reach of our comprehension. The modern improvements of optical science, which have expanded our prospects into the more distant regions of the universe, have likewise brought within our range of vision the more diminutive objects of creation, and have revealed to us many of the secrets of their structure and arrangement. But, farther, our reason tells us that, from the infinite divisibility of space, there still exist worlds far removed from the cognizance of every human sense, however assisted by the utmost refinements of art; worlds occupied by the elementary corpuscles of matter, composing, by their various configurations, systems upon systems, and comprising endless diversities of motions, of complicated changes, and of widely extended series of causes and effects, destined for ever to remain invisible to human eyes, and inscrutable to human science.

Thus, in whatever field we pursue our inquiries, we are sure to arrive at boundaries within which our powers are circumscribed. Infinity meets us in every direction, whether in the ascending or descending scale of magnitude; and we feel the impotence of our utmost efforts to fathom the depths of creation, or to form any adequate conception of that supreme and Dominant Intelligence, which comprehends the whole chain of being extending from that which is infinitely small to that which is infinitely great.

It is incumbent on us, before engaging in a study of such vast importance, and extending over so wide a field as that which lies before us, to examine with attention the nature of those processes of reasoning, by which we are conducted to the knowledge of the peculiar class of truths we are seeking. Such a preliminary inquiry is the more necessary, inasmuch as the investigation of these truths is beset with many formidable difficulties and liable to various sources of fallacy, which are not met with in the study of other departments of philosophy.

The proper objects of all human knowledge are the relations that exist among the phenomena of which the mind has cognizance. The phenomena of the universe may be viewed as connected with one another either by the relation of *cause* and *effect*, or by that of *means* and *end;* and accordingly these two classes of relations give rise to different kinds of knowledge, each of which requires to be investigated in a peculiar mode and by a different process of reasoning. The foundation of both these kinds of knowledge is, indeed, the same; namely, the constant uniformity which takes place in the succession of events, and which, when traced in particular classes of phenomena, constitutes what we metaphorically call the *Laws of Nature*. It is the province of philosophy, strictly so called, to discover the circumstances or laws which regulate this uniformity, and to arrange the observed changes according to their invariable antecedents, or *causes:* the unknown links by which these causes are connected with their respective consequents, or *effects*, being denominated the *powers of Nature*. With reference to phenomena which are purely mechanical, that is, to changes which consist in the sensible motions of material bodies, these powers are denominated *forces;* and the intensities, the operations, and the characters of these forces admit of exact definition, according to the qualities of the corresponding effects they produce. It is by pursuing the method of philosophical induction, so well explained by Bacon, that the physical sciences, which the misdirected efforts of former ages had failed to advance, have, within the last two centuries, been carried to a height of perfection which affords just grounds for exultation in the achievements of the human intellect.

In the investigation of the powers which are concerned in the phenomena of living beings we meet with difficulties incomparably greater than those that attend the discovery of the physical forces by which the parts of inanimate matter are actuated. The elements of the inorganic world are few and simple; the combinations they present are in most cases easily unravelled; and the powers which actuate their motions, or effect their union and their changes, are reducible to a small number of general laws, of which the results may, for the most part, be anticipated, and exactly determined by calculation. What law, for instance, can be more simple than that of gravitation, to which all material bodies, whatever be their size, figure, or other properties, and whatever be their relative positions, are equally subjected; and of which the observations of modern astronomers have rendered it probable that the influence extends to the remotest regions of space? The most undeviating regularity is exhibited in the motions of those stupendous planetary masses, which continually roll onwards in the orbits prescribed by this all-pervading force. Even the slighter perturbations occasioned by their mutual influence are but direct results of the same general law, and are necessarily restrained within certain limits, which they never can exceed, and by which the permanence of the system is effectually secured. All the terrestrial changes dependent on these motions partake of the same constancy. The same periodic order governs the succession of day and night, the rise and fall of the tides, and the return of the seasons: which order, as far as we can perceive, is incapable of being disturbed by any existing cause.

Equally definite are the operations of the forces of cohesion, of elasticity, or of whatever other mechanical powers of attraction or repulsion there may be, which actuate, at insensible distances, the particles of matter. We see liquids, in obedience to these forces, collecting in spheroidal masses, or assuming, at their contact with solids, certain curvilinear forms, which are susceptible of precise mathematical determination. In different circumstances, again, we behold these particles suddenly changing their places, marshalling themselves in symmetric order, and constructing by their union solid crystals of determinate figure, having all their angles and facets shaped with mathematical exactness.

The forces by which dissimilar particles are united into a chemical compound have been termed *Chemical Affinities*; and the operation of these peculiar forces is as definite and determinable as the former. They are now known to be regulated by the law of definite proportions; a law, the discovery of which has conferred on Chemistry the same character of precision which appertains to the exact sciences, and which it had never before attained. The phenomena of Light, of Heat, of Electricity, and of Magnetism have been, in like manner, reduced to laws of sufficient simplicity to admit of the application of mathematical reasoning, and to furnish the accurate results derived from such application.

Thus to whatever department of physical science our researches have extended, we every where meet with the same regularity in the phenomena, the same simplicity in the laws, and the same uniformity in the results. All is strictly defined, and subjected to rigid rule: all is subordinate to one pervading principle of order. The great Creator of the universe has exercised in its construction the severest and most refined geometry, has traced with unerring precision the boundaries of all its parts, and has prescribed to each element and each power its respective sphere and limit.

Far different is the aspect of living Nature. The spectacle here offered to our view is every where characterised by boundless variety, by inscrutable complexity, by perpetual mutation. Our attention is solicited to a vast multiplicity of objects, curious and intricate in their mechanism, exhibiting peculiar movements, actuated by new and unknown powers, and gifted with high and refined endowments. In place of the simple combinations of elements, and the simple properties of mineral bodies, all organic structures, even the most minute, present exceedingly complicated arrangements, and a prolonged succession of phenomena, so varied and so anomalous, as to be utterly irreducible to the known laws which govern inanimate matter. Let us hasten, with fresh ardour, to explore this new world that here opens to our view.

Turning, then, from the examination of the passive objects of the material world, we now direct our attention to the busy theatre of animated existence, where scenes of wonder and enchantment are displayed in endless variety around us; where life in its ever-changing forms meets the eye in every region to which our researches can extend; and where every element and every clime is peopled by multitudinous races of sensitive beings, who have received from the bounteous hand of their Creator the gift of existence and the means of enjoyment. Our curiosity is powerfully excited by phenomena in which our own welfare is so intimately concerned, as are all those that relate to animal life; and we cannot but take a lively and sympathetic interest in the history of beings in many respects so analogous to ourselves like us possessing powers

FINAL CAUSES. 11

of spontaneous action, impelled by passions and desires, and endowed with capacities of enjoyment and of suffering. Can there be a more gratifying spectacle than to see an animal in the full vigour of health, and the free exercise of its powers, disporting in its native element, revelling in the bliss of existence, and testifying by its incessant gambols the exuberance of its joy?

We cannot take even a cursory survey of the host of living beings profusely spread over every portion of the globe without a feeling of profound astonishment at the inconceivable variety of forms and constructions to which animation has been imparted by creative power. What can be more calculated to excite our wonder than the diversity exhibited among insects, all of which, amidst endless modifications of shape, still preserve their conformity to one general plan of construction? The number of distinct species of insects already known and described cannot be estimated at less than 100,000; and every day is adding to the catalogue.* Of the comparatively large animals which live on land, how splendid is the field of observation that lies open to the naturalist! What variety is conspicuous in the tribes of Quadrupeds and of Reptiles;

* Four-fifths of the insects at present known have been discovered within the last ninety years: for in 1743, Ray estimated the total number of species at 20,000 only. See his work on " The wisdom of God as manifested in the Creation," p. 24.

and what endless diversity exists in their habits, pursuits, and characters! How extensive is the study of Birds alone; and how ingeniously, if we may so express it, has nature interwoven in their construction every possible variation compatible with an adherence to the same general model of design, and the same ultimate reference to the capacity for motion through the light element of air. What profusion of being is displayed in the wide expanse of the ocean, through which are scattered such various and such unknown multitudes of animals! Of Fishes alone the varieties, as to conformation and endowments, are endless. Still more curious and anomalous, both in their external form, and their internal economy, are the numerous orders of living beings that occupy the lower divisions of the animal scale; some swimming in countless myriads near the surface; some dwelling in the inaccessible depths of the ocean: some attached to shells, or other solid structures, the productions of their own bodies, and which, in process of time, form, by their accumulation, enormous submarine mountains, rising often from unfathomable depths to the surface. What sublime views of the magnificence of creation have been disclosed by the microscope, in the world of infinite minuteness, peopled by countless multitudes of atomic beings which animate almost every fluid in nature? Of these, a vast variety of species has been discovered, each animalcule being provided with appropriate organs, endowed with spontaneous powers of motion, and giving unequivocal signs of individual vitality. The recent observations of Professor Ehrenberg have brought to light the existence of *Monads*, which are not larger than the 24,000th of an inch, and which are so thickly crowded in the fluid as to leave intervals not greater than their own diameter. Hence he has made the computation that each cubic line, which is nearly the bulk of a single drop, contains 500,000,000 of these monads, a number which equals that of all the human beings existing on the surface of the globe.

Thus, if we review every region of the globe, from the scorching sands of the equator to the icy realms of the poles, or from the lofty mountain summits to the dark abysses of the deep; if we penetrate into the shades of the forest, or into the caverns and secret recesses of the earth; nay, if we take up the minutest portion of stagnant water, we still meet with life in some new and unexpected form, yet ever adapted to the circumstances of its situation. Wherever life can be sustained, we find life produced. It would almost seem as if Nature* had been thus

---

* In order to avoid the too frequent, and consequently irreverent, introduction of the Great Name of the SUPREME BEING into familiar discourse on the operations of his power, I have,

lavish and sportive in her productions with the intent to demonstrate to Man the fertility of her resources, and the inexhaustible fund from which she has so prodigally drawn forth the means requisite for the maintenance of all these diversified combinations, for their repetition in endless perpetuity, and for their subordination to one harmonious scheme of general good.

The vegetable world is no less prolific in wonders than the animal. In this, as in all other parts of creation, ample scope is found for the exercise of the reasoning faculties, and at the same time abundant sources are supplied of intellectual enjoyment. To discriminate the different characters of plants, amidst the infinite diversity of shape, of colour, and of structure, which they offer to our observation, is the laborious, yet fascinating, occupation of the Botanist. Here, also, we are lost in admiration at the neverending variety of forms successively displayed to view in the innumerable species which compose this kingdom of nature, and at the energy of that vegetative power, which, amidst such great differences of situation, sustains the modified life of each individual plant, and which continues its species in endless perpetuity. Wherever circum-

throughout this Treatise, followed the common usage of employing the term *Nature* as a synonym, expressive of the same power, but veiling from our feeble sight the too dazzling splendour of its glory.

stances are compatible with vegetable existence, we there find plants arise. It is well known that, in all places where vegetation has been established, the germs are so intermingled with the soil, that whenever the earth is turned up, even from considerable depths, and exposed to the air, plants are soon observed to spring, as if they had been recently sown, in consequence of the germination of seeds which had remained latent and inactive during the lapse of perhaps many centuries. Islands formed by coral reefs, which have risen above the level of the sea, become, in a short time, covered with verdure. From the materials of the most sterile rock, and even from the yet recent cinders and lava of the volcano, Nature prepares the way for vegetable existence. The slightest crevice or inequality is sufficient to arrest the invisible germs that are always floating in the air, and affords the means of sustenance to diminutive races of lichens and mosses. These soon overspread the surface, and are followed, in the course of a few years, by successive tribes of plants of gradually increasing size and strength; till at length the island, or other favoured spot, is converted into a natural and luxuriant garden, of which the productions, rising from grasses to shrubs and trees, present all the varieties of the fertile meadow, the tangled thicket, and the widely spreading forest. Even in the desert plains of the torrid zone, the eye of the traveller is often refreshed by the appearance of a few hardy plants, which find sufficient materials for their growth in these arid regions: and in the realms of perpetual snow which surround the poles, the navigator is occasionally startled at the prospect of fields of a scarlet hue, the result of a wide expanse of microscopic vegetation.*

But whatever charms the naturalist may find in the occupations in which he is engaged, and however wide may be the field of his exertions, they still are insufficient to satisfy the more enlarged curiosity of a philosophic mind. The passive emotion of astonishment, in which inferior intellects are content to rest, serves but to awaken, in him who has learned to think, a desire of further knowledge. Filled with an ardent spirit of inquiry, he cannot but be impatient under the feeling that, while Nature has placed before his eyes this splendid spectacle of animation, she has thrown a dense veil over the interior machinery of life, and has concealed from his view the springs by which she sets it in motion. With the hope of discovering her

---

* The red snow, discovered in Baffin's Bay on the 17th of August, 1818, during the Northern Expedition, under the command of Captain Ross, was found to owe its colour to minute fungi, or microscopic mushrooms, which vegetate on the surface of snow, as their natural abode. See Phil. Trans. for 1820, p. 165.

proceedings, he hastens to explore the several parts which compose the organized fabric, to examine in minute detail the anatomy of its structure, and to ascertain the nature of the several actions that take place within it. But, overwhelmed by the multiplicity of objects, and lost amidst the complication of phenomena, he soon becomes dismayed by the magnitude and arduous nature of the investigation. He finds that his labours will be of no avail, unless, previously to any attempt at theory, he takes a careful and accurate account of all the circumstances attending the history and conditions of life, from the dawn of its existence to its appointed close. On tracing living beings to their origin, he learns that every individual vegetable and animal takes its rise from an atom of imperceptible minuteness, and gradually increases in bulk by successive accretions of new matter, derived from foreign sources, and, by some refined, but unknown process, transmuted into its own substance. Then, following the progressive developement of the organs, he observes them undergoing various modifications, as they are assuming new forms, which characterise certain definite epochs in the general growth of the system. In a great number of instances, especially among the lower orders of animals, he witnesses the same individual being acting, in its time, a variety of different parts; often re-appearing on the stage of life with new organs, new faculties, and new conditions of existence, and undergoing metamorphoses as complete as any that have been depicted in the fables of antiquity.

The period at length arrives when the animal, having completed its growth, attains the maturity of its being, and acquires the full possession of its powers. Every organ in succession has received its entire developement, and has united its energies with those which had been before perfected. Yet, however complete the arrangements that have thus been established, it is still necessary, in order to preserve the whole system in a state in which it may be capable of exercising the functions of life, that the materials which compose its fabric should undergo a certain slow, but constant renovation; and the same circle of actions and reactions, which have brought it to its state of perfection, must continue to be repeated, in order that a due proportion may be maintained between the consumption and the supply of these materials. In the course of a certain time, however, even under the most favourable circumstances, this equilibrium begins to fail: the energies of the system decline: and the processes of nutrition are insufficient to repair the waste in the substance of the body. The fluids are dissipated faster than they can be renewed; the channels through which they circulate are more and more obstructed, and at length cease to be pervious: and the solids gradually become hard and rigid. As in a machine of which the wheels are worn, and the springs have lost their elastic force, so in the animal body, at an advanced age, the slightest additional impediment that occurs will stop the movements of the whole system: and, when once stopped, their renewal is impossible. Nature has thus assigned to every living being a certain period as the utmost extent of its duration. Even when exempt from external interference, all are doomed to perish, sooner or later, by the slow but unerring operation of the same internal causes which originally effected their developement and growth, and which are inseparably interwoven with the conditions of their existence.

Numerous, however, are the extraneous and accidental causes that may hasten or precipitate their destruction, long before the period of natural decay. How striking is the contrast, on those occasions, between the scene we have just beheld of an animal in the full vigour of its powers, either rapidly bounding across the plain, or gliding beneath the wave, or soaring in the elevated regions of air, and the spectacle of the same animal lying, the next moment, extended at our feet, bereft at once of activity and of sense— of all the faculties and powers that constitute life. Can we contemplate without amazement so complete and instantaneous a change; so sudden and awful a catastrophe? Must we not be animated by an eager desire to penetrate so great a mystery, and resolve the many questions which so striking a phenomenon must naturally suggest? What, we are led to ask, is the nature of this extraordinary revolution, extending over the whole of that frame which had so long delighted the eye by its beauty, and producing this sudden and irretrievable extinction of the powers of life? How comes it that all those mighty energies which the animal had so lately displayed, and which had called forth our admiration, perhaps even excited our envy, are at once and for ever annihilated? What was the bond, thus suddenly dissevered, which held together the various parts of that compound frame? What potent spell has been dissolved, which could retain in combination for so long a period the multifarious elements of that exquisite organization; and from the control of which being now released, these elements hasten to resume their wonted attractions, and entering into new forms of combination, are scattered into dust, or dissipated in air, leaving no trace of their former union? What mechanism has been employed in its construction? What refined chemistry has been exerted in assimilating new particles of matter to those previously organized, and in appropriating them to the nourishment of the parts with which they became identified? By what transcendent power, above all, did this assemblage of material particles first become animated by the breath of life; and from what elevated source did they derive those higher energies, apparently so foreign to their inherent properties, and investing these once lifeless and inert materials with the exalted attributes of activity, of sensation, of perception, of intelligence? Shall we ever comprehend the nature of this subtle and pervading principle, by the agency of which all these wonderful phenomena of life are produced, and which, combining into one harmonious system so many heterogeneous and jarring elements, has led to the formation of this exquisite frame, this elaborate machine, this miraculous assemblage of faculties?

The discovery of a clue, if any such can be found, to the mazes of this perplexing labyrinth can be hoped for only from the successful cultivation of the science of physiology. But before engaging in this arduous study, we ought previously to inquire into the methods of reasoning by which it is to be conducted.

The object of physiology is, by the diligent examination of the phenomena of life, to ascertain the laws which regulate those phenomena, both as they apply to the individual beings endowed with life, and also as they relate to the various assemblages that constitute the species, the genera, the families, the orders, and the classes of those beings; and, lastly, as they concern the whole collective union of the organized world.

These peculiar laws, which it is the province of physiology to investigate, are, as I have before observed, of two kinds, each founded upon relations of a different class. The first, which depend upon the simple relation of cause and effect, are concerned merely with the natural powers of matter. They are the laws that regulate the succession of phenomena purely physical in all their stages. These phenomena consist in changes among material particles, which are either of a mechanical or chemical nature; or in the affections of imponderable physical agents, such as heat, light, electricity, and magnetism; and they include also the phenomena that take place in organized bodies, and which are referable to the operation of certain physical powers, appertaining to particular structures, such as muscular contraction and nervous irritation; phenomena which, as we shall afterwards find, are not reducible to any of the former laws, but are peculiar to the living state. The second class of laws comprise those which are founded on the relation of means to an end; and which are usually denominated *final causes*. They involve the operations of mind, in conjunction with those of matter. They presuppose intention or design; a supposition which implies intelligence, thought, motives, volition,—particular purposes to be answered, requiring the agency of powers and of instruments adapted to the production of the intended effects:—the knowledge of the properties of matter, the selection and choice of particular means, and the power of employing them in an effective manner. These purposes may themselves be subservient to more general objects, and these objects again subordinate to remoter ends; so that the whole shall comprehend a systematic plan of operations, conducive, on the most enlarged views, to ultimate and general utility.

The study of these final causes is, in some measure, forced upon our attention by even the most superficial survey of nature. It is impossible not to recognise the character of intention, which is so indelibly impressed upon every part of the structure both of vegetable and animal beings, and which marks the whole series of phenomena connected with their history. Microscopic observations teach us that the embryo of an organic being contains within itself the rudiments of the future vegetable or animal structure, into which it is gradually transformed by the slow and successive expansion and developement of all its parts. The processes of nutrition do nothing more than fill up the outlines already sketched on the living canvass. Every organ, nay every fibre, resulting from this developement, contributes its share in the production of certain definite effects, which we constantly witness taking place around us, as well as experience in our own persons. But these effects, though so familiar to us, are not on that account the less involved in mystery, or the less replete with wonder. To say that they are the results of chance conveys no information; and is equivalent to the assertion that they are wholly without a cause. Every one who is accustomed to reflect upon the operations of his own mind must feel that such a conclusion is contrary to the constitution of human thought; for if we are to reason at all, we can reason only upon the principle that for every effect there must exist a corresponding cause; or, in other words, that there is an established and invariable order of sequence among the changes which take place in the universe.

But though it be granted that all the phenomena we behold are the effects of certain causes, it might still be alleged, as a bar to all further reasoning, that these causes are not only utterly unknown to us, but that their discovery is wholly beyond the reach of our faculties. The argument is specious only because it is true in one particular sense, and that a very limited one. Those who urge it, do not seem to be aware that its general application, in that very same sense, would shake the foundation of every kind of knowledge, even that which we regard as built upon the most solid basis. Of causation, it is agreed that we know nothing; all that we do know is, that one event succeeds another with undeviating constancy. Now, if we were to probe this subject to the bottom, we should find that, in rigid strictness, we have no certain knowledge of the existence of any thing, save that of the sensations and ideas which are actually passing in our minds, and of which we are necessarily conscious. Our belief in the existence of external objects, in their undergoing certain changes, and in their possessing certain physical properties, rests on a different foundation, namely, the evidence of our senses; for it is the result of inferences which the mind is, by the constitution of its frame, necessarily led to form. We may trace to a similar origin the persuasion, irresistibly forced upon us, that there exist not only other material objects beside our own bodies, but also other intellectual beings beside ourselves. We can neither see nor feel those extraneous intellects, any more than we can see or feel the cause of gravitation, or the subtle sources of electricity or magnetism. We nevertheless believe in the reality both of the one and of the other; but it is only because we infer their existence from particular trains of impressions made upon our senses, of which impressions alone our knowledge can, in metaphysical strictness, be termed certain.

Upon what evidence do I conclude that I am not a solitary being in the universe; that all is not centered in myself; but that there exist other intellects similar to my own? Undoubtedly no other than the observation that certain effects are produced, which the experience I have had of the operations of my own mind lead me, by an irresistible analogy, to ascribe to a similar agency, emanating from other beings; beings, however, of whose actual intellectual presence I cannot be conscious, whose nature I cannot fathom, whose essence I cannot understand. I can judge of the operations of other minds only in as far as those operations accord with what has passed in my own. I cannot divine processes of thought to which mine have borne no resemblance, I cannot appreciate motives of which I have never felt the influence, nor comprehend the force of passions never yet awakened in my breast: neither can I picture to myself feelings to which no sympathetic chord within me has ever vibrated.

Our own intelligence, our own views, and our own affections, then, furnish the only elements by which it is possible for us to estimate the analogous powers and attributes of other minds. The difficulty of applying this scale of measurement will, of course, increase in proportion to the difference between the objects compared; and although we may conceive that there are powers and intelligences infinitely surpassing our own, the conceptions we can form of such superior essences must necessarily be indefinite and obscure, and must partake of the same kind of imperfection as our notions of the distances of the heavenly bodies, however familiar we may be with the units of the scale by which those distances are capable of being expressed. When, on the other hand, the objects contemplated are more within the range of our mental vision; when, for instance, they are phenomena that we can assimilate to our own voluntary acts, and in which we can clearly trace the connexion between means and end, then does our recognition of the agency of intellect become most distinct, and our conviction of its real and independent existence become most intimate and assured.

Such is the kind of evidence on which rests our belief of the existence of our fellow men. Such, also, is the foundation of our assurance that there exists a mighty Intellect, who has planned and executed the stupendous works of creation, with a skill surpassing our utmost conceptions; by powers to which we can assign no limit, and the object of whose will is universal good.*

* The view here taken is, of course, limited to *Natural Theology*; that being the express and exclusive object of these Treatises.

It will argue no undue presumption, therefore, if, in our earnest endeavours to form just ideas of the attributes of the Deity from the examination of nature, we are led to institute comparisons between His works and those of man; and strive to gather some faint notions of the divine intelligence by applying the only standard of admeasurement which we possess, and are permitted to employ, namely, that derived from the operations of human intellect. Our interpretations of the designs of the Creator must here be obtained through the medium of human views; and our judgment of His benevolence can be formed only by reference to our own affections, and by their accordance with those ardent aspirations after good, which the Author of our being has deeply interwoven with our frame.

The evidence of design and contrivance in the works of nature carries with it the greatest force whenever we can trace a coincidence between them and the products of human art. If in any unknown region of the earth we chanced to discover a piece of machinery, of which the purpose was manifest, we should not fail to ascribe it to the workmanship of some mechanist, possessed of intelligence, actuated by a motive, and guided by intention. Farther, if we had a previous experience of the operation of similar kinds of mechanism, we could not doubt that the effect we saw produced was the one intended by the artificer. Thus, if in an unexplored country, we saw, moving upon the waters of a lake, the trunk of a tree, carved into the shape of a boat, we should immediately conclude that this form had been given to it for the purpose of enabling it to float. If we found it also provided with paddles at its sides, we should infer, from our previous knowledge of the effects of such instruments, that they were intended to give motion to this boat, and we should not hesitate to conclude that the whole was the work of human hands, and the product of human intelligence and design. If, in addition, we found this boat furnished with a rudder and with sails, we should at once understand the object of these contrivances, and our ideas of the skill of the artificer would rise in proportion to the excellence of the apparatus, and the ingenuity displayed in its adaptation to circumstances.

Let us suppose that in another part of this lake we found an insect,* shaped like the boat, and moving through the water by successive impulses given to that medium by the action of levers, extending from its sides, and shaped like paddles, having the same kind of movement, and producing the same effects. Could we resist the persuasion that the Artificer of this insect, when

* Such as the *Notonecta glanca*, Lin., or water boatman, and the *Dytiscus marginalis*, or water beetle.

forming it of this shape, and providing it with these paddles, had the same mechanical objects in view? Shall we not be confirmed in this idea on finding that these paddles are constructed with joints, that admit of no other motion than that of striking against the water, and of thus urging forwards the animal in its passage through that dense and resisting medium? Many aquatic animals are furnished with tails which evidently act as rudders, directing the course of their progressive motion through the fluid. Who can doubt but that the same intention and the same mechanical principles which guide the practice of the ship-builder, are here applied in a manner still more refined, and with a master's hand? If Nature has furnished the nautilus with an expansible membrane, which the animal is able to spread before the breeze, when propitious, and by means of which it is wafted along the surface of the sea, but which it quickly retracts in unfavourable circumstances, is not her design similar to that of the human artificer, when he equips his bark with sails, and provides the requisite machinery for their being hoisted or furled with ease and expedition?

The maker of an hydraulic engine places valves in particular parts of its pipes and cisterns, with a view to prevent the retrograde motion of the fluids which are to pass through them. Can the valves of the veins, or of the lymphatics, or of the heart have a different object: and are they not the result of deliberate and express contrivance in the great Mechanist of the living frame?

The knowledge of the laws of electricity, in its different forms, is one of the latest results which science has revealed to man. Could these laws, and their various combinations, have been unknown to the Power who created the torpedo, and who armed it with an energetic galvanic battery, constructed upon the most refined scientific principles, for the manifest purpose of enabling the animal to strike terror into its enemies, and paralyse their efforts to assail it.

Does not the optician, who designedly places his convex lens at the proper distance in a darkened box, for the purpose of obtaining vivid pictures of the external scene, evince his knowledge of the laws of light, of the properties of refracting media, and of the refined combinations of those media by which each pencil is brought to a separate focus, and adjusted to form an image of remote objects? Does it not, in like manner, argue the most profound knowledge and foresight in the divine Artist, who has so admirably hung the crystalline lens of the eye in the axis of a spherical case, in the fore part of which He has made a circular window for the light to enter, and spread out on the opposite side a canvass to receive the picture? Has no thought been exercised in darkening the walls of this camera obscura, and thus preventing all reflection of the scattered rays, that might interfere with the distinctness of the image?

But we farther observe in the eye many exquisite refinements of construction, by which various defects, unavoidable in all optical instruments of human workmanship, are remedied. Of this nature are those which render the organ achromatic, which correct the spherical aberration, and which provide for the adjustment of its refracting powers to the different distances of the objects viewed; not to speak of all the external apparatus for the protection, the preservation, and the movements of the eye-ball, and for contributing in every way to the proper performance of its office. Are not all these irrefragable proofs of the continuity of the same design; and are they not calculated still farther to exalt our ideas of the Divine Intelligence, of the elaborate perfection impressed upon His works, and of the comprehensive views of His providence?

These facts, if they stood alone, would be sufficient to lead us irresistibly to this conclusion: but evidence of a similar kind may be collected in abundance from every part of living nature to which our attention can be directed, or to which our observations have extended. The truths they teach not only acquire confirmation by the corroborating tendency of each additional fact of the same description, but the multitude of these facts is so great, that the general conclusion to which they lead must be considered as indubitable. For the argument, as it has been justly remarked, is cumulative; that obtained from one source being strengthened by that derived from another; and all tending to the same conclusion, like rays converging to the same point, on which they concentrate their united powers of illumination.

The more we extend our knowledge of the operations of creative power, as manifested in the structure and economy of organized beings, the better we become qualified to appreciate the intentions with which the several arrangements and constructions have been devised, the art with which they have been accomplished, and the grand comprehensive plan of which they form a part. By knowing the general tendencies of analogous formations, we can sometimes recognise designs that are but faintly indicated, and trace the links which connect them with more general laws. By rendering ourselves familiar with the hand-writing where the characters are clearly legible, we gradually learn to decypher the more obscure passages, and are enabled to follow the continuity of the narrative through chapters that would otherwise appear mutilated and defaced. Hence the utility of comprehending in our studies the whole range of the organized creation, with a view to the discovery of final causes, and obtaining adequate ideas of the power, the wisdom, and the goodness of God.

Chapter II.

The Functions of Life.

THE intentions of the Deity in the creation of the animal kingdom, as far as we are competent to discern or comprehend them, are referable to the following classes of objects. The first relates to the individual welfare of the animal, embracing the whole sphere of its sensitive existence, and the means of maintaining the vitality upon which that existence is dependent. The second comprises the provisions that have been made for repairing the chasms resulting, in the present circumstances of the globe, from the continual destruction of life, by ensuring the multiplication of the species, and the continuity of the race to which each animal belongs. The third includes all those arrangements which have been resorted to in order to accommodate the system to the consequences that follow from an indefinite increase in the numbers of each species. The fourth class relates to that systematic economy in the plans of organization by which all the former objects are most effectually secured. I shall offer some observations on each of these general heads of enquiry.

With reference to the welfare of the individual animal, it is evident that in the brute creation, the great end to be answered is the attainment of sensitive enjoyment. To this all the arrangements of the system, and all the energies of its vital powers must ultimately tend. Of what value would be mere vegetative life to the being in whom it resides, unless it were accompanied by the faculty of sensation, and unless the sensations thence arising were attended with pleasure? It is only by reasoning analogically from the feelings we have ourselves experienced that we ascribe similar feelings to other sentient beings, and that we infer their existence from the phenomena which they present. Wherever these indications of feeling are most distinct, we find that they result from a particular organization, and from the affections of a peculiar part of that organization denominated the *nervous substance*. The name of *brain* is given to a particular mass of this substance placed in the interior of the body, where it is carefully protected from injury.

The sensations, for exciting which the brain is the material instrument, or immediate organ, are the result of certain impressions made on particular parts of the body, and conveyed to that organ by the medium of filaments, composed of a similar substance, and termed *nerves*. In this way, then, it has been provided that a communication shall be established between the sentient principle and the external objects, by which its activity is to be excited, and on which it is to be dependent for the elements of all its affections, both of sensation and of intellect. A considerable portion of this treatise will be occupied with the developement of the series of means by which impressions from external objects are made on the appropriate organs that are provided to receive and collect them, so as not only to give rise to varied sensations, but also to convey a knowledge of the existence and different qualities of the objects that produce them. This latter faculty is termed *Perception*.

But in the formation of animals it was not the intention of Providence to endow them with the mere capacity of being affected by surrounding objects, and of deriving from them various sensations of pleasure and of pain, without granting them the power of controlling these effects, and of acting on those objects in return. The faculties of sensation and perception, in beings destined to be merely passive, and the sport of every contingent agency, would have been not merely useless, but even baneful endowments. The same beneficent power which has conferred these gifts has conjoined that of voluntary motion, by which the animal may not only obtain possession of such objects as minister to its gratification, and reject those which are useless or hurtful, but may also move from place to place, and enlarge the sphere of its perceptions and of its power. The same mass of nervous substance which, under the name of brain, we have recognised as the organ of sensation, is also, as will afterwards be shown, the organ of volition; and the medium, by which the commands of the will are transmitted from the brain to the mechanical apparatus employed for motion, is again certain filaments of nerves; but these nervous filaments are distinct from those which are subservient to sensation.

Next in importance, then, to the organs of sensation and perception, are those of *Voluntary Motion*. They comprise two kinds of objects; first, the establishment of a certain mechanism, having the cohesion, the strength, and the mobility requisite for the different actions which the animal is to perform; and, secondly, the provision of a power, or agent, which shall be capable of supplying the mechanical force for setting this machinery in motion. With these objects must be combined various subsidiary arrangements relating to the connexions, the support, the protection, and other mechanical conditions of the organs of the body. It will be convenient to comprehend these under one general head, considering them as composing the *Mechanical Functions* of the animal economy. They will engage a considerable share of our attention in this work, as affording the clearest and most palpable proofs of contrivance and design.

From the peculiar conditions of the living body, not only with regard to the mechanical properties of its various parts, and the powers by which their movements are affected, but also with regard to the chemical laws which regulate the combinations of elements composing the substance of the body, there is required, as will be more fully explained in the sequel, a continual renovation of that substance. For this purpose new materials are perpetually wanted, and must be as regularly supplied. Hence arises a new class of functions, comprising a great extent of operations, opening a wide field of curious and interesting enquiry, and furnishing abundant evidence of the wise and beneficent operations of nature. These may be comprehended under a separate class bearing the general title of *Nutritive Functions*. They are often, also, spoken of under the designation of the *Vital Functions*, from their more immediate relation to the continuance of vitality, that is, of mere vegetative life, as distinguished from the exercise of the higher faculties of sensation, perception, and voluntary motion, which are the ultimate ends of animal existence, and which are emphatically termed the *Animal Functions*.

The vital as well as the animal functions require for the execution of their various objects certain instruments of an appropriate mechanical construction, adapted to those objects. To the contrivances of the mechanist must be added a refined hydraulic apparatus for the conveyance of fluids, and for the regulation of their movements; and with these must be conjoined the skilful combinations of the laboratory, by which the powers of the most subtle chemistry are exercised in effecting all the transmutations required by this elaborate system of operations. As far as they involve mechanical principles, these objects again arrange themselves under the mechanical functions : and I shall accordingly include them under that head, when giving an account of this branch of the subject.

There is another, and a most important consequence that flows from the peculiar chemical conditions of the materials of which animal structures are composed. The mode in which their elements are combined is so complex as to require a long and elaborate process to accomplish that purpose; and neither the organs with which animals are furnished, nor the powers with which those organs are endowed, are adequate to the conversion of the materials furnished by the inorganic world into the substances required for the construction of their bodies, and the maintenance of their powers. These inorganic elements must have passed through intermediate stages of combination, and must have been previously elaborated by other organized beings. This important office is consigned to the vegetable kingdom. Receiving the simple food furnished by nature, which consists chiefly of water, air, and carbonic acid, together with a small proportion of other substances, plants convert these aliments into products, which not only maintain their own vitality, but serve the further purpose of supporting the life of animals. Thus was the creation and continuance of the vegetable kingdom a necessary step towards the existence of the animal world; as well as a link in the great chain of being, formed and sustained by Almighty power. The Physiology of Vegetables presents many topics of great interest with relation to final causes, and will in this Treatise be reviewed with special reference to this important object.

Nutrition, both in the vegetable and animal systems, comprises a very extended series of operations. In the former it includes the absorption of the crude materials from the surrounding elements,—their transmission to organs where they are aerated, that is, subjected to the chemical action of the air;—their circulation in the different parts of the plant,—their further elaboration in particular vessels and receptacles—their deposition of solid materials—and their conversion into peculiar products, as well as into the substances which compose the several organs;—and, finally, the growth and developement of the whole plant. Still more various and complicated are the corresponding functions in animals. Their objects may be arranged under the following general heads; each, again, admitting of further subdivision. The first end to be accomplished is to animalize the food; that is, to convert it into a matter having the chemical properties of the animal substances with which it is to be afterwards incorporated. The entire change thus effected is termed *Assimilation*, of which *Digestion* forms a principal part. The second object is to collect and distribute this prepared nutriment, which is the blood, to the different organs, or wherever it may be wanted. The necessary motions for these purposes are given to the blood by the organs of *Circulation*, consisting of the *Heart*, which impels it through a system of pipes called *Arteries*, and receives it back again by means of another set of tubes called *Veins*. In the third place it is necessary that the circulating blood should continually undergo purification by the chemical action of oxygen: a purpose which is answered by the function of *Respiration*. The fourth stage of nutrition relates to the more immediate application of this purified material to the wants of the system, to the extension of the organs, to the reparation of their losses, and to the restoration of their exhausted powers.

Life, then, consists of a continued series of actions and reactions, ever varying, yet constantly tending to definite ends. Most of the parts of which the body consists undergo continual and progressive changes in their dimensions, figure, arrangement, and composition. The materials which have been united together and fashioned into the several organs, are themselves successively removed and replaced by others, which again are, in their turn, discarded, and new materials substituted, though without any perceptible change of external form. Perpetual mutation appears to constitute the fundamental law of living nature; and it has been further decreed by the power which gave the first impulse of animation to this organized fabric, that its movements and its powers shall be limited in their duration, and that, even when they are not destroyed by extraneous causes, after continuing for a certain period, they shall come to a close. The law of Mortality, to which all the beings that have received the gift of life are subjected, is a necessary consequence of the law of mutation; and the same causes that originally effected the developement and growth of the system, and maintained it in the vigour of its maturity, by continuing to operate, are certain to lead to the demolition of the fabric they had raised, and to the exhaustion and final extinction of its powers. The individual dies; but it is only to give place to other beings, alike in nature and in form, equally partaking of the blessings of existence, and destined, after having, in their turn, given rise to a new race of successors, to run through the same perpetual cycle of changes and renovations.

Thus the continuance and multiplication of each species may be assigned as the second of the great ends which are to be accomplished in the system of living nature. A portion of the vital power of the parent is for this purpose employed to give origin and birth to the offspring. The process itself, by which the germs of living beings originate, is veiled in the most impenetrable mystery. But we are permitted to trace many of the subsequent steps in the gradual developement both of vegetable and animal organizations; and certainly no part of the economy of animated nature is more calculated to impress us with exalted ideas of the immensity of the scheme of Providence, and the vigilant care with which the most distant consequences have been anticipated, than the history of the early periods of their existence. Nothing can be more admirable than the progressive architecture of the frame; nothing more beautiful than the setting up of temporary structures, which are required only at an early stage of growth, and which are afterwards removed to give place to more permanent and finished organs.

The utmost solicitude has been shown in every part of living nature to secure the perpetuity of the race, by the establishment of laws, of which the operation is certain in all contingent circumstances. It has also been manifestly the object of various provisions to diffuse the races as widely as possible over a great surface of the habitable globe.

We are next to advert to the important consequences which, in the animal kingdom more especially, flow from this law of indefinite production. As animals are ultimately dependent on the vegetable kingdom for the materials of their subsistence, and as the quantity of these materials is, in a state of nature, necessarily limited by the extent of surface over which vegetation is spread, a time must arrive when the number of animals thus continually increasing is exactly such as the amount of food produced by the earth will maintain. When this limit has been attained, no farther increase can take place in their number, except by resorting to the expedient which we find actually adopted, namely, that of employing the substance of one animal for the nourishment of others. Thus the identical combinations of ele-

THE FUNCTIONS OF LIFE.   45

ments, effected by the powers of vegetation, are transformed in succession from one living being into another, and become subservient to the maintenance of a great number of different animals before they finally, by the process of decomposition, revert to their original inorganic state.

> " See dying vegetables life sustain,
> See life dissolving vegetate again;
> All forms that perish other forms supply,
> By turns we catch the vital breath and die."—POPE.

Hence has the ordinance been issued to a large portion of the animal world that they are to maintain themselves by preying upon other animals, either consuming their substance when already dead, or depriving them of life in order to prolong their own. Such is the command given to the countless hosts of living beings which people the vast expanse of ocean; to the unnumbered tribes of insects which every spot of earth discloses; to the greater number of the feathered race; and also to a more restricted order of terrestrial animals. To many has the commission been given to ravage and to slaughter by open violence; others are taught more insidious, though no less certain arts of destruction; and some appear to be created chiefly for the purpose of quickly clearing the earth of all decomposing animal or vegetable materials, which might otherwise have filled the air with noxious exhalations and contaminated the sources of vitality.*

This new law of animal existence must necessarily introduce new conditions of organization and of functions. Structures adapted to rapid locomotion must be supplied for the pursuit of prey, and powerful weapons for attack and destruction. But nature has not left the weaker animals unprovided with the means of repulse, of defence, or of escape. For these purposes various expedients, either of force, of swiftness, or of stratagem, have been resorted to in different cases.

That a large portion of evil is the direct consequence of this system of extensive warfare, it is in vain to deny. But although our sensibility may revolt at the wide scene of carnage which is so generally presented to our view, our more sober judgment should place in the other scale the great preponderating amount of gratification which is also its result. We must take into account the vast accession that accrues to the mass of animal enjoyment from the exercise of those powers and faculties which are called forth by this state of constant activity; and when this

* As specially appointed for the performance of this useful task may be cited, among the larger beasts of prey, the hyæna, the jackall, the crow, and the vulture: among marine animals, the crustacea, and numerous mollusca; and among the lower orders innumerable tribes of insects, such as ants, flesh flies, &c.

consideration is combined, as it ought to be, with that of the immense multiplication of life which is admissible upon this system alone, we shall find ample reason for acknowledging the wisdom and the benevolent intentions of the Creator, who, for the sake of a vastly superior good, has permitted the existence of a minor evil.

From this system of hostilities there must also arise new relations among the different races of animals. It affords a ready and effectual means of preserving the proper balance between different races. Each separate species of animals, far from being isolated and independent, performs the part assigned to it in the system of nature, and, however apparently insignificant, may have a sensible influence on the rest of the animal creation. Man, above all other animals, has effected a most important change in the condition of a multitude of other races, in every region where his numbers have multiplied, where the arts of civilization have enlarged his dominion, and where science has armed him with still more extensive power.

In every department of nature it cannot fail to strike us that boundless variety is a characteristic and predominant feature of her productions. It is only when the object to be attained is dependent upon certain definite conditions, excluding the possibility of modification, that these conditions are uniformly and strictly adhered to.

But wherever that absolute necessity does not exist, and there is afforded scope for deviation, there we are certain to find introduced all those modifications which the occasion admits of. Not only is this tendency to variety exemplified in the general appearance and form of the body, but it also prevails in each individual organ, however minute and insignificant that organ may seem. Even when the purpose to be answered is identical, the means that are employed are infinitely diversified in different instances, as if a design had existed of displaying to the astonished eyes of mortals the unbounded resources of creative power. While the elements of structure are the same, there is presented to us in succession every possible combination of organs, as if it had been the object to exhaust all the admissible permutations in the order of their union.

Some wise purpose, though dimly perceptible to our imperfect understandings, is no doubt answered by this great law of organic formation, the *law of variety*. That it is not blindly or indiscriminately followed, is apparent from its being circumscribed within certain limits, and controlled by another law, which we have next to consider—that of *conformity to a definite type*.

The most superficial survey of nature is sufficient to show that there prevail certain general resemblances among great multitudes of species, which lead us to class them into more or less comprehensive groups. Thus in the animal kingdom, quadrupeds, birds, fishes, reptiles, shell-fish, and insects, compose natural assemblages or classes, and each of these is readily divisible into subordinate groups or families. Now it results from a closer examination of the structure and economy of plants and animals, that the formation of all the individual species comprehended in the same class, has been conducted in conformity with a certain ideal model, or *type*, as it is called. Of this general type all the existing forms appear as so many separate copies, differing, indeed, as to particulars, but agreeing as to general characters. The same observation applies to the families, the genera, and other subordinate groups of living beings.

The more extensive our acquaintance is with the anatomy and physiology of both plants and animals, the more striking do these analogies appear; so that amidst endless diversity in the details of structures and of processes, the same general purpose is usually accomplished by similar organs and in similar modes. So firmly is this principle established, that we may venture with confidence to predict many circumstances relating to an unknown animal, of which only a few fragments are presented to us, from our general knowledge of the characters and economy of the tribe or family, on the type of which it has been modelled. Thus the discovery of a mutilated portion of the skeleton of a fossil animal, gives to the physiologist, who is conversant with the details of comparative anatomy, a knowledge of the general structure and habits of that animal, though all other traces of its existence may have been swept away, amidst the primeval revolutions of the globe.*

Not only does this tendency to conform to particular types obtain in all organic formations, but further inquiry leads to the conclusion that the deviations from these standard forms, far from being arbitrary, are themselves referable to particular laws. The regulating principle of the variations is subordinate to higher views, and has reference to the respective objects and destination of each particular species in the general system of created beings. Nature, as far as we can discern, appears, in conformity with these intentions, first to have laid down certain great plans of functions to which she has adapted the structure of the organs; the minor objects and more subordinate functions being accommodated to this general design. Hence arises the necessary and reciprocal dependence of each organ and of each function on every other; and hence are deduced what have been termed the

* See Cuvier's " Discours sur les révolutions de la surface du globe," p. 47, prefixed to the first volume of his " *Ossemens Fossiles.*"

laws of the co-existence of organic forms. By attention to these laws we may often explain how each variation that is observed in any one organ, common to a natural group of animals, entails certain necessary and corresponding variations in other parts, and extends its influence in modifying, in a greater or less degree, the whole fabric. It is in comparative anatomy as in mechanics, where any alteration made in the position of one part of a system of bodies occasions a change in the centres of gravity, of gyration, and of oscillation; and evolves new mechanical forces and conditions of equilibrium, which render new adjustments in other parts necessary, in order to restore the equipoise, and preserve the harmony of their movements.

We may conclude from these inquiries that the numerous classes or assemblages of beings, which science has formed, are by no means arbitrary creations of the human mind, invented merely with a view to facilitate the study and to recognise the identity of species, or calculated only to supply the imperfections of our memory; but that they have a real foundation in nature. To regard any of the beings in the creation as isolated from the rest, would be to take a very narrow and a false view of their condition; for all are connected by mutual relations. Even among the leading types which represent the great divisions of the animal kingdom we may trace several points of resemblance, which show them to be parts of one general plan, and to have emanated from the same Creator. In the progress of discovery we are continually meeting with species which occupy intermediate places between adjacent types, and appear as links of connexion in the chain of being. It often happens, as I shall hereafter have occasion to point out, that throughout an extensive series of organic forms, the steps of gradation by which one type passes into another, are so numerous and so regular, as to preclude the possibility of drawing a decided line of demarcation between those that properly appertain to each.

All these apparent anomalies and gradations of structure tend still farther to demonstrate the generality of the plans of nature, and the comprehensiveness of her design, which embraces the whole series of animated beings. These views are strongly corroborated by the discoveries that are continually being made of species now no longer in existence, but which, in former ages of the world, helped to fill up many of the chasms which now interrupt the continuity of that series. This knowledge has been revealed to us by the examination of their fossil remains, those monuments of former epochs, which have thrown such important light on the most interesting questions in Geology as well as in Physiology.

THE FUNCTIONS OF LIFE.   53

The notion has long prevailed that the beings composing the vegetable and animal kingdoms, might, if we were thoroughly acquainted with their structure and economy, be arranged in a linear series, commencing with the simplest and regularly ascending to the most refined and complicated organizations, till it reached its highest point in man, who is unquestionably placed at the summit of the scale. Bonnet, in particular, cherished with enthusiastic ardour the hypothesis that all organic beings formed a continuous gradation, each member of which, like the successive links of a chain, was connected with that which preceded, and with that which followed it; and he pursued this idea by applying it even to the productions of the mineral world. But, divesting ourselves of these hypothetical views and figurative images, we find, on sober observation, that instead of one continuous series, we are presented with only detached fragments and interrupted portions of this imaginary system: so that, if, for the sake of illustration, we must employ a metaphor, the natural distribution of animals would appear to be represented, not by a chain, but by complicated net-work, where several parallel series are joined by transverse and oblique lines of connexion. A multitude of facts, however, tend to show that the real types or models of structure, are more correctly represented by circular or recurring arrangements.* But as the discussion of these and other topics relating to the plans and designs of nature in the formation of organic beings requires a previous acquaintance with the details of comparative anatomy and physiology, I shall defer all further observations respecting them till I have finished the review I propose to take of the several structures and functions of the animal and vegetable economy. There are, however, some views that have been entertained respecting the procedure of nature in the formation of the different races of animals, which it will be proper to notice in this place, as they will occasionally be referred to when the facts that more particularly illustrate and support them come to be noticed.

An hypothesis has been advanced that the original creation of species has been successive, and took place in the order of their relative complexity of structure; that the standard types have arisen the one from the other; that each succeeding form was an improvement upon the preceding, and followed in a certain order of developement, according to a regular plan traced by the great Author of the universe for bestowing perfection on his works. This grada-

* Mr. M'Leay is the author of this ingenious theory, which he has developed in his " *Horæ Entomologicæ,*" and which appears to be verified to a great extent by the modern discoveries in comparative anatomy.

tion of structure was necessarily accompanied by a gradation of faculties: the object of each change of type being to attain higher objects, and to advance a further step towards the ultimate ends of the animal creation. Many apparent anomalies which are inexplicable upon any other supposition, are easily reconcilable to this theory. The developements of structure belonging to a particular type being always prospective, are not completed in the inferior orders of the groupe formed upon that model, but remain more or less imperfect, although each organ always fully answers the particular purpose of the individual animal. But it sometimes happens that the imperfection of an organ is so great, in consequence of its developement having proceeded to a very small extent, as to render it wholly useless in that particular species, although in a higher race of animals it fully performs its proper function. Thus we shall find that rudiments of feet are contained within the bodies of various kinds of serpents, which can obviously not be serviceable as organs of progression. In the young of the whale, before its birth, there is found in the lower jaw, a row of small teeth, which do not rise above the gums, and can, therefore, be of no use as instruments of mastication. Their farther growth is arrested and they are afterwards obliterated. This imperfect or *rudimentary* condition of an organ indicates its relation to other species belonging to the same type, and demonstrates the existence of a general plan in their formation. I shall have occasion to mention several striking instances of this kind, both in the animal and vegetable kingdom.

In following the transitions from one model of structure to another, we often observe that a particular organ has been very greatly enlarged, or otherwise modified to suit some particular purpose, foreign to its usual destination, or to qualify it for performing some new office, rendered necessary by the particular circumstances in which the animal is placed. Thus the ribs, which in quadrupeds are usually employed for respiration, are in serpents converted into auxiliary organs of progressive motion: and in the *Draco volans*, or flying lizard, they are extended outwards from the sides to serve as wings. The teeth, usually intended for mastication, are in many animals enlarged in order to serve as weapons of offence, as in the *Elephant*, the *Boar*, the *Narwal*, and the *Pristis*. In like manner in the Crustacea, organs of the same general structure are converted sometimes into jaws, sometimes into feelers, (or palpi) and sometimes into feet; and the transition from the one to the other is so gradual that it is difficult to draw a proper distinction between them.

In pursuing the ascending series of animal structures we meet also with instances of a contrary change, yet still resulting from the continued application of the same principle. An organ which has served an important purpose in one animal, may be of less use in another, occupying a higher station in the scale, and the change of circumstances may even render it wholly useless. In such cases we find that it is gradually discarded from the system, becoming continually smaller, till it disappears altogether. We may often, however, perceive some traces of its existence, but only in a rudimental state, and as if ready to be developed, when the occasion may demand it.

In the greater number of organic structures we may trace a tendency to the repetition of certain organs, or parts, and the regular arrangement of these similar portions either round a central axis, or in a longitudinal series. The former is apparent in the verticillated organs of plants, and in the radiated forms of zoophytes. The linear arrangement is exhibited in the similar segments of annulose and other articulated animals, and also in the pieces which compose the spinal column of vertebrated animals. In these two latter classes, also, a remarkable law of symmetry obtains in the formation of the two sides of the body, which exhibits the lateral junction of similar but reversed structures. The violations of this law are extremely rare; yet some remarkable instances of anomalous formations in this respect will hereafter be noticed.

In treating of the particular functions of the animal and vegetable economy I shall follow a different order from that in which I have presented them in the preceding sketch. As the Mechanical functions depend upon the simpler properties of matter and the well known laws of mechanism, I think it best to commence with the examination of these. Our attention will next be directed to the highly interesting subjects which relate to the Nutritive or Vital functions both of vegetable and animal structures: for as they involve the chemical properties of organized substances, and are, therefore, of a more refined and intricate nature than the preceding, I conceive they will be best understood after the general mechanism of the frame has been explained. These studies will prepare us for the consideration of living animals as sentient and active beings, endowed by their bounteous Creator with the exalted faculties of perception and of volition, which alone give value to existence, and which raise them so far above the level of the vegetable world. I shall lastly give a very brief account of the reproductive functions, and of the phenomena of animal developement, in which the discoveries of modern times have revealed to us so considerable a portion of those extensive plans which an all-wise providence has beneficently devised for the general welfare of animated beings.

PART I.

THE MECHANICAL FUNCTIONS.

CHAPTER I.—ORGANIC MECHANISM.

§ 1. *Organization in General.*

LIFE, which consists of a continued series of actions directed to particular purposes, cannot be carried on but by the instrumentality of those peculiar and elaborate structures and combinations of material particles which constitute *organization*. All these arrangements, both as respects the mechanical configuration and the chemical constitution of the elements of which the organized body is composed, even when apparently most simple, are, in reality, complex and artificial in the highest possible degree. Let us take as a specimen the crystalline lens, or hard central part, of the eye of a cod fish, which is a perfectly transparent, and to all appearance homogeneous, spherule. No one, unaccustomed to explore the wonders of nature, would suspect that so simple a body, which he might suppose to be formed of a uniform material cast in a mould, would disclose, when examined under a powerful microscope, and with the skill of a Brewster, the most refined and exquisite conformation. Yet, as I shall have occasion to specify more in detail in its proper place, this little spherical body, scarcely larger than a pea, is composed of upwards of five millions of fibres, which lock into one another by means of more than sixty-two thousand five hundred millions of teeth. If such be the complication of a portion only of the eye of that animal, how intricate must be the structure of the other parts of the same organ, having equally important offices! What exquisite elaboration must those textures have received whose functions are still more refined! What marvellous workmanship must have been exercised in the organization of the nerves and of the brain, those subtle instruments of the higher animal faculties, and of which even the modes of action are to us not merely inscrutable, but surpassing all our powers of conception!

It is from the energies of life alone that organic forms are produced. No fabric achieved by human power ever approached in refinement the simplest of nature's works. The utmost efforts of the ingenuity or skill of man in the construction of the most delicate machinery is infinitely surpassed by the most ordinary of the

ORGANIC MECHANISM.

mechanisms which are presented to our view in living bodies. However successful may be human artists in their attempts to contrive automata, which shall exactly imitate different animal movements, there will always be wanting that internal principle of action, derived from a higher source than mechanism can supply, and without which these highly wrought works of man, like the unvivified statues of Prometheus, must remain for ever mere masses of insentient and inert materials.

As the living functions imply the mechanical action and re-action of parts which cohere in some definite order of arrangement, so as to preserve that determinate form to which they constantly tend to return on being displaced, it is impossible to conceive that a mere fluid can exercise these functions; because the particles of a fluid, being equally moveable in every direction, have no determinate relative situations, and possess no character of permanence. All organic and living structures, therefore, must be composed of solid as well as fluid parts; although the proportion between these is, in different cases, almost infinitely varied. A dormant vitality may, indeed, exist in a system of organs which have been brought into a perfectly dry state: as is proved by the examples of vegetable seeds, and also of many species of animalcules, and even of some of the more highly developed *Annelida,* or worms, which may be kept in a dry state for an indefinite length of time, and, when moistened with water, resume their activity, as if restored to life. The germination of seeds under these circumstances is matter of common observation; but the revivification of animalcules is a more curious phenomon, for it takes place more rapidly, and is more striking in its results. The *Rotifer redivivus,* or wheel animalcule,* (Fig. 1.) which was first observed by Lewenhoeck, and was afterwards rendered celebrated by the experiments made upon it by Spallanzani, can live only in water, and is commonly found in that which has remained stagnant for some time in the gutters of houses. But it may be deprived of this fluid,

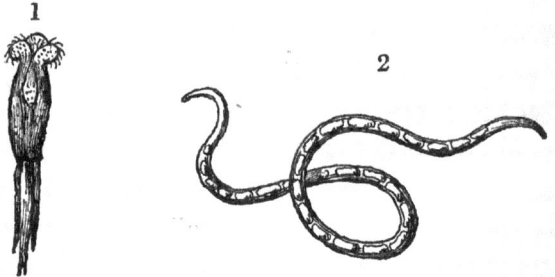

and reduced to perfect dryness, so that all the functions of life shall be completely suspended, yet without the destruction of the vital principle;

* *Vorticella rotatoria* of Gmelin, and *Furcularia* of Lamark.

for this atom of dust, after remaining for years in a dry state, may be revived in a few minutes by being again supplied with water. This alternate suspension and restoration of life may be repeated, without apparent injury to the animalcule, for a great number of times. Similar phenomena are presented by the *Vibrio tritici*, (Fig. 2.) or the animalcule, resembling an eel in its shape, which infests diseased wheat, and which, when dried, appears in the form of a fine powder: on being moistened, it soon resumes its living and active state.* The *Gordius aquaticus*, or hair worm, which inhabits stagnant pools, and which remains in a dry, and apparently lifeless state when the pond is evaporated, will, in like manner, revive, in a very short time, on being again immersed in water. The same phenomenon is exhibited by the *Filaria*, a thread-like parasitic worm, infesting the cornea of the eye of the horse.†

Both the composition of the fluid and the texture of the solid parts of animal and vegetable bodies are infinitely varied, according to the purposes they are designed to serve in the economy. Scarcely any part is perfectly homogeneous; that is, composed throughout of a single uniform material. Few of the fluids are entirely

* See a paper on this subject by Mr. Bauer, Phil. Trans. for 1823, p. 1.
† Blainville, Annales des Sciences Naturelles; X. 104.

limpid, and none are perfectly simple in their composition; for they generally contain more or less of a gelatinous matter, which, when very abundant, imparts to them viscidity, constituting an approach to the solid state. Many fluids contain minute masses of matter, generally having a globular shape, which can be seen only by means of the microscope, and which float in the surrounding liquid, and often thicken it in a very sensible manner.* We next perceive that these globules have, in many instances, cohered, so as to form solid masses; or have united in lines, so as to constitute fibres. We find these fibres collecting and adhering together in bundles; or interwoven and agglutinated, composing various other forms of texture; sometimes resembling a loose net-work of filaments; sometimes constituting laminæ or plates; and, at other times, both plates and filaments combining to form an irregular spongy fabric. These various tissues, again, may themselves be regarded as the constituent materials of which the several organs of the body are constructed, with different degrees of complication, according to the respective functions which they are called upon to perform.

We shall now examine the several kinds of

* Globules of this description have been found in the lymph, the saliva, and even in the aqueous humor of the eye.

texture in relation to these functions, in the order of their increasing complexity; beginning with those of vegetables, which are apparently the simplest of all.

§ 2. *Vegetable Organization.*

PLANTS, being limited in their economy to the functions of nutrition and reproduction, and being fixed to the same spot, and therefore in a comparatively passive condition, require for the performance of these functions mechanical constructions of a very different kind from those which are necessary to the sentient, the active, and the locomotive animal. The organs that are essential to vegetables are those which receive and elaborate the nutritive fluids they require, those which are subservient to reproduction, and also those composing the general framework, which must be superadded to the whole for the purpose of giving mechanical support and protection to these finer organizations. As plants are destined to be permanently attached to the soil, and yet require the action both of air and of light; and, as they must also be defended from the injurious action of the elements, so we find these several objects provided for by three descriptions of parts : namely, first, the *Roots*, which fix plants in their situation; secondly, the *Stems*, which support them in the proper position, or raise them to the requisite height above the ground; together with the branches, which are merely subdivisions of the stem; and thirdly, the *external coverings*, which correspond in their office to the teguments, or skin of animals.

The simplest and apparently the most elementary texture met with in vegetables is formed of exceedingly minute vesicles, the coats of which consist of transparent membranes of extreme tenuity. Fig. 3 is a highly magnified representation of the simplest form of these vesicles.* But they generally adhere together more closely, composing by their union a species of vegetable cellular tissue, which may be regarded as the basis or essential component material of every organ in the plant. This cellular structure is represented in figures 4 and 5, as it appears in the *Fucus vesiculosus;* the first being a horizontal, and the second a vertical section of that plant.† The size of these cells differs considerably in different instances. Kieser states that the diameter of each individual cell varies from the 330th to the 55th part of an inch; so

---

* These cells are well represented in the engravings which illustrate Mr. Slack's memoir on the elementary tissue of plants, contained in the 49th volume of the Transactions of the Society of Arts.

† De Candolle, Organographie Végétale.

that from 3,000 to 100,000 cells would be contained in an extent of surface equal to a square inch. But they are occasionally met with of different sizes, from even the 1000th part of an inch to the 30th.

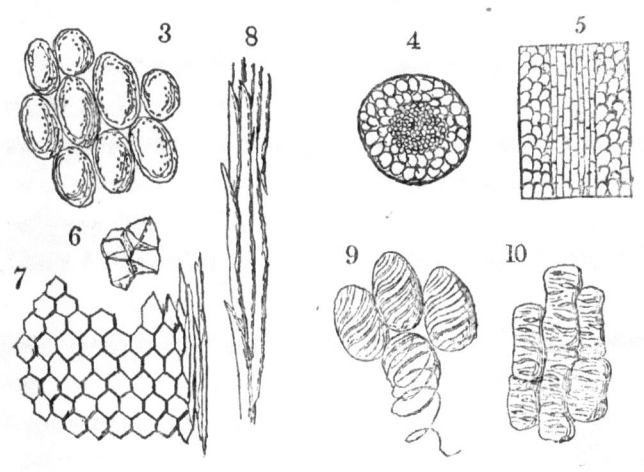

In their original state, these vesicles have an oval or globular form; but they are soon transformed into other shapes, either by the mutual compression which they sustain from being crowded into a limited space, or from unequal expansions in the progress of their developement. From the first of these causes they often acquire angles, assuming the forms of irregular rhomboidal dodecahedrons, and often of hexagonal prisms, like the cells of a honeycomb; and by the second, they are elongated into cylinders, or slowly tapering cones, thus passing by insensible gradations into the tubular form. Figures 6, 7, and 8, are representations of some of these different states of transition from the one to the other. These various modifications of the same elementary texture have been distinguished into several classes of cells, and dignified by separate technical denominations, which I shall not stop to specify, as it does not appear that they have as yet thrown any light on vegetable physiology.

Many of the cells are fortified by the addition of elastic threads, generally disposed in a spiral course, and adhering to the inner surfaces of the membranous coats of the cells, which they keep in an expanded state. (See Fig. 9.) When the membranes are torn, the fibres, being detached, unrol themselves, and being loosely scattered among the neighbouring cells, give the appearance of fibrous connexions among these cells, which did not originally exist. Simple membranous cells, containing no internal threads, are often found intermixed with these fibrous cells. In many of the cells, again, the original spiral threads appear to have coalesced by their edges; thus presenting a more uniform surface, excepting that a few interstices are left, where the pellucid membrane, having no internal lining, presents the appearance of transverse fissures or oval perforations. (Fig. 10.) Cells of this description are said to be *reticulated* or *spotted*, and, together with those having more regularly formed spiral threads, are very abundantly met with in plants belonging to the tribe of *Orchideæ*.

It has been much disputed whether the cells of the vegetable texture are closed on all sides, or whether they communicate with one another. Mirbel has given us delineations of what appeared to him, when he examined the coats of the cells with the microscope, to be pores and fissures. But subsequent observations have rendered it probable that these appearances arise merely from darker portions of the membranes, where opaque particles have been deposited in their substance. Fluids gain access into these cells by transuding through the membranes which form their sides, and not by any apertures capable of being detected by the highest powers of the microscope.

If all the cells consist of separate vesicles, as the concurring observations of modern botanists[*] appear to have satisfactorily established, the partitions which separate them, however thin and delicate, must consist of a double membrane, formed by the adhesion of the coats of the two contiguous vesicles. But as these coats can

[*] In particular, Treviranus, Kieser, Link, Du Petit Thouars, Pollini, Amici, Dutrochet, and De Candolle.

hardly be supposed to adhere in every point, we may expect to find that spaces have been left in various parts between them; and that communications exist to a certain extent between all these spaces ; so as to compose what may be regarded as one large cavity. These have been denominated the *intercellular spaces ;* and they have been supposed to perform, as will hereafter be seen, an important part in the function of Nutrition.

Fluids of different kinds occupy both the cells and the intercellular spaces. The contents of some is the simple watery sap; that of others consists of peculiar liquids, the products of vegetable secretion : and very frequently they contain merely air. In many of the cells there are found small opaque and detached particles of the substance termed by chemists, *Fecula,* of which starch is the most common example. In several parts, and more especially in the leaves, and in the petals of flowers, the material which gives them their peculiar colour is contained in the cells in the form of minute globules. De Candolle has given it the name of *Chromule.**

The cells of the ligneous portion of trees and shrubs are further encrusted with particles of a more dense material, peculiar to vegetable organization, and termed *Lignine.* It is this substance

* Organographie, Tom 1, p. 19.

which principally contributes to the density and mechanical strength of what are called the *Woody Fibres*, which consist of collections of fusiform, or tapering vessels, hereafter to be described, surrounded by assemblages of cells thus fortified, and the whole cohering in bundles, so as to present greater resistance to forces tending to displace them, in the longitudinal direction than in any other.

Most of the plants which are included in the Linnean class of Cryptogamia have a structure exclusively composed of cells, as has been already shown in the *Fucus vesiculosus*. But the greater number of other plants have, in addition to these cells, numerous ducts or vessels, consisting of membranous tubes of considerable length, interspersed throughout every part of the system. These tubes exhibit different modifications of structure, more especially with regard to the form of the fibres, or other materials, which adhere to the inner surface of their membranes; and these modifications correspond very exactly with those of the vesicles already described as constituting the simpler forms of vegetable tissue. There can be little doubt, indeed, that the vessels of plants take their origin from vesicles, which become elongated by the progress of developement in one particular direction; and it is easy to conceive that where the extremities of these elongated cells meet, the partitions which separate their cavities may become obliterated at the points of junction, so as to unite them into one continuous tube with an uninterrupted interior passage. This view of the formation of the vessels of plants is confirmed by the gradation that may be traced among these various kinds of structures. Elongated cells are often met with applied to each other endwise, as if preparatory to their coalescence into tubes. Sometimes the tapering ends of fusiform cells are joined laterally (as seen in Fig. 12), so that the partitions which divide their cavities are oblique. At other times their ends are broader, and admit of their more direct application to each other in the same line, being separated only by membranes passing transversely; in which case they present, under the microscope, the appearance of a necklace of beads (Fig. 13). When, by the destruction of these partitions, their cavities become continuous, the tubes they form exhibit a series of contractions at certain intervals, marking their origin from separate cells. In this state they have received the names of *moniliform, jointed* or *beaded vessels.** Traces of the membranous partitions sometimes remain where their obliteration has been only partial, leaving transverse fibres. The conical terminations occasionally

* Mirbel gave them the name of " *Vaisseaux en chapelet.*"

observable in the vessels of plants also indicate their cellular origin.*

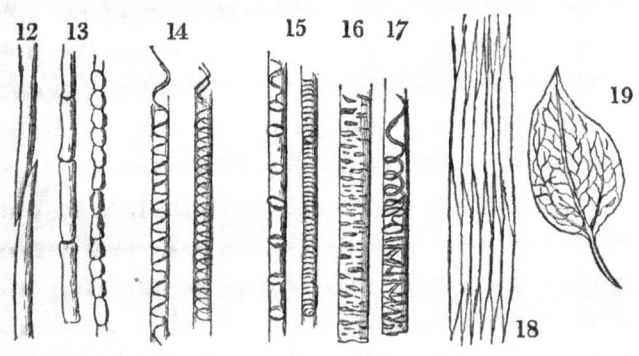

The membrane constituting the tube is sometimes simple, like those of the simple cells: but it frequently contains fibres, or other internal coatings, corresponding to those met with in the more compound cells. The vessels in which the internal fibres run in a spiral direction (Fig. 14), are denominated *tracheæ*, or *spiral vessels;* or, from their being found very constantly to contain air, they are often called *air tubes*. Their diameter is generally between the 1000th and the 300th part of an inch. These spiral, or air vessels, pervade extensively the vegetable system. The threads they contain are frequently double, treble, quadruple, or even still more numerous: they are of great length, and when the external membrane of the vessel is divided, they may

* This theory of the derivation of vessels from cells was first advanced by Treviranus.

easily be drawn out and uncoiled, their elasticity enabling them to retain their spiral shape. The object of this structure appears to be that of keeping the cavity of the tube always pervious, by presenting resistance to any external force tending to compress and close it.*

In many instances the inner fibres of the tube, instead of forming a continuous spiral, appear in the shape of rings, succeeding one another at regular intervals, and constituting what are called *annular vessels* (Fig. 15). They are generally larger than the spiral vessels. In other cases, as was first observed by Hedwig, the adjacent coils are found to be closely coherent throughout the greatest part of their course; leaving, however, occasional intervals, where the external membrane, being unprotected, appears, from its transparency, as if spotted or perforated in various places (Fig. 16). Every intermediate stage may occasionally be seen in the transition from one of these forms to the other, in consequence of the various kinds of convolution, of branchings, or of transverse junctions of fibres, as well as the greater or less extent of their lateral adhesions. All these varieties are met with, not only in different vessels, but, as was observed by Moldenhawer and Kieser, even in the dif-

* Vessels are sometimes met with which appear to be formed simply by the coils of a spiral fibre in close juxtaposition, and unattached to any external envelope, or connecting membrane.

ferent portions of the same vessel, when followed by the eye throughout a great extent of its length. Thus, in the course of the same tube, (as seen in Fig 17), we find parts exhibiting spiral fibres, which, in other parts, bifurcate and again unite; and in others, again, form rings: these may afterwards, by a closer junction, present a reticulated appearance, or a series of transverse lines, which, becoming smaller and smaller, are at length mere points, arranged in circular rows around the cylindrical surface of the vessel.*

What are called the *woody fibres* have their origin, like all other parts of plants, in cells. These are generally fusiform, that is, of the shape of a double cone, very greatly elongated, and placed close and parallel to one another, with the narrow extremities of one set wedged in between those of another set (Fig 18). Their coats are more firm and elastic than those of ordinary vessels, but do not appear to contain any internal fibres, although they receive, in the progress of their developement, large additions of solid matter. These fibres are generally collected together into bundles or layers, and are accompanied by cells and vessels of

* Many distinguished botanists, such as Rudolphi, Link, Treviranus, and Dutrochet, consider these spots as being produced not by the deficiency of the internal coating, but by the addition of granular bodies. See De Candolle's Organographie Végétale, tom. 1, p. 56.

various descriptions, and in different stages of transition. The density of the woody fibres increases in proportion as these incrustations are formed, till they have become nearly impervious; and have acquired a degree of rigidity peculiarly fitting them for the office of giving mechanical support to the fabric of the plant.* Their assemblage thus constitutes a kind of frame-work for the whole system, which may be regarded as the skeleton of the plant. Thus, what are called the *fibres* of leaves (Fig. 19), are principally composed of these woody fibres, distributed in the manner best adapted to support the expansion of the soft and pulpy substance of those important organs.

Besides the minute cavities of the cellular tissue, there occur, in various parts of a plant, much larger spaces, apparently serving the purpose of reservoirs of particular fluids; but sometimes containing only air. Large air cells are, in particular, met with very commonly in aquatic plants, where they probably contribute to impart the requisite degree of buoyancy.

There are also contained, in the interior of

* By drying different specimens of wood in a stove, Count Rumford was led to the conclusion that the specific gravity of the solid matter which constitutes timber is nearly the same in all trees. He found that the woody part of oak, in full vegetation, constitutes only two-fifths of the whole bulk: and that ordinary dry wood contains above one-fourth of its weight of water. Thomson's Annals of Philosophy, I. 388.

vegetables, certain organs, denominated *Glands*, which are composed of closely compacted cells, and which perform the function of *secretion*, that is, the conversion of the nutritious juices into particular products required for various purposes in the economy of the plant.

The external parts of a living plant require protection against the injurious effects of the atmosphere, and of the moisture it deposits. For this purpose there is provided a membrane, termed the *Cuticle*, which is spread over the whole surface, investing the leaves and flowers, as well as the stem and branches, and interposing a barrier to the action of fluids, or other extraneous bodies, on the living organs. The cuticle is formed originally by the condensation of a layer of cellular tissue, of which the cells, being consolidated by exposure to the air, and by compression, compose a thin but impervious pellicle. Amici has distinctly shown, by means of his powerful microscope, the cellular structure of the cuticle, and also that the layer of cells of which it consists is independent of the subjacent cellular tissue.* Fig. 20 is intended to show this circumstance, the shaded part representing the cuticle with its series of cells.

Oval orifices, or *stomata*, as they have been termed, are discoverable on almost every part of

* Annales des Sciences Naturelles, II. 211.

the surface of the cuticle, but more especially in those that have a green colour.* They are placed at nearly equal distances from one another, and are particularly numerous in the cuticle of the leaves, where they occupy the intervals between the fibres. These orifices conduct into the interior of the plant, probably into the general cavity of the intercellular spaces. It is evident, from the functions they perform, that they must occasionally open and close; but the minuteness of their size precludes any accurate observation as to the nature of the apparatus provided for the purpose of performing these motions. Amici describes their margins as formed by two cells, by the movements of which, combined perhaps with those of the adjoining cells, he conceives these orifices are opened and closed.† Great variety, however, is observable in the structure of the stomata in different species of plants.

Many plants have no stomata, either on the cuticle of the leaves, or on that of the stem. This is the case with such aquatic plants as are habitually immersed in water. In those that are only partially immersed, stomata are met

* Fig. 22 is a magnified representation of the appearance in the cuticle of the *Lycopodium denticulatum*, taken in the central part of the lower surface of the leaf, from De Candolle. Fig. 21 is a still more magnified view of the stomata in the leaf of the *Lilium candidum*, from Amici.

† Ibid. II. 215.

VEGETABLE ORGANIZATION. 79

with in those parts exclusively which are above the water. The leaves of the *Ranunculus aquaticus*, when made to grow in the air, acquire stomata, but lose them entirely when growing under water. Stomata are wanting in all plants whose structure is wholly cellular.

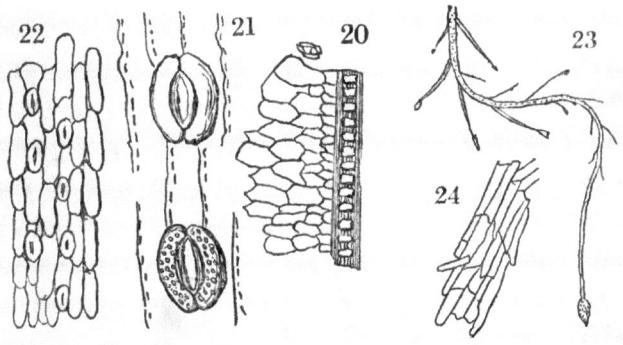

Botanists are far from being agreed as to the precise functions which the stomata perform. Their usual office undoubtedly is to exhale water; but they probably also absorb air under certain circumstances, and in particular exigences.

The principal organs through which the fluids that serve for nourishment are received into the system of plants, are those situated at the extremities of the roots, where they are termed, from their peculiar texture, *spongioles*.*

* Fig. 23 exhibits the termination of a root of a willow in a spongiole; the arrangement of the cells composing which is shewn in Fig. 24, from De Candolle.

Of the functions of spongioles in absorbing fluids I shall have occasion to speak when treating of nutrition. But as the roots exercise a mechanical as well as a nutrient office, we should here consider them in the light of organs adapted to procure to the plant a permanent attachment to the soil, upon which it is wholly dependent for its supply of nourishment. It is scarcely necessary to point out how effectually they perform this office. Our admiration cannot fail to be excited when we contemplate the manner in which a large tree is chained to the earth by its powerful and widely spreading roots. By the firm hold which they take of the ground, they procure the most effectual resistance to the force of the winds, which, acting upon so large a surface as that presented by the branches covered with dense foliage, must possess an immense mechanical power.

The principal seat of the vitality of a plant is the part which intervenes between the root and the stem. Injuries to this part are always fatal to the life of the plant.

As the roots penetrate downwards into the earth to different distances in order to procure the requisite nourishment, so the stem grows upwards for the purpose of obtaining for the leaves and flowers an ample supply of air, and the influence of a brighter light, both of which are of the highest importance to the maintenance

VEGETABLE ORGANIZATION.

of vegetable life. The stems of the grasses are hollow tubes; their most solid parts, which frequently consist of a thin layer of silex, occupying the surface of the cylinder. Of all the possible modes of disposing a given quantity of materials in the construction of a column, it is mathematically demonstrable that this is the most effective for obtaining the greatest possible degree of strength.*

The graceful continuous curve with which the stem of a tree rises from the ground, is the form which is best calculated to give stability to the trunk. Evidence of express mechanical design is likewise afforded by the manner in which the trunk is subdivided into its branches, spreading out in all directions, manifestly with a view to procure for the leaves the greatest extent of surface, and thus enable them to receive the fullest action of both light and air. The branches, also, are so constructed as to yield to the irregular impulses of the wind, and again, by their elasticity, to return to their natural positions, and by these alternate inflexions on opposite sides, to promote the motion of the sap in the vessels and cellular texture of the liber and

* Galileo, the most profound philosopher of his age, when interrogated by the inquisition as to his belief in a Supreme Being, replied, pointing to a straw on the floor of his dungeon, that from the structure of that object alone he would infer with certainty the existence of an intelligent Creator.

alburnum. Nothing can exceed the elegance of those forms which are presented in every part of the vegetable kingdom, whether they be considered with reference to their direct utility for the support of individual life, and the continuance of the species, or whether they be viewed as component parts of that beauty which is spread over the scenery of nature, and is so delightfully refreshing to the eye of every beholder alive to its fascinating charms. How enchanting are all the varieties of flowers, that decorate in gay profusion every part of the garden of creation; and into which the farther we carry our philosophic scrutiny, the more forcibly will our hearts be impressed with the truth of the divine appeal that " EVEN SOLOMON IN ALL HIS GLORY WAS NOT ARRAYED LIKE ONE OF THESE."

§ 3. *Developement of Vegetables.*

FARTHER proofs of design may be collected from an examination into the modes in which these structures, so admirably adapted to their objects, have been gradually formed. Confining our attention to vascular plants, in which the process of developement has been studied with the greatest attention and success, we find that Nature has pursued two different plans in conducting their growth.* In the greater number, the successive additions to the substance of the stem are made on the exterior side of the parts from which they proceed. This mode is adopted in what are called *Exogenous plants*. In others, the growth is the result of additions made internally; a plan which is followed in all *Endogenous plants*. The Oak, the Elm, the Beech, the Pine, and all the trees of these northern regions, belong to the first of these divisions. The Palm tribe, such as the Date, the Cocoa-nut tree, and, indeed, a large proportion of the trees of tropical climates, together with the sugar-cane, the bamboo, and all gramineous and liliaceous plants, belong to the latter. We shall first inquire into the endogenous mode of growth, as being the simplest of these two kinds of vegetable developement.

A Palm tree may be taken as an example of the mode of growth in endogenous plants. The stem of this tree is usually perfectly cylindrical, attains a great height, and bears on its summit a tuft of leaves. It is composed of an extremely dense external cylindric layer of wood; but the texture of the interior becomes gradually

* The tribe of *Filices*, or ferns, the structure of which is vascular, constitute an exception to this rule: as they differ in their mode of developement, both from exogenous and endogenous plants.

softer and more porous as it comes nearer to the centre; though with regard to its essential character it appears to be uniform in every part, having neither medullary rays, nor true outward bark, nor any central pith; in all which respects it differs totally from the ordinary exogenous trees.

The first stage of its growth consists in the appearance of a circle of leaves, which shoot upwards from the neck of the plant, and attain, during the first year, a certain size. The following year, another circle of leaves arises; but they grow from the interior of the former circle, which they force outwards as their vegetation advances, and as ligneous matter is deposited within them. Thus each succeeding year brings with it a fresh crop of leaves, intermixed with ligneous matter, which leaves, exerting an outward pressure, stretch out the preceding layers that enclose them; until the latter, acquiring greater density, no longer admit of further distention, and remain permanently fixed. This happens first to the outermost layer, which is the oldest: then each succeeding layer becomes consolidated in its turn. As soon as the outer layer has become too hard to yield to the pressure from within, the growth of the inner layers is immediately directed upwards; so that they each rise in succession by distinct stages, always proceeding from the interior; a mode of developement which has been compared by De Candolle to the drawing out of the sliding tubes of a telescope. The whole stem, whatever height it may attain, never increases its diameter after its outward layer has been consolidated. A circle of leaves annually sprouts from the margin of the new layer of wood; these, when they fall off in autumn, leave on the stem certain traces of their former existence, consisting of a circular impression round the stem. The age of the tree may accordingly be estimated by the number of these circles, or knots, which appear along its stem. The successive knots which are seen in the stems of other endogenous plants, as may be observed in growing corn, and also in various grasses, may be traced to a similar origin.

The structure of exogenous trees is more complicated: for, when fully grown, they are composed of two principal parts, the *wood* and the *bark*. The woody portion exhibits a further division into the *pith*, which occupies the centre, and consists of large vesicles, not cohering very closely, but forming a light and spongy texture, readily permeable to liquids and to air; the *harder wood*, which surrounds the pith in concentric rings, or layers; and the softer wood, or *alburnum*, which is also disposed in concentric layers on the outer side of the former. Each of these concentric layers of wood and of alburnum may be further distinguished into an inner and an outer portion; the former being of less density than the latter, and consisting of a lighter cellular tissue: while the outer portion is composed of the denser woody fibres resulting from the union of numerous vessels with a cellular envelope. The bark is formed by concentric layers of cortical substance, of which the innermost are denominated the *Liber;* and the whole is surrounded by an outer zone of cellular tissue, termed the *cellular envelope.* Of this envelope the exterior surface is called the *Epidermis.*

All these concentric zones may be readily distinguished in a horizontal section of the stem; which also presents a number of lines called *Medullary Rays,* radiating from the pith to the circumference. They are composed chiefly of large cells, extending transversely, or in the direction of the diameter of the tree, and composing by their union continuous vertical planes the whole length of the trunk.

Every vegetable stem, and also every branch which arises from it, is developed from a germ, or bud, which is originally of inconceivable minuteness, and totally imperceptible by any optical means of which we have the command. As soon as it becomes visible, and its structure can be distinguished, it is found to contain within itself the parts which are to arise from it, in miniature, and folded up in the smallest possible compass. The portion destined to form the stem is gradually expanded both in breadth and height, but principally the latter, so that it rises as it grows, during a certain period, until the fibres acquire the solidity and strength necessary not only for their own support, but also for sustaining the parts which are to be further added. In trees this process generally occupies one whole season; during which the growth of the first layer of wood, with its central pith, and its covering of a layer of bark, is free and unrestrained. On the second year, a fresh impulse being given to vegetation, a new growth commences from the upper end of the original stem, as if it were the developement of a new bud: and at the same time a layer of cellular tissue is formed by the deposition of new materials on the outside of the former wood, and between it and the bark. This is followed by a second layer of wood, enveloping the new layer of cellular tissue.

The effect of this new growth is to compress the layer of wood which had been formed during the first year, and to impede its further extension in breadth. But as its fibres, consisting of vessels and cells, are not yet consolidated, and admit of still greater expansion as long as they are supplied with nourishment, their growth, which is restrained laterally, is now directed upwards, and there is no farther enlargement of their diameter. From the same cause the pith cannot increase in size ; and is even found to diminish by the pressure of the surrounding wood. Thus the vertical elongation of the entire stem continues during the whole of the second year, and the trunk becomes sufficiently strengthened by the addition of the second layer on its outside to bear this increase of its height.

While this process is going on in the wood, corresponding changes take place in the bark, and a new layer is added on its inner surface, or that which is contiguous to the wood. This layer constitutes the *liber*. All these new depositions must of course tend to stretch the outer portions of the bark, which had been first formed, and which yield to this pressure to a certain extent; but, becoming themselves consolidated by the effects of the same pressure, they acquire increasing rigidity; and, the same cause continuing to operate, they at length give way, in various places, forming those deep cracks, which are observable in the bark of old trees, and which give so rugged an appearance to their surface. The cuticle has, long before this, peeled off, and has been succeeded by the consolidated layers of cortical envelope which form the *epidermis*. But the epidermis, which is continually splitting by the expansion of the parts it encloses, itself soon decays, and is constantly succeeded by fresh layers, produced by the same process of consolidation in the subjacent cortical substance.

During the third and each succeeding year, the same process is repeated; new layers of cellular texture and of woody fibres are deposited around those of the preceding year's growth, and a new internal coating is given to the liber of the bark. The compressing power continues to be exerted on the internal layers of wood, directing their growth vertically, while they are capable of elongation, and can be supplied with nourishment. In time, however, by continued pressure, and accumulating depositions of solid matter, the vessels and the cells become less and less pervious to fluids; till at length all further dilatation is prevented. But the tree still continues to enlarge its trunk by the annual accessions of vigorous and expansible alburnum, and to take its station among its kindred inhabitants of the forest; till, arriving at maturity, its majestic form towers above all the junior or less vigorous trees.*

The developement of each branch takes place in the same manner, and by the same kind of

---

* It is contended by Dr. Darwin and other writers on vegetable physiology that each annual shoot should be regarded as a collection of individual buds, each bud being a distinct individual plant, and the whole tree an aggregation of such individuals. I shall have occasion to revert to this question when I come to consider the subject of vegetable nutrition.

process, as that of the trunk. The buds from which they originate, spring from the angle formed by the stalk which supports a leaf, and which is termed by botanists the *axilla* of that leaf. A law of symmetry is established by nature in the developement of all the parts of plants. The leaves, in particular, are frequently observed to arise in a circle, or symmetrically round the parent stem; forming what is termed a *whorl*, or, in botanical language, a *verticillated* arrangement. In other cases they are found to have their origins at equal intervals of a spiral line, which may be conceived to be drawn along the stem, or the branch from which they grow. When these intervals correspond to the semi-circumference of the stem, the leaves alternate with one another on its opposite sides.

The stems of most plants, even those that are perfectly erect, exhibit a tendency to a spiral growth. This is observable in the fibres of the wood of the pine, however straight may be the direction of the whole trunk. This tendency is shown even in the epidermis of the cherry tree, for it may be stripped off with more facility in a spiral direction than in any other. The primitive direction of the leaves of endogenous plants is a spiral one. It is particularly marked also in the stems of creepers and of parasitic plants, which are generally twisted throughout their whole length; a disposition evidently conducive to the purpose of their formation, namely, that of laying hold of the objects with which they come in contact, and of twining round them in search both of nourishment and of support. The twisted stems of the hop and of ivy show this structure in a remarkable degree, and the purpose for which this tendency was given cannot be mistaken.

A conjecture has been offered that this tendency to a spiral growth might be the effect of the influence of the sun's light, acting successively on different sides of the plant, in the course of its diurnal motion. In these northern latitudes the direction of that motion is from east to west; or, to an observer facing the south, from left to right. That light has a powerful influence in determining the direction of the growth of all the parts of the plant which are above ground, is manifest to every one who has observed the habits of vegetables. If a growing plant be placed in a situation where the light reaches it only on one side, it will always, by degrees, turn itself to that side, as if eagerly pressing forward to obtain the beneficial action of that agent. The leaves, whose functions in a more especial manner require its operation, will always be found turned towards the light. The branches of a tree, which have naturally a tendency to rise vertically, have this tendency modified by the superior attraction of the light, when it can reach them only laterally. Thus while those on the upper part spread out in full luxuriance in all directions, those below them are obliged to expand more in a lateral direction : and this is still more the case with the lowest branches, which shoot out horizontally to a considerable distance before they turn upwards, and present their leaves to the light. Often, however, from the deficiency of this necessary agent, their growth is much stinted, or entirely prevented. The operation of this cause is extensively seen in the interior of a dense forest.

It may be objected to the theory of the spiral growth being the result of the sun's motion, that were it so, the direction of the spiral would always be the same, that is, ascending from left to right with reference to the axis. But this is not found to be the case, for the direction of the turns, though generally constant in the same plant, is far from being the same in all. Dr. Wollaston ingeniously suggested that a verification of the theory would be obtained were it found that plants transported from the southern to the northern hemispheres, would have this direction reversed ; for it is evident that the motion of the sun's light in the two hemispheres is in opposite directions; being, in the southern hemisphere, from right to left, to a spectator facing the meridian position of the sun, which in those regions is to the north. But, the facts are not in accordance with this view of the subject; so that we may consider the hypothesis as untenable.

The roots differ considerably from the stems both in their structure, and in their mode of growth. They exhibit, indeed, the appearance of medullary rays and of concentric layers, but they are destitute of any central pith, and they have no tracheæ; neither does their surface present any appearance of stomata. They increase in thickness in the same way as the stem increases. This law obtains both in exogenous and endogenous plants: they do not, however, grow in length by the elongation of any of their parts, but simply by additions made to their extremities. Their ramifications are not the result of the developement of buds, as are the branches of the stem; but they arise merely from the additional deposits taking different directions. Almost every part of the surface of the stem or branches may shoot forth roots if they are covered with earth, and properly moistened, and if they are supplied with sap from the circulating system of the plant itself. It is observed, however, that they generally grow from certain points on the surface of the bark, which appear as dark spots, and are termed *Lenticellæ.** Great variety exists in the form and disposition of roots in different families of plants, according to the particular purposes they are intended to serve, conformably to their general functions of

* This name was given to them by De Candolle, Annales des Sciences Naturalles, VII, 1. and Organographie, I, 94.

absorption and of mechanical support. Both these purposes are promoted by their sending out from their sides numerous fibrils, or lesser roots, which increase their firm hold upon the soil, as well as multiply the channels for the introduction of nourishment.

Nature has supplied various plants with certain appendages to the above mentioned structures, the use of which are for the most part sufficiently obvious. Of this description are the *tendrils*, which assist in fixing and procuring support to the stems of the weaker plants; the *stipulæ*, which protect the nascent leaves; and the *bracteæ*, which perform a similar office to the blossom. The different kinds of hairs, of down,* of thorns, and prickles, which are found on the surface of different plants, have various uses; some of which are easily understood, particularly that of defending the plant from molestation by animals. The sting of the nettle is of this class; and its structure bears a striking analogy, as we shall afterwards have occasion to notice, to that of the poisonous fangs of serpents.

The purposes answered by the down, which covers a great number of plants, are not very obvious. It perhaps serves as a protection from the injurious effects of cold winds on the tender surface: or it may have a relation to the depo-

---

* The finer hairs, and filaments of down, are composed of elongated cells, either single, or several conjoined end to end.

sition of moisture ; or, as it may be further conjectured, the number of points which are thus presented to the air may be designed to convey electricity from the atmosphere, or to restore the electric equilibrium, which may have been disturbed by the processes of vegetation.

In the smaller parts of plants, as in the general fabric of the whole, we find, on examination, the most admirable provision made, according to the particular circumstances of the case, for the mechanical objects of cohesion, support and defence. Thus the substance of the leaf, of which the functions require that a large surface be expanded to the air and light, is spread out in a thin layer upon a frame work of fibres, like rays, connected by a net-work of smaller fibrils, and constituting what is often called the skeleton of the leaf.

In all these vegetable structures, while the objects appear to be the same, the utmost variety is displayed in the means for their accomplishment, in obedience, as it were, to the law of diversity which, as has been already observed, seems to be a leading principle in all the productions of nature. It is more probable, however, judging from that portion of the works of creation, which we are competent to understand, that a specific design has regulated each existing variation of form, although that design may in general be utterly beyond the limited sphere of our intelligence.

§ 4. *Animal Organization.*

THE structures adapted to the purposes of vegetable life, which are limited to nutrition and reproduction, would be quite insufficient for the exercise of the more active functions and higher energies of animal existence. The power of locomotion, with which animals are to be invested, must alone introduce essential differences in their organization, and must require a union of strength and flexibility in the parts intended for extensive motion, and for being acted upon by powerful moving forces.

The animal, as well as the vegetable fabric is necessarily composed of a union of solid and fluid parts. Every animal texture appears to be formed from matter that was originally in a fluid state; the particles of which they are composed having been brought together and afterwards concreting by a process, which may, by a metaphor borrowed from physical science, be termed animal crystallization. Many of those animals, indeed, which occupy the lowest rank in the series, such as *Medusæ*, approach nearly to the fluid state; appearing like a soft and transparent jelly, which by spontaneous decomposition after death, or by the application of heat, is resolved almost wholly into a limpid watery fluid.* More accurate examination, however, will show that it is in reality not homogeneous, but that it consists of a large proportion of water, retained in a kind of spongy texture, the individual fibres of which, from their extreme fineness and uniformity of distribution, can with difficulty be detected. Thus even those animal fabrics, which on a superficial view appear most simple, are in reality formed by an extremely artificial and complex arrangement of parts. The progress of developement is continually tending to solidify the structure of the body. In this respect the lower orders of the animal kingdom, even when arrived at maturity, resemble the conditions of the higher classes at the earliest stages of their existence. As we rise in the scale of animals, we approximate to the condition of the more advanced states of developement which are exhibited in the highest class.

Great efforts have been made by physiologists to discover the particular structure which might be considered as the simplest element of all the animal textures; the raw material, as it were, with which the whole fabric is wrought: but

* Thus a Medusa, weighing twenty or thirty pounds, will, by this sort of general liquefaction, be found reduced to only a few grains of solid matter. Péron, Annales du Musée, tom. XV, p. 43. See also a memoir by *Quoy* and *Gaimard,* Annales des Sciences Naturalles, tom. I. p. 245.

their labours have hitherto been fruitless. Fanciful hypotheses in abundance might be adduced on this favourite topic of speculation; but they have led to no useful or satisfactory result. Haller, who pursued the inquiry with great ardour, came to the conclusion that there existed what he calls the simple or primordial fibre, which he represents as bearing to anatomy the same relation that a line does to geometry. Chemical analysis alone is sufficient to overturn all these hypotheses of the uniformity of the proximate elementary materials of the animal organs: for they are found to be extremely diversified in their chemical composition. Neither has the microscope enabled us to resolve the problem: for although it has been alleged by many observers that the ultimate elements of every animal structure consists of minute globules, little confidence is to be placed in these results obtained by the employment of high magnifying powers, which are open to so many sources of fallacy. That globules exist in great numbers, not only in the blood, but in all animal fluids, there can be no doubt: and that these globules, by cohering, compose many of the solids, is also extremely probable. But it is very doubtful whether they are essential to the composition of other parts, such as the fibres of the muscles, the nerves, the ligaments, the tendons, and the cellular texture: for the most recent, and apparently most accurate microscopical observations tend to show that no globular structure exists in any of these textures.*

The element which we can recognise without difficulty as composing the greater portion of animal structures, is that which is known by the name of the *cellular texture*. Although bearing the same designation as the elementary material of the vegetable fabric, it differs widely from it in its structure and mechanical properties. It is not, like that of plants, composed of a union of vesicles; but is formed of a congeries of extremely thin laminæ, or plates, variously connected together by fibres, and by other plates 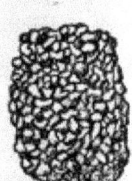 which cross them in different directions, leaving cavities or cells. (Fig. 25). These cells, or rather intervening spaces, communicate freely with one another; and, in fact, may be considered as one common cavity, subdivided by an infinite number of partitions into minute compartments. Hence the cellular texture is throughout readily permeable to fluids of all kinds, and retains these fluids in the manner, and on the same principle, as a sponge.

The cellular texture is not only the element, or essential material employed by nature in the

* See the Appendix to Dr. Hodgkin and Dr. Fisher's translation of Edwards's work on the Influence of Physical Agents on Life, p. 440.

construction of all the parts of the animal fabric; but, in its simplest form, it constitutes the general medium of connexion between adjacent organs, and also between the several parts of the same organ. Like the mortar which unites the stones of a building, the cellular texture is the universal cement employed to bind together all the solid structures. Its properties are admirably adapted to the mechanical purposes which are required in different parts of the frame: and these properties are variously modified and adjusted to suit the particular exigencies of the case. When, for instance, different parts require to be moveable upon each other, the cellular substance interposed between them has its state of condensation adapted to the degree of motion required. That which connects the muscles, or surrounds the joints, and all other parts concerned in extensive action, has a looser texture, being formed of broad and extensible plates, with few lateral adhesions, and leaving large interstices; while in the more quiescent organs, the plates of the cellular substance are thin and small, the fibres short and slender, and their intertexture closer and more condensed.

Besides being flexible and extensible, the cellular texture is also highly elastic, a property which is exceedingly advantageous in the construction of the frame. Not only the displacement of parts is resisted by their elasticity, but, when displaced, they tend to return to their natural position. This property performs a more important part in the mechanism of the animal than of the vegetable system; as might, indeed, have been anticipated from the more active and energetic movements required by the functions of the former.

The cellular texture, in its simple form, admits of the ready transmission of fluids through it; but it is necessary, on many occasions, to interpose a barrier to their passage. Such barriers are provided in *membranes*, which are merely modifications of the same material, spread out into a continuous sheet of a closer texture, after the surfaces of the plates have been brought to cohere so as to obliterate all the cellular interstices, and become impervious to fluids. Though equally flexible and elastic with the original texture of which it is formed, the membrane has acquired, by this consolidation, greater strength and firmness, properties which adapt it to a great number of important purposes.*

Membranes are extensively employed to connect distant organs, and often serve to determine the direction and extent of their relative motions.

* With a view of ascertaining the actual strength of membranes, Scarpa stretched a portion of peritoneum, (which is a very thin membrane lining the abdominal cavity), over a hoop, and placing weights upon its surface, found it did not give way till it was loaded with fifteen pounds.

They furnish strong coverings for the investment, the support, and the protection of all the important organs of the body. What Paley has termed the *package* of the organs is effected principally by their intervention. Membranes are also employed to line the interior of all the large cavities of the body, as those of the chest, and of the abdomen, or lower part of the trunk containing the organs of digestion. These membranes, after lining the sides of their respective cavities, are reflected back upon the organs which are enclosed in those cavities, so as to furnish them with an external covering. Their inner sides present every where a smooth and polished surface, over which the organs contained in the cavity may glide without injury. In all these cases, a thin fluid, called *serum*, is provided, which moistens and lubricates the surfaces that are in contact with one another, and obviates the injury that would otherwise arise from friction. From this circumstance, the linings of these cavities have been termed *serous membranes.* In the neighbourhood of joints, closed cavities of the same description, but of smaller size, are met with, for the obvious purpose of facilitating motion; and here also friction is prevented by a highly lubricating fluid, termed *synovia*, which is poured out between the surfaces of the membrane lining the cavities.

Membranes, being impermeable to fluids, are

ANIMAL ORGANIZATION. 103

extensively employed as receptacles for retaining them: forming, in the first place, sacs, or pouches of various kinds for that purpose. The ink-bag of the cuttle fish, the gall-bladder, and even the stomach itself, are examples of this kind of structure. The coats of these sacs, being very extensible and elastic, readily accommodate themselves to the variable bulk of their contents.

In the second place, we find membranes composing tubes of various descriptions for conducting fluids. Thus, in the higher classes of animals, the whole of the body is traversed by innumerable canals conveying different kinds of fluids. These canals, when uniting into trunks, or subdividing into branches, are called *Vessels* (Fig. 26).

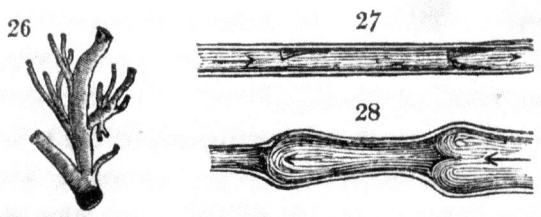

The fluids contained in vessels are never stagnant, but are almost always carried forwards in one constant direction. For preventing the retrograde motions of the fluids passing along these canals, recourse is had to the beautiful contrivance of valves. The inner membrane of the vessel is employed to construct these valves; for which purpose it is extended into a fold having the shape of a crescent; fixed by its convex edge to the sides of the vessel, while the other edge floats loosely in its cavity. Whenever the fluid is impelled in a direction contrary to its proper course, it raises the loose edge of the valve, which, being applied to the opposite side of the canal, effectually closes the passage. On the contrary, it presents no obstacle to the natural flow of the contents of the vessel, both edges being then closely applied to the same side. Frequently two, or even three valves are used at the same part, their edges being made to meet in the middle of the passage, like the floodgates, or locks of a canal.* Among the numberless instances of express contrivance which are met with in the examination of the fabric of animals, there is perhaps none more striking and more palpable, than this admirable mechanism of the valves.

As we ascend from the simpler to the more complicated systems of organization, adapted to a greater range of faculties, we find greater diversity in the mechanical means employed

* Fig. 27, representing the section of a vessel, is intended to show the position of the valves when applied to the sides of the vessel, by the stream moving onwards in the direction pointed out by the arrow. In Fig. 28, they are seen closing the passage by the retrograde pressure of the current.

for carrying on the functions of life. Textures of greater strength than can be constructed by membranes alone become necessary for the security, the support, and the defence of important organs; and more especially for the execution of extensive movements. For obtaining these advantages a peculiar species of fibres is provided, formed of a much denser substance than even the most consolidated forms of cellular texture. The animal product termed *albumen* possesses a much stronger cohesive power than *gelatin*, which is the basis of membrane. The addition of albumen, therefore, procures the quality required: and the fibres that are produced by its combination with gelatin are opaque, and of a glistening white colour. By interlacing fibres thus composed, a close texture is formed, which is exceedingly tough and unyielding. These *fibrous textures*, as they are termed, while they retain the flexibility of membranes, greatly surpass them in strength; but, being at the same time incapable of extension, they are necessarily devoid of elasticity. Hence they are adapted to form external tunics for the investment of such organs as are not intended to vary in their size. Occasionally these *fibrous capsules*, as they are called, send down processes into the interior of those organs, for the purpose of giving them mechanical support. This is the case, for instance, with the membranes surrounding the brain of quadrupeds, and which form two partitions, the one vertical, the other horizontal; both being firmly stretched in their respective positions, and serving to divide the pressure. In other cases these sheets of fibrous membrane are employed as bandages, tightly bracing the muscles, and retaining them in their relative situations. The joints are surrounded by similar bandages, known by the name of *Capsular Ligaments*.

In following the series of animal structures in the order of their increasing density, we find the proportion of albumen which enters into their composition becoming greater, while that of the gelatin and mucilage diminishes. When the product is more uniform in its composition it is in general less elastic than when it consists of a more complex combination of ingredients. A great preponderance of albumen tends also to diminish the elasticity. Thus the densest kinds of fibrous texture present, instead of thin and broad expansions of elastic membrane, the thick and elongated form of inextensible cords, constituting the ordinary *Ligaments*, and the *Tendons*. These structures resist with great power any force calculated to extend them : a property which of course excludes elasticity, but, when united with flexibility, implies great toughness. In a word, they possess all the qualities that can be desired in a rope. It will hardly be credited how great a force is required to stretch, or rather rend asunder a ligament; for it will not yield in any sensible degree until the force is increased so enormously as at once to dissever the whole contexture of its fibres. Nothing can be more artificially contrived than the interweaving of the fibres of ligaments; for they are not only disposed, as in a rope, in bundles placed side by side, and apparently parallel to each other: but, on careful examination, they are found to be tied together by oblique fibres curiously interlaced, in a way that no art can imitate. It is only after long maceration in water, that this complicated and beautiful structure can be unravelled.

The mechanical properties of these fibrous structures, which are strictly inextensible ligatures, render them applicable to purposes of connexion where motion is to be restrained. Many cases, however, occur in which a substance is wanted, uniting great compactness and strength with a considerable degree of elastic power. For this purpose a different texture is fabricated, consisting of twisted fibres, which impart this required elasticity. Such is the structure of the *elastic ligaments* of animals, which are very generally employed for the support of heavy parts that require being suspended. An instance occurs in quadrupeds, in that strong ligament which passes along the back and neck to be fixed to the head, and to support its weight when the animal stoops to graze. This, the *ligamentum nuchæ*, as it is termed, is capable of great extension, and by its elasticity reacts with considerable force in recovering its natural length, after it has been stretched. This ligament is particularly strong in the Camel, whose neck is of great length.* Another example of an elastic ligament occurs in that which connects the two shells of bivalve mollusca (as those of the oyster and muscle), and which keeps them open when the animal exerts no force to close them. The claws of the Lion, and other animals of the cat tribe, are retracted within their sheaths by means of two strong elastic ligaments. Structures of this kind are employed very extensively in the fabric of insects.†

* Many birds are provided with strong elastic ligaments connecting the vertebræ of the neck with those of the back; ligaments of the same kind are also employed for retaining the wings close to the body, where they are not used in flying: and a similar provision is made in the wings of bats. The weight of the bulky organs of digestion in herbivorous quadrupeds require some permanent support of this kind; and this is furnished by a broad, elastic, fibrous band extended across the lower part of the abdomen. It is particularly strong in the elephant, which remains more constantly in the horizontal position than most quadrupeds: and it has been remarked that the general cellular texture in this animal has an unusual degree of elasticity.—Hunter on the Blood, &c. p. 112.

† Chabrier, Mémoires du Musée, tom. vi. p. 416.

The animal substance which comes next in the order of density is *Cartilage*. The purposes for which this kind of structure is employed are those in which a solid basis is required for the support of softer or more flexible parts, and where the mechanical properties that are wanted are firmness, conjoined with some degree of elasticity. Cartilage (or gristle) is composed of a finer and more uniform material than any of the preceding structures. It consists almost wholly of albumen, with a slight proportion of calcareous matter. Unlike membrane in any of its forms, it contains no fibres, but, on being cut with a sharp knife, presents the appearances of a dense homogeneous substance of a white pearly hue. Its surface is smooth, and where it is exposed to friction, as in the joints, is often highly polished.

In all the inferior tribes of animals Nature employs cartilage to supply the place of bone when rigidity is required to be given to the fabric. In an extensive order of fishes, including the shark, the sturgeon, and the ray, we find the whole skeleton constructed of cartilage. In the fabric of very young quadrupeds cartilage is substituted for bone; and in the adult animal, various organs, such as the external ears, the eye-lids, the nostrils, and different parts of the apparatus of the throat and windpipe, are composed of flexible cartilage, which gives them a determinate shape and firmness. In all these cases bone, which, besides being three times as heavy, is devoid of elasticity, and liable to fracture, would have been much less suitable. Cartilage is often employed as an intermedium for connecting different bones, as for instance, between the ribs and the sternum, or breast-bone; whereby, besides the advantage of greater lightness, the pliancy of the material diminishes those jars which are incident to the frame in all its violent actions.

In the construction of cartilage, nature seems to have attained the utmost degree of density which could be given to an internal texture composed merely of the usual animal constituents. But substances of still greater hardness, united with perfect rigidity, are wanted, in numberless instances, for giving effectual protection to soft and delicate structures, for supplying a firm basis to the framework of the body, and for constructing levers of various kinds to be employed in the more energetic movements of the higher animals. For all these purposes it was necessary to superadd a material endowed with stronger cohesive powers, and capable by its dense concretion of forming solid and inflexible organs. The substances which nature has selected for this office are the salts of lime. Sometimes the Carbonate, and sometimes the Phosphate of lime is employed for forming these hard and unyielding structures; and often both these calcareous substances are united together in different proportions in the same solid fabric. When the carbonate of lime predominates, or is the sole earthy ingredient, it constitutes *Shell:* when there is a greater proportion of the phosphate, it is called a *Crust*, as is the case with the coverings of the lobster and the crab : when the earthy matter consists almost wholly of phosphate of lime, it composes the different forms of *Bone*. I shall have occasion to describe the formation and properties of each of these structures in the sequel.

The protection of the delicate structure of the fabric from the injurious influence of external agents is an object of great importance in the animal economy, and is one which nature has shown extreme solicitude to secure. For this purpose she has provided the *integuments*, under which designation are included not merely the skin, but also all the parts that are immediately connected with it, and are formed and nourished by the same vessels. No parts of the animal structure present greater diversity in their form and outward appearance than the integuments; yet it is easy to discover, amidst all these varieties, that the same general plan has been followed in their construction, and that each particular formation is the result of a combination of the same elementary structures. Of these elements the most important, and that which generally composes the chief bulk of the skin, is the *Corium*, or true skin. The outermost layer is termed the *Epidermis, Cuticle,* or *scarf-skin;* and between these there is often found an intermediate layer denominated the *Rete Mucosum,* or the *Pigmentum.*

The corium is generally of considerable thickness, and is composed of strong and tough fibres, closely compacted together, and pervaded by innumerable ramifications of blood-vessels of every kind. It is endowed with great flexibility, and is capable of being considerably extended; properties which fit it for readily accommodating itself to all the movements of the body and limbs, and to the variable bulk of the parts it covers. Being also very elastic, it soon regains its natural form and dimensions when left to itself after being stretched. The skin is connected with the subjacent muscles and other parts by a large quantity of cellular texture, which, according to the particular intentions of its formation, sometimes binds it tightly over these parts, and on other occasions allows of a free and extensive motion. This latter property is remarkably exemplified in the *Racoon,* an animal in which the skin hangs loosely on the limbs, and encloses the body like a wide elastic

ANIMAL ORGANIZATION. 113

garment; so that, however firmly a person may attempt to grasp the animal by the neck, it can easily turn its head completely round, and bite the fingers that are holding it. In like manner the skin of the frog is attached to the body only at a few places, and may be readily stripped off. A thin layer of muscular fibres is often found lying immediately underneath the skin, and is provided for the purpose of moving it over the subjacent parts. In animals that roll themselves into a ball, as the hedge-hog, these muscles are of great size and importance. We shall see that in the mollusca, this muscular apparatus is inseparably blended with the integument, and composes a peculiar structure, termed the *mantle*. Immediately covering the corium is the Rete Mucosum, which is a very thin layer of soft animal matter, composed of a net-work of delicate fibres, and containing more or less of the material from which the colour of the skin is derived.

The *Epidermis* is a membrane of a very peculiar nature, consisting of a thin expansion of albuminous matter, apparently homogeneous in its texture and composition. It is impervious to fluids, although capable of imbibing moisture, and of slowly transmitting a portion to the subjacent textures. Its thickness varies exceedingly in different parts; being adapted to the kind of protection it has to afford against pressure, friction, or other causes of injury. As it is not nourished by vessels, its outer layer is liable to wear away, or to become, by drying, unfit for use: and accordingly a separation of this outward layer generally takes place from time to time, the loss being speedily repaired by a fresh growth from the surface in contact with the skin. This process is often performed periodically, as is most remarkably exemplified in serpents.

Special provisions are made for preserving the cuticle in a healthy condition; and more particularly for defending it from the injurious action of the surrounding element. These sometimes consist of a supply of oily fluid, prepared in small cavities that are situated in the skin itself, and have minute ducts opening upon the surface. These cavities, termed *sebaceous follicles*, are generally interspersed in great numbers on different parts of the body, abounding more especially in those places where folds occur, and where there is the greatest friction. In fishes, mollusca, and other aquatic animals, the skin is at all times defended from the action of the water by a viscid or glutinous secretion, prepared in this manner, and continually poured out on the surface, through ducts, the orifices of which are easily seen with the naked eye, disposed in a line on each side of the body.

Connected with the skin, and more particularly with the cuticle, are structures of very various forms, intended for giving additional protection, occasionally contributing their aid in progressive motion, and sometimes fashioned into weapons of offence. In this class should be included all the varieties of hair, such as wool, fur, feathers, bristles, quills, and spines, as well as the more ordinary kinds of hair. All these resemble the cuticle in their chemical composition, differing only in their degrees of hardness and condensation. Horn is formed of the same material as hair; as are also the nails, the hoofs, and the claws of quadrupeds, and the scales of fishes, reptiles, and other animals. The integuments of insects, and especially their more solid and horny coverings, contain, however, as will hereafter be noticed, a peculiar chemical principle termed *Entomoline*.

All these parts seem to be but remotely connected with the vital actions of the system with which they are associated; and it is doubtful how far they are to be considered as appertaining to the living portion of the body, or as mere extraneous appendages. Yet, however they may differ in their forms, uses, and external appearance, they all are produced by the same kind of vascular structure, variously arranged to suit the particular circumstances in each case: and the mode of their developement and growth is essentially the same in all.

An extremely delicate and finely organized pulp, composed partly of a congeries of minute vessels, and partly of a gelatinous substance, in which these vessels are embedded, constitutes the apparatus by which the nutrient particles are selected, combined and elaborated into the materials of the intended structure. The original form, situation, and disposition of this vascular pulp, determines the future figure and extent of growth of the production which is to arise from it. The materials which compose it are deposited sometimes in masses, as in the scales of the crocodile; more generally in layers, as in

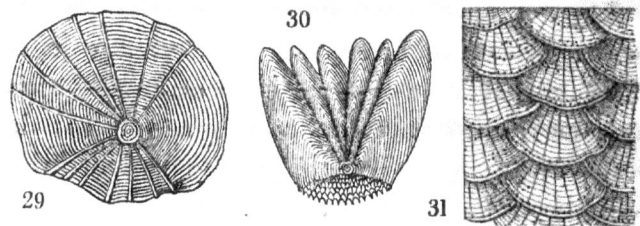

hoofs and nails, and also in the scales of fishes;* and occasionally in filaments, as in hair; which latter, again, are often agglutinated together by a strong cement, uniting them into a hard and solid structure, of which the horn of the rhinoceros is a remarkable example. In all cases, the portions thus successively produced,

* The laminated structure of the scales of fishes is easily distinguished by applying to them a high magnifying power. As the breadth of each new layer is greater than the last, its edges project further, the whole surface having that concentric striated appearance which renders it an interesting object for microscopic examination. Fig. 29 exhibits the striated surface of the scale of the *Cyprinus alburnus*, and Fig. 30 that of the *Perca fluriatilis*. The imbricated arrangement of these scales, resembling that of the tiles on the roof of a house, is shown in Fig. 31. All these figures represent the objects highly magnified.

ANIMAL ORGANIZATION. 117

are no longer susceptible of being nourished, and from the moment of their deposition, undergo no further change, except from the action of external agents. By the continual additions that are made to them at their base, or root, where the vessels deposit fresh materials, they gradually increase in size, protrude through the skin, and continue to grow by the same process, as long as these vessels continue in activity.

The nature of this process is well exemplified in the growth of hair. Fig. 32 shows the apparatus employed in its construction, in an imaginary section of the root, on a magnified scale. Every hair takes its rise from a minute vascular pulp, P, of an oval shape, which is implanted below the corium, or true skin, D.* This pulp is

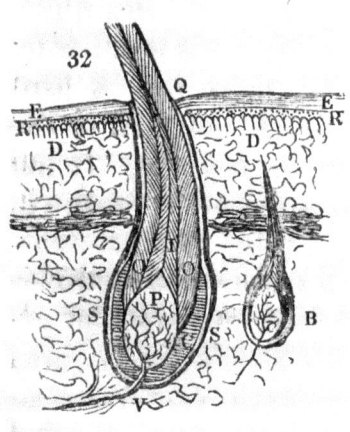

invested by a sheath or capsule, c, which, together with the contained pulp, and the root of the hair that grows from it, composes the *bulb* of the hair. The bulb itself is contained in a small cell formed by condensed membranes, s, to which it has no

---

* In the above figure E is a section of the Epidermis, or cuticle; the dotted part, R, represents the situation of the subjacent *rete mucosum*, and D, the derm, or corium.

attachment excepting at the lower part, v, where the vessels and nerves of the pulp are passing into it. The hair, growing by depositions from the inside of the capsule, which forms the outer part, o, of the shaft, and from the outside of the pulp, which forms the inner or central part, I, is forced upwards till it has pierced the skin; and in the course of its passage a canal is formed for it in the skin itself, and continuous with that which encloses the bulb: and the course of this canal is generally oblique. In the elephant, where the thickness and density of the hide, present considerable obstacles to the passage of the hairs through it, we may discover, on minute examination, many hairs that have only penetrated a certain way, as shown at B, without ever succeeding in reaching the surface.

An opinion has been very commonly entertained that each hair, on its protruding from underneath the cuticle, E, at the point Q, carries up along with it a portion of this outer integument, which, stretching as the hair increases in length, forms over it a very fine external tunic. But later observations have shown that this is not the case, and that there is simply an adhesion of the edge of the cuticle to the origin of the hair, without any accompanying prolongation; so that if the whole bulb be destroyed, and its pulp absorbed, the hair may be detached by the slightest force.

From this account it will be seen that a hair is, in its origin, tubular; the inner part being occupied by the pulp. But as the pulp extends only to that portion of the hair which is in a state of growth, it never rises above the surface of the skin; and the cavity in the axis of the hair is either gradually obliterated, or is filled with a dry pith, or light spongy substance, probably containing air. After a certain period, the bulb diminishes in size, from the collapse of the vessels, whose powers of supplying nutriment become exhausted. The first deficiency in its nourishment appears in the cessation of the deposit of colouring matter, and the hair in consequence becomes grey. After a time, the vessels becoming quite impervious, the bulb shrivels, the hair is detached, and the canal which its root occupied in the skin becomes obliterated.

The hair of different animals, and even of different parts of the same animal, is very various in its shape, texture, and mechanical properties. Sometimes, instead of being cylindrical, the filaments are more or less flattened, striated, deeply grooved, or even beaded. Instead of being solid, they may even be tubular: and they exhibit also the greatest diversity in their length, fineness, tenacity, rigidity, and disposition to curl. All these varieties may be traced to corresponding differences in the form, and the relative actions of the component parts of the bulb, namely, the pulp and its capsule.*

The structure of the organs by which hairs are formed is not easily distinguished, in the ordinary kinds of hair, on account of their minuteness: it is readily seen, however, in the large whiskers of the feline species, and also of the seal, which are subservient to more extended uses than those of merely covering the body, and which are even supplied with nerves, converting them into instruments of a sense of touch.

In the quills of the porcupine a still more complicated organization has been detected. Fig. 33 shows a quill with its bulbous root, detached from the body; and Fig. 34, a transverse section magnified. The bulb itself is contained in a distinct cell, shown at A, Fig. 35, which represents a longitudinal section of these organs. This cell contains a portion of fat in which the numerous vessels supplying its pulp and capsule are embedded. The bulb is itself surrounded by an outer sheath, s, into the cavity of which, B, there opens a duct, D, proceeding from a small cell or follicle, F, lodged in the cellular substance on the outside of the sheath. This upper cell communicates below with another cavity, c,

---

* See F. Cuvier's Memoir on the Formation of the Quills of the Porcupine, in the Nouvelles Annales du Muséum, I. 429.

ANIMAL ORGANIZATION. 121

containing an unctuous matter. During the formation of the quill this unctuous matter is supplied through this channel, and probably enters as an ingredient in its composition. The capsule of the pulp consists of two membranes, the one enveloping the other. Fig. 36 shows

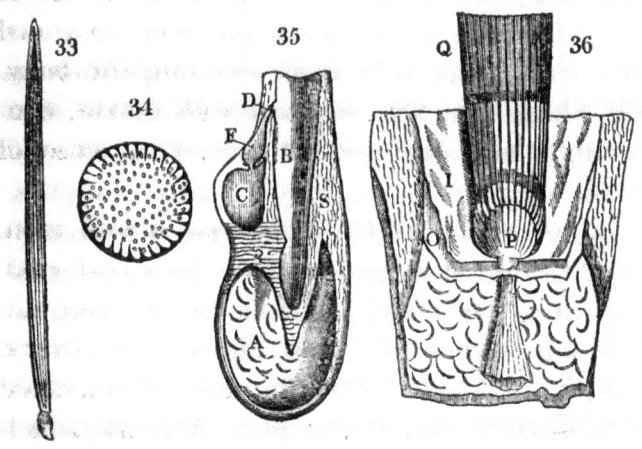

the bulb laid open by dividing the membranes and turning them aside. The horny portion of the quill is secreted by the internal membrane, I, and deposited in successive laminæ. The external membrane is seen at o. The pulp itself, seen at p, is still more curiously organized; its surface being fluted, or formed into longitudinal processes. The horny matter, being deposited on these processes, is moulded to their shape, and concretes into laminæ which converge from the circumference of the cylinder towards the centre. The section (Fig. 36) shows these converging laminæ, which being of a dark colour, give to the surface of the quill the appearance of being grooved; this, however, is merely an optical illusion, occasioned by the dark laminæ being seen through the transparent exterior covering; as may readily be detected by viewing the surface with a magnifying glass.* After a certain period of the growth of the quill, the pulp ceases to supply the materials for forming the spongy substance which occupies the interior of the quill. But although it no longer secretes, it still retains its place; and the capsule continuing to deposit horn, the quill becomes a hollow tube of considerable diameter. When it has attained a certain size, the pulp begins to shrink, and the diameter of the tube diminishes; so that it exhibits a tapering form at both ends. Thus mere variations in the bulk and the action of the pulp, accompanied with changes in that of the capsule, are sufficient to account for every diversity in the form and condition of the resulting structures.

Among the mechanical uses of the integument, that of serving as a cushion for relieving the more prominent parts of the frame, and especially of the bones, from unequal pressure, ought

* It is observed by F. Cuvier, that this striated appearance is peculiar to the quills of porcupines of the old world. Those from America have no such arrangement of laminæ.

not to be overlooked. This object is promoted by the interposition of a layer of *fat*, which is another animal substance entitled to be enumerated among the elements of its structure. It consists of an oily fluid, composed, according to the analysis of Chevreuil, of two constituent principles, which he has distinguished by the terms *stearine* and *elaine*. In warm blooded animals the temperature of the body is always sufficient to preserve this compound substance in a fluid form: but it is prevented from being diffused through the cellular texture by being contained in separate vesicles of extreme minuteness.* Hence the whole mass of the fat, which is thus formed of an aggregation of these vesicles, has not the appearance of being fluid, but seems to be composed of small grains united by membranous investments into larger masses; a structure peculiarly adapted to the purposes of a soft cushion, retaining only a small share of elasticity, and yielding only in a certain limited degree to pressure.

* Dr. Monro estimated their diameter at between the 800th and 600th of an inch. But their size varies in different animals.

§ 5. *Muscular Power*.

IN Machines contrived by human skill the chief art consists in devising expedients for regulating and directing the given moving power, so that it may bear, in the proper degree, and in the proper order, upon some particular objects, and produce some particular effect. The whole of the apparatus employed with this intention, however numerous may be its parts, however various the forms of its wheels, its levers, or its pulleys, and however complicated may be their connexions, resolves itself into a series of intermediate instruments for the transferrence of motion from the source of power, or the point where its action is impressed, to the parts which are designed ultimately to receive the action of the force employed. It is an established principle in physics, that mere machinery is incapable of generating mechanical force; and that such force must always be originally derived from some extraneous source. Some impulse from without, whether it be the pressure of the wind, the fall of a stream of water, or the action of men or horses, or any other kind of foreign agency, must be resorted to, both to set the engine in motion, and to continue its movements when they are once begun. Nor is the case essentially different when the source of motion apparently resides in some internal part of the machine itself; in a watch, for instance, which is actuated by the main spring; or in a steam engine, which is set in motion by the elastic vapour contained in its cylinder: the spring in the one case, and the vapour in the other, although they may in one sense be regarded as impelling powers, are, in reality, but intermediate agents in the distribution of a force originating from other sources. In the watch, the force may be traced to the hand which coiled the spring: in the steam-engine, to the fire, which has imparted elasticity to the vapour.

The living body differs from inorganic machinery in containing within itself a principle of motion not referable, as far as we can perceive, to any of the primary forces which exist in the inanimate world. This principle has been termed *contractility*. In animals of the simplest construction, every part of the substance of the body seems to be equally endowed with this contractile property, although exhibiting no distinct appearance of a fibrous structure. This is the case with all the lower zoophytes, such as the *Infusoria, Polypi, Medusæ*, and the simpler kinds of *Entozoa*.

Among the Polypi and Infusoria we meet with a singular mode of acting upon the surrounding fluid by means of very minute and generally microscopic filaments, which the animal, by some unknown power, causes to vibrate with great rapidity. Occasionally these organs are found even in animals belonging to the higher classes. Wherever they are met with they perform, as will hereafter be shown, very important functions; sometimes assisting in respiration, at other times contributing to the supply of food, and very generally serving as instruments of progressive motion.

In animals placed a little higher in the scale, we begin to trace the formation of fibres, which at first are irregularly scattered through the soft substance: but as the organization becomes more refined, these fibres are collected into bundles, and compose what are properly called *muscles*. Muscular fibres are attached at their extremities to the parts intended to be moved. In the lower animals these attachments are principally to the skin, or other external parts, which are subservient to the purposes of progressive motion. In the higher classes, the solid parts, or skeleton, being disposed more in the centre of the system, the muscles are applied to them in the interior of the body, and are more distinctly separated into masses, each having its proper function in the movements of the frame.

The peculiar property which characterises

the muscular fibre is that of suddenly shortening itself, so as to bring its two ends, and the parts to which those ends are connected, nearer to one another. This contraction is performed with astonishing quickness and force, and the accumulated effect of a large collection of these fibres, such as constitutes a muscle, is therefore capable of overcoming great resistances, or of raising enormous weights. Those muscles, which, by means of their nerves, as will hereafter be noticed, are subservient to voluntary motion, are excited into action by an exertion of the will of the animal. There are, however, a great number of other muscles, the contractions of which are involuntary, that is, are produced by other causes than the will.*

Muscular contractility, of which there exists no trace in the vegetable kingdom,† has been established by nature as the primary moving power of the animal machine. This agent is

* These two classes of muscles do not differ in their outward appearance: but Dr. Hodgkin has lately pointed out a curious difference in the microscopic structure of the fibres of some of the involuntary muscles. See Appendix to his Translation of Edwards on the influence of Physical Agents in Life, p. 443.

† The principal instances, which have been adduced in support of the opinion that muscularity occasionally exists in vegetable structures, are the alternate movements of the leaflets of the *Hedysarum gyrans*, which have been fancifully compared to the movements of the ribs in respiration; the quick motions of the stamina of the *Berberis*, *Opuntia*, and many plants of the genera *Carduus*, and *Centaurea*; the closing of the

resorted to on all occasions where considerable mechanical force is wanted; just as in a great manufactory, where an immense quantity of machinery is to be set in motion, and a great variety of work is to be executed, the human mechanist avails himself of some constant moving force, such as that of water, or steam. The laws of inorganic matter furnish no power that could conveniently have been applied in the animal body for that purpose; but muscular power, from its high intensity, is adequate to every object, and has been accurately adjusted, by the most refined application of the laws of mechanism, to all the degrees and kinds of effects intended to be produced.

Although the power be the same, yet the mode of its application is exceedingly diversified; and the comparison of these diversities is the more interesting, inasmuch as there are few of the animal functions in which the ends to be answered are so definite, and the operation of the expedients employed is so plain and intelligible. For while the intricate chemical

---

leaves of the *Dionæa muscipula;* and the shrinking of those of the *Mimosa pudica*, or sensitive plant. On a superficial view, it must be acknowledged that these motions bear a resemblance to the effects of muscular contractility; but I believe that naturalists are now generally agreed that there is no real analogy between these phenomena, and that there is no substantial evidence for the existence of that property in the vegetable kingdom.

processes of the living system generally elude our research, and the higher faculties of sensation and perception are dependent on still more recondite and mysterious powers of nature, the mechanical functions are effected by the simpler properties of matter, and allow us a clearer insight into the wonderful art which has been exerted in their accomplishment.

Muscles, during their contraction, increase in thickness in the same proportion as they diminish in length.* It is on this account, more

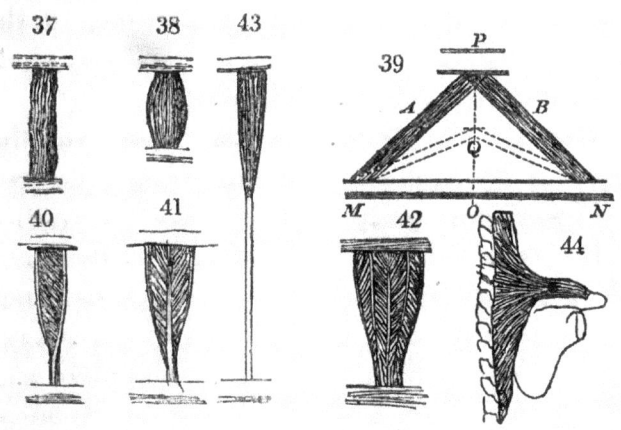

especially, that a knowledge of anatomy is so necessary to the painter and the sculptor. In every movement and attitude of the body, some particular sets of muscles are in action,

* This is illustrated by the annexed figures, 37 and 38, the former showing the relaxed and elongated, and the latter the contracted and swollen state of the same muscle.

and consequently tense and prominent, while others are relaxed and flattened; differences which it is requisite that the artist should faithfully express, in order to give a correct representation of the living figure.

The dilatation of the muscular fibres in thickness, which accompanies their contraction in length, would, if these fibres had been loose and unconnected, have occasioned too great a separation and displacement, and have impeded their co-operation in one common effect. Nature has guarded against this evil by collecting a certain number of the elementary fibrils, and tying them together with threads of cellular substance; thus forming them into a larger fibre; and again packing a number of these fibres into larger bundles: always surrounding each packet with a web of cellular tissue; which thus forms a separate investment for each. This plan of successive reunion into larger and larger assemblages is carried on through several gradations of size, till the entire muscle is completed.

That we may be the better able to appreciate the excellence of the plans adopted in the mechanism of the animal frame, let us inquire what arrangements would occur to us, prior to an acquaintance with those actually adopted, as the most advantageous dispositions of the muscular power. It is evident, that the simplest mode would be that of extending the fibres of the muscle in a straight line between the points intended to be brought nearer to each other. This direct application of the power, however, is seldom compatible with convenience, unless the parts to be moved are of very small size, and require very delicate adjustments. Straight muscles, accordingly, are employed chiefly for the movements of the minuter parts of the apparatus belonging to the senses, such as the eye, and the ear, and also that of the voice. In insects, when the hard case, or skeleton, is wholly external, this direct application of the moving force is also very generally employed. The shells of the bivalve mollusca, as of the *Oyster* and the *Cardium*, are closed by one or two straight muscles, the fibres of which pass immediately from the inner surface of the one to that of the other.

In the greater number of cases it is more convenient to place the muscle in a situation which causes it to act obliquely with respect to the direction of the motion produced in the part to which it is attached. This will, of course, be attended with a loss of force corresponding to the degree of obliquity; but there are, at the same time, advantages gained, both in point of velocity of motion, and also in the effect being produced by a smaller extent of contraction in the fibres of the muscle. Oblique muscles are frequently employed in pairs, and are made to act on opposite sides of the line of the intended motion, which is, in this case, the diagonal between the direction of the two equal forces. Thus, in order to bring a bone at P, Fig. 39, down to the point Q, the two muscles A and B, extending from the fixed points M and N, may be employed; for as they exert forces in the directions P M and P N, there will result a force in the intermediate direction P O: and the effect desired will be accomplished more quickly, and with a smaller extent of contraction in the muscles producing it, than if the same power had been applied by means of a straight muscle in the direction P O.* It is by means of two sets of muscles, acting thus obliquely, that the ribs are brought in closer approximation every time that the chest is elevated in breathing. Thus carefully does nature dispose the muscular fibres so as to obviate the necessity of their being contracted beyond a certain extent: and thus does she economize, as much as possible, the expenditure of muscular power, wherever there is a constant call for its exertion.

The principle which I have just explained, whereby certain advantages result from the ob-

* See a paper by Dr. Monro, in the Transactions of the Royal Society of Edinburgh. Vol. iii. p. 250.

liquity of the action of muscular fibres, is applied, not only to the entire muscle, but also to the internal arrangement of its fibres. Thus, we generally find that, in a flat muscle, its upper and under surfaces are covered by a thin sheet of fibrous texture, or thin expansion of ligament or tendon; and that the muscular fibres which are attached to them are directed obliquely from the one to the other, in the manner represented by the section, Fig. 40. There is frequently a middle tendinous layer interposed between those that are on the surface (as shown in Fig. 41), in which case the muscular fibres pass obliquely from the former to the latter, but in different directions on each side; like the fibres proceeding from the shaft of a pen. A muscle thus constructed has accordingly been termed a *penniform muscle;* as is exemplified in the straight muscle inserted into the knee-pan (the *rectus extensor cruris*), and also in the muscle which bends the great toe (the *flexor pollicis pedis longus*). The arrangement first described, Fig. 40, forms the *semi-penniform muscle;* an instance of which occurs in the muscle of the leg, which is termed the *semimembranosus*. Frequently the structure is rendered still more complex, by the interposition of several tendinous layers among the fleshy fibres. This arrangement, which constitutes a *complex muscle,* (as shown in Fig. 42) occurs, for example, in the *Solæus,* or large muscle, which raises the heel, and forms the thickest part of the calf of the leg.

It very commonly happens in the animal frame, as it does in other machines, that the presence of the moving agent in the spot where its action is wanted, would be exceedingly inconvenient. The usual plan adopted for transferring the effect of the moving power to a distant point is the employment of a rope, or strap. Such is precisely the office of the *tendons*, which are long straps, attached at one end to the muscle, and at the other to the bone, or other part intended to be moved. (See Fig. 43). If the hand, for instance, had been encumbered with all the muscles which are necessary for the movements of the fingers, it never could have performed its office as a delicate mechanical instrument. These muscles, accordingly, are disposed high up on the arm, and their tendons are made to pass along the wrist to the joints of the fingers which are to be moved.

The employment of tendons is accompanied with this farther advantage, that by their intervention the united power of all the fibres of the muscle may be obtained, and concentrated upon any particular point. In this respect, likewise, they resemble a rope, at which a great number of men are pulling at the same moment, and whose combined strength is thus brought into action. Another principal use of tendons is that a different direction may, by their means, be given to the moving power, without altering its position. Many instances occur of their application in this manner, by their being made to pass round corners of bones, and along grooves, or channels, expressly formed for their transmission, and producing the effect of pullies.

In a great number of muscles, the fibres, instead of running parallel to one another, are made either to converge, or to diverge, in order to suit particular kinds of movements: and we frequently find that different portions of the same muscle have the power of contracting independently of the rest, so as to be capable of producing very various effects, according as they act separately or in combination. This is exemplified in the muscle of the back, called the *Trapezius*, represented in Fig. 44. In many instances, the fibres radiate in all directions from a common centre: this is the case with the delicate muscle of the ear-drum, as shown in Fig. 45. In that of the elephant, which is about an inch and a half in diameter, these radiating fibres are very conspicuous, even to the naked eye: and they are also visible in the membrane of the human ear, when viewed with a good microscope.[*]

At other times, the muscular fibres run in a

---

[*] Home Phil. Trans. for 1800, p. 1.

circular direction, forming what is called an *orbicular*, or *sphincter muscle*, of which an example occurs in that which surrounds and closes the eye. (Fig. 46.) Very frequently these two last modes of arrangement are united in some part, as appears to be the case in the membrane of the eye, called the *Iris*. (Fig. 47.) The circular fibres of the iris surround the central aperture, or pupil, the size of which they diminish when they contract; while on the contrary, the radiating fibres, acting on the inner circle, and drawing it nearer to the outer circumference, which is fixed, lessen the breadth of the ring, and consequently enlarge the circular aperture.

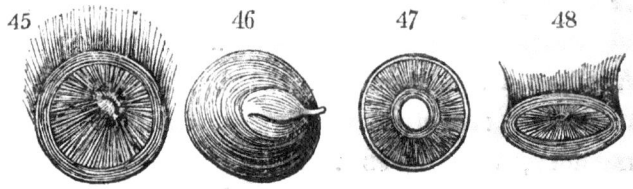

A similar combination of radiating and circular fibres is employed in the construction of flat, or slightly concave muscular disks, which are thus rendered capable of exerting a strong force of adhesion to the surfaces on which they are applied. In these organs the circular fibres are placed at the circumference, and the radiating fibres in the interior of the sucker, (see Fig. 48); so that, while the margin of the disk is closely applied to the object, the force resulting from the contraction of the circular fibres is exerted to remove the central portions from the surface of attachment, and thereby tends to create a vacuum underneath the disk ; the two surfaces remain, therefore, strongly attached by the atmospheric pressure, which acts on their outer sides. An apparatus of this kind, as we shall afterwards find, is met with very frequently among the lower orders of the animal kingdom.

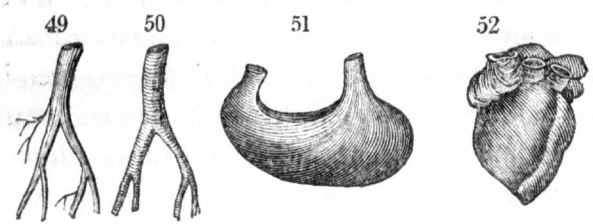

Another kind of circular disposition of fibres is that which occurs in the muscular coats surrounding canals of various kinds, such as the blood vessels and the alimentary tube. Their action tends to contract the diameter of the canal, and to exert pressure on its contents. In these cases, there is generally at the same time provided another layer of fibres, disposed longitudinally, as shown in Fig. 49 ; the circular fibres being seen in Fig. 50. The action of the longitudinal fibres is evidently to shorten the canal ; while that of the circular fibres, by the yielding and the partial reaction of the contents of the vessel, has a tendency to extend it. The *Ascidia*, which is a species of marine worm, is an example of an animal whose skin contains a union of straight and circular fibres, by which all its movements are readily performed. Many instances occur in the cylindrical envelopes of animals, of the combination of a third series of fibres, passing obliquely, with those which have transverse and longitudinal directions. In the muscular skin of the *Leech*, for example, besides two internal layers of longitudinal fibres, an external one has lately been discovered, which is composed of oblique or spiral fibres, crossing one another in opposite directions, and greatly facilitating the varied movements of the animal.*

A variety of still more complicated arrangements may be traced in the fibres of those muscles which invest hollow sacs, or receptacles, such as the stomach, (Fig. 51,) and the heart, (Fig. 52). We find, in the substance of these organs, sets of fibres, which pass in a spiral direction, and which, consequently, unite the effects of both longitudinal and circular fibres; and, when combined with either of these, they serve to modify and regulate the actions of each organ in a great variety of ways.†

---

* Carus, Tabulæ Anat. Comp. fol. Tab. I. Fig. 6.

† The muscular fibres of the heart are disposed in two layers; each set passing in a spiral course from the basis, or broad part, to the point or apex; but the direction of the turns being different in each, the two layers cross or decussate, producing the

The infinite mechanical skill, with which the moving power has been applied to the purposes to be accomplished, is displayed not only in the larger organs, where great force is to be exerted, but also, in a still more conspicuous manner, in the execution of the smaller motions, requiring the most accurate regulation, and the nicest adjustments. We cannot but be struck with the accordance which may often, in these instances, be traced with human contrivances, when the greater motions are rapidly executed by one set of agents, acting with considerable power and velocity, while the minuter approximations to the exact positions are effected by a distinct part of the apparatus, capable of more delicate action, though with a smaller force. Thus, while the astronomer brings his telescope round by powerful machinery, so as to direct it to that part of the heavens, where the object he wishes to view is situated, a more nice mechanism is employed to direct the instrument accurately to the exact point; and again another is provided for making the proper focal adjustments. Many parallel cases occur in the mechanism of the animal frame; one set of powerful muscles being em-

effect and procuring the advantages of a combination of oblique muscles already explained. Thus beautifully is the arrangement of the muscular fibres of the heart calculated to produce the rapid and complete expulsion of its contained blood, with the smallest amount of contraction in the individual fibres.

ployed for the larger movements, and another set provided for the accurate regulation of the more delicate inflexions and nicer positions. This we shall find exemplified in the movements of the fingers, and of many of the organs of the finer senses.

In general, however, we may observe that the mechanical expedients devised by Nature for effecting each particular purpose are characterised by the most admirable simplicity. In this respect, also, as well as in all others, we cannot fail to recognise their infinite superiority over every corresponding invention of man.

> " In human works, though labour'd on with pain,
> A thousand movements scarce one purpose gain;
> In God's, one single can its ends produce,
> Yet serves to second too some other use." Pope.

We may generally observe, in the mechanism of the joints, that the muscles are made to act, either directly or by means of their tendons, at a point much nearer to the axis of motion than the resistance to be overcome. With regard to the direct force, therefore, it is evident that they must act with a great mechanical disadvantage; and this disadvantage is still farther increased by the obliquity of the action with reference to the direction of the motion. But the contractile power, which is inherent in the muscular fibre, is so enormous, as amply to afford these losses, great as they necessarily are; while, on the other hand, full compensation is made by the greater freedom and velocity of motion thereby obtained. Strength is sacrificed without scruple to beauty of form or convenience of purpose; and that disposition of the force is always adopted, from which, on the whole, the greatest practical benefit results. Every where do we find the wisest adaptation of muscular power to the objects proposed, whether it be exerted in laborious efforts of the limbs and trunk; whether employed in balancing the frame, or urging it into quick progression; or whether it be applied to direct the delicate evolutions of the fingers, the rapid movements of the organs of speech, or the more exquisite adjustments of the eye, or of the internal ear. Amidst the endless combinations of machinery exhibited in different parts of the animal kingdom, although the mode of application be diversified in ten thousand ways, the original power is still of the same kind, and is regulated by the same physical laws; and similar instruments are employed in effecting this infinite variety of purposes, by the all-wise and omnipotent Architect of animated creation.

Chapter II.

THE MECHANICAL FUNCTIONS IN ZOOPHYTES.

§ 1. *General Observations.*

The mechanism of an organized being is designed to fulfil various important objects. These we may distinguish into two classes; the one having reference to its internal welfare, the other to its relations with external bodies. The different parts of its system must, in the first place, be mechanically united and supported, as well as protected from injurious external impressions; and they must at the same time be so constructed as to admit of all the internal movements, which the performance of their functions renders necessary. They must, in the second place, be made capable of exerting upon external matter the actions which conduce to their well being; and in order to enlarge their sphere of action, they must have the power of transferring the whole body from one place to another; or, in other words, of effecting its *progressive motion*.

The objects included in the first of these

branches of the mechanical functions are answered by the organization both of the vegetable and the animal systems: but those of the latter belong exclusively to the functions of animal life. The power of locomotion, more especially, constitutes the most general and palpable feature of distinction between these two classes of beings. A plant, during the whole period of its existence, is fixed to the spot where it was first produced, and is dependent for the continuance of its life on local circumstances; such as the nature of the soil in which its roots are embedded, and the qualities of the air and water in its immediate vicinity. It is exposed to the action of the surrounding elements, and affected by their vicissitudes, without the means of retreat, and without the power of reaction. With respect to all external agents, indeed, vegetables may be regarded as passive beings. Very different are the condition and destination of animals. Excepting a few among the lower orders of the creation, such as Zoophytes and Mollusca, all animals are gifted with the power of spontaneously changing their situation, according to their several wants and necessities, and are thus enabled to seek and to choose those objects which are salutary, and to avoid or reject those which are injurious. Nature has, for these purposes, furnished them with a more complex organization and more varied powers, adapted to a greater diversity of pursuits, and to a higher and more expanded sphere of existence.

The power of progressive motion is enjoyed in very different degrees by different races of animals, according to the particular model on which they are constructed, and the relations which their organization bears to the element assigned as their residence. All the mechanical circumstances in their economy, indeed, are so closely linked together, as scarcely to admit of being considered separately. Thus we find, in one animal, a variety of mechanical effects accomplished by one and the same instrument; while, in others, they are each produced by a separate and distinct organ. In some, the leading principle of the construction is simplicity; in others, the most elaborate mechanism is displayed. But the means have constant reference to the design, and are ever varied in exact conformity with the change of purpose. The relative advantages of each plan of structure appear to have been carefully estimated, and studiously balanced. Each quality has been bestowed in different degrees of perfection; so that in following the series of gradation among the successive tribes of animals, we occasionally meet with favoured species, endowed with great superiority in some particular faculty. Some animals excel in swiftness; others in strength. Some are qualified to dive into the recesses of the deep; others to flutter in the light regions of air; while, in many of the inferior ranks, we find all these objects renounced for the more certain advantage of security, which the softer texture of the organs renders one of paramount importance. That construction of limbs which favours certain movements will necessarily interfere with the ready performance of others, and must preclude the developement of the organs which would be necessary for facilitating them. Different kinds of prey require dexterity in particular actions for their pursuit and seizure. The animal is, in one case, formed for climbing trees; in another, for burrowing in the earth: in a third, for perforating wood. Some are provided with organs for penetrating into the bodies of other animals; others with the means of ensnaring their captives; while others, again, instil into the veins of their victims a deadly poison. Hence it is necessary, in studying the organization of animals, to bestow particular attention on the habits and mode of life for which each respective tribe and species has been destined.

In the examination of the mechanical functions which will form the first part of this treatise, I shall keep in view, as the leading object of inquiry, the faculty of *progressive motion*, noticing its different degrees of perfection as we follow the ascending series of animals; but adverting, also, occasionally, to the other topics which belong to this class of functions.

It may be observed in general, that the mechanical construction of animals which constantly inhabit a watery element is more simple than the construction of those which live on land, and are encompassed by a lighter medium. Differing but little in their specific gravity from the fluid in which they are immersed, aquatic animals are necessarily supported, on all sides, by a powerful hydrostatic pressure, which nearly balances the force of gravity, and counteracts the tendency of their bodies to descend in the fluid. Many of the obstacles to progressive motion are thus removed; and there is no necessity for the compactness of frame, and the rigidity and cohesion of substance which are required in terrestrial animals.

The animals that occupy the lower divisions of the scale can exist only in a liquid element. Their forms present many analogies with vegetables; and hence they have been denominated *Zoophytes*, that is, animated plants: but as it is now well ascertained that they possess the essential characters of animals, the term of *Phytozoa*, or plant-like animals, which has been given to them by some modern writers, would appear to be a more appropriate designation. It is, however, scarcely worth while, at the present day, to change a name so generally received as that of Zoophytes, and the application of which is not likely to lead to any misunderstanding.

§ 2. *Porifera, or Sponges.*

AMONG Zoophytes, the lowest station in the scale of organization is occupied by the tribes of *Porifera*, the name given by Dr. Grant to the animals which form the various species of sponge, and which are met with in such multitudes on every rocky coast of the ocean, from the shores of Greenland to those of Australia. Sponges grow to a larger size within the tropics, and are found to be more diminutive, and of a firmer texture, as we approach the Polar circles. Dr. Grant observes[*] that they are met with equally in places covered perpetually by the sea, as in those which are left dry at every recess of the tide. They adhere to, and spread over the surface of rocks and marine animals, to which they are so firmly attached that they cannot be removed without lacerating and injuring their bodies. "Although they thrive best," he farther remarks, " in the sheltered cavities of rocks, they come to maturity in situations exposed to

[*] Edinburgh Philosophical Journal, vol. xiii. p. 94.

the unbroken fury of the surge. They cover the nakedness of cliffs and boulders; they line with a variegated and downy fleece the walls of submarine caves, or hang in living stalactites from the roof."

In their general appearance they resemble many kinds of plants, but in their internal organization they differ entirely from every vegetable production; being composed of a soft flesh, intermixed with a tissue of fibres, some of which are solid, others tubular; and the whole being interwoven together into a curious and complicated net-work. The substance of which this solid portion, or basis, is formed, is composed partly of horn, and partly of siliceous or calcareous matter. It has been termed the *axis* of the Zoophyte; and as it supports the softer substance of the animal, it may be regarded as performing the office of a skeleton, giving form and protection to the entire fabric.

The material of which the fleshy portion is composed is of so tender and gelatinous a nature that the slightest pressure is sufficient to tear it asunder, and allow the fluid parts to escape; and the whole soon melts away into a thin oily liquid. When examined with the microscope the soft flesh is seen to contain a great number of minute grains, disseminated through a transparent gelly. Every part of the surface of a living sponge (as may be seen in Fig. 53) presents to the eye two kinds of orifices; the larger having a rounded shape, and generally raised

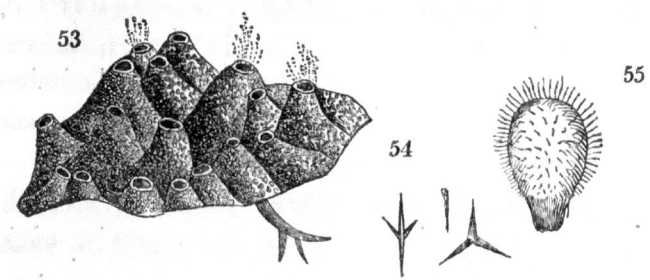

margins, which form projecting papillæ; the smaller being much more numerous, and exceedingly minute, and constituting what are termed the *pores* of the sponge.

It has, for a long time, been the received opinion among naturalists that this superficial layer of gelatinous substance was endowed with a considerable power of contractility: it was generally believed that it shrunk from the touch, and that visible tremulous motions could be excited in it by punctures with sharp instruments, or other modes of irritation. It is extraordinary that errors like these should have crept into the writings of modern zoologists of the highest authority, such as Lamarck, Bruguiere, Gmelin, Bosc, and Lamouroux.* The notion that the

* This mistaken view was adopted by Cuvier in the first edition of his " Regne Animal," T. iv. p. 88.; but Dr. Grant's rectification of the error is noticed in the second edition of that work.— T. iii. p. 322.

sponge contracts when touched is of very ancient date, for it may even be traced beyond the time of Aristotle; and it has been handed down by succeeding naturalists, and echoed from the one to the other, so as to have gained admission, without being questioned, in all the recent systematic works on Zoology.

The alleged spontaneous palpitation of the flesh, occurring in particular parts, had its origin in the views taken of the nature of sponges by Marsigli, an Italian naturalist, who, in the year 1771, announced that he had seen movements of dilatation and contraction in the round apertures visible on the surface of sponges. This statement, so confidently advanced, seems to have made a strong impression on Ellis, who, while pursuing a similar train of observations, came to persuade himself that he could see, not only the movements described by Marsigli, but also the passage of water to and fro, through the same apertures. He communicated this account to the Royal Society in 1765; it was published in its Transactions,* and will ever remain an instructive proof of the degree in which our very perceptions may be influenced by preconceived views, and by the force of the imagination. Pallas immediately admitted, without examination, the hasty assertion of Ellis, into his " *Elen-*

---

* Vol. lv. p. 284.

chus Zoophytorum;" whence it was copied by succeeding authors, and the error became at length so widely disseminated, that for more than half a century it was received as an established fact in natural history. The elaborate and accurate researches of Dr. Grant on these subjects have at length dispelled the prevailing illusion, and have clearly proved that the sponge does not possess, in any sensible degree, that power of contraction which had, for so many ages, been ascribed to it.*

Dr. Grant has also shown the true nature of the currents of fluid issuing at different points from the surface of these animals, as well as the absence of all visible movements in the orifices which give exit to the fluid. Never did he find, in his experiments, the slightest appearance of contraction produced in any part of the sponge, by puncturing, lacerating, burning, or otherwise injuring its texture, or by the application of corrosive chemical agents. Of his discovery of the fluid currents, he gives the following interesting account: "I put a small branch of the *Spongia coalita*, with some sea-water, into a watch-glass, under the microscope, and, on reflecting the light of a candle through the fluid,

---

* See his papers on this subject in the Edinburgh Philosophical Journal, vol. xiii. p. 95 and 333, from which most of the facts mentioned in the above account are taken.

I soon perceived that there was some intestine motion in the opaque particles floating through the water. On moving the watch-glass, so as to bring one of the apertures on the side of the sponge fully into view, I beheld, for the first time, the splendid spectacle of this living fountain, vomiting forth, from a circular cavity, an impetuous torrent of liquid matter, and hurling along, in rapid succession, opaque masses, which it strewed everywhere around. The beauty and novelty of such a scene in the animal kingdom, long arrested my attention, but after twenty-five minutes of constant observation, I was obliged to withdraw my eye from fatigue, without having seen the torrent for one instant change its direction, or diminish, in the slightest degree, the rapidity of its course. I continued to watch the same orifice, at short intervals, for five hours, sometimes observing it for a quarter of an hour at a time, but still the stream rolled on with a constant and equal velocity." About the end of this time, however, the current became languid, and, in the course of another hour, it ceased entirely. Similar currents were afterwards observed by Dr. Grant in a great variety of species. They take place only from those parts that are under water, and immediately cease when the same parts are uncovered, or when the animal dies.

It thus appears that the round apertures in

the surface of a living sponge are destined for the discharge of a constant stream of water from the interior of the body; carrying away particles, which separate from the sides of the canals, and which are not only seen, under the microscope, constantly issuing from these orifices, but may even be perceived by the naked eye, propelled occasionally in larger masses.*

For the supply of these constant streams, it is evident that a large quantity of water must be continually received into the body of the sponge. It is by the myriads of minute pores, which exist in every part of the surface, that this water enters, conveying with it the materials necessary for the subsistence of the animal. These pores conduct the fluid into the interior, where, after percolating through the numerous channels of communication which pervade the substance of the body, it is collected into wider passages, terminating in the fecal orifices above described, and is finally discharged. The mechanism by which these currents are produced is involved in much obscurity. There can be no doubt that they are occasioned by some internal movements; and the analogy of other zoophytes

* The currents issuing from the larger orifices are best seen by placing the living animal in a shallow vessel of sea water, and strewing a little powdered chalk on the surface, the motions of which will render the currents very sensible to the eye. Fig. 53 exhibits these phenomena.

would lead us to ascribe them to the action of fibrils, or *cilia*, as they are termed, projecting from the sides of the canals through which the streams pass; but these cilia have hitherto eluded observation, even with the highest powers of the microscope.

The organization of sponges is as regular and determinate as that of any other animal structure, and presents as systematic an arrangement of parts. In some species, such as the common sponge, the basis is horny and elastic, and composed of cylindric tubes, which open into each other, and thus form continuous canals throughout the whole mass.

Others have a kind of skeleton, composed of a tissue of needle-shaped crystals of carbonate of lime, or of silex. These hard and sharp-pointed fibres, or *spicula*, are disposed around the internal canals of the sponge, in the order best calculated to defend them from compression, and from the entrance of foreign bodies. Some of these spicula are delineated in Fig. 54: but their forms, although constant in each species, admit of considerable diversity in the different kinds of sponge.

Although sponges, in common with the greater number of zoophytes, are permanently attached to rocks, and other solid bodies in the ocean, and are consequently destined to an existence as completely stationary as that of plants, yet such is not the condition of the earlier, and more transitory stages of their developement. Nature, ever solicitous to provide for the multiplication of each race of beings, and for their dissemination over the habitable globe, has always provided effectual means for the accomplishment of these important ends. The seeds of plants are either scattered in the immediate neighbourhood of the parent, and take root in the adjacent soil, or are carried to more distant situations by the wind or other agents. In the animal kingdom, the young offspring of those races which are endowed with a wide range of activity, are reared on the spot where they were produced, either by the fostering care of the parent, or by means of the nourishment with which they are surrounded in the egg, and there remain until the period when, by the acquisition or extension of locomotive powers, they are enabled, in their turn, to go in quest of food. But in the tribes of animals at present under our consideration, this order is reversed. It is the parent that is chained to the same spot from an early period of its growth, and it is on the young that the active powers of locomotion have been conferred, apparently for the sole purpose of seeking for itself a proper habitation at some distance from the place of its birth; and when once it has made this selection, it there fixes itself unalterably for the remaining term of its existence.*

The parts of the *Spongia panicea*, which are naturally transparent, contain at certain seasons a multitude of opaque yellow spots, visible to the naked eye, and which, when examined by means of a microscope, are found to consist of groups of ova, or more properly *gemmules*,† since we cannot discover that they are furnished with any envelope. In the course of a few months these gemmules enlarge in size, each assuming an oval or pear-like shape, and are then seen projecting from the sides of the internal canals of the parent, to which they adhere by their narrow extremities. In process of time, they become detached, one after the other, and are swept along by the currents of fluid, which are rapidly passing out of the larger orifices. Fig. 55 represents one of these gemmules detached

* Phenomena, which appear to bear some analogy with these, have been noticed in the vegetable kingdom. The tribe of *Zoocarpia*, produce a kind of fruit, which when detached from the parent, appears to possess powers of spontaneous motion, until the period of its taking root, and growing like a vegetable structure. These singular productions, which seem, in their progressive developements, to possess alternately the characters of vegetables and of animals, may perhaps be regarded as connecting links between the two great kingdoms of living nature.

† *Gemmule* is a term derived from the Latin word *gemma*, a bud: and its meaning, as applied to zoophytes, is that of a young animal, not contained within an envelope, or egg.

from the parent sponge. When thus set at liberty, they do not sink by their gravity to the bottom of the water, as would have happened had they been devoid of life; but they continue to swim, by their own spontaneous motions, for two or three days after their separation from the parent. In their progression through the fluid they are observed always to carry their rounded broad extremity forwards. On examining this part with the microscope, we find that it is covered with short filaments, or *cilia*, which are in constant and rapid vibration. These cilia are spread over about two thirds of the surface of the body, leaving the narrower portion, which has a whiter and more pellucid appearance, uncovered. They are very minute transparent filaments, broadest at their base, and tapering to invisible points at their extremities: they strike the water by a rapid succession of inflexions, apparently made without any regular order, but conspiring to give an impulse in a particular direction. When the body is attached by its tail, or narrow end, to some fixed object, the motion of the cilia on the fore part of the body determines a current of fluid to pass in a direction backwards, or towards the tail; but when they are floating in the water, the same action propels them forwards in the opposite direction, that is, with the broad ciliated extremity foremost. They thus advance, without appearing to have any definite object, by a slow gliding motion, totally unlike the zig-zag course of animalcules in search of prey. Yet they appear to have a consciousness of impressions made on them; for on striking against each other, or meeting any obstacle, they retard a little the motion of their cilia, wheel for a few seconds round the spot, and then, renewing the vibrations, proceed in their former course.

In about two or three days after these gemmules have quitted the body of the parent, they are observed to fix themselves on the sides or bottom of the vessel in which they are contained; and some of them are found spread out, like a thin circular membrane, on the surface of the water. In the former case, they adhere firmly by their narrow extremity, which is seen gradually to expand itself laterally, so as to form a broad base of attachment. While this is going on, the cilia are still kept in rapid motion on the upper part, scattering the opaque particles, which may happen to be in the fluid, to a certain distance around. But these motions soon become languid, and, in the course of a few hours, cease; and the cilia, being no longer wanted, disappear. The gemmule then presents the appearance of a flattened disk, containing granules, like the flesh of the parent sponge; and also several spicula interspersed through the central part. In less than twenty-four hours, a transparent colourless margin has extended round the whole gemmule, and continues to surround it during its future growth. The spicula, which were at first small, confined to the central part, and not exceeding twenty in number, now become much larger and more numerous; and some of them shoot into the thin homogeneous margin. It is a remarkable circumstance that the spicula make their appearance completely formed, as if by a sudden act of crystallization, and never afterwards increase their dimensions.

When two gemmules, in the course of their spreading on the surface of a watch-glass, come into contact with each other, their clear margins unite without the least interruption; they thicken and produce spicula : in a few days we can detect no line of distinction between them, and they continue to grow as one animal. The same thing happens, according to the observation of Cavolini, to adult sponges, which, on coming into mutual contact, grow together and form an inseparable union. In this species of animal grafting we again find an analogy between the constitution of zoophytes and that of plants.

In the course of a few weeks, the spicula are assembled in groups, similar to those of the parent sponge; assuming circular arrangements, and presenting distinct openings at the points they enclose. The young animal now rapidly spreads and enlarges in every direction, becoming more convex, and at the same time more opaque, and more compact in its texture; and before it has attained the tenth of an inch in diameter, it presents, through the microscope, a miniature representation of its parent.

Thus has a power of spontaneous motion been given to what may be regarded as the embryo condition of animals, which are afterwards so remarkable for their inertness, and for the privation of all active powers : and this has been conferred evidently for the purpose of their being widely disseminated over the globe. Had not this apparatus of moving cilia been provided to the gemmules of such species as hang vertically from the roofs of caves, they would have sunk to the bottom of the water and been crushed or buried among the moving sand, instead of supporting themselves while carried to a distance by the waves and tides of the ocean. Many species which abound in the Red Sea and Indian Ocean have, in this way, been gradually transported, by the Gulf stream, from the shores of the east to corresponding latitudes of the new world.

§ 3. *Polypifera.*

THE next step in the organic series introduces us to the extensive family of *Polypifera*. The transition from the structure of the sponge to that of the polypus may be thus conceived. Suppose the absorbing orifices of the former to be enlarged, and their number to be at the same time reduced: and let these orifices be drawn out into tubes, and provided with vibratory cilia; in addition to which, let there be placed around their margin a circular row of larger filaments, extremely flexible, and capable of twining round any object that comes within their reach, and of conveying it to the central orifice, which performs the office of a mouth. Each tube, thus furnished with a circle of radiating filaments, or *tentacula*, as they are called, is denominated a *Polype.** The animal structure thus composed has received the name of *Lobularia* (Fig. 56), and is the genus among this tribe that approaches the nearest in its character to the sponge, which it resembles in the

---

* For the sake of greater distinctness I shall employ the term *polype* to denote the single tube with its tentacula; and shall designate by the Latin term *polypus* the entire animal mass composed of an aggregation of these polypes. *Polypifera*, the name of the order, expresses animals bearing polypes.

nature of its internal texture. Each of the polypes with which its surface is studded has eight serrated tentacula. Fig. 57 represents one of these polypes detached. Polypes may thus be united in immense numbers in one mass, having mutual organic connexion. In other cases they may form smaller clusters, or be even totally unconnected. Sometimes the detached polypes are still disposed to assemble in groups, as is the case with the *Zoanthus* of Cuvier* (Fig. 58): at other times they are altogether isolated, as in the *Hydra viridis* (Fig. 59).

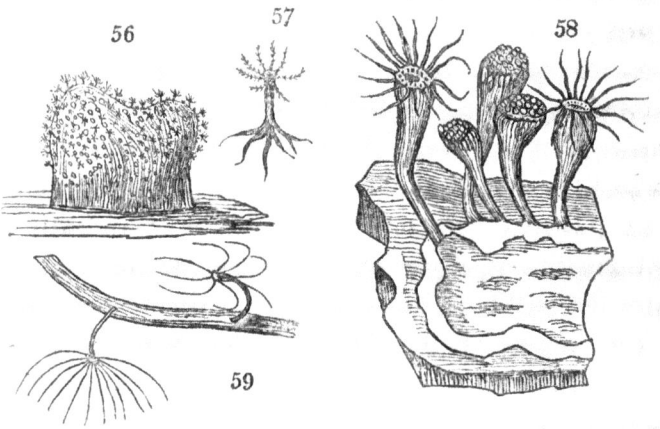

Polypi form a very extensive order of zoophytes, abounding in every part of the ocean, but growing in greatest luxuriance in the

---

* The *Hydra sociata* of Gmelin; the *Actinia sociata* of Ellis.

warmer regions of the globe. Their flesh exhibits the same granular appearance as that of the sponge, but it is generally firmer, and often intermingled with masses of calcareous matter. The tentacula, which may be compared to arms, vary in number and in length in different species of polypi, and sometimes, instead of a single row, each of the mouths has two or more series of tentacula placed around it. They are formed of a prolongation of the soft substance of the polypus, and are sometimes tubular; and their cavities are then continuous with that of the general internal cavity into which the several mouths open. Besides being flexible in every direction, the tentacula are also capable of being lengthened or shortened at the pleasure of the animal. Their elongation is produced by the propulsion of a fluid into their interior, derived from the general cavity of the body; and their retraction is effected by the return of the same fluid.

The whole arrangement of the tentacula on the margin of the projecting mouths bears a striking resemblance to a flower, especially to those which, like the daisy, or china-aster, have the corolla composed of slender radiating petals. We find, indeed, that as the organs of zoophytes become more developed, the affinities which these lower departments of the animal kingdom retain with plants, are more marked and more predominant. In the construction of zoophytes, nature seems still to keep in view the models of vegetable forms, the characters of which, while effecting the transition from one kingdom to the other, she continues to impress on her productions. Zoophytes, both in their outward form, and in the disposition of their internal organs, preserve the symmetrical arrangement round a common centre so generally exhibited in plants, and especially in flowers, and in the verticillated leaves and branches.* Hence the radiated or star-like forms which predominate in most of the animals composing this class: and hence they have obtained the title of *Radiata*, by which Cuvier has designated them.

Like the animals of the sponge tribe, Polypi are for the most part attached to some inorganic shell or base, which may be either of a horny or calcareous nature. The form of this shell admits of almost infinite variety. In some it constitutes the external surface of the animal, and encloses the flesh in a general sheath, leaving only openings at the extremities of the tubes for the expansion of each set of tentacula surrounding the respective mouths. Sometimes these tubes are placed parallel to each other, like the pipes of an organ, with transverse partitions at regular intervals: such is the structure of the *Tubipora*

---

* See page 90.

musica, as shown in Fig. 61. In Fig. 62, a portion of the tubes is seen highly magnified, and laid open, to show the polypes in their interior. At other times the tubes are joined together endwise, like the branches of a tree, leaving lateral apertures for the protrusion of the tentacula of each separate polype: this is the case in the *Sertularia*. (Fig. 60.)

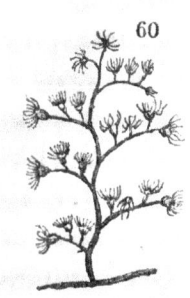

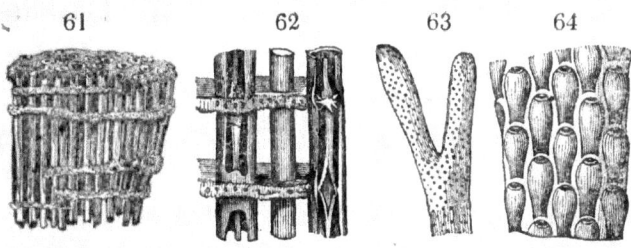

In some species the horny base is fashioned into a number of cells, each of which serves for the protection of its respective polype. These cells are generally placed at the extremity of the branches, presenting the greatest similitude to flowers. The *Flustra* (Fig. 63) is composed of minute and almost microscopic cells, spread over a flat membraneous substance, resembling, in the flexibility of its texture, and its mode of subdivision, the leaves of plants. These cells are arranged in rows, with great regularity, like those of a honey-comb, as is seen in the magnified view of them, Fig. 64.

In other tribes the inorganic base of support is internal, constituting a kind of skeleton or *axis;* the polypous mouths being spread at intervals over the surface of the fleshy layer which covers this skeleton. This is the case with the *Gorgonia, Antipathes,* and the *Coral,* which exhibit still closer resemblances to the branched forms of vegetable stems. The flesh contains granules of calcareous matter, which, in the dried specimens, adhere to the surface of the stems. Fig. 65 is a branch of the *Corallium*

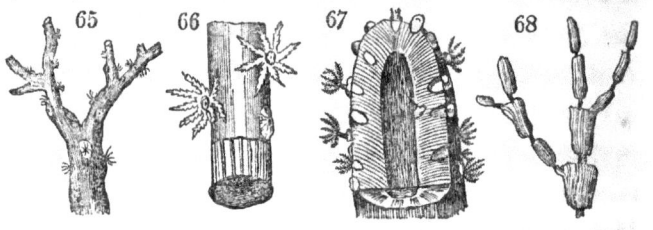

rubrum, of which Fig. 66 is a magnified portion, showing the appearance of the polypes in their expanded and contracted states. The way in which the polypes are embedded in the flesh is seen in Fig. 67, which represents a section of the *Gorgonia Briareus.*

In many cases the polypes are lodged in cup-like depressions in the surface of the calcareous axis, which affords them some degree of protection. In *Madrepores* these depressions are crossed by radiating plates, adapted to the form and number of the tentacula. In *Millepores* the cells are closer and more minute, and exhibit none of these star-like radiations. In some species the plates have more of a parallel arrangement; and in others they form a network.

The material of which this axis, to which the polypes are attached, is composed, is of various kinds. Sometimes it is horny, flexible, and elastic, corresponding in its nature to animal membrane: at other times it is hard and calcareous, being composed principally of carbonate of lime, with a small quantity of the phosphate; the proportion of this latter ingredient varying in different species. In all cases the particles of calcareous matter are united together by some portion of animal substance which may be obtained by dissolving out the former by an acid. We always find the materials arranged in concentric layers, indicating that their deposition has been successive; and the surface is marked by longitudinal lines, corresponding to the figure of the animal covering of flesh. Sometimes the stem consists of horny and calcareous parts disposed alternately, composing a jointed structure, which some have fancied might be considered as making an approach to an articulated skeleton; for it is capable of considerable flexion, and readily yields to the impulse of the waves, without the risk of being broken. This is the case with the *Isis hippuris*, commonly known by the name of *jointed coral*. (Fig. 68.) There is, in short, hardly any possible combination of these parts which does not occasionally occur amidst the infinite diversities of condition displayed in this department of the animal creation.

These structures are generally attached to submarine rocks by an expansion of the base into a kind of foot, or root, which has a strong power of adhesion. In this respect, therefore, as in so many others, these animals preserve an analogy with plants.

It has been ascertained that, in a great number of instances, these fixed zoophytes are multiplied, like the sponge, by the detachment of gemmules, or imperfectly formed portions of their soft substance. These gemmules require to undergo the same kind of metamorphosis in order to bring them to their perfect state; and when newly detached from the parent, they exhibit the same singular spontaneous motions, buoying themselves in the water, and swimming in various directions, by the rapid vibrations of their cilia, till they find a place favourable to their growth. On becoming fixed, they spread out to form a base for the future superstructure; and, after the foundation has thus been laid, they proceed in their upward growth, depositing a calcareous or horny axis in successive layers, until it has acquired the requisite thickness; and they then gradually assume the forms characteristic of the particular species to which they belong. The materials thus deposited are permanent structures, not capable of modification or removal, and not possessing any vital properties; for these properties belong exclusively to the animated flesh with which these structures are associated. The polypes themselves are not developed till after the formation of the root and stem; their growth being in this respect analogous to that of the leaves and flowers of a plant.

The gemmules of the *Flustra carbasea* may be selected in illustration of these phenomena. These have been observed by Dr. Grant,* to swim about in the water as soon as they have escaped from the cells of the parent; each moving with its narrow end foremost, while the opposite broad end, which is covered with cilia, expands into a flat circular zone. These gemmules are very irritable, and are frequently seen to contract the circular margin of their broad extremity; and, while swimming, to stop suddenly in their course. They swim with a gentle gliding motion, at other times they appear stationary, all the while revolving rapidly round their longer axis, with their broad end uppermost: they often bound forwards, either in straight lines, or describing

---

* Edinburgh Philosophical Journal, XVII. 107 and 337.

circles, with no other apparent object than to keep themselves afloat, until they shall arrive at a favourable spot for fixing their permanent abode, and proceeding in their further developement. The time of their remaining in this free and moving state varies according to circumstances, from a few hours to about three days. When about to fix, the slightest agitation of the water causes them to desist, and to recommence their gliding motions, which they continue for some time longer. If, when any of these gemmules has begun to fix, it be again disturbed, and separated from the surface to which it had become attached, it generally remains free, and perishes. During the process of fixing, it exhibits no peculiar appearance or change of form; it simply lies on its side; and the cilia continue to vibrate over the whole surface, producing a constant current in the water, apparently for the purpose of cleaning the space immediately surrounding the gemmule. It remains for three days in this attitude, without undergoing any perceptible change of form, and without relaxing the vibrations of its cilia. At the end of this time, the cilia cease to move, and shortly after disappear: then the gemmule begins to swell, the surrounding margin becomes more transparent, and the whole gradually assumes the form of a cell, surrounded by a delicate white opaque line, which is the rudiment of the calcareous wall of the future cell. Towards the base of this rudimental cell, the gelatinous substance in the interior may be perceived to become more consistent and opaque at a particular point; from this dull spot within the cell, short straight tentacula begin to bud, extending upwards in the direction of the future aperture. The gelatinous spot, from which the tentacula originated, assumes the vermiform appearance of the body of a polype; and we may distinctly perceive the bundles of fibres which connect its head with the base of the cell. The structure of the polype is perfected by the addition of a closed capsule; and when it is first detected protruding from the cell, it possesses all the parts of an adult polype, and vibrates the cilia of its tentacula with as much regularity and velocity as at any future period. Before the polype is capable of protruding from the aperture of the first cell, the upper part of the cell has already extended outwards to form the rudiment of a second: and so on, in succession, till the whole structure is completed.

The tentacula of polypi are exquisitely sensible, and are frequently seen, either singly or altogether, bending their extremities towards the mouth, when any minute floating body comes in contact with them. When a polype is expanded, a constant current of water is observed to take place, directed towards the mouth. These currents are never produced by the motions of the tentacula themselves; but

172 THE MECHANICAL FUNCTIONS.

are invariably the effects of the rapid vibrations of the cilia placed on the tentacula. In the polypes of the *Flustra carbasea*, (Fig. 69), the tentacula have each a single row of cilia, extending along both the lateral margins, from their base to their termination.* Each polype has usually twenty-two tentacula; and there are about fifty cilia on each side of a tentaculum, making 2200 cilia on each polype. As there are above 1800 cells in each square inch of surface, and the branches of an ordinary specimen present about ten square inches of surface, we may estimate that an ordinary specimen of this zoophyte presents more than 18,000 polypes, 396,000 tentacula, and 39,600,000 cilia. But other species certainly contain more than ten times these numbers.†

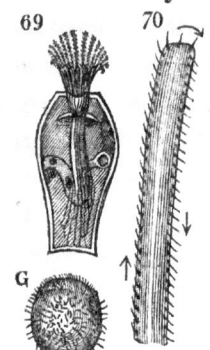

The vibrations of these cilia are far too rapid to be followed by the quickest eye, even when assisted by the most powerful microscope, and can be detected only at the times when they have become comparatively languid, by the di-

---

* A portion of one of these tentacula is represented, highly magnified, in Fig. 70. The lower figure (G) is the delineation of one of the gemmules of the same polypus, also greatly magnified.

† Dr. Grant has calculated that there are about 400,000,000 cilia on a single *Flustra foliacea*. Transactions of the Zoological Society of London, Vol. i. p. 11.

minished vigour of the animal: their motions may then be seen, ascending on one side of the tentaculum and descending on the other. (Fig. 70.) All the cilia appear to commence and to cease their motions at the same moment. The constancy with which they continue would seem to exclude the possibility of their being the result of volition; and they are, therefore, more probably determined by some unknown physical cause, dependent, however, on the life of the animal. But so retentive are they of the power of motion, whatever may be its cause, that if any one of the tentacula be cut off, its cilia will continue to vibrate, and will propel it forward in the fluid for a considerable time, as if it had become itself an individual animal.

A question arises with regard to the constitution of these zoophytes, similar to that which has been proposed with regard to trees, namely, what limits should be assigned to their individuality? Is the whole mass, which appears to grow from one root, and which consists of multitudes of branches, proceeding from a common stem, to be considered as one individual animal, or is it an assemblage or aggregation of smaller individuals: each individual being characterised by having a single mouth, with its accompanying tentacula, and yet the whole being animated by a common principle of life and growth? The greater number of naturalists have adopted this latter view, regarding each portion, so provided with a distinct circle of tentacula, as a separate animal, associated with its neighbours in the construction of a common habitation, and contributing its quota to the general nourishment of this animal republic. As the determination of this question involves the consideration of the function of nutrition, I shall postpone its further discussion to a future part of this treatise. As far, indeed, as regards the mechanical condition of animals which are so completely stationary, it matters little, whether the whole mass be regarded as one individual animal, or as an aggregate of distinct individuals. But the question becomes of some importance when applied to detached zoophytes, such as *Pennatula*, which are formed of a multitude of polypes connected with a common stem, but which float at liberty in the sea.

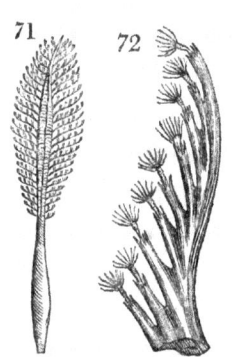

The Pennatula (Fig. 71) has been termed the *sea pen*, from the circumstance of its calcareous axis, or stem, having a double set of branches, extending in the same plane from both the sides, like the vane of a quill, and of its series of polypes being set along one edge of each branch, like the filaments which arise from the fibres of the feather. Some of these polypes are seen magnified in Fig. 72. Immense numbers of these curious animals are met with in different parts of the ocean. If they possessed in any degree the power of locomotion, which many naturalists have ascribed to them, we should be able to ascertain whether all their movements are conducted by a common volition, or whether they are performed independently of one another. It has often, indeed, been asserted, that pennatulæ swim through the water by their own spontaneous movements, consisting either in the waving up and down of the lateral branches, or in the simultaneous impulses of the tentacula of all the polypes. Cuvier even represents the polypes of the pennatula as having the power of keeping time, while they are waving the mass through the water, as if they were all actuated by a single undivided volition. But Dr. Grant, who has watched the motions of these animals with great care, is led by his observations to the conclusion that pennatulæ are not in reality possessed of any such locomotive faculty; but that they are carried to and fro in the ocean, like the gulf weed, without the slightest voluntary power of directing their course. Whatever may be the result of the combined movements of the tentacula, the arms are certainly incapable of those inflexions which have been supposed to supply the means of progressive motion.

It is only when the contractile flesh of the polypus is released from the restraint which the solid axis imposes upon its movements, that the animal becomes capable of any distinct power of locomotion. Such is the condition of the animals belonging to the genus *Hydra*, of which the *Hydra viridis*, or fresh water polype, (Fig. 59, p. 162) may be taken as the type. This singular animal presents us with perhaps the simplest kind of structure that exists in the animal kingdom. It would almost seem as if Nature had formed it with the design of exhibiting to us the resources of vitality in carrying on the functions of animal life without the aid of the complicated apparatus which she has bestowed upon the higher orders of the creation. The Hydra consists merely of a fleshy tube, open at both ends, one of which, being more dilated, may be regarded as the head, and has for a mouth the aperture of the tube, which is furnished at its margin with a single row of tentacula. It thus corresponds to the general definition of a polypus, and exemplifies its most simple form.

The whole body may, on the one hand, be considerably elongated, and on the other, so much retracted, as to appear a mere globule; and these movements are the effect of a voluntary power in the animal directed to specific ends. The number of tentacula varies from six to twelve; they are slender tubular filaments, capable of being extended to a great length, and of being bent in all directions. In this way, they can quickly surround and grasp any small object which they may happen to touch; and whenever irritated they instantly retract, so as hardly to be visible without the aid of a magnifier. Each tentaculum may be moved independently of the rest, at the pleasure of the animal. The remainder of the body tapers gradually from the head to the other extremity, becoming very slender, and having at its termination a flat surface, which has been termed the foot; for although every portion of the surface has the power of adhering to the bodies to which it is applied, it is principally by this extremity that the animal chooses to attach itself to the sides or bottom of the vessel in which it is kept. No trace of the existence of cilia can be met with on any part of the surface of these animals.

It is to Mr. Trembley of Geneva that we are indebted for the discovery of this singular animal, the examination of which has contributed to throw great light on the natural history of polypiferous animals.* While observing some aquatic plants, which he had collected and put into water, his attention was called to the appearance of filaments adhering to them, which he at first conceived to be parasitic vege-

---

* Mémoires pour servir à l'Histoire d'un genre de Polypes d'eau douce, à bras en forme de cornes. Par A. Trembley, 1744.

tables: but farther observation convinced him that they were endowed with powers of spontaneous motion, and that they preyed upon small insects: and he, therefore, could no longer doubt their animal nature. He found that they always placed themselves on the side of the glass next to the light; and by watching their changes of position, he discovered the mode in which they effect their progressive motions. If the hydra be standing in the erect position, its foot being applied to the bottom of the glass (Fig. 73), it slowly bends the body in the direction in which it intends to advance till its head touches the vessel, as shown in Fig. 74. It then adheres to the surface by the mouth, or by one or two of its tentacula, and, detaching the foot, bends the body into a curve, at the same time slightly retracting it, so that the foot is brought near the head (Fig. 75). The foot is then again fixed, preparatory to a new step, which it takes by detaching the head and projecting it forwards as before (Fig. 76).

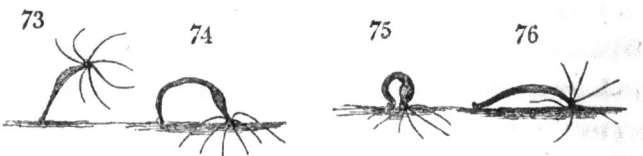

The progress made by these successive efforts is but slow: for the hydra often pauses in the midst of a step, as if deliberating whether it should proceed: so that the traversing a distance of seven or eight inches is to these animals a very good day's journey, even in summer. But a mode of travelling rather more expeditious than this is occasionally resorted to. It consists of a succession of somersets: the hydra, while adhering firmly by the mouth, detaches its foot, and, making it describe a semicircle, throws it over its head, and places it foremost in the line of progression. Having attained this situation, the foot is then fixed, and a similar semi-revolution is performed by the head, the body continuing all the while elongated.

By these and other manœuvres these animals contrive to walk with equal facility in any direction, either on the bottom or sides of the vessel, or along the stems of aquatic plants, to which they are most frequently found attached. The position in which they appear to take most delight, is that of remaining suspended from the surface of the water by means of the foot alone: and this they effect in the following manner. When the flat surface of the foot is exposed for a short time to the air, above the surface of the water, it becomes dry, and in this state exerts a repulsive action on the liquid: so that when dragged below the level of the surface by the weight of the body it still remains uncovered, and occupies the bottom of a cup-shaped hollow in the fluid, thereby receiving a degree of buoyancy sufficient to suspend it at the surface. The principle is the same as that by which a dry needle is supported on water in the boat-like hollow which is formed by the cohesive force of the liquid, if care be taken to lay the needle down very gently on the surface. If, while the hydra is floating in this manner, suspended by the extremity of the foot, a drop of water be made to fall upon that part, so as to wet it, this hydrostatic power will be destroyed, and the animal will immediately sink to the bottom.

While in this state of suspension from the surface, the hydra is capable of performing several curious evolutions, and with the assistance of the tentacula, by which it lays hold of objects within its reach, is able to cross over from one side of the vessel to the other. It does not appear that these animals ever employ the tentacula as instruments for swimming; but they frequently use them as cables, or anchors, to enable them to retain their positions in security, however violently the water may be agitated. Great use is also made of the tentacula as organs of prehension for seizing and detaining their living prey, and for conveying it to the mouth, where it is quickly swallowed. On the other hand, when alarmed, or exposed to irritation, the hydra suddenly shrinks, by the gradual contraction of all the tentacula, and of the body also, into a small globule, which might easily escape notice, unless its previous situation were accurately observed.

It might be asked by what power is this animal, occupying so low a place in the scale of organization, enabled to perform these actions? To this question, however, no satisfactory answer has yet been given. The substance of the hydra, when examined by the microscope, appears to be nearly homogeneous, except that a number of grains are intermixed with the pulpy and gelatinous matter composing the principal bulk of the body. These grains, when pressed out of the flesh into water, are scattered indiscriminately; and appear to have been united in the living animal, by means of this glutinous material.

No perceptible fibres, either muscular, or of any other kind, can be detected in the flesh of the polypus: nor is there the least indication of the formation of transverse rings, similar to those which exist in worms, and which, in these latter animals, contribute to progressive motion. Every portion of the substance of the body is equally irritable and contractile, and its movements appear to be governed by some voluntary power belonging to the animal, and directed to the attainment of certain ends. The softness and pliancy which it possesses allow of its being closely fitted to all the inequalities of the surface of the bodies to which it is applied; and perhaps this cause alone occasions it to adhere with great force to these bodies, without the aid of any glutinous fluid. A conjecture, which has much appearance of probability, has been offered, that this power of adhesion is derived from the presence of a great number of exceedingly minute disks, interspersed over every part of the surface, constituting so many suckers, and resembling, though on a very diminutive scale, the sucking apparatus on the arms of the cuttle-fish.

The *Zoanthus* (Fig. 58) belongs to a tribe of larger polypi, which are generally met with assembled in clusters; on which account it is termed by Ellis the *Actinia sociata*, or cluster-animal flower. It consists of a globular body, having a mouth surrounded by one or two rows of tentacula; and connected below with a firm and fleshy tube, which adheres strongly to the rocks at the bottom of the sea; so that it remains permanently fixed in the same place.

The genus *Vorticella* is formed by a small tribe of animals, which, although they have been usually included under the present order, differ from Polypi in having no tentacula, but only cilia, surrounding the margin of a bell-shaped body, which is mounted upon a long and slender foot-stalk (Fig. 77).* Currents are,

---

* They also differ from Polypi in having a distinct intestinal canal, with numerous stomachs.

as usual, excited by the vibrations of the cilia; which in the simpler species, such as the 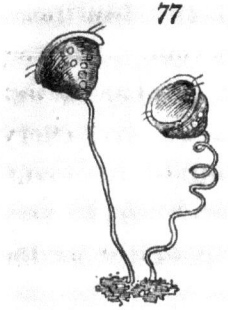 *Vorticella cyathina,* here delineated, are the efficient instruments of progressive motion. When attached by its foot-stalk, the vorticella advances in search of food, by the extension of the foot-stalk into a straight line; but quickly retreats from danger, by suddenly throwing it into spiral folds. Many of the species of vorticellæ are so exceedingly diminutive as to be imperceptible without the aid of the microscope. They conduct us, therefore, by a natural gradation, to the next order we have to notice, and which is composed wholly of microscopic animals.

§ 4. *Infusoria.*

THE Infusory animalcules, or *Infusoria,* were so named by Muller, a Danish naturalist, from the circumstance of their swarming in all infusions of vegetable or animal substances that have been kept for a sufficient time. They are, in general, far too minute to be perceptible to the naked eye: it is to the microscope alone, therefore, that we owe our knowledge of their existence, and of the curious phenomena they present: yet even the best instruments afford us but little insight into their real organization and physical conditions. On this account it is extremely difficult to assign their true place in the scale of animals. By most systematic writers they have been regarded as occupying the very lowest rank in the series, and as exemplifying the simplest of all possible conditions to which animal life can be reduced. *Monads,* which are the smallest of visible animalcules have been spoken of as constituting " the ultimate term of animality;" and some writers have even expressed doubts whether they really belong to the animal kingdom, and whether they should not rather be considered as the elementary molecules of organic beings, separated from each other by the effects of chemical decomposition, and retaining the power of spontaneous, but irregular and indeterminate motion. It was conceived that all material particles belong to the one or the other of two classes; the first, wholly inert and insusceptible of being organized; the second, endowed with a principle of organic aptitude, or capability of uniting into living masses, and constituting, therefore, the essential elements of all organization. According to this view, all vegetables or animals in existence would be mere aggregations of infusory animalcules, which gradually accumulate by continual additions to their numbers, derived from organic matter in the food: so that the body of man himself would be nothing more than a vast congregation of monads!

This bold and fanciful hypothesis, devised by Buffon, and recommended by its seductive appearance of simplicity, as well as by the glowing style and brilliant imagination of its author, has had many zealous partisans. The new world, which was disclosed to the wondering eyes of naturalists by the microscope, abounding in objects and in phenomena of which no conception could have been formed previously to the invention of that instrument, was peculiarly calculated to excite curiosity, and to inspire the hope of its revealing the secret of the living principle in the arrangement of the atoms of organic bodies. During the greater part of the last century, infusory animalcules were the subject of frequent and laborious microscopical research, and gave rise to endless conjecture and speculation as to their origin, their vitality, and their functions in the economy of nature. Notwithstanding their minuteness, considerable differences of organization were perceived to exist among them: but many naturalists still clung to the idea that monads, the most diminutive of the tribe, and whose very presence can be detected only by the application of the highest magnifying powers, are homogeneous globules of living matter, without organization, but endowed with the single attribute of voluntary motion: and even this property was denied to them by some authors.

All these fanciful dreams have been dispelled by the important discoveries of Ehrenberg, who has recently found that even the *Monas termo* is possessed of internal cavities for the reception and the digestion of its food; and who has rendered it probable that their organization is equally complex with that of the larger species of infusoria, such as the *Rotifera*, in which he has succeeded in distinguishing traces of a muscular, a nervous, and even a vascular system.

Those animalcules, whose form can be at all distinguished, exhibit a great diversity of shapes, and variety of modes of progressive motion. Many, as the *Cyclidium*, have the appearance of a thin oval pellicle, smoothly gliding in all directions through the fluid: some, as the *Volvox*, are globular; others, as the *Cercaria*, are shaped like a pear, tapering at one end, and often terminating in a slender tail, so as to resemble a tadpole. In many, this tail is of great length; in some, as the *Furcocerca*, it is forked; in others, it takes spiral turns, like a corkscrew. The *Kerona* has processes like horns. The shape of the *Vibrio* is cylindrical, and more or less pointed at one or both ends, like an eel, or a serpent, which animals it also resembles in its undulatory mode of swimming.* Some, as the *Gonium*, have an angular, others, as the *Kolpoda*, a waving outline. Some, as the *Urceolaria*, present the likeness of a bell or funnel, and appear to be analogous to the Vorticella, in which genus they should probably be included.

Forms still more irregular are exhibited by other infusoria. Of these the most singular is the *Proteus* (Fig. 78), which cannot, indeed, be

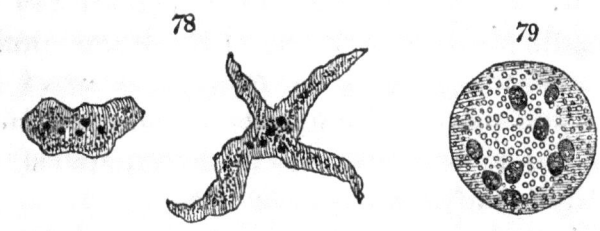

said to have any determinate shape, for it seldom remains the same for two minutes together. It looks like a mass of soft gelly, highly irritable and contractile in every part; at one time wholly shrunk into a ball, at another stretched out into a lengthened ribbon; and again, at another moment, perhaps, we find it doubled upon itself like a leech. If we watch its motions for any time, we see some parts shooting out, as if sud-

* Animalcules referable to this genus are met with in great numbers in blighted wheat, (Fig. 2, p. 62) in sour paste, and in vinegar which has lost the whole of its alcohol. In this last fluid they sometimes attain so large a size as to be visible to the naked eye.

denly inflated, and branching forth into star-like radiations, or assuming various grotesque shapes, while other parts will, in like manner, be as quickly contracted. Thus the whole figure may, in an instant, be completely changed, by metamorphoses as rapid as they are irregular and capricious.

The *Volvox globator* (Fig. 79) is found in prodigious numbers at the surface of many stagnant pools. Its figure is perfectly spherical; and its movements consist in a continual and rapid rotation round its axis, frequently remaining all the while in the same spot. Another species, the *Volvox conflictor*, moves by turning alternately to the right and to the left.

The progressive movements of infusory animalcules are of two kinds, the one consisting in a smooth and equable gliding through the fluid, produced apparently by the vibrations of cilia, which are set on various parts of the body, and often seem to cover the whole surface: the other, more rapid and energetic, when the animalcule darts forward in a particular direction, as if in pursuit of prey, and proceeds by sudden and irregular starts, like a vivacious insect or fish. The voluntary nature of their motions is evident from the dexterity they display in avoiding obstacles, while swimming together in myriads in a single drop.

The great agent in the movements of the animal frame being the muscular fibre, it was

WHEEL ANIMALCULES.

natural to suppose that a texture analogous to that of muscles might exist in these latter genera of infusoria. It was not till very recently, however, that the actual presence of contractile fibres could be recognised. But this problem has at length been solved by the discoveries of Ehrenberg, who, in his observations of the larger and more highly organized species belonging to the order of *Rotifera*, has, with a magnifying power of 380, distinctly seen muscular bands running in pairs between the two layers of transparent membrane which envelope the body. When the animalcule throws itself into its violent lateral contortions, these fibrous bands are observed to become broader and thicker, as well as shorter, on the side towards which the contractions take place. There can, therefore, be no doubt that these are muscular organs, and that they are the real agents by which the motions witnessed are effected.

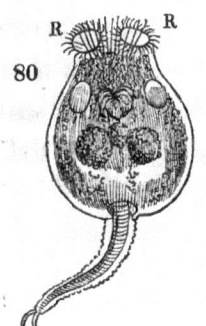

These *Rotifera*, or wheel animalcules, are so named from their being provided with an apparatus for creating a perpetual eddy, or circular current in the surrounding fluid. The remarkable organs, by which this effect is produced, are generally two in number, (Fig. 80, R, R) and are situated on the head, but do not surround the opening of the mouth, as is the case with the tentacula of polypes. They consist of circular disks, the margins of which are fringed with rows of cilia, bearing a great resemblance to a crown wheel. This wheel appears to be incessantly revolving, and generally in one constant direction; giving to the fluid a rotatory impulse, which carries it round in a continual vortex. The constancy of this motion would seem to indicate that it is related to some function of vital importance, such as respiration. But even considered as a mechanical action, which is the view we have now to take of it, this phenomenon is of a nature to excite much curiosity; for the continued revolution round an axis of any part or appendage to the body, is quite inconsistent with any notion we can form of the solid organic attachment of such appendage; and we can have no conception of organization extending through the medium of a fluid, or of any substance, which, like a fluid, admits of the continual displacement of its parts. Mr. Dutrochet has offered an ingenious solution of this difficulty. He suggests that the revolution of the wheels of the Rotifera may not be real, but apparent only.* The indented margin of each wheel being composed of a material so exceedingly flexible as to be capable of assuming quickly all kinds of curvatures, may be conceived to be thrown into undulations, which follow one another round the

* The same opinion was advanced long ago by Vicq. d'Azyr.

circumference; each part, in succession, becoming alternately convex and concave, and thus producing the appearance of the actual advance of the portions that are raised; while their real motions are only those of elevation and depression, by the elongation and contraction of their perpendicular fibres.

Besides possessing extensive powers of locomotion, the infusoria manifest in several of the vital functions, as we shall hereafter find, a degree of complication, which appears to entitle them to a higher station in the animal scale, than that which most naturalists have assigned to them. They are certainly superior to the sponges or the polypi, doomed by nature to be permanently fixed, like plants, to the same spot; and of which, if we consider them as compound beings, the individual animals are often so minute as to be scarcely visible without the aid of the microscope. Mere size, indeed, is of all the circumstances attendant on organized beings, that which should least be assumed as the criterion of complication or refinement of structure. An object is great or small, only in relation to the standard of our own limited and imperfect senses; but with reference to the operations of creative power, all such distinctions must vanish. There is not, as far as we have the means of judging, in the colossal fabric of the elephant, any structure more complicated than exists in the minutest insect that crawls unheeded at our feet.

§ 5. *Acalepha.*

FLOATING masses of living gelatinous matter are met with in every part of the ocean; often in vast numbers, and of various forms; and having but little the appearance of belonging to the animal kingdom. They compose the order *Acalepha*, of which the  *Medusa* (Fig. 81) may be taken as the type. They appear, from their organization, to be raised but a single step above polypi; and in point of activity and locomotive powers, they rank among the lowest of those Zoophytes which are not permanently fixed to the spot where they were first developed. They are almost wholly passive beings, floating on the surface of the sea, or remaining at a small depth below it, carried to and fro by the motion of every tide and current, and destined to be the unresisting prey of innumerable tribes of animals which people every part of the ocean.

The usual form of a Medusa is that of a hemisphere, with a marginal membrane, like the fold of a mantle, extending loosely downwards from the circumference; together with a central pedicle descending from the lower surface, like the stalk of a mushroom, and terminating below in several fringed laminæ, or processes, which have sometimes been denominated tentacula.

The whole substance of the body of these medusæ is semi-transparent and gelatinous, without any distinct fibrous structure; yet it has considerable elasticity, and possesses also some degree of contractile power. The animal is seen alternately to raise and depress the margin of its hemispherical body, and to flap with the fringed membrane or mantle, which descends from it, in a manner somewhat similar to the opening and shutting of a parasol. This pulsatory movement is performed about fifteen times in every minute, with great regularity: and by the reaction of the water, the animal is sustained at the surface; or by striking the water obliquely, it may even perform a slow lateral movement. They descend in the water by simply contracting their dimensions in every direction. Sometimes, in order to sink more quickly, they turn themselves over, so that their convex part is undermost.

Medusæ are met with of very various sizes; the larger abound in the seas around our coast; but immense numbers of the more minute and often microscopic species occur in every part of the ocean.* In some parts of the Greenland seas they swarm to such an extent that they give a visible tinge to the colour of the waves for hundreds of miles. The total number of these animals dispersed over that space surpasses the utmost stretch of the imagination. In these situations a cubic foot of water, taken indiscriminately, was found by Mr. Scoresby to contain above 100,000 of these diminutive medusæ.

Belonging to the tribe of Medusaria is a singular genus, denominated the *Beroë*, (Fig. 82 and 83,) which is remarkable for its organs of

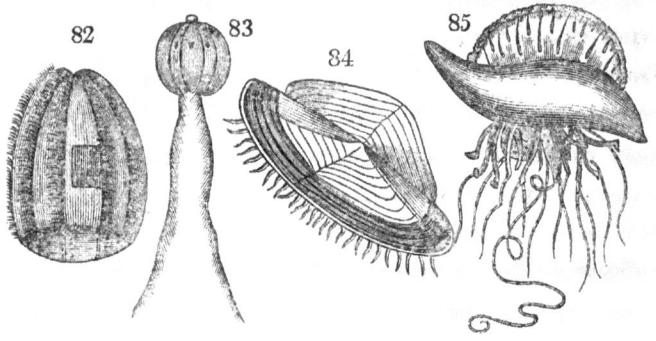

progressive motion. Its body is either globular, or oblong, and it swims with its axis in a vertical position. Eight longitudinal bands or ridges, which have been sometimes compared to ribs,

* The luminous property of sea water, or its *phosphorescence*, as it is sometimes called, generally arises from the presence of minute medusæ, which are met with in greatest numbers at the surface, being specifically lighter than the surrounding fluid.

extend down its sides, like those of a melon; and along each of these is attached a set of little membranes, extended horizontally, and supported on radiating fibres; so that they bear a pretty exact resemblance to the fin of a fish. Their action is not unlike that of the wings of a bird; for they are made to flap up and down, striking the water vertically, and communicating an ascending impulse to the body. This animal is also provided with two very long and slender processes, which come out from the sides of the body, and from these a great number of still finer filaments, or *cilia*, proceed: the whole apparatus is highly sensitive and irritable, and on the slightest touch the filaments are thrown into spiral coils, and retract rapidly within the body. They thus act the part of tentacula, or delicate organs both of touch and of prehension.* It was observed by Fabricius, that when a Beroe is cut into many pieces, each piece continues to live, and to swim about by the action of the cilia, which still continue their vibratory motions.

In two other genera of Acalepha, the *Porpita* and the *Velella*, provision is made for the mechanical support of the soft gelatinous mass, by means of an internal cartilage. In the former, this cartilage is of a circular form; in the latter,

* See a description of the *Beroe pileus*, Lam. by Dr. Grant, in the Transactions of the Zoological Society of London, vol. i. p. 9.

(Fig. 84), it is oval, and bears upon its upper edge a thin pellucid membrane of a triangular shape, which extends the whole length of the upper surface of the body. As this membrane is connected with the cartilage at its middle part only, while its edges are loose and floating, it is peculiarly adapted, when above the surface of the water, to catch the wind and act as a sail. Such, indeed, appears to be the purpose for which it was given to the animal; enabling it to steer its course by means of the loose edges, and also of the tentacula, which extend from the lower side of the body, and act as a rudder, while the sail is impelled by the wind.

A construction still more artificial is provided in another family of the same order, denominated the *Physalida*, or *Hydrostatic Acalepha*. They have attained this latter appellation from their being rendered buoyant by means of vesicles filled with air, which enable them to float without the necessity of using any exertion for that purpose. The *Physalia*, or Portuguese Man-of-War, as it is called, (Fig. 85,) is furnished with a large air-bladder, of an oval shape, placed on the upper part of the body: and also with a membrane of a beautiful purple colour, which, as in the Velella, serves as a sail. These Zoophytes are met with in great numbers in the Atlantic Ocean, and more especially in its warmest regions, and at a considerable distance from land. In calm weather they float on the surface of the sea, rearing their purple crests, and appearing at first like large air bubbles, but distinguishable by the vivid hues of the tentacula which hang down beneath them. Nothing can exceed the beauty of the spectacle presented by a numerous fleet of these animals, quietly sailing in the tropical seas. Whenever the surface is ruffled by the slightest wind, they suddenly absorb the air from their vesicles, and becoming thus specifically heavier than the water, immediately disappear, by diving into the still depths of the ocean. By what process they effect these changes of absorption and of reproduction of air yet remains to be discovered. Other genera, as the *Physsophora*, have several of these air-bladders; but in other respects resemble the ordinary Medusæ, in having no membranous crest.

The *Actiniæ* are a tribe of Zoophytes, which, from the general resemblance of their forms to those of Polypi, are by most naturalists included under that order. But they exhibit a much greater developement in their organization; having very distinct muscular fibres, endowed with strong powers of contraction. Their digestive organs, also, as I shall have afterwards occasion more fully to notice, are constructed upon a more complicated plan than in the polypus. Fig. 86 exhibits an Actinia in its contracted state. When their tentacula, which surround the mouth, and are very numerous, are fully expanded, (as shown in Fig. 87,) these

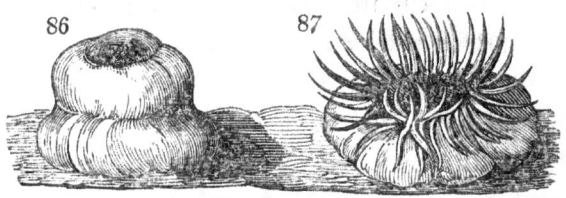

animals present a striking analogy of form to many of the compound flowers; and accordingly the particular species are named from these resemblances, the *sea-anemone*, the *sea-marygold*, the *sea-carnation*, the *sun-flower*, *daisy*, &c. Actiniæ are seen in great numbers on many shores, adhering by their flat surfaces to rocks, and being generally permanently fixed to their abode. When the weather is fine, and the sea calm, it is very amusing to watch the rapid expansions and retractions of their many coloured tentacula, while they are moving in search of food: to observe the quickness with which they seize on whatever prey comes within their reach, and to notice the suddenness with which they collapse into a round contracted mass, on receiving the slightest injury.

Yet these animals are not of necessity confined to the particular spots where we see them fixed; for they are capable, when disturbed, of seeking, by a slow progressive motion, a more

ECHINODERMATA. 199

secure abode. Reaumur has minutely examined the arrangements of their muscular fibres, and has described the actions by which they either attach themselves to the surfaces of rocks, or effect their sluggish movements.*

§ 6. *Echinodermata.*

ASCENDING in the scale of organization we come to the *Echinodermata*, a class which comprehends the families of the *Asterida*, the *Echinida*, the *Holothurida*, and the *Crinoidea*, together with other tribes of less note.

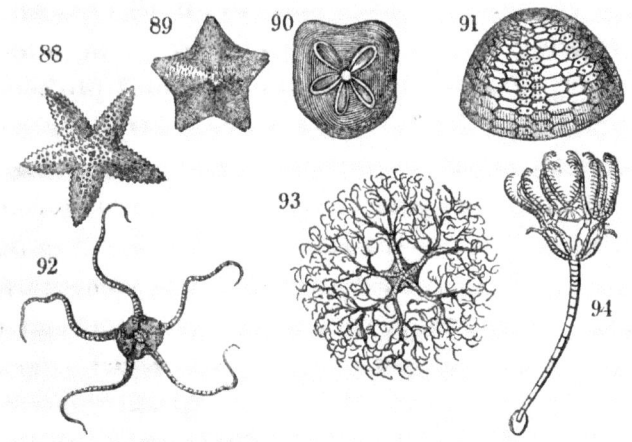

These animals, both in their general form, and in the arrangement of their internal organs,

* Mémoires de l'Académie des Sciences, 1710, p. 490.

retain, in a very marked manner, the radiated disposition so characteristic of Zoophytes: for we find all their parts symmetrically arranged either in lines, or in compartments, which proceed from a common centre, or axis, and which are repeated, in regular succession, all round the circumference (See Fig. 88 to 94). Besides an external horny, or semi-calcareous covering, there is also provided, for the support of the softer parts, a kind of internal skeleton, or jointed frame-work. The organs in the interior of the body are further supported by membranous walls, which impart mechanical firmness to the fabric.

The *Asterias*, or star-fish (Fig. 88), is so named from its star-like form; and the number of rays composing the star is generally five. Besides the tough coriaceous integument, which protects the mass of the body, each ray is farther supported by a series of calcareous pieces, resembling those which compose the spinal column of vertebrated animals, and forming an articulated axis, constructed with the evident design of combining the greatest strength with a proper degree of flexibility. Cartilaginous plates are also added for the more special support of the integument. This integument itself is irritable, and has the power of changing its form, although the muscular fibres by which its motions are effected are not easily distinguished. Calcareous grains, of a solid consistence, are thickly interspersed throughout its texture; and these, in various parts of the body, both in the upper and the under side, often project from the surface in the form of spines or prickles. They are particularly large around the mouth of the animal, which opens at the centre of the under side. These calcareous masses have a crystalline arrangement, and exhibit in fracture the exact oblique angles characteristic of the primitive rhomboid of carbonate of lime.

The under side of each ray (Fig. 95) has a

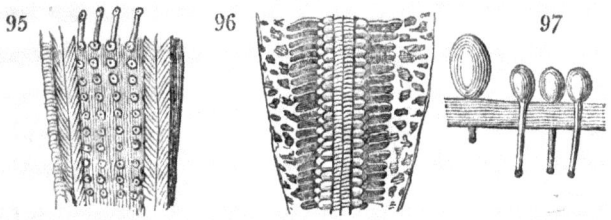

groove termed, by Linneus, the *ambulacrum*, or *avenue*, a name which it has received from its fancied resemblance to a walk between rows of trees: for each groove contains a quadruple row of perforations, like pin holes, through which small fleshy cylindrical processes pass. These processes extend but a short distance from the surface; but they admit of being elongated, or retracted, at the pleasure of the animal, by a very curious mechanism, which I shall presently describe. By bending them on either side, in their expanded state, the Asterias is capable of effecting a slow progressive motion; so that these processes may be regarded as corresponding to feet, being levers for the advance of the body. This, it may be remarked, is the first time that we meet with organs of that description in our progress through the animal kingdom. Each of these feet is terminated by a concave disk, which when applied to any flat surface acts as a sucker, on the principles already adverted to.* Reaumur counted 304 of these feet in each of the five rays of the star fish, making 1520 in all.† Each foot consists of a tube, closed at the outer end, and the stem of which, after passing through the aperture in the integument, is dilated into a bag or reservoir of fluid; as is shown in Fig. 97. By the contraction of this reservoir, the fluid it contains is propelled into the outer portion of the tube, which protrudes by being thus distended; the foot fixes itself by means of its terminal fleshy disk to the point it touches, and then, by retracting, draws the body along for a short distance. By the retreat of the fluid into its reservoir, the foot is again detached, and ready to be moved forwards, and is thus made instrumental in taking another step, by a repetition of the same

* Page 137.
† Mémoires de l'Académie des Sciences, 1710, p. 487.

process.* From the shortness of these feet, notwithstanding their great number, the advance which this animal can make in any particular direction is excessively slow.

Besides this movement of creeping, the Asterias is capable of bending and unbending each of its rays; actions, however, which it can perform but very slowly, and not to an extent sufficient to accomplish its removal from one place to another.†

The skeleton of the *Echinus* or sea-urchin, (Fig. 91), is still more artificially framed than that of the Asterias. It has a spheroidal form, like that of an orange; the calcareous material

---

* The mechanism by which the feet are protruded and retracted is illustrated by the diagram, Fig. 97, which exhibits the bladders connected with them, in different states of distention and contraction. Fig. 96 shows the upper side of the ambulacra, and of the bladders connected with the feet. Dr. Grant, from some observations which he made on the structure of the cilia of the Beroë pileus, is led to suspect that the rapid vibrations of these singular organs in the lowest animals may depend on the undulations of water conveyed through elastic tubes along their bases, in a manner resembling the injection of the tubular tentacula of Actiniæ and Asteriæ. If this conjecture were verified, he remarks, one of the most remarkable phenomena of animal motion, though one of the most frequent, would lose much of its present marvellous character.

† In addition to these larger tubes, there exists also a smaller set, which pierce the skin in different places, and are channels for the absorption of the water used in respiration. These I shall have occasion to notice more particularly hereafter.

employed in its construction, instead of forming isolated grains, is accumulated and extended into polygonal plates (Fig. 98), the edges of which are dovetailed into each other. The form of each piece is that of a lengthened hexagon; and the whole are regularly arranged in rows, like a mosaic or tesselated pavement. Ambulacra are also seen on the surface of the shell, passing vertically down the sides of the sphere, similar to the meridians of a globe; and containing, like those of the Asterias, a double row of perforations.*

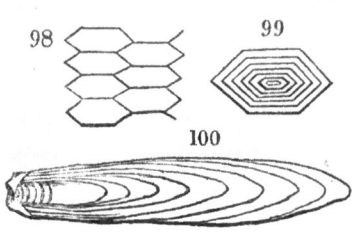

On the outer spherical surface of the external crust, there are formed a great number of calcareous tubercles, arranged with beautiful regularity and symmetry in double lines, passing, like meridian circles, from the upper to the lower pole of the sphere. Each appears, when magnified, to be a smooth and solid ball, projecting from the surface of one of the polygonal plates of the crust. These balls serve for the

---

* An architecture of a still more curious description is exhibited in the calcareous frame-work that has been provided for the support of the teeth, and other organs of mastication, with which this animal is furnished. The structure of these organs will be noticed when treating of that function.

support of the spines,* which have grooves or sockets at their base, allowing of their accurate application to the spherical surface of the tubercles. They thus constitute ball-and-socket joints, allowing of free motion in all directions. Each joint is connected with the plate on which it turns, by means of the integument, which acts the part of a capsular ligament; and sets of radiating muscular fibres are provided for effecting the movements of the spines. By employing these spines as levers, the Echinus advances with great facility along plane surfaces at the bottom of the sea. This animal is also aided in its progressive motion by the employment of suckers, which are placed at the end of the slender tubes, protruding from the pores of the ambulacra, and analogous to those of the Asterias.

The *Spatangus*, a genus belonging to this order, buries itself in the sand by the action of its spines, which on its under surface are short, thick, and expanded at the ends, like the handle of a spoon, with the convexity downwards; and which have a limited rotatory motion. Those which grow from the sides are more slender,

---

* It has been ascertained by Mr. Haidinger, that the structure of these spines is crystalline, and that their cleavage presents the exact rhomboidal angles characteristic of carbonate of lime. See his Translation of Mohs's Mineralogy, vol. ii. p. 91.

and taper towards the extremities, and when not in use they fall flat upon the body with their points directed backwards. Besides these, there are a few longer bristles, arranged in a crescent on the back, and converging till their points meet, but capable of being erected to a perpendicular position. The animal, when placed on sand, commences its operations by revolving the lower spines, thus soon creating a hollow quicksand, into which it sinks by its own weight so far as to enable the lowest of the lateral spines to cooperate with them, by scattering and throwing up the loosened particles; while these, at the same time, contribute, by their reaction, still farther to depress the body. As the animal sinks, a greater number of spines are brought into action, and its progress becomes more rapid; while the sand, that had been pushed aside, flows back, and covers the body, when it has sunk below the level of the surface. In this situation the long dorsal bristles come into play, preventing the sand from closing completely, and preserving a small round hole for the admission of water to the mouth and respiratory organs.*

Whenever, in following the series of organic structures, new forms are met with, we always

---

* The account here given is taken from Mr. Osler's papers in the Philosophical Transactions for 1826, p. 347.

find them accompanied by corresponding modifications in the processes of developement. The organization of the animals belonging to the lowest division of the series is not sufficiently perfect to afford the means, which are supplied in the higher animals, of removing or modifying the substances that have at any time been deposited, and suffered to harden. Hence the structures composed of these substances remain unchanged during the life-time of the animal, although they may continue to receive additions of new layers of the same material, deposited upon their surface by the soft parts in contact with them; for it is through the medium of the soft parts alone that these materials are supplied. All the solid structures of zoophytes are formed by this process, and they are subjected to all the consequences of this law of increase. As these consequences are important in their relation to the conditions of growth, and to the forms which result, it will be necessary to direct our attention to them more particularly.

The influence which this mode of increase by superficial depositions may have, in changing the form of the original structure, will depend altogether upon the relative situations of the soft secreting organ and the hard part on which it is to deposit new layers: for, as every new layer must occupy the situation of the soft organ which has formed it, it must displace the latter, and push it back for a space equal to its own thickness. In process of time, the addition of numerous layers having led to successive encroachments of the solid substance, the latter will have been displaced to an extent which must sooner or later become sensible. If the soft organs have sufficient room for their expansion, as is the case when they are external to the hard axis of the zoophyte, the growth of that axis may go on without impediment; and no change need take place in the general figure of the parts, since their relative proportions and situations may be preserved unaltered. But this cannot happen when the new materials are to be deposited on the internal surface of a membrane, or a shell, which completely encloses the soft parts: for the additions thus made to the thickness of the layer must encroach upon the space within; and, that space being limited, the soft parts contained in it will not merely cease to grow, but will be actually contracted in their dimensions: and if the process of deposition were to go on, the space occupied by the soft organs would at last be entirely filled up with solid matter, and the cavity be obliterated. Accordingly it is necessary, whenever cells, intended for the lodgement of soft organs, are to be constructed of hard materials, that the foundation of these cells should be laid, and their construction begun, upon a scale of the same size as that which they are intended to have at all future periods; because, as we have just seen, after the innermost layer has been deposited, they admit not of any future enlargement of their cavity. Thus we find that, in the case of polypes which are lodged in cells, the walls of these cells must be completed before the soft polypous portion has attained its full expansion; for were it at first built of a smaller size, proportioned to that of the young polype, it would prevent all farther growth.

The globular shell of the Echinus, which is external to the soft parts that nourish it, and which yet grows from a very minute sphere to one of large dimensions, keeping pace with the gradual expansion of the internal organs, might appear to be an exception to the general law. Nature has, however, accomplished her purpose without deviating from her usual plan; first, by dividing the shell of the Echinus into a great number of small pieces; and secondly, by giving to each piece the polygonal form, which is best adapted to their mutual and perfect junction, without leaving any intervening spaces. Thus has she provided for the enlargement of the whole structure, by admitting of additions being made to the margins of each of the separate polygonal pieces; fresh layers of calcareous substance being deposited on the under side, and on the edges of each, in proportion as the expansion of the contents of the shell causes their separation. That such a succession of deposits has taken place, may easily be seen, by minutely examining the texture of the plates, which will be found marked by concentric polygonal lines. (Fig. 99.)

The spines of the Echinus must be formed by the successive deposition of layers on their outer surface, as appears from the examination of their structure, when a longitudinal section of them has been made. The lines exhibiting the succession of layers are seen in Fig. 100, which represents such a section. Hence they are probably deposited by the membrane which covers them during the whole period of their growth.

There is probably no series of animals that exemplify in so marked a manner as the Echinodermata, the gradations which nature has observed in passing from one model of construction to another of a totally different aspect, through every intermediate form. What shapes can be more diversified, and apparently irreducible to a common standard, than those of the star-like Asterias, (Fig. 88) of the globular Echinus, (Fig. 91) and of the lily-shaped Pentacrinus; (Fig. 94) and yet we find these passing the one into the other by the most gradual transitions? Setting out from the star with five slender rays, which is the standard form of the Asterias; we find the rays, in succeeding species, assuming gradually a greater breadth at their base, and their sides joining at more obtuse angles: the star-like form is gradually effaced, and the outline is rather a pentagon, with its sides curved inwards (**Fig. 89**). We soon perceive this curvature giving place to a straight line, so that the shape becomes an exact pentagon. The next change effected is in the angles of this pentagon, which by degrees are lost in a general rounded outline; still, however, preserving its flatness. This stage is attained in the *Scutella*, and the *Clypeaster*. (**Fig. 90.**) We next find that, in the *Spatangus*, the thickness increases; though at first with an oval outline, and with several changes in the situation of the mouth of the animal. At length, after passing through many intermediate steps, we arrive at the perfectly circular and spheroidal *Echinus*. (**Fig. 91.**) If we might be permitted to conjecture the objects of all these changes, which occur in this continuous gradation, we might not unreasonably suppose them to be the concentration of the internal organs into one compact mass, and the retrenchment of all the external appendages. It is also curious to observe, how, amidst all these modifications, the double rows of perforations, which constitute the ambulacra, retain their situations, diverging in five equidistant lines from one of the extremities of the axis, and winding round to the other.

Returning to the Asterias, we can trace changes equally gradual, though in an opposite sense, in another series, which presents a striking contrast with the former. Here, instead of the retrenchment of the appendages, we find them greatly developed, and amplified in every possible degree. The rays of the Asterias become narrower, while their length is at the same time increased; the vital organs, and also the tubular feet, are gradually withdrawn from them, and retire within a central disk, to which the slender rays, now bereft of feet, become mere appendages. Such is the condition of the *Ophiura*. (Fig. 92.) By the prolongation and tapering of these rays to slender filaments, they acquire a greater prehensile power, and twine with ease round their prey. We next find their number augmented; it is at first doubled, then tripled, and at length indefinitely augmented. They also become branched, subdividing by simple bifurcations, as in the *Euryale palmiferum* (Fig. 93); next into minuter ramifications, as in the *Caput Medusæ*, where the thousands of filaments have the appearance of a tangled web, which defies all attempts at unravelling.

The steps are but short from the Comatula to the *Crinoidea*, or lily-shaped tribe, (of which, Fig 94, representing the *Pentacrinus europæus*, is an example); for they consist chiefly in the addition of a jointed stalk, which is made to proceed downwards from the centre of the whole assemblage of rays, and which is to serve as a common stem for sustaining the whole mass; while the branches themselves are carried up, and folded inwards. The lower joint of the foot-stalk is a little expanded, in order to procure a more extensive base of support; and the whole structure thus presents a remarkable resemblance to a liliaceous plant.

Chapter III.

MOLLUSCA.

§ 1. *Mollusca in general.*

THE series of animal structures, arranged according to their mechanical functions, conducts us next to the *Mollusca;* an assemblage of beings which was first recognised as constituting one of the primary divisions of the animal kingdom by Cuvier, the greatest naturalist of modern times. A vast multitude of species, possessing in common many remarkable physiological characters are comprehended in this extensive class. In all, as their name imports, the body is of soft consistence; and it is enclosed more or less completely in a muscular envelope, called the *mantle*, composed of a layer of contractile fibres, which are interwoven with the soft and elastic integument. Openings are left in this mantle for the admission of the external fluid to the mouth and to the respiratory organs, and also for the occasional protrusion of the head and the foot, when these organs exist. But a large proportion of the animals of this class are *acephalous*, that is, destitute of a head, and the mantle is then occasionally elongated to form tubes, often of considerable length, for the purpose of conducting water into the interior of the body.

Mollusca, with the exception of a few among the higher orders, are but imperfectly furnished with organs of locomotion. The greater number, indeed, are formed for an existence as completely stationary as the Zoophytes attached to a fixed base. The Oyster, the Muscle, and the Limpet, for example, are usually adherent to rocks at the bottom of the sea, and are consequently dependent for their nourishment on the supplies of food casually brought within their reach by the waves and currents of the ocean. This permanent attachment to the solid body on which they fix their abode, does not, however, take place till they have arrived at a certain period of their growth: for at the commencement of their separate existence, that is, immediately after they are hatched, they are free to move in the water, and to roam in search of a habitation. In this respect, therefore, they preserve an analogy with the gemmules of sponges, and of polypi, which exercise locomotive powers only in the early stages of their developement.*

The organization of the Mollusca being unfitted for the construction of an internal skeleton, Nature has ordained that the purposes of mechanical support and protection shall be answered by the formation of hard calcareous coverings, or *shells*, the result of a peculiar process of animal production. These shells are formed either of one piece, or of several; the separate pieces, in either case, being termed *valves;* so that shells

* This analogy is strengthened by the circumstance that the movements of many of these animals, in the first periods of their existence, are effected by the same mechanism of vibratory cilia which we found to be instrumental in the progression of the infusory animalcules, and of the young of polypi. On observing the first evolution of the ova of the *Buccinum undatum*, Dr. Grant found them to consist of groups of spherical gelatinous bodies, which soon become covered on one side with a transparent envelope, the rudiment of the future shell; while, on the other side, the gelatinous matter is extended outwards, so as to form the margin of an internal cavity, of which the entrance is surrounded with vibratory cilia, and in the interior of which a revolution of particles is seen, indicating a constant current of fluid. The vibrations of these cilia are perceived long before the pulsations of the heart, and even before any appearance of that organ is visible;

may be either *univalve, bivalve*, or *multivalve*, according as they consist of one, two, or more pieces. Univalve shells have generally more or less of a spiral form, and are then called *turbinated shells*. In a few, the cavity of the shell is divided by transverse partitions into numerous compartments. Some Mollusca have internal shells for the defence and support of particular organs; and others have shells which are partly external, and partly internal. As respects their shape, colour, and appearance, shells admit of infinite diversity; yet, as will presently be shown, all are composed of the same kind of material; and their production and increase are regulated by the same uniform laws.

they are, indeed, the first indications of life in the embryo. The cilia are in activity even before the animal is hatched; for while confined within the egg, it is seen almost continually revolving round its centre; a motion which appears destined to bring a constant supply and renewal of sea water into the interior of the organization, in order to perfect the formation of the shell before the animal is, as it were, launched into the ocean. Possibly, also, the continued friction of the cilia against the interior of the egg may tend to abrade it, and open a passage for the young animal. No sooner has the animal effected its escape, than it darts rapidly forwards by the motion of its cilia. The same appearances have also been observed by Dr. Grant in the young of different Mollusca, such as the *Doris, Eolis*, &c. which have no shell.—Edin. Journal of Science, Vol. vii.

§ 2. *Acephala.*

The Mollusca which inhabit bivalve shells, such as the *Oyster*, the *Muscle*, and the *Cockle*, are all acephalous. The two valves of the shell are united at the back by a hinge joint, often very artificially constructed, having teeth that lock into each other : and the mechanism of this articulation varies much in different species. The hinge is secured by a substance of great strength.

It is seen in Fig. 101, which shows the valves of the *Unio batava*, with the connecting ligament. This ligament is composed of two kinds of texture : the one, which is always external, is strictly ligamentous; that is, perfectly inelastic : the other has more of the properties of cartilage, being highly elastic, and formed of parallel series of condensed transverse fibres, directed from the hinge of one valve to the similar part of the other, and having generally a deep black colour, and a pearly lustre. The cartilage is always situated within the ligament, sometimes in immediate contact, and forming with it one and the same mass: at other times placed at a distance, in a triangular cavity, amongst the teeth of the hinge. The closing of the valves produces, in all cases, a compression of the cartilage, the elasticity of which tends, therefore, to separate the valves from each other; that is, to open the shell.

During the life of the animal, the usual and natural state of its shell is that of being kept open for a little distance, so as to allow of the ingress and egress of the water necessary for its nourishment and respiration. But as a security against danger, it was necessary to furnish the animal with the means of rapidly closing the shell, and retaining the valves in a closed state. These actions being only occasional, yet requiring considerable force, are effected by a muscular power: for which purpose sometimes one, sometimes two, or even a greater number, of strong muscles are placed between the valves, their fibres passing directly across from the inner surface of the one to that of the other, and firmly attached to both.—

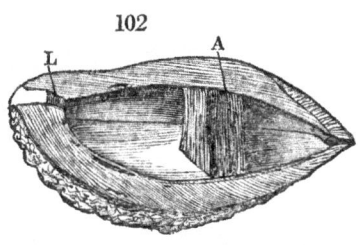

They are named, from their office of bringing the valves towards each other, the *adductor muscles*.

Fig. 102, which represents the section of an oyster, shows the situation of the hinge L, the adductor muscle A, and the transverse direction of its fibres, with respect to the valves. When these muscles are not in action, the elasticity of the cartilage attached to the hinge is sufficient to separate the valves; but as they were not intended to open beyond a certain extent, it was necessary to provide some limitation to the action of the cartilage. The adductor muscle might, it is evident, be called into play to counteract that action; but this would require a constant muscular exertion, and a great expenditure, therefore, of vital force. Nature has always shown a solicitude to economize muscular power, whenever a substitute could be had, and such a substitute she has here provided, by uniting with the muscle an elastic ligament, of a peculiar construction. It has a texture similar to that of the *ligamentum nuchæ*, and being placed on the side of the muscle next to the hinge, allows the valves to separate to the proper distance only.* When the animal dies, the muscular force ceases, but the ligament, with which the muscle is associated, retaining its elasticity, allows the shell to open, but only to a certain extent; and accordingly, this is the state in which we find bivalve shells that are cast upon the shore, after the soft flesh of the animal has

---

* This remarkable structure was first described by Dr. Leach, in a paper read before the Royal Academy of Paris. Bulletin des Sciences, 1818, p. 14. See also Gray, in Zoological Journal, I. 219.

decayed and been washed out, provided the cartilage and the ligament of the hinge are still preserved.*

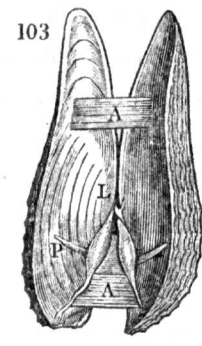

The simple actions of opening and closing the valves are capable of being converted into a means of retreating from danger, or of removing to a more commodious situation, in the case of those bivalves which are not actually attached to rocks or other fixed bodies. Diquemare long ago observed that even the oyster has some power of locomotion, by suddenly closing its shell, and thereby expelling the

---

* The *Pholas* is an exception to this rule; for instead of its valves being united, as usual, by an elastic ligament, they are connected chiefly by means of muscles. This departure from the ordinary structure is probably occasioned by a new condition introduced into the economy of the animal in consequence of its being fitted for excavating passages through hard rocks. It is furnished, for this purpose, with a complicated boring apparatus moved by many muscles, and requiring great freedom of action. Fig. 103 represents the shell of the *Pholas candida* extremely expanded, in order to show the hinge, together with the ligament, L; the long and thin process of shell, P, to the ends of which, on each side, a pair of fan-shaped muscles, more particularly employed in boring, are attached; and the two adductor muscles, A A, which retain the valves in contact independently of the ligaments. For a full description of this apparatus, I must refer to a paper by Mr. Osler, on burrowing and boring marine animals, contained in the Phil. Trans. for 1826, p. 342, from which the above figure has been taken.

contained water, with a degree of force, which by the reaction of the fluid in the opposite direction, gives a sensible impulse to the heavy mass. He notices the singular fact that oysters, which are attached to rocks occasionally left dry by the retreat of the tide, always retain within their shells a quantity of water sufficient for respiration, and that they keep the valves closed till the return of the tide : whereas those oysters which are taken from greater depths, where the water never leaves them, and are afterwards removed to situations where they are exposed to these vicissitudes, of which they have had no previous experience, improvidently open their shells after the sea has left them, and by allowing the water to escape, soon perish.*

Many bivalve mollusca are provided with an instrument shaped like a leg and foot, which they employ extensively for progressive motion. Its form in the *Cardium*, or cockle, is seen in Fig. 104. This organ is composed of a mass of muscular fibres, interwoven together in a very complex manner, and which may be compared to the muscular structure of the human tongue : the effect in both is the same, namely, the con-

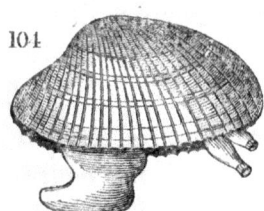

* Journal de Physique, xxviii. 244.

ferring a power of motion in all possible ways; thus it may be readily protruded, retracted, or inflected at every point. The *Solen*, or razor-shell fish, has a foot of a cylindrical shape, tapering at the end, and much more resembling in its form a tongue than a foot. In some bivalves the dilatation of the foot is effected by a curious hydraulic mechanism: the interior of the organ is formed of a spongy texture, capable of receiving a considerable quantity of water, which the animal has the power of injecting into it, and of thus increasing its dimensions.

The foot of the *Mytilus edulis,* or common muscle, can be advanced to the distance of two inches from the shell, and applied to any fixed body within that range. By attaching the point to such body, and retracting the foot, this animal drags its shell towards it; and by repeating the operation successively on other points of the fixed object, continues slowly to advance.

This instrument is of great use to such shellfish as conceal themselves in the mud or sand, which its structure is then peculiarly adapted for scooping out. The *Cardium* continually employs its foot for this purpose: first elongating it and directing its point downwards, and insinuating it deep into the sand; and next, turning up the end, and forming it into a hook, by which, from the resistance of the sand, it is fixed in its position, and then the muscles which usually retract it are thrown into action, and the whole shell is alternately raised and depressed, moving on the foot as on a fulcrum. The effect of these exertions is to drag the shell downwards. When the animal is moderately active these movements are repeated two or three times in a minute. The apparent progress is at first but small; the shell, which was raised on its edge at the middle of the stroke, falling back on its side at the end of it; but when the shell is buried so far as to be supported on its edge, it advances more rapidly, sinking visibly at every stroke, till nothing but the extremity of the tube can be perceived above the sand. Mr. Osler, who has given us this account,* observes that the instinct, which directs the animal thus to procure a shelter, operates at the earliest period of its existence. The *Mya truncata*, when fully grown, will not attempt to burrow; but on placing two young ones, which were scarcely more than a line in length, and apparently but just excluded, on sand, in a glass of sea-water, he found that they buried themselves immediately.

By a process exactly the inverse of this, that is, by doubling up the foot, and pushing with it downwards against the sand below, the shell

* Philos. Trans. for 1826, p. 349.

may be again made to rise by the same kind of efforts which before protruded the foot. By this process of burrowing the animal is enabled quickly to retreat when danger presses: and when this is past, it can, with equal facility, emerge from its hiding place.

The *Cardium* can also advance at the bottom of the sea along the surface of the soft earth, pressing backwards with its foot, as a boatman impels his boat onwards, by pushing with his pole against the ground, in a contrary direction. It is likewise by a similar expedient that the Solen forces its way through the sand, expanding the end of its foot into the form of a club. The course of these locomotive bivalves may readily be traced on the sand by the furrows which they plough up in their progress.

This, as well as many other of the bivalve mollusca, are enabled by the great size and flexibility of this organ to execute various other movements, of which, from the habitual inactivity of animals of this class we should scarcely have supposed them capable. The Tellina is remarkable for the quickness and agility with which it can spring to considerable distances by first folding the foot into a small compass, and then suddenly extending it; while the shell is at the same time closed with a loud snap.

The *Pinna*, or Marine Muscle, when inhabiting the shores of tempestuous seas, is furnished, in addition, with a singular apparatus for withstanding the fury of the surge, and securing itself from dangerous collisions, which might easily destroy the brittle texture of its shell. The object of this apparatus is to prepare a great number of threads, which are fastened at various points to the adjacent rocks, and then tightly drawn by the animal; just as a ship is moored in a convenient station to avoid the buffeting of the storm. The foot of this bivalve is cylindrical, and has, connected with its base, a round tendon of nearly the same length as itself, the office of which is to retain all the threads in firm adhesion with it, and concentrate their power on one point. The threads themselves are composed of a glutinous matter, prepared by a particular organ. They are not spun by being drawn out of the body like the threads of the silk-worm, or of the spider, but they are cast in a mould, when they harden, and acquire a certain consistence before they are employed. This mould is curiously constructed; there is a deep groove which passes along the foot from the root of the tendon to its other extremity; and the sides of this groove are formed so as to fold and close over it, thereby converting it into a canal. The glutinous secretion, which is poured into this canal, dries into a solid thread; and when it has acquired sufficient tenacity, the foot is protruded, and the thread it contains is applied to the object to which it is to be fixed; its extremity being carefully attached to the solid surface of that object. The canal of the foot is then opened along its whole length, and the thread, which adheres by its other extremity to the large tendon at the base of the foot, is disengaged from the canal. Lastly, the foot is retracted, and the same operation is repeated.

Thread after thread is thus formed, and applied in different directions around the shell. Sometimes the attempt fails in consequence of some imperfection in the thread; but the animal, as if aware of the importance of ascertaining the strength of each thread, on which its safety depends, tries every one of them as soon as it has been fixed, by swinging itself round, so as to put it fully on the stretch: an action which probably also assists in elongating the thread. When once the threads have been fixed, the animal does not appear to have the power of cutting or breaking them off. The liquid matter out of which they are formed is so exceedingly glutinous as to attach itself firmly to the smoothest bodies. It is but slowly produced, for it appears that no Pinna is capable of forming more than four, or at most five threads in the course of a day and night. The threads that are formed in haste, when the animal is disturbed in its operations, are more slender than those that are constructed at its leisure. Reaumur, to whom we are indebted for these interesting observations, states also that the marine muscles possess the art of forming these threads from the earliest periods of their existence; for he saw them practising it, when the shells in which they were inclosed were not larger than a millet seed.* In Sicily, and other parts of the Mediterranean, these threads have been manufactured into gloves, and other articles, which resemble silk.

§ 3. *Gasteropoda.*

THE Mollusca which inhabit univalve or turbinated shells, belong to the order of *Gasteropoda,* and have a more highly developed organization than the Acephala. The part which performs the office of a foot is a broad expansion of fleshy substance, occupying nearly the whole under surface of the animal, and forming a flat disk, capable of being applied to the plane along which it moves. This is seen in the *Planorbis* (Fig. 105, D). In some species it is fashioned into a pro-

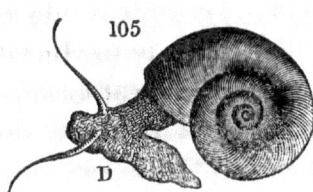

* Mémoires de l'Académie des Sciences: 1711, p. 118 to 123. Poli conceived that these threads are dried muscular fibres; an opinion which has been adopted by Blainville.

jecting ridge which cuts its way, like a ploughshare, along the surface on which it moves. The bands of muscular fibres, which compose the principal part of its structure, are short, and are interlaced together in a very intricate arrangement. All the columns of their fibres terminate at the surface of the disk; so that when the animal is crawling their successive actions produce a visible undulatory motion of that surface. The effect of these actions is that different parts of the plane on which it moves are laid hold of in succession, and each corresponding portion of the animal is dragged along, so that the body advances by a slow and uniform gliding motion. The operation of this mechanism may easily be seen in a snail, by making it crawl on a pane of glass, and viewing the movement of its disk from the other side of the glass: the regular undulations which advance in the direction of the motion of the snail, but with twice the velocity, present a curious and interesting spectacle.

A mucilaginous secretion generally exudes from the surface of the disk, and tends to increase considerably its power of adhesion, both when the animal is crawling, and also when it fixes itself on any surface. In the *Patella*, or limpet, this adhesion is greatly favoured by the conical form of the shell, which, having a circular base, enables the muscles of the disk, by their efforts to create a vacuum underneath it, to command the whole hydrostatic pressure of the superincumbent water, as well as of the atmosphere above the water. Besides the muscular bands contained in the substance of the foot, other sets of fibres are provided for the purpose of protruding or of retracting the whole member, and of moving it in different directions.

The foot of the *Buccinum undatum,* or Whelk, is capable of great dilatation by means of four tubes, which open from the surface near the gullet, and convey into it a large quantity of water. It may, by this means, be distended to a size even greater than the shell itself; so that the opening which it forms in the sand is large enough to receive the shell, when the latter is drawn down by the contraction of the muscles which are attached to the foot.* The foot of the *Scyllæa* is grooved, for the purpose of enabling the animal to lay hold of the stems and branches of marine plants, and advance along them by a gliding motion.

The head is generally furnished with tubular tentacula, which the animal protrudes for the purpose of feeling its way as it advances, and which are quickly retracted, by the reversion of the tube, when they are touched or irritated. This mechanism is matter of familiar observa-

* Osler, Phil. Trans. for 1826, p. 352.

230 THE MECHANICAL FUNCTIONS.

tion in the tentacula, or horns, of the snail and of the slug, which are terrestrial mollusca belonging to this order. The former of these has a turbinated shell of the ordinary structure: the latter, though extremely similar in its internal structure to the snail, is destitute of any external shell; but is furnished, instead of it, with a small internal plate of cartilage, giving support to some of the vital organs.

§ 4. *Structure and Formation of the Shells of Mollusca.*

THE structure and formation of the shells of molluscous animals is a subject of much interest in comparative physiology, as presenting many beautiful illustrations of the laws by which the inorganic parts of the living system are increased in their dimensions.

All shells are composed of two portions, the one consisting of particles of carbonate of lime, the other having the character of an animal substance, and corresponding in its chemical properties either to albumen or to gelatine. The mode in which these two constituent parts are united, as well as the nature of the animal portion, differ much in different kinds of shell; and it is chiefly in reference to these circumstances

STRUCTURE OF SHELLS. 231

that shells have been divided into two classes, namely, the *membranous* and *porcellaneous shells.*

In shells belonging to the first of these classes, the carbonate of lime is united with a membranous substance deposited in layers, which may be separated from one another, either by mechanical division with a sharp instrument, or by the slow actions of air, water, or other decomposing chemical agents. The shells of the limpet, of the oyster, and of almost all the larger bivalve mollusca which reside in the ocean are of this kind. They are usually covered with a thick outer skin, or *epidermis;* and their texture is of a coarser grain than that of other shells.

If a shell of this description be immersed in an acid capable of dissolving carbonate of lime, such as the muriatic or nitric acids properly diluted, at first a brisk effervescence is produced, but this soon slackens, and the carbonate of lime contained in the shell is slowly dissolved; the membranous layers being left entire, and sufficiently coherent to retain the figure of the shell, but, having lost the earthy material which gave them hardness, they assume their natural form of soft and flexible plates.

Many membranous shells exhibit, on several parts of their internal surface, a glistening, silvery, or iridescent appearance.* This appear-

* Examples of this *nacreous structure*, as it is termed, occur in the shells of the *Haliotis*, or Sea-ear, and of the *Anodon*, or fresh water muscle.

ance is caused by the peculiar thinness, transparency, and regularity of arrangement of the outer layers of the membrane, which, in conjunction with the particles of carbonate of lime, enter into the formation of that part of the surface of the shell. The surface, which has thus acquired a pearly lustre, was formerly believed to be a peculiar substance, and was dignified with the appellation of *mother of pearl*, from the notion that was entertained of its being the material of which pearls are formed. It is true, indeed, that pearls are actually composed of the same materials, and have the same laminated structure as the membranous shells; being formed by very thin concentric plates of membrane and carbonate of lime, disposed alternately, and often surrounding a central body, or nucleus: but Sir David Brewster has satisfactorily shown that the iridescent colours exhibited by these surfaces are wholly the effect of the parallel grooves consequent upon the regularity of arrangement in the successive deposits of shell.* The appearance of these grooves or striæ when highly magnified is shown in Fig. 106.†

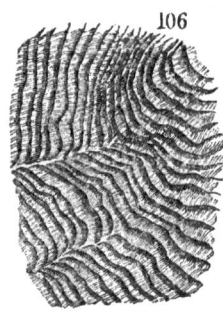

* Philosophical Transactions for 1814, p. 397.

† See also a paper on this subject by Herschel in the Edinburgh Philosophical Journal, ii. 114, from which the annexed figure is taken.

STRUCTURE OF SHELLS.

This iridescent property may be communicated to shell lac, sealing wax, gum Arabic, balsam of Tolu, or fusible metal, by taking an accurate cast or impression of the surface of mother of pearl with any one of these substances.*

Porcellaneous shells have a more uniform and compact texture than those of the former class. The animal matter which unites the carbonate of lime is less in quantity and not so evidently disposed in layers; but it is more equally blended with the earthy particles, with respect to which it appears to perform the office of a cement, binding them strongly together, although it has of itself but little cohesive strength. The *Cyprœa* and the *Volute* are examples of porcellaneous shells.

In shells of this kind the carbonate of lime assumes more or less of a crystalline arrangement; the minute crystals being sometimes in the form of rhombs, and sometimes in that of prisms. In the former case they are composed of three distinct layers, as may be seen by making sections of any of the spiral univalve shells, or simply by breaking them in various

---

* When these shells decay and fall to pieces, they separate into numerous thin scales of a pearly lustre. The fine scales thus obtained from the *Placuna*, or window oyster, are employed by the Chinese in their water-colour drawings to produce the effect of silver. Some of this powder has been brought to England and used for this purpose. See Gray, Phil. Trans. for 1833.

directions. Each layer is composed of very thin plates, marked by oblique lines, which show the direction of the crystalline fibres.* The direction of the layers and fibres is also rendered manifest by the planes of cleavage, when they are broken into fragments. The plates of the outer and inner layers are always directed from the apex of the cone to its base, so as to follow the direction of the spire : while, on the contrary, those of the intermediate plate form concentric rings round the cone parallel to its base. Thus the fibres of each layer are at right angles to those of the layer which is contiguous to it; an arrangement admirably calculated for giving strength to the shell, by opposing a considerable cohesive resistance to all forces tending to break it, in whatever direction they may be applied.* We here find that a principle, which has only of late years been recognised and applied to the

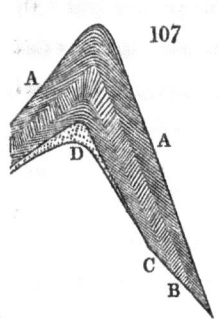

* These lines are shown in the diagram, Fig. 107, which represents a longitudinal section of a shell of this kind. A is the outer layer, of which the fibres pass obliquely downwards. B is the middle layer, having fibres placed at right angles with the former. C is the third, or inner layer, the fibres of which have a direction similar to the outer layer. Within this layer there is frequently found a deposit of a hard, transparent, and apparently homogeneous calcareous material, D. Of this latter substance I shall afterwards have occasion to speak.

building of ships, namely, that of the diagonal arrangement of the frame-work, and the oblique position of the timbers, is identical with that which, from the beginning of creation, has been acted upon by nature in the construction of shells.

When the form of the crystals is prismatic, the fibres are short, their direction is perpendicular to the surface, and the prisms are generally hexagonal. This structure is observable in the *Teredo gigantea* from Sumatra,* and also in many bivalves, such as those belonging to the genera *Avicula* and *Pinna*.

When porcellaneous shells are subjected to the solvent action of acids, the animal matter in their composition offering but little resistance, there is a considerable and long continued effervescence. The solution of the carbonate of lime proceeds rapidly, in consequence of the speedy disintegration of the animal substance, which is broken up, and partly dissolved. The remainder is reduced to minute fragments, which subside in the form of flakes or scales to the bottom of the fluid. Poli has given a minute and elaborate description of the appearances of these fragments of membrane, when seen under the microscope.†

* In this shell the crystalline appearance is so perfect, that when some fragments were sent to England, they were mistaken for a mineral production. Home; Lectures, I. 53.

† See his folio work on the Testacea of the Two Sicilies.

The difference between the textures of these two kinds of shell is further illustrated by the impression made upon them by fire. Porcellaneous shells, when exposed to a red heat, give out neither smell nor smoke: they lose indeed their colour, but retain their figure unaltered. Membranous shells, on the contrary, emit a strong fetid odour, and become black; after which the plates separate, and the structure falls to pieces.

This variety in the composition and structure of different kinds of shell is accompanied by corresponding modifications of their mechanical properties. The toughness of the fibrous basis of membranous shells imparts to them greater strength than is possessed by the porcellaneous shells, which, in consequence of the tenuity and uniform intermixture of the animal cement with the calcareous particles, present a harder and more transparent, but at the same time more brittle compound. It is these qualities, together with their smooth enamelled surface, often beautifully variegated with brilliant colours, and presenting altogether a close resemblance to porcelain, that have procured them the name they bear.

When the transparency and brittleness of these shells are very great, they have been considered as forming another class, and they have been termed *Vitreous shells*, from their making a nearer approach to glass. Some shells present interme-

FORMATION OF SHELLS.

diate textures between the membranous and the porcellaneous.

All those surfaces of the shell on its outer side which are not in contact with any part of the animal, are originally covered with an epidermis:* which, however, is frequently rubbed off by friction.

The process employed by nature for the formation and enlargement of the shells of the mollusca was very imperfectly understood prior to the investigations of Reaumur, who may be considered as having laid the first solid foundations of the theory of this branch of comparative physiology.† His experimental inquiries have fully established the two following general facts: first, that the growth of a shell is simply the result of successive additions made to its surface; and secondly, that the materials constituting each layer, so added, are furnished by the organized fleshy substance, which he termed the skin of the animal, but which is now known by the name of *the mantle*, and not by any vessels or other kind of organization belonging to the shell itself.

If a portion of the shell of a living snail, for instance, be removed, which can be done without injury to the animal, since it adheres to the flesh

---

* This membrane has been termed the *Periostracum*.

† Mémoires de l'Académie des Sciences, 1709, p. 367, and 1716, p. 303.

only in one point, there is formed, in the course of twenty-four hours, a fine pellicle, resembling a spider's web, which is extended across the vacant space, and constitutes the first stratum of the new shell. This web, in a few days, is found to have increased in thickness, by the addition of other layers to its inner surface; and this process goes on until, in about ten or twelve days, the new portion of shell has acquired nearly the same thickness as that which it has replaced. Its situation, however, is not exactly the same, for it is beneath the level of the adjacent parts of the shell. The fractured edges of the latter remain unaltered, and have evidently no share in the formation of the new shell, of which the materials have been supplied exclusively by the mantle. This Reaumur proved by introducing through the aperture a piece of leather underneath the broken edges, all round their circumference, so as to lie between the old shell and the mantle: the result was that no shell was formed on the outside of the leather; while, on the other hand, its inner side was lined with shell.

The calcareous matter which exudes from the mantle in this process is at first fluid and glutinous; but it soon hardens, and consolidates into the dense substance of the shell. The particles of carbonate of lime are either agglutinated together by a liquid animal cement, which unites them into a dense and hard substance, resembling porcelain; or they are deposited in a bed of membranous texture, having already the properties of a solid and elastic plate. This explains the laminated structure possessed by many shells of this class, such as that of the oyster, of which the layers are easily separable, being merely agglutinated together like the component leaves of a sheet of pasteboard.

It has long been the prevailing opinion among naturalists that no portion of a shell which has been once deposited, and has become consolidated, is capable of afterwards undergoing any alteration by the powers of the animal that formed it. Very conclusive evidence has, in my opinion, been adduced against the truth of this theory, by Mr. Gray, in a paper lately read to the Royal Society. From a variety of facts, it appears certain that on some occasions the molluscous animal effects the removal of large portions of its shell, when they interfere with its own growth, or are otherwise productive of inconvenience. We should at the same time regard these cases in the light of exceptions to the ordinary rule that a portion of shell once formed remains ever after unchanged, while it continues to be connected with the animal which produced it. In a general way, indeed, we may consider the connexion between the animal and the shell as mechanical, rather than vital; and the shell itself as an extraneous inorganic body, forming no part of the living system: for whatever share of vitality it may have possessed at the moment of its deposition, all trace of that property is soon lost. Accordingly we find that the holes made in shells by parasitic worms are never filled up, nor the apertures of the cavities so made covered over, unless the living flesh of the animal be wounded; in which case an exudation of calcareous matter takes place, and a pearly deposit is produced. The worn edges of shells, and the fractures, and other accidents which befall them, are never repaired, except as far as such repairs can be made by the addition of materials from the secreting surfaces of the mantle. It is found that shells may be impregnated with poisonous metallic salts, such as those of copper, without any detriment to the animals they enclose.

The power of secreting the materials of shell does not usually extend to the whole of the surface of the mantle, but is generally confined to the parts near the margin, composing what is termed *the collar*. The calcareous substance is always poured out underneath the epidermis,* that is, between this outermost layer of integu-

---

* Mr. Gray considers the external membrane of the shell, or epidermis, as formed by the outer edge of the plates of animal substance, which have scarcely any calcareous matter in their composition, and which are soldered together into a membranous coat.

ment, and the subjacent corium, which is incorporated with the mantle, and may be regarded as forming one and the same organ.*

The shape of the shell depends altogether on the extent and particular form and position of the secreting organ. The animal, on its exclusion from the egg, has already a small portion of shell formed. The simplest case is that in which this rudiment of shell is a concave disk. We may conceive the animal, covered by its mantle, to expand the border of this organ, and extend it beyond the edge of the shell, where it then forms a new layer of shell; and this new layer, being applied to the inner or concave surface of the original shell, will, of course, extend a little way beyond its circumference. The same happens with the succeeding layers, each of which being larger than the one which has preceded it, projects in a circle beyond it; and the whole series of these conical layers, of increasing diameters, forms a compound cone, of which the outer surface exhibits transverse lines, showing the successive additions made to the

* A secreting power is also, in some instances possessed by the foot, as is exemplified in some of the gasteropoda, where it forms an operculum, or calcareous covering to the mouth of the shell. Mr. Gray also ascertained that in the *Cymbia*, the *Olivæ*, and the *Ancillariæ*, shell is deposited, and most probably secreted by the upper surface of the foot, which is very large, and not by the mantle, which is small, and does not extend beyond the edge of the mouth.

shell in the progress of its increase. The *Patella*, or limpet, is an example of this form of structure.

But in by far the greater number of mollusca which inhabit univalve shells, the formation and deposition of the earthy material does not proceed equally on all sides, as happens in the patella. If the increase take place in front only, that is, in the fore part of the mantle, the continual deflexion thence arising necessarily gives the shell a spiral form, the coils being simply in one plane. This is the case in the *Planorbis*, (Fig. 105) the *Spirula* and the *Nautilus*. Most commonly, however, as in the *Buccinum*, and *Achatina*, (Fig. 108) the deposit of shell takes place laterally, and more on one side than on the other; hence the coils produced descend as they advance, giving rise to a curve, which is continually changing its plane, being converted from a

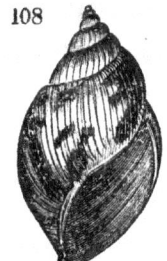 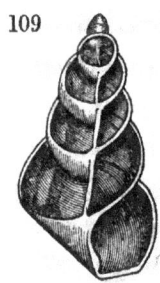

spiral to a *helix*, a term of Geometry borrowed from the Latin name of the common snail, which, as is well known, has a shell of this form. Fig. 108, which represents the shell of the *Achatina zebra*, and of which Fig. 109 shows a longitudinal section, may serve as an example of a shell of this kind. The axis of revolution is termed the *Columella*, and the turns of the spiral are denominated *whorls*. In consequence of the situation of the heart and great blood-vessels relatively to the shell, the left side of the mantle is more active than the right side, so that the lateral turns are made in the contrary direction, that is, towards the right.* There are a few species, however, where, in consequence of the heart being placed on the right side, the turns of the spiral are made to the left. Such shells have been termed *sinistral*, or *reversed* shells: but this left-handed convolution seldom occurs among the shells of land or fresh-water mollusca.

It results from this mode of formation that the apex both of the simple and of the spiral cone is the part which was formed the earliest, and which protected the young animal at the moment of its exclusion from the egg. This portion may generally be distinguished by its colour and appearance from that which is afterwards formed. The succeeding turns made by the shell in the progress of its growth, enlarging in diameter as they

---

* The terms right and left have reference to the position of the animal when resting on its foot; the head being of course in front. See Gray, Zool. Journal, i. 207.

descend from the apex, form by degrees a wider base. During the growth of the animal, as the body extends towards the mouth of the shell, its posterior end often quits the first turn of the spire, and occupies a situation different from that which it had originally. In these cases the cavity at the apex of the spire is filled up with solid calcareous matter of a hardness not inferior to that of marble.

Such is the general form of turbinated shells. It sometimes happens, however, as in the *Conus*, that the upper surface of the spiral scarcely descends below the level of the original portion of the shell, which in the former disposition of its parts would have been the apex: while the lower portions of the spiral turns shoot downwards so as to form a pointed process; thus the whole is still a cone, but reversed from the former, the part last formed being the outer surface of the cone and the circumference of the apparent base, or flat surface, of which the central part is the one first formed.

Various causes may occur to disturb the regularity of the process of deposition, by which the shell is enlarged in its dimensions: at one time accelerating, and at another retarding, or totally arresting its growth. These irregularities are productive of corresponding inequalities in the surface of the shell, such as transverse lines, or striæ. Whenever an exuberance of materials

FORMATION OF SHELLS. 245

has led to a sudden expansion of growth, which has again soon subsided, a projecting ridge is produced in the direction of the margin of the mantle at the time this happens. This change generally recurs at regular periods, so that these ridges, or ribs, as they are often called, succeed one another at equal distances along the course of the spiral turns.

It not unfrequently happens, that at different periods, a sudden developement takes place in particular parts of the mantle, which become in consequence rapidly enlarged, shooting out into long slender processes. Every part of the surface of these processes has the power of secreting and forming shell, so that the portion of shell they construct, being consolidated around each fleshy process, must necessarily have at first the shape of a tube closed at the extremity. As fresh deposits are made by the secreting surface, which are in the interior of the tube, the internal space is gradually filled up by these deposits; the process of the mantle retiring to make way for their advance towards the axis of the tube. In the course of time, every part of the cavity is obliterated, the process of the shell becoming entirely solid. Such is the origin of the many curious projecting cones or spines which several shells exhibit, and which have arisen periodically during their growth from their outer surface. In the *Murex* these processes are often exceedingly numerous, and occur at regular intervals, frequently shooting out into various anomalous forms. In many shells of the genus *Strombus* these spines are of great length, and are arranged round the circumference of the base, being at first tubular, and afterwards solid, according to the period of growth. This is exemplified in the *Pterocera scorpio* (Lamarck) of which Fig. 110 shows the early, and Fig. 111 the later period of growth.

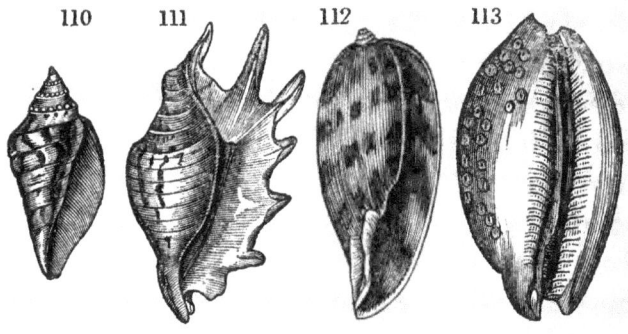

A limit has been assigned by nature to the growth of molluscous animals, and to the shells which they form: and there is a certain epoch of their existence, when considerable changes take place in the disposition of the mantle, and in its powers of secretion. Often we find it suddenly expanding into a broad surface, adding to the shell what may be termed a large lip. Sometimes no sooner has this been accomplished than the same part again shrinks, and the mantle retires a little way within the shell, still continuing to deposit calcareous layers, which give greater thickness to the adjacent part of the shell: and at the same time narrow its aperture, and materially alter its general shape and aspect. Thus it happens that the shells of the young and of the old individuals of the same species are very different, and would not be recognised as belonging to the same tribe of mollusca. This is remarkably the case with the shell of the *Cypræa*, or Cowrie, which in the early stage of its growth, (Fig. 112) has the ordinary form of an oblong turbinated shell: but from the process just described taking place at a certain period, the mouth of the shell (as shown in Fig. 113), becomes exceedingly narrow, and the edges of the aperture are marked by indentations, moulded on corresponding processes of the mantle.* But in this instance the change does not stop here; for both edges of the mantle next take a wider expansion, turning over the outer surface of the shell, and passing on till they meet at the upper convex part, or back of the shell, forming what has been termed the *dorsal line*. They deposit, as they proceed,

* Similar changes occur in the shells of the *Ovula* (spindles), *Erato* (tear-shells), and *Marginella*, (dates). Gray, Phil. Trans. for 1833.

a dense and highly polished porcellaneous shell, beautifully variegated with coloured spots, which correspond exactly with the coloured parts of the mantle that deposits them. This new plate of shell completely envelopes the original shell, giving it a new covering, and disguising its former character. A transverse section (Fig. 114) at once shows the real steps by which these changes have taken place.*

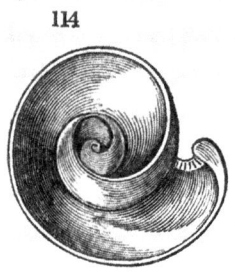

114

Changes equally remarkable are observed to occur in the interior of the shell at different stages of its growth. On the inner surface of the *Mitra*, the *Volute*, and other shells of a similar kind, there is deposited a layer of a hard semi-transparent calcareous material, having a vitreous appearance.† The thickness of the layer, which thus lines the cavity of the shell, is greater as it approaches the apex; and where the spire is

---

* According to Bruguiere, there is reason to believe that the animal of the *Cypræa* after having completed its shell, in the manner above described, still continuing to grow, and being incommoded for want of space, quits its shell altogether, and sets about forming a new one, better suited to its enlarged dimensions. It is stated also that the same individual is even capable of forming in succession several shells. Blainville, however, considers it impossible that the living animal can ever quit its shell. Malacologie, p. 94.

† This is the substance represented at D, Fig. 107, p. 234.

much elongated, or *turrited*, as it is called,* this deposition entirely fills the upper part, which, in the early condition of the shell, was a hollow space with thin sides. The purpose answered by this deposit is evidently to give solidity and strength to a part which, by remaining in its original state, would have been extremely liable to be broken off by the action of the sea.

In other cases a different expedient is adopted. The animal, instead of fortifying the interior of the apex by a lining of hard shell, suddenly withdraws its body from that part, and builds a new wall or partition across the cavity, so as to protect the surface thus withdrawn. That portion of the shell, which is thus abandoned, being very thin and brittle, and having no support internally, soon breaks off, leaving what is termed a *decollated* shell; examples of this occur in the *Cerithium decollatum*, the *Bulimus decollatus*, &c. The young of the genus *Magilus* has a very thin shell of a crystalline texture; but when it has attained its full size, and has formed for itself a lodgment in a coral, it fills up the cavity of the shell with a glassy deposit, leaving only a small conical space for its body; and it continues to accumulate layers of this material, so as to maintain its body at a level with the top of the coral to which it is attached, until the

* As in the genera *Turritella, Terebra, Cerithium,* and *Fasciolaria.*

original shell is quite buried in this vitreous substance.

The forms of the *Cone* and *Olive shells* are such as to allow but a small space for the convolutions of the body of the animal, which accordingly becomes, in the progress of its enlargement, excessively cramped. In order to obtain more space, and at the same time lighten the shell, the whole of the two exterior layers of the inner whorls of the shell are removed, leaving only the interior layer, which is consequently very thin when compared with the other whorl, that envelopes the whole, and which, retaining its original thickness, is of sufficient strength to give full protection to the animal. That this change has actually been effected is very distinctly seen in the *Conus* (Fig. 115) by examining a vertical section of that shell, as is represented in Fig. 116. All the inner partitions of

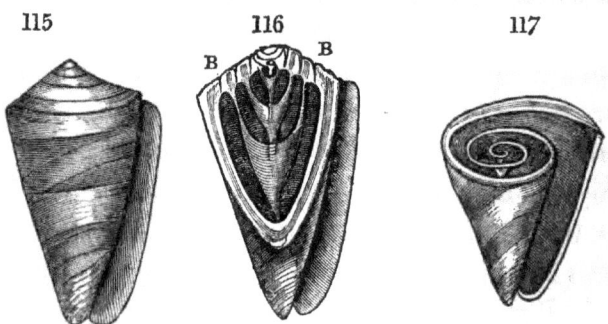

the cavity thus laid open are found to be extremely thin and transparent, and to consist only of the innermost lamina of the original shell; as will appear on tracing them up to that outer portion of the section B B, which lies on each side of the proper apex of the shell, and which forms the apparent base. The lines on this part of the section indicate the thickness which each successive whorl had originally, and when it was itself the outermost whorl. The section also shows the vitreous deposit which lines the upper parts of the cavity, and which completely fills up the smaller turns of the spire, near the apex.*

There are, indeed, instances among shells of the total removal of the interior whorls. This is found to occur in that of the genus *Auricula*, which are molluscous animals, respiring by means of pulmonary organs. In the young shell of this tribe, the partitions which separate the cavities of the whorls are incomplete, and twine parallel to each other; but they wholly disappear as the animal approaches to maturity. In other cases, the animal is found to remove exterior portions of shell formerly deposited, when they lie in the way of its farther growth, and when the mouth of the spire is advancing over the irregular sur-

* Fig. 117, which is a transverse section of the same shell, shows the spiral convolutions, and the comparative thinness of the inner portions. It also forms a striking contrast with a similar section of the Cypræa, Fig. 114.

face of the preceding whorls. Thus we often find that the ridges, ribs, or processes which had been deposited on the surface of the shells of the *Triton*, *Murex*, &c. are removed to make way for the succeeding turn of the spire. In other cases, however, no such power of destroying portions of shell previously deposited seems to exist; and each successive whorl is moulded upon the one which it covers.

It may also be observed, that some mollusca have the means of excavating the shells of other animals on which they may choose to fix, for the purpose of forming a convenient lodgement for themselves. The *Pileopsis* (or fool's cap) has this faculty in a remarkable degree; and it is also met with occasionally in *Siphonariæ* and *Patellæ*. The common *Patella*, or limpet of our own coasts, often, indeed, forms for itself, by some unknown process, a deep cavity out of a calcareous rock.

When the animal which inhabits a spiral shell retires within it, the only part of its body that is exposed to injury is that which is situated at the mouth of the shell. With a view to its protection, it constructs, in many instances, a separate plate of shell, adapted to the aperture, and denominated an *Operculum*. This piece is constructed by a process similar to that by which the rest of the shell is formed; that is, by the deposition of

FORMATION OF SHELLS. 253

successive layers on the internal surface, sometimes in an annular, and sometimes in a spiral form. If an operculum were to be constructed of a considerable size, and were connected to the shell itself by a regular hinge, it would be entitled to be considered as a distinct valve. Here, therefore, we perceive, as was remarked by Adanson, a connecting link between the univalve and the bivalve testacea. A *Clausium* is another kind of covering, serving also for protection, and consisting of a thin spiral plate of shell, attached to the columella by an elastic spring, by which the plate is retracted when the animal retires into its shell. It thus corresponds exactly in its office to a door, opening and closing the entrance as occasion requires. An *Epiphragma* is a partition of a membranous or calcareous nature, constructed merely for temporary use. It is employed for closing the aperture of the shell during certain periods only, such as the winter season, or a long continued drought. Fig. 118 exhibits the lines which appear on the inner side of the epiphragma, of the *Helix pomatia*, or garden snail, and which indicate the succession of deposits by which it has been formed.

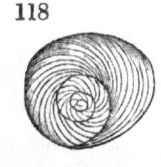

It is remarkable in how short a time this

species of Helix will construct this covering, when circumstances occur to urge its completion. On the approach of winter, the animal prepares itself for passing that season in a state of torpidity, first, by choosing a safe retreat; and next by retiring completely within its shell, and then barricading its entrance by constructing the epiphragma just described, and of which the outer surface is represented in Fig. 119. Having formed this first barrier, the animal afterwards constructs a second, of a membranous nature, situated more internally than the first, and at a little distance from it. If at any other season, while the snail is in full vigour, the experiment be made of surrounding it with a freezing mixture, it will immediately set about constructing a covering for its protection against the cold; and it works with such diligence, that in the course of an hour or two, it will have completed its task, and formed an entire epiphragma.* When the genial warmth of returning spring has penetrated into the abode of the snail, the animal prepares for emerging from its prison, by secreting a small quantity of a mucous fluid, which loosens the adhesion that had taken place between the epiphragma and the sides of the aperture; and the former is, by the pressure of the foot of the snail, thrown off. The whole of this

* Gray, Zoological Journal, i. 214.

process of construction has to be renewed, on every occasion when another covering is required.*

One great use of these coverings is to prevent evaporation from the surface of the body of the animal. It is thus that Snails, Bulimi, &c. may be preserved for months, and even years in a torpid, but living state, ready to be restored to the active functions of life, when sufficient water is supplied.†

The enlargement of bivalve shells is conducted on the same principles as that of univalves; the augmentation of bulk taking place principally at the outer margin of each valve, and corresponding with the growth of the included animal. The order of succession in which the layers are deposited is clearly indicated by the lines on the surface, which frequently appear of different hues from the addition of colouring particles secreted at particular periods by the mantle.

The shells of Oysters and other acephalous mollusca which adhere to rocks, are often moulded, during their growth, to the surfaces to which they are applied. The mantle, being ex-

* An epiphragma differs from true shells in having no adhesion in any part to the animal which formed it.

† A remarkable instance of this apparent reviviscence of snails, which had lain for many years in a dormant state in a cabinet of shells, and which crawled out on being accidentally put into warm water, is recorded in the Philosophical Transactions for 1774, p. 432.

ceedingly flexible, accommodates itself to all the inequalities it meets with, and depositing each successive layer of shell equally on every part, the figure of the surface is assumed, not only by the valve in contact with it, but also by the other valve, which is formed by the opposite surface of the mantle,* and which during its formation was immediately superposed on the thin edge of the other valve, while it was deflected by the irregular surface on which it grew. As the enlargement of the shell proceeds, it was necessary that the muscle, which closes the valves, and is attached to their inner surface, should be gradually removed to a greater distance from the hinge, so that it may preserve its relative situation with regard to the whole shell, and retain undiminished its power of acting upon the valves. For this purpose its adhesions are gradually transferred, by some unknown process, along the surface of the valves; and the progress of the removal may generally be distinctly traced by the marks which are left in the shell at the places before occupied by the attachments of the muscular fibres. The same process takes place when there are two or three muscles instead of one.

A few genera of Mollusca, such as the *Pholas*, have, in addition to the two principal valves, small supplementary pieces of shell. They have

---

* Defrance, Annales des Sciences Naturelles, ii. 16.

been accordingly comprised in the order of *Multivalves*, which also comprehends Cuvier's order of *Cirrhopoda*, including the several kinds of *Barnacles*, (the genus *Lepas* of Linnæus), which are furnished with a great number of jointed filaments, or *cirrhi*, and form an intermediate link of connexion between the *Mollusca* and the *Articulata*. But the limits of this treatise will not allow me to dwell on the endless diversities of structure which this subject presents.

§ 5. *Pteropoda*.

IN the Mollusca belonging to the two orders which have now passed under our review, namely, the *Acephala* and *Gasteropoda*, the mantle, while it folds over the principal viscera of the body, leaves apertures for the admission of water to the gills, or organs of respiration. But there exist a few genera having the sac formed by the mantle closed on every side; a structure which renders it necessary to adopt a different arrangement with regard to the gills, and to place them externally, and we then find them spreading out like a pair of wings, on each side of the neck. Since this general closing of the mantle precludes, also, the formation of any organ of progressive motion corresponding to a foot, advantage is taken of the projection of the gills to employ them as oars for the purpose of enabling the animal to swim through the water.

Mollusca of this description are found in great abundance in the colder regions of the ocean surrounding both the north and south poles; and other species are also met with, though in smaller numbers, in the tropical seas. The *Clio borealis*, of which Fig. 120 is a representation, is the most perfect specimen of this form of construction. It swarms in the Arctic seas, and constitutes the principal food of the whale. The position of its gills, which perform the office of oars or feet, at the same time that they resemble in their shape and action the wings of an insect, are characters which have suggested the title of *Pteropoda*, given by Cuvier to this order of Mollusca.

§ 6. *Cephalopoda.*

FOLLOWING the progress of organic developement, we now arrive at a highly interesting family of Mollusca, denominated the *Cephalopoda*, and distinguished above all the preceding orders by being endowed with a much more elaborate organization, and a far wider range of faculties.

MOLLUSCA CEPHALOPODA.

The Cephalopoda have been so named from the position of certain organs of progressive motion, which are situated on the head, and like the tentacula of the Polypus, surround the opening of the mouth. (See Fig. 121). These feet, or arms,

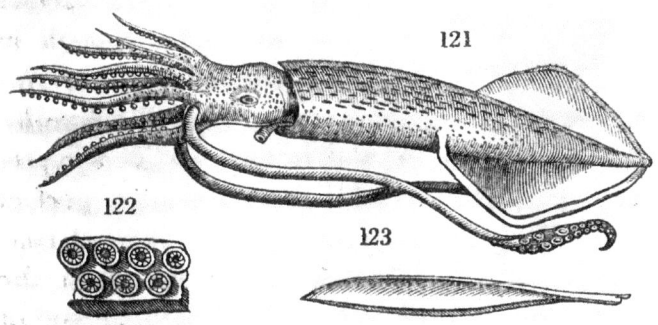

or *tentacula*, if we choose so to call them, are long, slender, and flexible processes, exceedingly irritable, and contractile in every part, and provided with numerous muscles, which are capable of moving and twisting them in all directions with extraordinary quickness and precision. They are thus capable of being employed as instruments, not only of progressive motion, but also of prehension. For this latter purpose they are in many species peculiarly well adapted, because, being perfectly flexible as well as highly muscular, they twine with ease round an object of any shape, and grasp it with prodigious force. In addition to these properties they derive a remarkable power of adhesion to the surfaces of bodies from their being furnished with numerous suckers all along their inner sides. Each of these suckers, as shown separately in Fig. 122, is usually supported on a narrow neck, or pedicle, and strengthened at its circumference by a ring of cartilage. Their internal mechanism is more artificial than the simple construc-

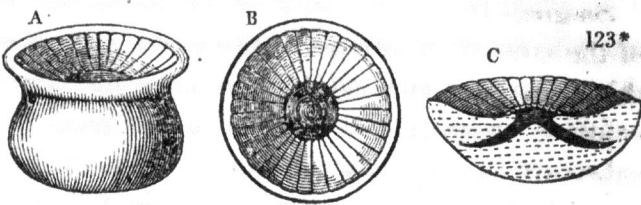

tion already described (p. 137): for when the surface of the disk is fully expanded, as shown in Fig. 123* B, we find that it is formed of a great number of long slender pieces, resembling teeth closely set together, and extending from the inner margin of the cartilaginous ring, in the form of converging radii, to within a short distance of the centre, where they leave a circular aperture. In the flattened state of the sucker, this aperture is filled by the projecting part of a softer substance, which forms an interior portion, capable of being detached from the flat circle of teeth, when the sucker is in action, and of leaving an intervening cavity. The form of this cavity is exhibited in Fig. c, which represents a perpendicular section of the whole organ, and where the central portion, or principal mass of the sucker is drawn away from the circular disk, the inner margin of which appears like a row of teeth. It is evident that by this mechanism, which combines the properties of an accurate valve, with an extensive cavity for producing rarefaction, or the tendency to a vacuum, the power of adhesion is considerably augmented.*

So great is the force with which the tentacula of the cuttle-fish adhere to bodies by means of this apparatus, that while their muscular fibres continue contracted, it is easier to tear away the substance of the limb, than to release it from its attachments. Even in the dead animal I have found that the suckers retain considerable power of adhesion to any smooth surface to which they may be applied.

Our attention must first be directed to the remarkable family of *Sepiæ*, which comprehends three principal genera, namely, the *Octopus*, the *Loligo*, or Calamary, (depicted in Fig. 121), and the common *Sepia*, or Cuttle-fish. The first of these, the Octopus, which was the animal denominated Polypus by Aristotle, has eight arms of equal length, and contains in its interior

* The description I have here given is the result of my own examination of a large Octopus, which I had lately an opportunity of dissecting: and the annexed figures 123*, A, B, C, are copied from drawings I made on that occasion. A represents the sucker in its usual form when not in action: B shows the sucking surface fully expanded: and c is a section of the whole, which had become somewhat flattened by the operation of dividing it.

two very small rudimental shells, formed by the inner surface of the mantle. This shell becomes much more distinct in the Loligo, where it is cartilaginous, and shaped like the blade of a sword. (Fig. 123). The internal shell of the common Sepia is large and broad, and composed wholly of carbonate of lime: it is well known by the name of the *cuttle-fish bone.* Its structure is extremely curious; and deserves particular attention, as establishing the universality of the principles which regulate the formation of shells, whether internal or external, and from which structures differing much in their outward appearance may result. It is composed of an immense number of thin calcareous plates, arranged parallel to one another and connected by thousands of minute hollow pillars of the same calcareous material, passing perpendicularly between the adjacent surfaces. This shell is not adherent to any internal part of the animal which has produced it; but is enclosed in a capsule, and appears like a foreign body, impacted in the midst of organs, with which at first sight, it would appear to have no relation. It, no doubt, is of use in giving mechanical support to the soft substance of the body, and especially to the surrounding muscular flesh; and thus probably contributes to the high energy which the animal displays in all its movements. It has been regarded as an internal skeleton; but it certainly has no pretensions to such a designation; for, although enveloped by the mantle, it is still formed by that organ; and the material of which it is composed is still carbonate of lime. On both these accounts it must be considered as a true shell, and classed among the productions of the integuments. It differs, indeed, altogether from bony structures, which are composed of a different kind of material, and formed on principles of growth totally dissimilar.*

Besides tentacula, the Sepia is also furnished with a pair of fleshy fins, extending along the two sides of the body. The Loligo has similar organs of a smaller size, and situated only at the extremity of the body which is opposite to the head. They have been regarded as the rudiments of *true fins,* which are organs, developed in fishes, and which are supported by slender bones, called *rays;* but no structure of this kind exists in the fins of the Cephalopoda.

In swimming, the organs principally employed by cuttle-fish for giving an effective impulse

---

* Some analogies have, indeed, been attempted to be traced between the cartilaginous lamina of the Loligo, and the spinal column of the lowest order of cartilaginous fishes: these I shall have occasion to point out in the sequel. Solid cartilaginous structures also exist in the interior of the body of the cephalopoda, which are considered by some naturalists as indicating an approach to the formation of an internal skeleton, analogous to that of vertebrated animals.

to the water, are the tentacula. These they employ as oars, striking with them from behind forwards, so that their effect is to propel the hinder part of the body, which is thus made to advance foremost, the head following in the rear. They also use these organs as feet for moving along the bottom of the sea. In their progress, under these circumstances, the head is always turned downwards, and the body upwards, so that the animal may be considered as literally walking upon its head. The necessity of this position for the feet arises probably from the close investment of the mantle over the body; for although the mantle leaves an aperture in the neck for the entrance of water to the respiratory organs, yet, in other respects, it forms a sac, closed in every part, except where the head, neck, and accompanying tentacula protrude.

In the Calamary, as well as in the common Sepia, two of the arms are much longer than the rest, and terminate in a thick cylindrical portion covered with numerous suckers, which may not unaptly be compared to a hand. These processes are employed by cuttle-fish as anchors for the purpose of fixing themselves firmly to rocks, during violent agitations of the sea; and accordingly we find that it is only the extremities of these long tentacula that are provided with suckers, while the short ones have them along their whole length.

The other genera of Cephalopodous Mollusca are, like the Sepiæ, provided with tentacula attached to the head. They comprehend animals differing exceedingly in their size: some being very large, but a great number very minute, and even microscopic.* The shells of these animals are often found to contain partitions dividing them into a number of chambers; hence they have been termed *camerated*, or *multilocular*, or *polythalamous* shells. The Spirula (Fig. 124) is a shell of this description, of which the cellular structure and numerous partitions are rendered visible by making a section through it: (Fig. 125). Some, however, as the

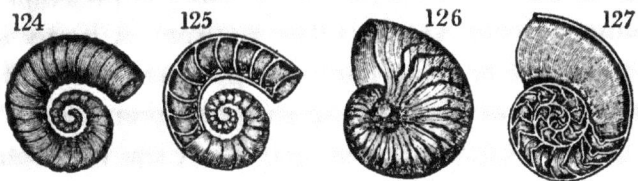

Argonaut, or *Paper Nautilus*, have shells undivided by partitions; and are accordingly termed *unilocular*, or *monothalamous*. The shell of the Argonaut is exceedingly thin, and almost pellucid, probably for the sake of lightness, for it is intended to be used as a boat. For the purpose of enabling the animal to avail itself of the im-

* A particular account has been given of the shells of these microscopic cephalopoda by M. D'Orbigny, in the Annales des Sciences Naturelles; vii. 96.

pulses of the air, while it is thus floating on the waters, nature has furnished it with a thin membrane, which she has attached to two of the tentacula, so that it can be spread out like a sail to catch the light winds which waft the animal forwards on its course. While its diminutive bark is thus scudding on the surface of the deep, the assiduous navigator does not neglect to ply its tentacula as oars on either side, to direct, as well as accelerate its motion. No sooner does the breeze freshen, and the sea become ruffled, than the animal hastens to take down its sail, and quickly withdrawing its tentacula within its shell, renders itself specifically heavier than the water, and sinks immediately into more tranquil regions beneath the surface.*

The common Nautilus, which is provided with a similar sailing apparatus, is an inhabitant of a polythalamous shell (Fig. 126), of which Fig. 127 represents the section. The formation of this, as well as of other shells of this description, presents very curious phenomena. The animal at certain periods of its growth, finding itself cramped in the narrow part of the spire, draws

* It must be confessed, however, that the habits of the Argonaut are still very imperfectly known. Considerable doubts are entertained whether the shell it inhabits is formed by the animal itself, or whether it is the production of some other, but unknown species of Mollusca, and is merely taken possession of by the Argonaut as a convenient habitation, which it can quit and enter again at pleasure.

up that portion of the mantle which occupied it, thus leaving a vacant space. The surface of the mantle which has receded immediately begins to secrete calcareous matter, which is deposited in the form of a partition, stretching completely across the area of the cavity. As the animal proceeds to increase in size, and to occupy a wider portion of the external shell, the same necessity soon recurs, and the same expedient is again resorted to. It withdraws its mantle from the narrower into the wider part of the shell; and then forms a second partition, at a little distance from the first, corresponding to the space left by the receding of the mantle. This process is repeated at regular intervals, and produces the multitude of chambers contained in polythalamous shells, of which the living animal occupies only the largest, or that which continues open.* The partitions are in general perforated either in the centre or at one side, for the purpose of giving passage to a ligament, which preserves the attachment of the mantle to the apex of the shell. This ligament is often surrounded either entirely or partially by shell, which forms a tube, denominated the *syphon:* and portions of which are seen in the section Fig. 127.

* This structure is extremely prevalent in fossil shells: some of which are spiral, such as the *Cornu Ammonis*, while others are straight cones, such as the *Bacculite* and *Orthoceratite*. In most of these the partitions are very numerous, and have undulating surfaces.

Chapter IV.

ARTICULATA.

§ 1. *Articulated Animals in general.*

From the Cephalopoda, the transition is easy to the lowest order of vertebrated animals. But previously to pursuing the analogies which connect these two divisions of the animal kingdom, we have to pass in review a very extensive series of animal forms, constructed upon a peculiar system, and occupying, as well as the Mollusca, a place intermediate between Zoophytes and the more highly organized classes.

We have seen that even in those Zoophytes which are distinguished from the rest by a more elaborate conformation of organs, the powers of progressive motion are always extremely limited. Nor are the Mollusca in general more highly favoured with respect to the degree in which they enjoy this faculty. But the greater number of the animals composing the series we are now to examine are provided with a complete apparatus for motion, and endowed with extensive capacities for using and applying it in various ways. While nature has preserved in the construction of their vital organs the simplicity which marks the primitive modes of organization, and has adhered to a definite model in the formation of the different parts of the system, she has nowhere displayed more boundless variety in the combinations of the forms which she has impressed upon the mechanical instruments, both of prehension and of progression.

All the tribes of Zoophytes, and by far the greater number of Mollusca, are limited by the constitution of their system, to an aquatic existence. But in following the series of *Articulated* animals, we very soon emerge from the waters, and find structures adapted to progression on land. For this we see that preparation is early made in the developement of the nascent structures. A farther design, also, soon becomes manifest; and instruments are given for elevating the body above the ground, and for traversing with rapidity the light and scarcely resisting atmosphere. This prospective design may be traced in the whole system of insects; every part of which is framed with reference to the properties of the medium through which these movements are to be performed.

§ 2. *Annelida.*

THE lowest division of articulated animals comprehends those which have a vermiform shape, and which compose the class of *Annelida*, or Annulose animals; of which the earth-worm may be taken as the type, and most familiar example. In the series of structures which constitute this division of the animal kingdom, we may trace remarkable gradations of developement, through which nature appears to pass in attaining the higher and more perfect conformations.

It may be remarked that, in effecting the transition from Zoophytes to the new model of construction here presented, nature seems to have wholly abandoned that radiated disposition of parts, and those star-like forms, so characteristic of the beings which are placed on the confines of the animal kingdom, and which still retain an analogy with vegetable structures. She now adopts a more regular law of symmetry; by which all the parts are referable to one longitudinal axis, and also to a vertical plane passing through that axis, and which has been termed the *mesial plane*. As a direct consequence of this law, we shall find that in the forms which are hereafter to pass under our review, as far as the external organs and general outline of the body are concerned, all that exists on one side is an exact counterpart, like a reflected image, of what is found on the other side. While in the Star-fish, and Echinus, nothing in point of situation was definite, excepting the upper and the lower surface, and there was no side which could be exclusively denominated

ANNELIDA. 271

either the right or the left side, and no end that could be properly said to be the front, or the back, in Articulated, as well as in Vertebrated animals, all these distinctions are clearly marked and easily defined.

In all the *Annelida* the firmest parts of the body, or those which give mechanical support to the rest, are external, and may be regarded either as appendages to the integuments, or as modifications of the integuments themselves. They consist of a frame-work, composed of a series of horny bands or rings: their assemblage having more or less of a lengthened cylindric shape, and constituting a kind of external skeleton, which encloses all the other organs. This is exemplified in the earth-worm; in the *Pont-obdella* (Fig. 128), which is a species of leech; and in the *Nereis* (Fig. 129). These rings

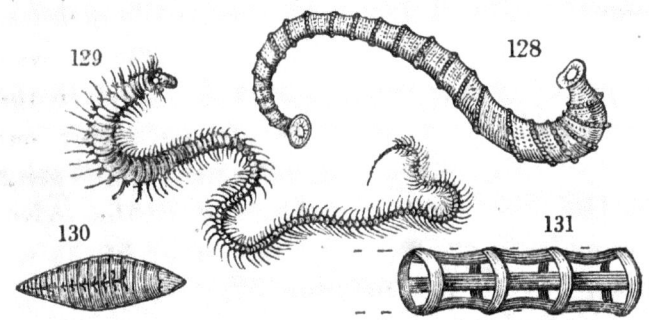

give rise to the division of the body into as many different segments. In some cases, however, we find all these rings compressed into the form of a flat oval disk. This is the case in the *Erpobdella*, of which Fig. 130 is an enlarged representation.

In general, the first of the segments into which the body is divided, contains the principal organs of sense, and is sufficiently distinct from those which follow to entitle it to the appellation of *the head;* while the lengthened prolongation of the opposite extremity, when such a form is present, may be denominated *the tail.*

The rings which encircle the body are connected laterally by a looser and more flexible portion of integument, and also by layers of muscular fibres, curiously collected into bands. The muscular flesh of insects, and other animals of this class, differs much from that of the larger animals, being soft and gelatinous in its texture, though endowed with a high degree of irritability, and contracting with great force. The fibres composing each band are all parallel to one another, and have seldom any tendinous attachments; being generally inserted directly on the parts they are destined to move. Thus the adjacent margins of the rings of worms (as shown in the diagram, Fig. 131) are connected together by these muscular bands, which pass transversely from the one to the other, immediately under the skin, and parallel to the axis of the body. There are generally four distinct bands provided; two running along the back, and two along the lower part of the body.

The effects which result from the action of these muscles are such as might easily be anticipated. The lower set must, when contracting, bring the rings nearer to one another at that lower part; and when the whole series occupying that situation are exerted in concert, they will raise the body in the form of an arch. An opposite curvature will be produced by the contraction of the upper bands; whereby the back will be bent downwards, and both ends of the body raised. In proportion as the two bands, situated on each side, act in concert, while the others are relaxed, the body will be bent laterally towards that side. When all the four muscular bands contract together equally, their joint effect will be to bring the rings near to each other, and to contract the length of the worm; the skin being at the same time wrinkled and swelled out between the rings.

Other muscular bands, attached to the rings, pass from the one to the other in more oblique directions. By means of these muscles the rings may be made to recede at some points, while they approach at others; so that the body may be either twisted laterally on its axis, or wholly elongated, according as the actions of these oblique muscles are partially or generally exerted.

The skin on the surface of the earth-worm is furnished, at the parts where it covers the rings, with very minute bristles, called *Setæ*, by means of which the animal is enabled to fix those parts on the ground, while the other portions of its body are in motion. Both in the anterior and posterior segments, these hairs are directed towards the centre of the animal; while those on the middle segments are perpendicular.* We almost constantly find, in animals belonging to the order of *Annelida*, some provision of this kind. Often it consists of tufts of hair regularly disposed in rows on each side of the under surface. In the *Nereis* (Fig. 129), a genus of sea-worms, there are often above a hundred pair of little tufts of strong bristles: and between these we find tentacula to prevent the animal from running against any thing by which it might be injured. They also raise the body from the ground, for which purpose, as they

* As an instance of the extraordinary multiplicity of species existing in every department of living nature, I may here notice, that of the common earth-worm, apparently so uniform in its shape, Savigny has lately, by a closer examination, been able to distinguish no less than twenty-two different species, among those found in the neighbourhood of Paris alone.

are used under water, very little support is necessary.* Sometimes the whole body is covered with hair; at other times these appendages are in the form of hooks, which, of course, give greater power of clinging to the objects on which they fasten. In some, again, they assume more the nature of feet, of which they exercise during progression all the functions; being furnished with several sets of muscles for adjusting and strengthening their actions.

The mode by which an animal of this description advances along the ground is very simple. It first protrudes the head by the elongation of the foremost segments of the body, while the others cling to the earth by means of the rings, and also of the bristles and other appendages to the integuments. The head is then applied to the ground, and made the fixed point, and the segments next to it, which had been elongated, are now contracted by the action of their longitudinal muscles; in doing which, equal portions of the succeeding segments are necessarily elongated: these are next contracted; and so on, in succession, till the whole is brought forwards to the head: after which the same series of actions is repeated, beginning with the advance of the head.

* Home; Lectures, &c. Vol. i. p. 115.

Worms often reverse this motion, and are thus enabled to move backwards, or with the tail foremost.*

Great variety exists in the forms of the animals referable to the type of Annelida. The *Gordius*, or hair-worm (Fig. 132) is that which exhibits the greatest developement in length compared with the breadth of the body. It has the form of a very long and slender thread: the annular structure being indicated only by very slight transverse folds of the integuments. No

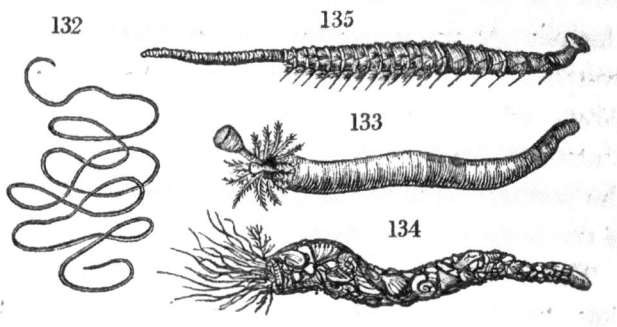

external members, nor even tentacula, have been given to this simplest of vermiform animals.

Many of the animals of this class being soft and defenceless, are obliged to consult their safety by retreating into holes and recesses, or by burrowing in the sand or mud. One genus

* See Home; Lectures on Comparative Anatomy, Vol. i. p. 114.

only, the *Serpula* (Fig. 133), forms for itself an external shell, which is shaped into a spiral tube. Others, as the *Sabella* and the *Terebella*, accomplish the same object by collecting grains of sand, or fragments of decayed shells, or other substances, which they agglutinate together by means of a viscid exudation, so as to form a firm defensive covering, like a coat of mail. Fig. 134 shows this rude architecture in the *Terebella conchilega*. These coverings, however, composed as they are of extraneous materials, and not being organic productions of the animals themselves, are structures wholly foreign to their systems. These inhabitants of tubes, the *Tubicolæ* of Cuvier, are generally furnished with tentacula, issuing from the head, which, when the rest of the body has retired within the tube, is the only part exposed.

The expedient resorted to for progressive motion by the *Lumbricus marinus* of Linnæus (*Arenicola piscatorum* of Lamarck), is very remarkable.* This worm, depicted in Fig. 135, swarms on all sandy shores, and is dug up in great numbers as bait by the fishermen. It bores its way through the sand by means of the peculiar construction of the rings of its head, which, when elongated, has the shape of a re-

* See the account given by Mr. Osler, Philosophical Transactions for 1826, p. 342.

gular cone. As each ring is so much smaller than the one behind it as to admit of being received within it, the whole head, when completely retracted, presents a flat surface. When this disk is applied to the sand, the animal, by gradually projecting the cone, and successively dilating the rings of which it is composed, opens for itself a passage through the sand, and then secures the sides of the passage from falling in by applying to them a glutinous cement, which exudes from its skin, and which unites the particles of sand into a kind of wall, or coating. This covering does not adhere to the body, but forms a detached coherent tube, within which the animal moves with perfect freedom, and which it leaves behind it as it progressively advances: so that the passage is kept pervious throughout its whole length by means of this lining, which may be compared to the brickwork of the shaft of a mine, or tunnel.

An apparatus of a more complex description is provided in the *Terebellæ conchilegæ*, belonging to a tribe of marine worms, which from the peculiar circumstances of their situation, inhabiting parts of the shore nearly midway between high and low water, are obliged often to prolong their tubes to a great length through the sand; for, in consequence of the frequent shifting of the sands in storms, these animals are sometimes buried to a considerable depth, and at others have several inches of their tubes exposed. In the one case, they must work their way speedily to the surface; in the other, they must dive deeper below it. The manœuvres of the terebella are best observed by taking it out of its tube and placing it under water upon sand. It is then seen to unfold all the coils of its body, to extend its tentacula in every direction, often to a length exceeding an inch and a half, and to catch, by their means, small fragments of shells, and the larger particles of sand. These it drags towards its head, carrying them behind the scales which project from the anterior and lower part of the head, where they are immediately cemented by the glutinous matter which exudes from that part of the surface. Bending the head alternately from side to side, while it continues to apply the materials of its tube, the terebella has very soon formed a complete collar, which it sedulously employs itself to lengthen at every part of the circumference with an activity and perseverance highly interesting. For the purpose of fixing the different fragments compactly, it presses them into their places with the erected scales, at the same time retracting the body. Hence the fragments, being raised by the scales, are generally fixed by their posterior edges, and thus overlaying each other, often give the tube an imbricated appearance.

Having formed a tube of half an inch, or an

inch in length, the terebella proceeds to burrow; for which purpose it directs its head against the sand, and contracting some of the posterior rings, effects a slight extension of the head, which thus slowly makes its way through the mass before it, availing itself of the materials which it meets with in its course, and so continues to advance till the whole tube is completed. After this has been accomplished, the animal turns itself within the tube, so that its head is next to the surface, ready to receive the water which brings it food, and is instrumental in its respiration. In summer, the whole task is completed in four or five hours; but in cold weather, when the worm is more sluggish, and the gluten is secreted more scantily, its progress is considerably slower.

Tentacula of various kinds are also met with in several of the more active and vivacious kinds of annelida, such as the *Nereis* (Fig. 129), proceeding from the margin of the mouth and other parts of the head. This animal swims with great facility by rapid, undulating inflexions of its body; and by practising a similar succession of movements in the loose sand at the bottom of the water, it quickly buries itself, and even travels to considerable distances through the sand, first extending the anterior rings, and then bringing up the posterior part of the body; its progress being also much assisted by the action of its numerous bristly feet.*

* Osler, Phil. Trans. 1826. p. 342.

Facilities for progression are also given by the addition of tubercles, arranged in pairs along the under side of the body, which serve the purposes of feet, and are often furnished with bristles or hooks. In the *Amphitrite*, and many other genera, tufts of hair occupy the place of feet on each side, and being moved by muscles specially provided for that purpose, serve as levers for effecting progressive motion.

We find the same object accomplished by very different means in other animals of this class. The leech, for instance, having the rings which encircle its body very numerous and close to each other, could not well have advanced by the ordinary modes of vermiform progression. As a substitute, accordingly, it has been furnished with an apparatus for suction at the two extremities of the body, which are formed into disks for that purpose. By fixing alternately the one and the other, and contracting or elongating the body as the occasion requires, the leech can move at pleasure either forwards or backwards. Thus, while the tail is fixed, the head may be advanced by lengthening the whole body, and when the head is fixed, the hinder sucker can be brought forwards by the contraction of the body, and applied to the ground near to the head, and preparation may thus be made for taking another step.

Most of the parasitic animals which inhabit the interior cavities of the body, and especially the alimentary canal, correspond in external form, as well as in many circumstances of internal conformation, to the Annelida. They compose an order denominated the *Entozoa*.

§ 3. *Arachnida*.

In passing from the Annelida to the *Arachnida*, an order which comprehends all the species of spiders, together with animals allied to them in conformation, we find that a considerable advance has been made in the progress of developement. The frame-work of the body is more consolidated: and the instruments provided for progressive motion are shaped into longer and more perfect levers, are united by a more refined system of articulation, and are moved by more distinct and more powerful muscles; so that the body is elevated from the ground, and enjoys a greater range of action, and a wider sphere of perception.

The rings, which always compose the framework of the Annelida, are here consolidated so as to form two principal divisions of the body, the one in front, termed the *Cephalo-thorax*, which contains the organs of sensation, and of mastication, and also the principal reservoir of circulating fluids; the other, which is behind, and contains the organs of digestion, is termed the *abdomen*. In the spider (Fig. 136, where c is the cephalo-thorax, and A the abdomen) these two portions of the body are separated by a deep groove, which leaves only a slender pedicle, or tube of communication between them.

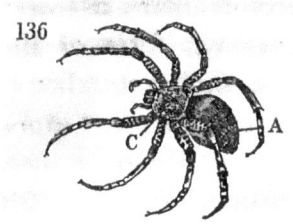

There are usually in the male four pair of legs, constantly articulated with the cephalo-thorax; but the female is furnished with an additional pair, to enable her to carry her eggs. For the purpose of obtaining an extensive base of support, the feet of the spider are spread out in diverging rays, so as to include a very wide circle. They are divided into several joints, those next to the body being termed the *haunches*, and the succeeding ones the *leg*, and the *tarsus*, and each foot is terminated by two, or sometimes three hooks. Besides these, there are other members, resembling feet, which are placed in front of the head, and have affixed to them either a moveable hook, or pincers, which are employed as organs of prehension, and of offence. Through the larger branches of these a canal passes, which opens near the point, and conducts a poisonous fluid into the wounds inflicted by this formidable weapon.

In common with all articulated animals, spiders, in the progress of their growth, cast off their outer skin several times, and at regular periods. In the earlier stages of their existence, although they have the general form of the mature insect, yet they have a smaller number of legs: the last pair not making their appearance till after the spider has attained a certain size. We may here trace the commencement of that system of metamorphosis, which, as we shall afterwards find, is carried to so great a length in winged insects.

Spiders are endowed with extensive powers of progressive motion, and display great activity and energy in all their movements. The long and elastic limbs on which the body is suspended, being firmly braced by their articulations, enable the muscles to act with great mechanical advantage in accelerating the progression of the body. Hence these animals are enabled to run with great swiftness, and to spring from a considerable distance on their prey; powers which were necessary to those tribes that live altogether by the chase. The greater number of species, however, as is well known, are provided with a curious apparatus for spinning threads, and for constructing webs to entangle flies and other small insects. Every species of spider weaves its web in a manner peculiar to itself: and, besides the principal web, they often construct in the neighbourhood a smaller one, in the form of a cell, in which they conceal themselves, and lie in ambush for their prey. Between this cell and the principal web they extend a thread of communication, and by the vibrations into which this thread is thrown, on the contact of any solid body, the spider is immediately acquainted with the event, and passes quickly to the spot, by the assistance of the same thread.

Some species have the power of conveying themselves to considerable distances through the air by means of threads which they dart out, and which are borne onwards by the wind, while the spider is clinging to the end of the thread which is next to it. In this manner these spiders are often carried up to a great height in the air: and it has been supposed that during their flight they often seize upon gnats and other flies; because the mutilated remains of these insects are often seen adhering to the threads: this point, however, is still open to much doubt.

The Natural History of the spider is in many points of view highly interesting, not only from the great extent to which the organic developement is carried, and the energy with which all the functions of animal life are performed; but also with reference to the wonderful instincts displayed in the construction of its web, in the surprise and destruction of its victims, and in the zealous guardianship of its young. It would be impossible, in so brief an outline as the one I am now tracing, to enlarge upon so fertile a topic, without being led too far from the object I have at present more particularly in view, namely the developement of organization with reference to the organs of progressive motion.

§ 4. *Crustacea.*

The plan which Nature appears to have commenced in the construction of the Arachnida, is farther pursued in that of the *Crustacea*. The portions into which the external frame-work of the body was divided in the former, are still further consolidated in the latter: they are composed of denser materials, and endowed with greater rigidity; thus not only offering more resistance to external forces, but also giving a firmer purchase to the muscles which are the moving powers. The limbs, as well as the whole body, are encased in tubes of solid carbonate of lime: they are articulated with great care, and almost always compose hinge joints. The muscles, by which these solid levers are moved, are lodged in the interior, and their fibres either pass directly from one point to another, across the joint; or else they are attached to cartilaginous plates, which, for the purpose of receiving the muscles, are made to project into the interior of the upper portion of the limb, being themselves immovably connected with the lower portion. By this expedient, not only is the employment of a tendon dispensed with, but a larger surface is presented for the attachment of the muscles, which by acting also upon a longer lever, obtain great mechanical advantage. It would be superfluous to occupy more time in explaining the minutiæ of structure in these joints, because the simple inspection of the limbs of a crab or lobster will give clearer ideas of this mechanism than can be conveyed by any laboured description. We must content ourselves with a brief sketch of the principal constituent parts of these external members of the Crustacea.

The number of pairs of legs is either three or four: each leg is divided into five pieces. The

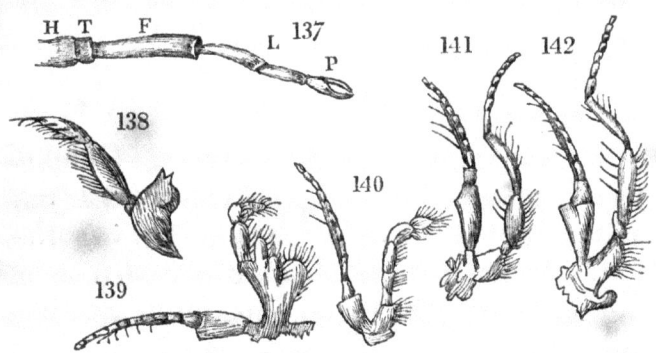

piece H (Fig. 137), next the trunk, is termed the *haunch*, to which is united the *trochanter*, T; after which come, in succession, the *femur* or *thigh*, F; two portions of the leg, L; and the *tarsus*, P. The haunch is usually short, being interposed merely as a base for increasing the extent of motion of the pieces which follow: and sometimes it is itself composed of more than one piece. The leg is usually divided into two pieces, by a joint. The tarsus is terminated by a single or double hook, and sometimes by a pincer, or claw.

New organs, not met with among the Arachnida, are here for the first time developed, namely, the *Antennæ*, of which there is one on each side of the head. They are denominated, in popular language, the *feelers;* although it is more than probable that they perform some function of higher importance than that of conveying perceptions of mere touch. The antennæ consist of slender filaments, composed of a great number of pieces articulated together: and they are infinitely diversified in their form in the different genera and species, both of Crustacea and of Insects.

The jaws, and other parts connected with the mouth, present a great complication of structure; and many of these parts are employed in various uses besides those of mastication; such as the seizing of objects, and turning them in various ways for examination; and, according to their suitableness as articles of food, conveying them into the mouth. These organs are called the

Palpi, and sometimes the *false feet*. They always exist in pairs, and take their rise from the lower lip, or some adjacent part of the head. The portions of which each is composed are articulated together and moved by muscles in the same manner as the ordinary or proper feet. It is worthy of notice, however, that sometimes the foremost pairs of palpi are shaped more like jaws, and actually perform the office proper to jaws, of compressing and dividing the food previously to its introduction into the mouth. These auxiliary jaws are then called *mandibles*. In other instances, we see them assuming every variety of intermediate form between that of mandibles and of false feet, so that it is often difficult, amidst these gradual transitions of structure, to decide to which of these two kinds of organs a specimen we meet with properly belongs. It is apparently with a view to evade this difficulty that a term has been invented which shall include them all, namely, that of *feet-jaws*. These transitions are illustrated by the annexed figures of several of these members in the *Mysis Fabricii*; Fig. 138 being that of a mandible, with its feeler, or palpus; Figures 139, 140, and 141, representing the first, second, and third pair of feet-jaws; and Fig. 142, the first pair of true feet. It would thus seem as if the same constituent element of the fabric is converted by nature into the one or other of these organs, according as best suits the exigencies of each particular case.*

In the lobster, the crab, and many other analogous crustacea, the foremost pair of true feet are also modified to suit a particular purpose; the pincers which terminate them being expanded into a claw, and constituting a powerful organ of prehension, and a formidable weapon of offence. It resembles a finger and thumb in its power of grasping and strongly compressing any object on which it seizes; and to enable it to do this with more effect, the inner edges of both parts of the claw are notched or serrated.

The large portion of shell which is consolidated into one piece, and covers the upper part of the body, is termed the shield, or *carapace*. The tail of the crab is very short, and is united with the body, appearing as if it had been folded under it. The feet-jaws are particularly large, but short: the articulations of the feet are such as to allow of scarcely any motion but in a transverse plane. This is the cause of the greater

---

* The labours of Savigny, Audouin and Latreille appear to have established a complete analogy in the respective component parts, not only of the feet, feet-jaws, jaws and mandibles, but also of the palpi and other appendices attached to the head, in all the articulated animals, whether belonging to the classes of arachnida, crustacea, myriapoda, or winged insects.

facility the crab finds in walking side-ways, which it can do with great quickness when urged by a sense of danger. The lobster, on the contrary, is better formed for swimming than for walking. The hinder part of its body is divided into segments, which play upon each other by a remarkable kind of mechanism, the margins of each portion overlapping the succeeding segment, and partly enclosing it. The tail is the principal agent used in swimming, and the whole force of the muscles is bestowed upon its movements. As it strikes the water from behind forwards, the lobster can only swim backwards; and it is assisted in this action by five pair of false feet, which are attached to the under side of the body, behind the true feet, and which terminate in a fin-shaped expansion, giving them the effect of oars. The extremity of the tail is still more expressly formed for giving effect to the stroke, being terminated by a number of flat scales, which, when expanded, present a broad surface to the water.

The calcareous coverings of these crustacea are analogous to shell both in structure and composition. They contain, however, some phosphate of lime, in addition to the carbonate. The calcareous particles are deposited on a membrane of considerable firmness; and they together compose a dense, but thin and fragile structure, which, in order to distinguish it from the shells of the mollusca, has been denominated a *crust*. A solid structure of this kind, as we have already seen, does not admit of increase by the extension of its own parts: so that in order to allow of the growth of the parts which it encloses, it is necessary that it be cast off, and exchanged for a new shell of larger dimensions.

The process by which this periodical casting and renewal of the shell are effected, has been very satisfactorily investigated by Reaumur. The tendency in the body and in the limbs to expand during growth is restrained by the limited dimensions of the shell, which resists the efforts to enlarge its diameter. But this force of expansion goes on increasing, till at length it is productive of much uneasiness to the animal, which is, in consequence, prompted to make a violent effort to relieve itself; by this means it generally succeeds in bursting the shell; and then, by dint of repeated struggles, extricates its body and its limbs. The lobster first withdraws its claws, and then its feet, as if it were pulling them out of a pair of boots: the head next throws off its case, together with its antennæ; and the two eyes are disengaged from their horny pedicles. In this operation, not only the complex apparatus of the jaws, but even the horny cuticle and teeth of the stomach, are all cast off along with the shell: and, last of all, the tail is extricated. But the whole process is not accomplished without long continued efforts. Sometimes the legs are lacerated or torn off, in the attempt to withdraw them from the shell; and in the younger crustacea the operation is not unfrequently fatal. Even when successfully accomplished it leaves the animal in a most languid state: the limbs, being soft and pliant, are scarcely able to drag the body along. They are not, however, left altogether without defence. For some time before the old shell was cast off, preparations had been making for forming a new one. The membrane which lined the shell had been acquiring greater density, and had already collected a quantity of liquid materials proper for the consolidation of the new shell. These materials are mixed with a large proportion of colouring matter, of a bright scarlet hue, giving it the appearance of red blood, though it differs totally from blood in all its other properties. As soon as the shell is cast off, this membrane, by the pressure from within, is suddenly expanded, and by the rapid growth of the soft parts, soon acquires a much larger size than the former shell. Then the process of hardening the calcareous ingredient commences, and is rapidly completed; while an abundant supply of fresh matter is added to increase the strength of the solid walls which are thus constructing for the support of the animal. Reaumur estimates that the lobster gains, during each change of its covering, an increase of one-fifth of its former dimensions. When the animal has attained its full size, no operation of this kind is required, and the same shell is permanently retained.

A provision appears to be made, in the interior of the animal, for the supply of the large quantity of calcareous matter required for the construction of the shell at the proper time. A magazine of carbonate of lime is collected, previous to each change of shell, in the form of two rounded masses, one on each side of the stomach. In the crab these balls have received the absurd name of crab's eyes; and during the formation of the shell they disappear.

It is well known that when an animal of this class has been deprived of one of the claws, that part is in a short time replaced by a new claw, which grows from the stump of the one which had been lost. It appears from the investigations of Reaumur, that this new growth takes place more readily at particular parts of the limb, and especially at the joints; and the animal seems to be aware of the greater facility with which a renewal of the claw can be effected at these parts; for if it chance to receive an injury at the extremity of the limb, it often, by a spontaneous effort, breaks off the whole limb at its junction with the trunk, which is the point where the growth more speedily commences. The wound soon becomes covered with a delicate white membrane, which presents at first a convex surface: this gradually rises to a point, and is found on examination to conceal the rudiment of a new claw. At first this new claw enlarges but slowly, as if collecting strength for the more vigorous effort of expansion which afterwards takes place. As it grows, the membrane is pushed forwards, becoming thinner in proportion as it is stretched; till at length it gives way, and the soft claw is exposed to view. The claw now enlarges rapidly, and in a few days more acquires a shell as hard as that which had preceded it. Usually, however, it does not attain the same size; a circumstance which accounts for our frequently meeting with lobsters and crabs which have one claw much smaller than the other. In the course of the subsequent castings, this disparity gradually disappears. The same power of restoration is found to reside in the legs, the antennæ, and the jaws.

We must naturally be curious to learn, if possible, from what source these astonishing powers of regeneration are derived. Reaumur hazarded the conjecture, that there might be originally implanted in each articulation a certain number of embryo limbs, ready to be developed as occasion might require; somewhat in the way in which the rudiments of the secondary teeth remain concealed in the jaw, in preparation for replacing the first set when these have been removed. But this hypothesis is overturned by the fact that if the animal loses only part of the limb, it is the deficient portion alone, and not the whole limb that is regenerated. The sprouting of the new claw bears a strong analogy to the budding of a plant; both having their origin from an imperceptible atom, or germ, which is either formed on the occasion, or had pre-existed in the organization. We are, however, totally destitute of the means of deciding which of these alternatives is nearest to the truth. It is but too probable that the agents which can effect such wonderful operations will ever baffle our most scrutinizing inquiries, and that they are of too refined an order to come within the reach of the most subtle conjectures that human imagination can devise.

CHAPTER V.

INSECTS.

§ 1. *Aptera.*

APTEROUS, or wingless insects form the next term in the series of articulated animals. Closely allied in their organization to many of the preceding families, they differ from them in being essentially formed for a terrestrial instead of an aquatic life. Most of the lower tribes of this order are parasitic, that is, derive their nourishment from the juices of other animals, the skin of which they infest and penetrate, and into which they insert tubes for suction. The various tribes of *Acari*, or mites, of *Pediculi*, or lice, of *Ricini*, or ticks, of *Pulices*, or fleas; together with the *Podura*, or spring-tail; the *Lepisma*, and the family of *Myriapoda*, or millepedes, are comprehended in this order. I shall be obliged to pass over these tribes very cursorily, noticing only a few of the more remarkable circumstances attending their mechanical conformation.

The *Pulex* is the only apterous insect that undergoes complete metamorphoses in the course of its developement. In the first stage of its existence, it has the form of a long worm, without feet, frequently rolling itself into a spiral coil. It consists of thirteen segments, having tufts of hair growing upon each. In its mature state it has six articulated legs, the hindmost of which are of great size, for the purpose of enabling the insect to take those prodigious leaps which astonish us in beings of so diminutive a size, and afford a striking proof of the exquisite mechanism pervading even the lowest orders of the animal creation.

The *Podura* leaps into the air by a mechanical contrivance of another kind; employing for this purpose the tail, which is very long, and forked at the end. In its ordinary state this organ is kept folded under the abdomen, where it is concealed in a groove. The pieces of which it is composed are articulated together in such a manner as to admit of their being rapidly unbent by the action of its muscles, the whole mechanism conspiring to produce the effect of a powerful spring, by which the body is propelled forwards to a considerable distance. In some species, this flexible tail has a flattened form, for the purpose of enabling the insect to leap from the surface of water, an action which it performs with apparently as much ease as if it sprung from a solid resisting plane.

The *Lepisma* leaps by means of moveable appendages, placed in a double row along the under side of the body, and acting like springs. There are eight pair of these members, corresponding in situation and structure to the false feet of the crustacea, and, like them, terminating in jointed filaments.

The *Julus* and the *Scolopendra*, which compose the family of the *Myriapoda*, so called from the immense number of their feet, undergo, to a certain extent, a kind of metamorphosis in the progress of their developement. When first hatched they have often no feet whatever, and resemble the simpler kinds of worms. Legs at length make their appearance; but they arise in succession, and it is not until the later periods of their growth that these animals acquire their full complement of segments, with their accompanying legs. The *Julus terrestris*, for example, (Fig. 143) has, at its entrance into the world, only eight segments and six feet; but acquires in the course of its developement, fifty segments and about two hundred feet. The anterior legs are directed obliquely forwards, and the rest more or less backwards. The mandibles have the form of small feet; as we have seen is frequently the case in crustaceous animals.

§ 2. *Insecta alata.*

OUR attention is now to be directed to the more highly developed Insects, which have been formed with a view to progression through the air. On these, which compose the most extensive class of the whole animal kingdom, Nature has lavished her choicest gifts of animal powers, as far as they are compatible with the diminutive scale to which she has restricted herself in their formation. The model she has chosen for their construction is that which combines the greatest security against injurious impressions from without, with the most extensive powers of locomotion; and which also admits of the fullest exercise of all those faculties of active enjoyment which are characteristic of animal life. She has provided for the first of these objects by enclosing the softer organs in dense and horny coverings, which perform the office of an external skeleton, sustaining and protecting the viscera, and furnishing extensive surfaces of attachment to the muscles, from the action of which all the varied movements of the system are derived.

The muscular system of perfect insects is exceedingly complex. Lyonet has described and delineated an immense number of muscular bands in the caterpillar of the *Cossus*, and the plates he has given have been copied in a variety of books in illustration of this part of the structure of insects. The recent work of Straus Durckheim affords an equally striking example of admirable arrangement in the muscles of the

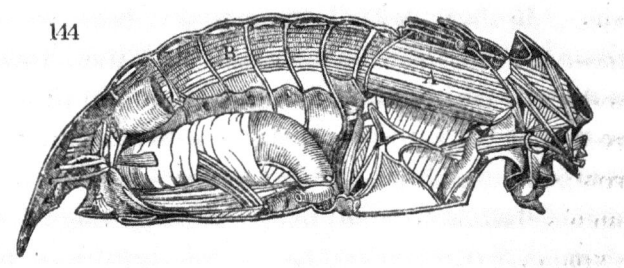

Melolontha vulgaris, or cockchaffer, the anatomy of which has been minutely investigated by

that distinguished entomologist. These muscles are represented in Fig. 144, which has been carefully reduced from his beautifully executed plates. The largest mass of muscular fibres is that marked A, which depress the wings, and are of enormous size and strength.

On examining the different structures which compose the solid frame-work of insects, we find them conforming in every instance to the general type of annulose animals, inasmuch as they consist of thickened portions of integument, encircling the body; but variously united and consolidated, for the manifest purpose of obtaining greater mechanical strength and elasticity than if they had remained detached pieces, joined only by membranous connexions. A long flexible body, such as that possessed by the Myriapoda, could not easily have been transported through the air; for every bend would have created a resistance, and have impeded its advance during flight. Hence the body of the insect, which is to be ultimately adapted to this mode of progression, has been shortened by a reduction in the number of its segments, and rendered more simple and compact. The segments destined to support the wings have been expanded for the purpose of lodging the powerful muscles that are to move them; and rendered dense and unyielding in order to support their action.

Nature has farther provided insects with instruments adapted to different kinds of external actions. They consist of articulated levers, variously combined together, and forming legs, claws, pincers, oars, palpi, and, lastly, wings, calculated for executing every variety of prehension, of progression, or whatever other action their wants and necessities require.

§ 3. *Developement of Insects.*

It would appear as if the final accomplishment of objects so numerous, so widely different, and so liable to mutual interference, could be attained only by the animal being subjected to a long series of modifications, and passing through many intermediate stages of developement. The power of flight is never conferred upon the insect in the earlier periods of its existence: for before its structure can obtain the lightness which fits it for rising in the air, and before it can acquire instruments capable of acting upon so light an element, it has to go through several preparatory changes, some of which are so considerable as to justify the term of *metamorphoses*, which has been generally given to them.* But

* Transformations quite as remarkable occur in several tribes of animals belonging to other classes: such as those of the *Frog* among reptiles, and of the *Lernæa* among parasitic worms.

transient is the state of perfection in every thing that relates to animal existence. When the insect has by a slow developement reached this ultimate elaboration of its organs, its life is hastening to a close; and the period of its perfect state is generally the shortest of its whole existence.

The history of the successive stages of developement of insects opens a highly interesting field of philosophical inquiry. For a certain period of the early life of these animals, the growth of all the parts appears to proceed equably and uniformly: but at subsequent epochs, some parts acquire a great and sudden increase of size, and others that were in a rudimental condition become highly developed, and constitute what appear to be new forms of organs, although their elements were in existence from a much earlier period. The modifications which the harder and more solid structures of insects exhibit in the progress of these changes, are particularly remarkable, as illustrating the principles on which the developement is conducted. The researches of modern entomologists have led to the conclusion that the frame-work, or skeleton of insects, is always formed by the union of a certain determinate number of parts, or elements, originally distinct from one another, but which are variously joined and soldered together in the progress of growth: frequently exhibiting a great disproportion in the comparative expansion of different parts. The enlargement of any one part, however, exercises a certain influence on all the neighbouring parts, and thus are the foundations laid of all the endless diversities which characterize the several species belonging to each tribe and family.

In the progress of developement, we may recognize two principles, which, though apparently opposite to each other, concur and harmonize in their operation: these are *expansion* and *concentration*. Thus while those segments of body which follow the head are greatly enlarged, in order to support the more recently developed organs of progressive motion, they are also more consolidated, and rendered stronger by the union of several pieces which were before separate. The hinder segments, having no such appendages to support, are less dilated, and the whole body is much shortened by the approximation of the segments, which in this way compose the abdomen, or hinder division of the insect.

The progress of the metamorphoses of insects is most strikingly displayed in the history of the *Lepidopterous*, or butterfly and moth tribe.*

---

* The four periods of the existence of the *Bombyx mori*, or the moth of the silk-worm, are shown in the annexed engravings, Fig. 145 are the eggs; Fig. 146, the *Larva*, or caterpillar; Fig. 147, the *Pupa*, or chrysalis; and Fig. 148, the *Imago*, or perfect insect.

DEVELOPEMENT OF INSECTS. 305

The egg, which is deposited by the butterfly, gives birth to a caterpillar; an animal, which, in out-

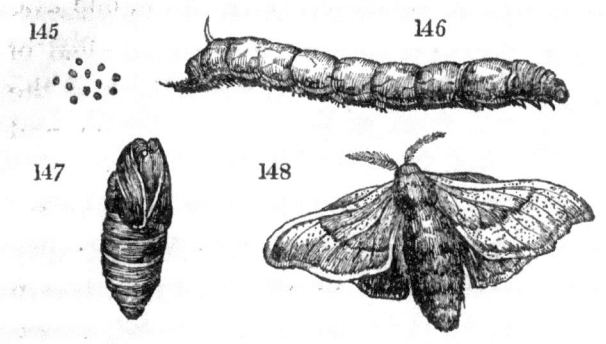

ward shape, bears not the slightest resemblance to its parent, or to the form it is itself afterwards to assume. It has, in fact, both the external appearance, and the mechanical structure of a worm. The same elongated cylindric shape, the same annular structure of the denser parts of its integument, the same arrangements of longitudinal and oblique muscles connecting these rings, the same apparatus of short feet, with claws, or bristles, or tufts of hairs, for facilitating progression; in short, all the circumstances most characteristic of the vermiform type are equally exemplified in the different tribes of caterpillars, as in the proper Annelida.

But these vermiform insects have this peculiarity, that they contain in their interior the rudiments of all the organs of the perfect insect. These organs, however, are concealed from view by a great number of membraneous coverings, which successively invest one another, like the coats of an onion, and are thrown off, one after another, as the internal parts are gradually developed. These external investments, which hide the real form of the future animal, have been compared to a mask; so that the insect, while wearing this disguise, has been termed *larva*, which is the Latin name for a mask.

This operose mode of developement is rendered necessary in consequence of the greater compactness of the integuments of insects, as compared with those of the annelida. In proportion as they acquire density, they are less capable of being further stretched, and at length arrive at the limit of their possible growth. Then it is that they obstruct the dilatation of the internal organs, and must be thrown off to make way for the farther growth of the insect. In the mean time a new skin has been preparing underneath, moulded on a larger model, and admitting of greater extension than the one which preceded it. This new skin, at first, readily yields to the distending force from within, and a new impulse is given to the powers of developement: until, becoming itself too rigid to be further stretched, it must, in its turn, be cast off in order to give place to another skin. Such is the process which is repeated periodically, for a great number of times, before the larva has attained its full size.

These successive peelings of the skin are but so many steps in preparation for a more important change. A time comes when the whole of the coverings of the body are at once cast off, and the insect assumes the form of a *pupa*, or *chrysalis*; being wrapt as in a shroud, presenting no appearance of external members, and retaining but feeble indications of life. In this condition it remains for a certain period: its internal system continuing in secret the farther consolidation of the organs; until the period arrives when it is qualified to emerge into the world, by bursting asunder the fetters which had confined it, and to commence a new career of existence. The worm, which so lately crawled with a slow and tedious pace along the surface of the ground, now ranks among the sportive inhabitants of air; and expanding its newly acquired wings, launches forward into the element on which its powers can be freely exerted, and which is to waft it to the objects of its gratification, and to new scenes of pleasure and delight.

Thus do the earlier stages of the developement of insects exhibit a recurrence of those structures which are found in the lowest department of this series of animals. The larva, or infantile stage of the life of an insect, is, in all its mechanical relations, a mere worm. The *imago*, or perfect state, on the other hand, exhibits strong analogies with the crustaceous tribes, not only in the general form of the body, but also in the consolidated texture of its organs, (especially of those which compose its skeleton) and in the possession of rigid levers, shaped into articulated limbs, and furnished with large and powerful muscles, from all which circumstances great freedom and extent of motion are derived. To this elaborate frame, nature has added wings, those refined instruments of a higher order of movements, subservient to a more expanded range of existence, and entitling the beings on which they have been conferred to the most elevated rank among the lesser inhabitants of the globe.

The mechanical functions of insects scarcely admit of being reduced to general principles, in consequence of the great diversity of forms, of habits and of actions, that is met with among the innumerable host of beings which rank under this widely extended department of the animal creation. In these minute creatures may be discovered all the mechanical instruments and apparatus required for the execution of those varied motions which we witness in the larger animals, and which, though almost peculiar to the different classes of these animals, are here frequently united in the same individual. Insects swim, dive, creep, walk, run, leap, or fly with as much facility as fishes, reptiles, quadrupeds, or birds. But besides these, a great number have also movements peculiar to themselves, and of which we meet with no example in other parts of the animal kingdom.

In attempting to delineate a sketch of the movements of insects, and of the mechanism by which they are performed, I am compelled, by the great extent of the subject, to confine myself to very general views; and must refer such of my readers as are desirous of fuller information on this subject to the works of professed entomologists.

The mechanical conditions of an insect in its several states of larva, pupa, and imago, are so widely different, that it will be necessary to consider each separately. In many tribes, however, the difference between the larva and the perfect insect is much less considerable than in others. Those belonging to the orders of Hemiptera and Orthoptera for example, come out of the egg with nearly the same form as that which they have in the mature state; excepting that they are without wings, these organs being added in the progress of their growth, and constituting, when acquired, their perfect or *imago* condition.

§ 4. *Aquatic Larvæ.*

MANY insects, which, when fully developed, are the most perfectly constructed for flying, are, when in the state of larvæ, altogether aquatic animals. Some of them are destitute of feet, or other external instruments of motion, swimming only by means of the alternate inflexions of the body from side to side, in the same manner as the Nais, and the Leech. Sometimes these actions are performed by abrupt strokes, giving rise to an irregular zig-zag course: this is the case with the larva of the gnat, and with many others which have no feet. In the structure of the larva of the *Libellula*, or dragon-fly, a singular artifice has been resorted to for giving an impulse to the body, without the help of external members. It is that of the alternate absorption of water into a cavity in the hinder part of the body, and its sudden ejection from that cavity, so that the animal is impelled in a contrary direction, upon the same principle that a rocket rises in the air by the reaction of that fluid. It has at various times been proposed to apply the power of steam to the production of an effect exactly similar to that of which Nature here presents us with so perfect an example, for the purpose of propelling ships, instead of the ordinary mode of steam navigation.

Some larvæ, such as that of the *Stratiomys*, collect a bubble of air, which they retain within a tuft of hair at the extremity of the tail, evidently with a view of diminishing the specific gravity of the body, and thus giving greater efficacy to the muscular actions which they employ in their progression through the water. Another use is also made of these tufts of hair; for by repelling the water, they allow of the insect's suspending itself from the surface of the fluid in the manner already noticed in giving the history of the evolutions of the hydra.*

The impulse given by the lateral inflexions of the body are in many cases assisted by short legs; but the larvæ of the *Ephemera*, though furnished with legs, do not use them for this purpose, and swim simply by the action of the tail. Those of the *Dytiscus* are furnished with a pair of very long members, projecting to a considerable distance from the sides, and flattened at the ends, to serve as oars. The larvæ of the *Hydrophilus* are also admirably formed for swimming; and they not only dart forwards with surprising velocity, but also turn in all directions with the utmost facility.

§ 5. *Terrestrial Larvæ.*

The movements of larvæ that are not aquatic are perfectly analogous to those of the Annelida, which they much resemble in their outward form and mechanical structure. The muscles by which the annular segments of the body are moved, are exceedingly numerous, and beauti-

* Page 179.

fully arranged with reference to the motions they are intended to effect. The investigation of the structure of these minute organs has long exercised the talents of the most skilful entomologists, and still offers much that remains to be explored. The researches of Lyonet, already alluded to, on the anatomy of the larva of the *Bombyx Cossus*,* of which he has published an elaborate description, accompanied by admirable engravings, will ever remain a splendid monument of patience and ingenuity in overcoming the difficulties which impede this kind of inquiry. In the body and the limbs of this caterpillar, Lyonet counted above 4000 separate muscular bands, all arranged with the most perfect symmetry, and adapted with wonderful precision to the performance of the required effects.

In these larvæ, as in the simpler forms of the Annelida, progression is often accomplished solely by the alternate contraction and extension of the annular segments, aided, in many cases, by short hairs, and frequently, also, by a slimy secretion which exudes from their bodies. Many larvæ which are destitute of feet, move onwards by first coiling the body into a circle, making the head and the tail meet, and then springing forwards by a sudden extension of the back, producing an effect like the un-

* *Cossus ligniperda.* Fabricius.

bending of a bow. By an artifice of the same kind, some larvæ contrive to leap to a considerable distance, by the violent effort which they make in unfolding the curvatures of their bodies.

Some larvæ avail themselves of their jaws in order to fix the head, and drag the rest of the body towards it. In this manner do the larvæ of the capricorn beetles advance along the winding passages which they have themselves excavated, holding by the jaws, and dragging themselves forwards. These movements are assisted by the resistance afforded by short tubercles which project from different parts of the back and under surface of the body; so that these insects advance in the passage by an act similar to that by which a chimney-sweeper, exerting the powerful pressure of his elbows, shoulders, and knees, manages to climb up a chimney.

For the purpose of enabling insects to take stronger hold of the surfaces they pass over, we often observe them furnished with spines, or hooks, which are moved by appropriate muscles, and they occupy different situations on the body. Modifications without end occur with regard to these and other external parts subservient, in various degrees, to progressive motion. Every possible gradation is also seen between the short tubercles already mentioned, and the more regularly formed feet or legs. Those which are regarded as *spurious legs*, or *prolegs*, as they have been called, occupy an intermediate place between these two extremes. They consist of fleshy and retractile tubercles, and are often very numerous; while the number of the *true legs*, as they are called, is limited to six. These last are the representatives of the legs of the future perfect insect; for they are attached to the three first segments of the thorax; and are formed of those portions articulated to each other, corresponding to the three principal joints of the imago. The true legs are generally protected by horny scales; but the coverings of the prolegs are wholly membranous. The office of these spurious legs is merely to serve as props to support the body while the insect is walking, and to prevent its hinder part from trailing on the ground. They are frequently terminated by single or double hooks; and also by a marginal coronet of recurved spines. These hooks, or spines, enable the insect to cling firmly to smooth surfaces; and also to grasp the most slender twig, which could not have been laid hold of by legs of the usual construction.

The speed with which these larvæ can advance is regulated by many circumstances independently of the mere possession of legs: for some caterpillars move slowly, while others can run very nimbly. The following is the order in which the legs are usually moved: namely, the anterior and the posterior leg on the same side are advanced at the same moment, together with the intermediate one on the other side; and this takes place alternately on both sides.

There is one tribe of caterpillars called *Surveyors*, or *Geometers*, (Fig. 148*, A) which walk

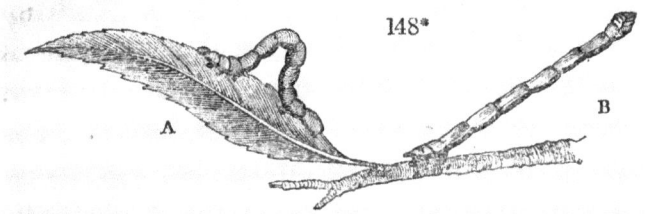

by first fixing the fore feet, and then doubling the body into a vertical arch; this action brings up the hind part of the caterpillar, which is furnished with prolegs, close to the head. The hind extremity being then fixed by means of the prolegs situated at that part, the body is again extended into a straight line; and this process being repeated, the caterpillar advances by a succession of paces, as if it were measuring the distance, by converting its body into a pair of compasses. At the same time that they employ this process, they further provide for their security by spinning a thread, which they fasten to different points of the ground as they go along.*

Many other species of caterpillar practise the

* The great force exerted by the muscles of many caterpillars is exemplified by their often fixing themselves to an object, and extending the body to a distance, as if it were a rigid cylinder: this attitude is shown in Fig. 148* B.

same art of spinning fine silken threads, which especially assist them in their progression over smooth surfaces, and also in descending from a height through the air. The caterpillar of the cabbage butterfly is thus enabled to climb up and down a pane of glass, for which purpose it fixes the threads that it spins in a zig-zag line, forming so many steps of a rope ladder. The material of which these threads are made is a glutinous secretion, which, on being deposited on glass, adheres firmly to it, and very soon acquires consistence and hardness by the action of the air.

Other caterpillars, which feed on trees, and have often occasion to descend from one branch to another, send out a rope made with the same material, which they can prolong indefinitely; and thus either suspend themselves at pleasure in the air, or let themselves down to the ground. They continue, while walking, to spin a thread as they advance, so that they can always easily retrace their steps, by gathering up the clue they have left, and reascend to the height from which they had allowed themselves to drop.

§ 6. *Imago, or Perfect Insect.*

THE process which nature has followed in the developement of the structure of insects, has for its object the gradual hardening and consolidation of texture, and the union and concentration of organs: for we find that the segments which were at a distance from one another in the larva, are approximated in the perfect insect, and often closely tied together by ligaments: and in other cases, adjoining segments cohere so as to form but a single piece. Thus the number of separate parts composing the solid fabric is considerably diminished. Other segments, again, fold inwardly, forming internal processes, and adding to the extent and complication of the skeleton.

The integuments of perfect insects, being designed to be permanent structures, are thicker and more rigid than those of their larvæ, and are formed of several layers, in which the component parts of the integuments of the larger animals may readily be distinguished. Their rigidity does not, like that of shells, arise from the presence of carbonate of lime; for they contain but a small proportion of this material: and whatever calcareous ingredient enters into their composition is in the form of phosphate of lime.

In external appearance their texture approaches nearer to that of horn than to any other animal product: yet in their chemical composition they differ from all the usual forms of albuminous matter. The substance to which they owe their characteristic properties is of a very peculiar nature; it has been termed *Chitine* by M. Odier,* and *Entomoline* by M. Lassaigne.† This substance is found in large quantity in the wings and elytra of coleopterous insects. It is remarkable for not liquefying, as horn does, by the action of heat; and accordingly the integuments of insects, even after having been subjected to a red heat, and reduced to a cinder, are found to retain their original form.‡

With this substance there is blended a quantity of colouring matter, which has usually a dull brown or black hue. But the colour of the external surface is generally owing to another portion of this matter, which is spread over it like a varnish, and being soluble in alcohol and in ether, may be removed by means of these agents. The colours which are displayed by insects, and

* Annales de Chimie, tom. 76.
† See the work of Straus Durckheim, p. 33.
‡ M. Odier had concluded from his experiments that no nitrogen enters into the composition of this substance. That this conclusion has been too hastily adopted has been proved by Mr. Children, who, by pursuing another mode of analysis, found that the chitine of cantharides contains not less than nine or ten per cent. of nitrogen. See Zoological Journal, i. 111—115.

which arise from the presence of this latter substance, are often very brilliant, and, as is the case with many other classes of animals, the intensity of the tints is heightened by the action of light. The elytra of tropical insects display a gorgeous metallic lustre depending on the reflexion of the prismatic colours; and the same variegated hues adorn the scales of butterflies of those regions.

Hair grows in various parts of the surface of insects. Where the integument is membranous and transparent, these hairs may be distinctly perceived to originate from enlarged roots, or bulbs, and to pass out through apertures in the skin; as is the case with the hair of the larger animals. Their chemical composition, however, is very different, for they are formed of the same substance as the integuments, namely entomoline. The purposes served by the hairs are not always obvious. In many cases they seem intended to protect the integuments from the water, which they repel from their surfaces. They also tend to prevent injury arising from friction; and are found to be more abundant in those parts, as the joints, which are liable to rub much against one another.

The divisions of the body are frequently marked by deep incisions; whence has originated the term *insect*, expressive of this separation into sections. It is, however, a character which they possess in common with all articulated animals, the typical form of which consists, as we have seen, of a series of rings, or segments, joined endwise in the direction of a longitudinal axis. The principal portions into which the body is divided are the *head*, the *trunk*, and the *abdomen:* each of which is composed of several segments. I have here given, in illustration, the annexed figures, showing the successive portions into which the solid framework, or skeleton, of one of the beetle tribe,

the *Calosoma sycophanta*,* may be separated. The entire insect, which presents the most perfect specimen of a complete skeleton in this class of animals, is represented in Fig. 149; and the several detached segments, on an enlarged scale, in Fig. 150. The head c, as seen in the latter figure, may be regarded as being composed of three segments; the trunk, x, y, z, of three; and the abdomen, b, of nine. Fig. 151, is a view of the head separated from the trunk, and seen from behind, in order to show that its form is essen-

* *Carabus sycophanta.* Linn.

STRUCTURE OF INSECTS. 321

tially annular, and that it resembles in this respect the rings of which the thorax consists, and to which it forms a natural sequel.

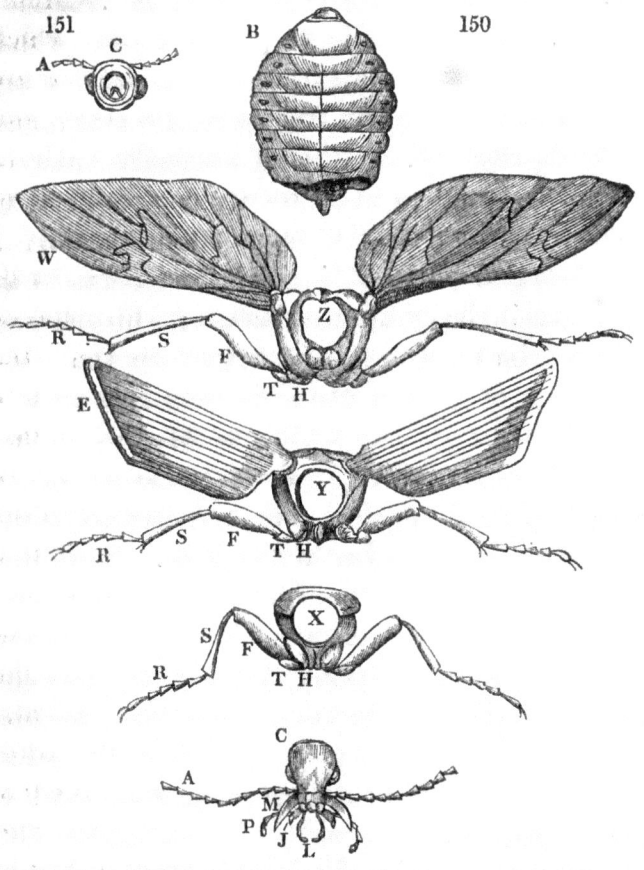

The *head* contains the brain, or principal enlargement of the nervous system, and the organs of sensation and of mastication. Its size, as compared with the rest of the body, varies much in

VOL. I. Y

different insects, and is in general proportionably larger than it is in the larva state. Its integument, which, from analogy with vertebrated animals, has been called the *skull*, or *cranium*, (c, Fig. 150), is usually the hardest part of the general crust. Although it may appear, a on superficial examination, to consist of a single undivided piece, yet, on tracing its gradual formation, it is found to be in reality composed of a union of several of the segments of the larva. Audouin and Carus distinguish three component segments in the cranium of insects; while Straus Durckheim considers it as formed by the consolidation of no less than six segments of the vermiform larva. According to this theory, the same elements which in the thoracic segments are developed into feet, are here employed to form parts having other destinations. From the segment adjacent to the thorax the antennæ are supposed to be developed. The two anterior segments belong properly to the face; the one giving origin to the mandibles (M), to the maxillæ, or proper jaws, (J), and also to the palpi (P); the other producing the processes called the labial palpi (L).

The mode in which the head is connected with the trunk varies much in different insects. Sometimes it is united by a broad basis of attachment, forming a joint between the adjacent surfaces: but usually it is only appended by a narrow filament, or neck; so that the articulation is effected by ligament alone. Occasionally it is placed at the end of a long pedicle, which removes it to a considerable distance from the trunk. In the *Hymenoptera* and *Diptera*, the head moves upon a pivot, so as to admit of its being turned completely round.

The trunk, or *Thorax*, is composed, as shown in the figure, of three segments, termed respectively the *Prothorax* (x); the *Mesothorax* (y); and the *Metathorax* (z).* The first of these, the prothorax, carries the first pair of legs; the second, or mesothorax, gives origin to the second pair of legs, and also to the first pair of wings, or to the Elytra (e), as in the example before us; and the third, or metathorax, supports the third pair of legs, and the second pair of wings (w). These two last segments are closely united together, but the original distinction into two portions is marked by a transverse line. Each of these three segments is divisible into an upper, a lower, and two lateral portions, which

* In these denominations I have followed the nomenclature of Victor Audouin (Annales des Sciences Naturelles, tom. i. p. 119), as being the simplest and the clearest: but other entomologists have applied the same terms to different parts. The first segment is termed by Straus Durckheim and other French writers, the *Corselet*. Mr. Kirby calls it the *Manitrunk*, and restricts the term *Prothorax* to its upper portion. The united second and third segments are the *Thorax* of Straus Durckheim, the *Tronc alifère* of Chabrier, and the *Alitrunk* of Kirby.

are joined together at the sides of the trunk; these again admit of further subdivision; but for the names and descriptions of these smaller pieces I must refer the reader to works on Entomology. The parts of the thorax to which the wings are attached indicate the situation of the centre of gravity of the whole insect; a point, which being in the line of the resultant of all the forces concerned in the great movements of the body, requires to be sustained by the moving powers under all circumstances either of action or repose.

Victor Audouin, who has made extensive researches on the comparative forms of all these parts in a great variety of insects, appears to have satisfactorily established the general proposition that, amidst the endless diversity of forms exhibited by the skeleton of insects, they are invariably composed of the same number of elements, disposed in the same relative situations and order of arrangement: and that the only source of difference is a variation in the proportional developement of these elements. He has also observed that the great expansion of one part is generally attended by a corresponding diminution of others.

The third division of the body is termed the *Abdomen* (B); it is composed of all the remaining segments, which join to form a cavity enclosing the viscera subservient to nutrition, respiration, and reproduction. The number of these abdominal segments is very various in different genera of insects. Sometimes there appear to be but three or four; while, in other cases, there are twelve, or even a greater number. In the *Calosoma* (Fig. 150, B), the abdomen has six complete, followed by three imperfect segments. Not being intended to carry any of the organs of progressive motion, they retain the form of simple hoops, which is the primitive type of the segments of annulose animals. Each segment has a ligamentous connexion with the next, which is often so close, as hardly to admit of any motion between them; but in other instances it is more lax, and allows of the abdomen being flexible. In the former case, which is the construction in all the *Coleoptera*, or beetles, the rings have an imbricated arrangement; that is, each overlaps the next, often to the extent of two-thirds of its breadth: so that they present a succession of spheroidal hoops, capable of being drawn out, to a certain extent, like the tubes of a telescope. This very artificial construction is manifestly designed to allow of a great variety of movements, determined by the position of the muscles they enclose: for since the surfaces which receive, as well as those which are received, are segments of spheroids, this structure admits of a twisting motion; and the latter segment may be pushed more or less into the cavity of the former, either generally, or on one side.

Each segment, besides being separate from the rest, is further divided into an upper, or dorsal, and a lower, or ventral portion; each portion having the form of a semicircle, or rather of an arch of a circle. These are connected at the sides by a ligamentous band, which runs the whole length of the abdomen. Great advantage results from this division of the circles, allowing of the upper and lower portions of the abdominal covering being at one time separated, and at another brought nearer together; for thus the cavity is capable of being enlarged or contracted in its dimensions, and adapted to the variable bulk of its contents. It is deserving of notice that, during the process of transformation, some of the abdominal segments, which are present in the larva, disappear entirely, or leave only imperfect traces of their former existence. Sometimes the posterior segments become so exceedingly contracted in their diameter as to give rise to the appearance of a tail: this is exemplified in the *Panorpa*.

The junction of the abdomen with the trunk is effected in various ways. In all the Coleoptera, it is united by the whole margin of its base, without having a narrower part: in other tribes there is a visible diminution of diameter, forming a groove all round, or an *incision*, as it is technically termed. In the Hymenoptera, this incision is so deep as to leave only a narrow pedicle, like a neck, connecting these two divisions of the body. In some this pedicle is short, in others long: in the former case, an exceedingly refined mechanism is resorted to for effecting the necessary movements in a part so bulky compared with the narrowness of the surface of attachment.*

Insects in their perfect state have constantly six legs, which are the developements of the six proper legs of the same animal in its larva condition: all the spurious legs having disappeared during its metamorphosis. We have seen that in the myriapoda, the result of developement is an increase in the number both of segments and of legs; the reason of which is that, being terrestrial animals, a lengthened form was more useful and accordant with their destination; but in winged insects, where the object is to procure the means of flight, the organs require to be concentrated, and all superfluous parts must be retrenched and discarded from the fabric. The multiplication of organs, which, in the former case, indicated the progress of a higher developement, would in the latter have been the source

* For the details of this structure I must refer to writers on entomology, and in particular to Kirby and Spence's "Introduction to Entomology," vol. iii. p. 701.

of imperfection. As long as the insect remains in its larva stage, its condition is analogous to that of the myriapode: but in the more elevated state of its existence, its structure is subject to new conditions and regulated by new laws.

While the number of members is thus reduced, ample compensation is given by their increased activity and power, derived from their augmented length, and the more distinct lever-like forms of the pieces which compose them.

These pieces (see Fig. 150) are named, from their supposed analogy to the divisions of the limbs of the higher orders of vertebrated animals, the haunch (H), the trochanter (T), the femur (F), the tibia (S), and the tarsus (R). In general the femur (or thigh) has nearly a horizontal, and the tibia (or leg) a vertical position, while the whole tarsus (or foot) is applied to the ground.

The haunch (H), which is supposed to correspond to the hip bone of quadrupeds, is a broad, but very short truncated cone. The mode of its articulation with the trunk admits of great variety; sometimes it is united by a ball and socket joint, as in the *Curculio* and *Cerambyx*; and it then has, of course, great freedom of motion: at other times the joint is of the hinge kind, as in the *Melolontha*. The trochanter (T), and the femur (F), though in reality distinct pieces, are usually so firmly united as to compose only one division of the limb. The articulation of this portion with the haunch is always effected by a hinge-joint. Joints of this description, when formed, as they are in insects, by the apposition of two tubular pieces, are constructed in the following manner. One of the tubes has, at the end to be articulated, two tubercles, which project from the margin, and are applied to the adjacent end of the other tube at two opposite points of its circumference; the line which passes through those two points being the axis of motion. On the side where the flexion is intended to be made both tubes are deeply notched, in order to admit of their being bent upon one another at a very acute angle: and the space left by these notches is filled up by a pliant membrane, which performs the office of a ligament. These articular tubercles and depressions are so adjusted to one another, that the joint cannot be dislocated without the fracture of some of its parts. As the different axes of motion in the successive joints are not coincident, but inclined at different angles to one another, the extent of motion in the whole limb is very greatly increased. Thus in the cases where the articulation of the haunch with the trunk is a hinge joint, the axes of this joint and of the next are placed at right angles to each other; so that there results, from the combination of both, a capability in the thigh of executing a circular motion in a manner almost as perfect as if it had revolved in a spherical socket. The principle of this compound motion is the same as that employed on ship-board for the mariner's compass, and other instruments which require to be kept steady during the motion of the ship. For this purpose what are called *gimbals* are used, the parts of which have two axes of rotation, at right angles to each other, so as to enable the compass to take its proper horizontal position, independently of any inclination of the ship.

The *tibia*, or *shank* (s), is joined at an acute angle with the femur; and is frequently either beset with spines, or else notched or serrated.

The *tarsus*, or foot (R), is the last division of the limb: it is divided into several joints, which have been supposed to represent those of the toes of quadrupeds. The joints are generally of the hinge kind, but some are met with of a more rounded form, and approaching to that of the ball and socket. The whole structure is most admirably adapted to its exact application over all the inequalities of the surfaces on which the insect treads. But as the habits and modes of life of this numerous class are exceedingly diversified, so the form of the feet admits of greater variety than that of any other part of the limb.

The feet of insects diverge, and spread over a wide surface; thus extending the base of support so as to ensure the stability of their bodies in the most perfect manner. When the legs are very long, as in the *Tipula*,* the body seems, indeed, more to be suspended than supported by them; contrary to what obtains in quadrupeds, where the feet are more immediately underneath the points at which they are connected with the trunk.

The last joint of the tarsus is generally terminated by a claw, which is sometimes single and sometimes double, and which contributes to fasten the foot, under a variety of circumstances, both of action and of repose. With feet thus armed the insect can ascend or descend the perpendicular sides of a rough body with the greatest ease; but it is scarcely able to advance a single step upon glass, or other polished surfaces, even when horizontal. The hooks at the ends of the anterior pair of feet are directed backwards, those of the middle pair inwards, and of the posterior pair forwards; thus affording the greatest possible security against displacement.

Many insects are provided with cushions at the extremity of the feet, evidently for the purpose of breaking the force of falls, and preventing the jar which the frame would otherwise have to sustain. These cushions are formed of

* It has been conjectured that the object in furnishing this insect with legs of so great a length is that of enabling it to walk among blades of grass.

dense velvetty tufts of hair, lining the underside of the tarsi, but leaving the claw uncovered; and the filaments, by insinuating themselves among the irregularities of the surfaces to which they are applied, produce a considerable degree of adhesion. Cushions are met with chiefly in large insects which suddenly alight on the ground after having leaped from a considerable height: in the smaller species they appear to be unnecessary, because the lightness of their bodies sufficiently secures them from any danger arising from falls.

Some insects are furnished with a still more refined and effectual apparatus for adhesion, and one which even enables them to suspend themselves in an inverted position from the under surfaces of bodies. It consists of suckers, the arrangement and construction of which are exceedingly beautiful; and of which the common house-fly presents us with an example. In this insect that part of the last joint of the tarsus which is immediately under the root of the claw, has two suckers appended to it by a narrow funnel-shaped neck, moveable by muscles in all directions. These suckers are shown in Fig. 152, which represents the under side of the foot of *Musca vomitoria*, or blue-bottle fly, with the suckers expanded. The sucking part of the apparatus consists of a membrane, capable of contraction and extension, and the edges of

STRUCTURE OF INSECTS. 333

which are serrated, so as to fit them for the closest application to any kind of surface. In

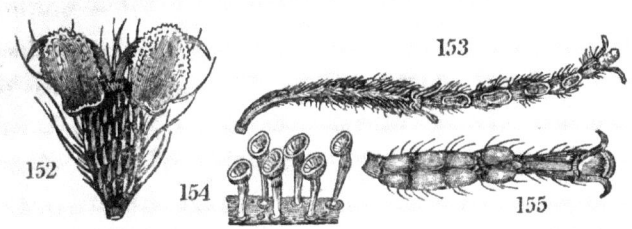

the *Tabanus*, or horse-fly, each foot is furnished with three suckers. In the *Cimbex lutea*, or yellow saw-fly, there are four, of which one is placed upon the under surface of each of the four first joints of the toes (Fig. 153); and all the six feet are provided with these suckers. In the *Dytiscus marginalis*, suckers are furnished to the feet of the male insect only. The three first joints of the feet of the fore-legs of that insect have the form of a shield, the under surface of which is covered with suckers having long tubular necks; there is one of these suckers very large, another of a smaller size, and a great number of others exceedingly small. A few of the latter kind are represented highly magnified in Fig. 154. In the second pair of feet, the corresponding joints are proportionally much narrower, and are covered on their under surface with a multitude of very minute suckers. The *Acridium biguttulum*, which is a species of grasshopper, has one large oval sucker, under the last joint of the foot, immediately between the claws. On the under surface of the first joint are three pair of globular cushions, and another pair under the second joint. Fig. 155 shows these parts. The cushions are filled with an elastic fibrous substance; which, in order to increase the elasticity of the whole structure, is looser in its texture towards the circumference.*

The mode in which these suckers operate may be distinctly seen, by observing with a magnifying glass the actions of a large bluebottle fly in the inside of a glass tumbler. A fly will, by the application of this apparatus, remain suspended from the ceiling for any length of time without the least exertion; for the weight of the body pulling against the suckers serves but to strengthen their adhesion: hence we find flies preferring the ceiling to the floor, as a place of rest.

Insects which, like the gnat, walk much upon the surface of water, have at the ends of their feet a brush of fine hair, the dry points of which appear to repel the fluid, and prevent the leg from being wetted. If these brushes be moistened with spirit of wine, this apparent repulsion no longer takes place; and the insect immediately sinks and is drowned.

* Philosophical Transactions for 1826, p. 324.

§ 7. *Aquatic Insects.*

Although many insects are inhabitants of water while in their larva state, few continue to reside in that element after they have undergone all their metamorphoses. When they have attained the imago state, indeed, every part of their bodies becomes permeated by air, which forms altogether a large portion of their bulk, and gives to the insect, when it is immersed in water, a strong buoyant force. As the largest volume of air is contained in the abdomen, this part is comparatively lighter than either the trunk or head; and the natural position of the insect in the fluid is oblique to the horizon, the head being depressed, and the abdomen elevated. Any force impelling the body forwards in the direction of its axis tends, therefore, to make it also descend. The effect of this downward force is counteracted by the sustaining pressure of the water, which is directed vertically upwards: so that the real operation of the force in question is to carry the body forwards nearly in a horizontal direction.

In insects destined to move in water, sometimes all the legs, but occasionally only one pair, are lengthened and expanded into broad triangular surfaces, capable of acting as oars:

and these surfaces are further extended by the addition of marginal fringes of hair, so disposed as to project and act upon the water every time the impulse is given, but to bend down when the leg is again drawn up, preparatory to the succeeding stroke; thus imitating the action which is called feathering an oar. The impulses are given with great regularity, all the feet striking the water at the same moment.

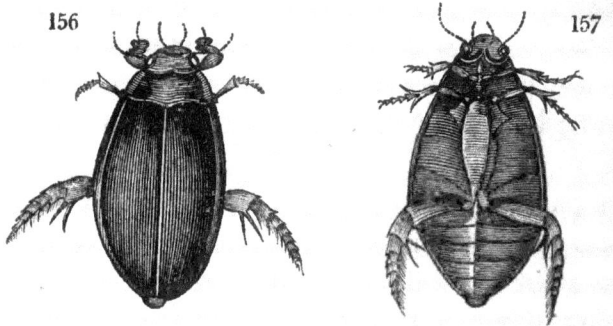

Of all the coleopterous insects, the *Dytiscus*, or water-beetle (of which Fig. 156 represents the upper, and Fig. 157 the under side), is the one best constructed for swimming: its body having a flattened form, very much resembling a boat, narrower before than behind, and its surface presenting no projecting parts. The upper surface in particular is extremely smooth, to enable it to glide under the water with the least possible friction. Its centre of gravity is placed very near the under surface. The posterior legs, which act as powerful oars, are attached to very large haunches, for the purpose of containing the thick muscular bands which are inserted into the trochanter, and by which these joints are moved with great power. As the motion of these oars is to be performed in a plane nearly parallel to the axis of the body, the haunches are not required to be moveable: and accordingly they are firmly united to the thorax; a structure which renders the motion of the other joints more regular and uniform. When the Dytiscus wishes to rise, it need only desist from all action, and abandon itself to the buoyant force of the fluid, which quickly carries it to the surface.

The *Notonecta,* or water-boatman (Fig. 158), is remarkable for always swimming on its back,  a peculiarity depending on the form of its body, which is semi-cylindrical, with the legs affixed to the flat surface; so that, when lying on its back in the fluid, the centre of gravity is below the centre of the whole figure, or the *metacentre,* as it is termed, and the equilibrium is maintained. It is evident that, under these circumstances, if it were placed in the water with its legs undermost, it would unavoidably tilt over, and resume its usual position. Its long legs extending at right angles to the body, present a striking resemblance to the oars of a boat; and they act, indeed, in the same manner, and on the same principles.

§ 8. *Progressive Motion of Insects on Land.*

THE actions of the limbs of insects in walking are quite different from what they are in swimming, and are very similar to those of the caterpillar, in which we have seen that the motions of the anterior and posterior legs on one side are combined with that of the middle one on the other side; and the two sets of legs are moved alternately. In consequence of their relative positions with the trunk, the anterior legs are advanced by the extension, and the posterior legs by the flexion of the corresponding joints. When the feet have fixed themselves on the ground, the contrary actions take place, and the body is brought forwards. During this period the legs which compose the other set are called into play, and are advanced; and the same succession of actions takes place with these as with the former. This can easily be seen when the insect walks very leisurely; but in a more quickened pace, the succession of actions is too rapid to be followed by the eye.

The action of leaping is performed by the

sudden extension of all the joints of the limb, which are previously folded as close as possible. The joints principally concerned in this action, are those of the thigh and tibia, as they furnish the longest and most powerful levers. Preparatory to the effort, the tibia is brought down as close as possible to the ground, by bending it over the tarsus; and the thigh also is bent upon the tibia, so as to form with it a very acute angle. In order to enable it to take this position with most advantage, we find in many of the Coleoptera, that the thigh has a longitudinal groove for the reception of the tibia, with a row of spines on each side of the groove. While the limb is in this bent position, the extensor muscles are violently exerted, and by producing a sudden unbending of this apparatus of folded springs, they project the whole body, by the accumulated impulse, to a considerable height in the air. The leaps of insects being generally forwards, all the legs do not participate equally in the effect; for the fore legs contribute much less to it than the hind legs, and are more useful in modifying the direction of the leap, than in adding to its force. The power of leaping is derived principally from the great size and strength of the extensor muscles of the legs, which, being contained within the femur, necessarily swell that division of the limb to an unusual thickness; and in order to procure sufficient velocity of action, both the femur and tibia are much elongated. Thus the locust, which is so constructed, leaps with ease to a distance two hundred times the length of its own body. We may in general, indeed, infer the particular kind of progressive motion for which the insect is intended by observing the comparative length of the different pairs of legs. When they are of equal size, the pace is uniform:—swiftest in those that have the longest legs,—slowest when they are short. When the anterior legs are much longer than the posterior, the power of prehension may be increased, but that of progression is impeded. The great prolongation of the posterior legs is generally accompanied by the power of jumping, unless, indeed, they are at the same time much bent, for such curvature disqualifies them from acting advantageously as levers.

Many insects have the extremity of the tibia armed with a coronet of spines, which assist in fixing this point against the plane from which they intend to spring, and which give to the limb a steady fulcrum. The *Cicada spumaria* has been known to leap to a distance of five or six feet; which is two hundred and fifty times its own length: this, if the same proportions were observed, is equivalent to a man of ordinary stature vaulting through the air the length of a quarter of a mile. When the same insect is laid on glass, on which the spines cannot fasten, it is unable to leap farther than six inches.*

The insects belonging to the genus *Elater* are provided with a peculiar mechanism for the special purpose of accomplishing a singular mode of leaping, independently of any action of the legs. The legs of this insect are so short, that when it is laid on its back, it cannot turn itself, being unable to reach with its feet the plane on which it is lying, and procure a fulcrum for the action of its muscles. It is apparently with the design of remedying this inconvenience, that nature has bestowed on this tribe of insects the faculty of springing into the air, and making a somerset, so as to light upon the feet; an effect which is accomplished by an exceedingly curious mechanism. The prothorax is prolonged beyond the length it usually has in other coleoptera, and it is articulated with the mesothorax on the dorsal side by two lateral tubercles, which form a hinge joint, limiting its motions to a vertical plane. The sternum, or pectoral portion of the prothorax is also extended backwards, and terminates in an elastic spine, which is received into a cavity in the mesothorax, and which, while the insect is lying on its back, with the prothorax bent upon the mesothorax, recoils with the force of

* De Geer, III. 178, quoted by Kirby and Spence.

a spring, and communicates to the body an impulse which carries it upwards to a considerable height. If the elater should fail in its first attempts to recover its feet, it repeats its leaps till it succeeds. We find no example of a similar structure in any other part of the animal kingdom.

The express adaptation of structure to the mode of life designed for each species of insect is nowhere more strongly marked than in those which are intended to burrow in the earth: and of these the *Gryllo-talpa*, or mole cricket, presents a remarkable example. A minute account of the anatomy of this insect has been given by Dr. Kidd,* from which it appears that being destined, like the mole, to live beneath the surface of the earth, and to excavate for itself a passage through the soil, it is furnished with limbs peculiarly calculated for burrowing, with a skin which, being covered with a fine down, effectually prevents the adhesion of the moist earth through which it moves; and with a form of body enabling it to penetrate with least resistance the opposing medium. By being endowed with the power of moving as easily in a backward as in a forward direction, it is enabled quickly to retreat in the narrow channel it has excavated: and as a safeguard in these retro-

* Phil. Trans. for 1825, p. 203.

PROGRESSIVE MOTION OF INSECTS. 343

grade movements, it is provided with a pair of posterior appendages, which are supplied with large nerves, and may be regarded as serving the purpose of caudal antennæ.

The fore-legs, (one of which is represented in Fig. 158*) are the burrowing implements, and 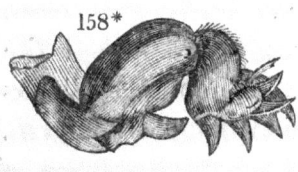 they are admirably calculated for their peculiar office, both in the shape and in the mode of articulation of their several divisions, which bear a considerable analogy to the corresponding member of the mole. Dr. Kidd observes, that, compared with the other legs, and with the general size of the animal, they are as if the brawny hand and arm of a robust dwarf were set on the body of a delicate infant; and the indications of strength which their structure manifests, fully answer to their extraordinary size. For a more particular description of the mechanism of this instrument I must refer the reader to the paper above quoted.

§ 9. *Flight of Insects.*

IF the excellence of a mechanic art be measured by the difficulties to be surmounted in the attainment of its object, none surely would rank higher than that which has accomplished the flight of a living animal. No human skill has yet contrived the construction of an automaton, capable, by the operation of an internal force, of sustaining itself in the air, in opposition to gravity, for even a few minutes; and far less of performing in that element the evolutions which we daily witness even in the lowest of the insect tribes. To the ultimate attainment of this faculty it would appear that all the transformations they undergo in external appearance, and all the developements of their internal mechanism, are expressly directed. Wings are added to the frame only in the last stage of its completion; after it has disencumbered itself of every ponderous material that could be spared, after it has been condensed into a small compass, and after it has been perforated in all directions by air-tubes, giving lightness and buoyancy to every part. Curiously folded up in the pupa, the wings there attain their full dimensions, ready to expand whenever the bandages that surround them are removed. No sooner is the insect emancipated from its confinement, than these organs, which are composed of duplicatures of a dense, but exceedingly fine membrane, identical in its composition with the general integuments, begin to separate from the sides of the body, and to unfold all their parts. Their moisture rapidly evaporates, leaving the delicate film dry and firm, so as to be ready for immediate action. The fibres, or *nervures*, as they are called, form a delicate net-work, for the support of this fine membrane, like the frame of the arms of a windmill, which supports the canvass spread over them. The microscope shows that these fibres are tubular, and contain air; a structure the most effectual for conjoining lightness with strength; and many entomologists are of opinion that the insect has the power, during the act of flying, of directing air into the nervures, so as to dilate them to the utmost, and render them quite tense and rigid.

In the great majority of insects the wings are four in number; of which the first pair are, as we have seen, affixed to the *mesothorax*, and the second to the *metathorax*. These two segments of the thorax, composing what has been termed the *alitrunk*, constitute the most solid portion of the skeleton, and are frequently strengthened by ridges, and other mechanical contrivances for support. The superior extremities of these supports, which have been compared to the clavicles, or furcular bones of birds, are always curved inwards. This part of the trunk requires to be alternately dilated and contracted during flight, and hence the several pieces of which its dorsal portion is composed are loosely connected together by ligaments.*

The shape of the wings is more or less triangular. They are moved by numerous muscles, which occupy a large space in the interior of the trunk, and consist of various kinds of flexors, extensors, retractors, levators, and depressors; the whole forming a very complicated assemblage of moving powers. The largest, and consequently most powerful of these muscles, are those which depress, or bring down the wings. They form a large mass, marked A in Fig. 144. All these muscles exert great force in their contractions, which are capable of being renewed in very rapid succession: for, indeed, unless they had this power, even so light a body as that of an insect could not have been sustained for a moment in so rare a medium as the atmosphere, far less raised to any height by its resistance.

The simple ascent and descent of the wings would be sufficient, without any other movement being imparted to them, to carry forwards the

* See Chabrier's " Essai sur le Vol des Insectes," Mémoires du Muséum d'Histoire Naturelle; vi. 410, vii. 297, and viii. 47 and 349. See also Zoological Journal; i. 391.

body of the insect in the air. The action in which the muscles exert the greatest force is in striking the air during the descent of the wing; an impulse in the opposite direction being the result of the reaction of the air. The axis of motion of the wings is a line inclined at a small angle to the axis of the body, and directed from before backwards, outwards, and downwards; and they move in a plane, which is not vertical, but inclined forwards. The angle which the plane of the wing forms with the horizon varies continually in the different positions of the wing, but the general resultant of all these successive impulses is a force directed forwards and upwards; the first part of this force produces the horizontal progression of the insect, while the second operates in counteracting the force of gravity, and during the advance of the insect, either maintains it at the same height, or enables it to ascend.

When the insect wishes to turn, or to pursue an oblique course, it effects its purpose very easily by striking the air with more force on one side than on the other; or, by employing certain muscles which bend the body to one side, it shifts the situation of the centre of gravity, so that the reaction of the air on the wings is exerted in a different direction to what it was before; and the motion of the body is modified accordingly.

By exerting a force with the wings just sufficient to balance that of gravity, insects can poise themselves in the air, and hover for a length of time over the same spot, without rising or falling, advancing or retreating; and the body may, all the while, be kept either in the horizontal, or in the erect position. In the latter case the motions are similar to those which take place in ordinary flying, only they are more feebly exerted, since all that is required is to sustain the weight of the body without urging it to a greater speed. *Libellulæ*, *Sphinxes*, and a great number of Diptera, exhibit this kind of action: among the latter the *Stratiomys* is most remarkable for its power of remaining long in the same fixed position.

The number, form, and structure of the wings have furnished entomologists with very convenient characters for their classification: on these are founded the orders of the *Coleoptera*, *Orthoptera*, *Rhipiptera*, *Hemiptera*, *Neuroptera*, *Hymenoptera*, *Diptera*, *and Lepidoptera*. To enter into any detail in a field of such vast extent as is presented by the infinitely diversified mechanism of the insect creation, would, it is obvious, far exceed the proper limits of this treatise. I must therefore confine myself to a few leading points in their structure and modes of progression.

In the *Coleoptera*, an order which comprehends

by far the largest number of genera of insects, the lower pair of wings (w, Fig. 150, p. 321) are light and membranous, and of a texture exceedingly fine and delicate. They are of great extent compared with the size of the body, when fully expanded : and are curiously folded when not in use. For the protection of these delicate organs, the parts which correspond to the upper pair of wings of other insects, are here converted into thick opaque, and hard plates (E), adapted to cover the folded membranous wings when the insect is not flying, and thus securing them from injurious impressions to which they might otherwise be exposed from heat, moisture, or the contact of external bodies. These wing cases, or *elytra* as they are termed, are never themselves employed as wings, but remain raised and motionless during the flight of the insect. They probably, however, contribute to direct the course of flight, by variously modifying the resistance of the air.*

In the *Orthoptera*, (Fig. 159), the coverings of the wings, or *tegmina*, instead of being of a horny texture, are soft and flexible, or semi-membranous. The wings themselves, being

---

* The Elytra of insects have been regarded by Oken as corresponding to the bivalve shells of the Mollusca, a notion which seems to be founded upon a fanciful and strained analogy.

broader than their coverings, are, when not in use, folded longitudinally, like a fan.

In the new Order of *Rhipiptera* of Latreille,* which includes only two genera, the tegmina are

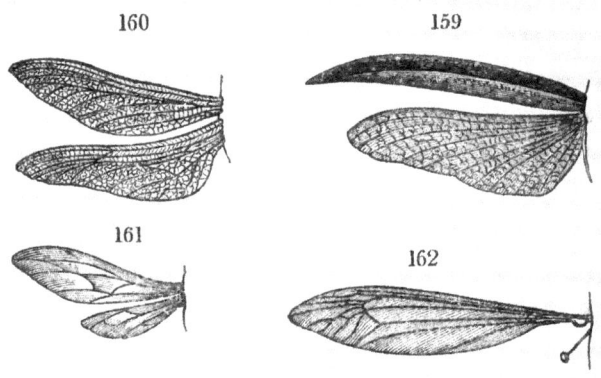

anomalous both in their situation and shape; being fixed at the base of the anterior legs, very long and narrow, and apparently incapable of protecting the wings. The wings themselves are of ample extent, forming, when expanded, a quadrant of a circle, with five or six nervures radiating from their base, and folded longitudinally.

In the *Hemiptera*, the tegmina, or as they are here called, the *hemi-elytra*, are coriaceous towards their base, but membraneous towards

* The *Strepsiptera* of Kirby. See Transactions of the Linnæan Society, XI. 86.

their extremity, and the true wings are folded transversely, so as to cross one another. These hemi-elytra are employed to strike the air in flight, and their movements accompany those of the wings.

Insects having four thin membranous and transparent wings are arranged under two orders; namely, the *Neuroptera* (Fig. 160), in which the lesser nervures form an interlacement of fibres, crossing one another nearly at right angles, like net-work, or lace: and the *Hymenoptera* (Fig. 161), in which they are disposed like the ramifications of arteries or veins, diverging at acute angles from the main trunks. The insects belonging to these two orders enjoy extensive powers of flight. *Libellulæ*, and *Æschnæ*, which are included in the first of these orders, never close their wings, but, when they are not flying, keep them constantly expanded, and ready for instant action. They fly with the greatest ease in all directions, sideways, or backwards, as well as forwards, and can instantly change their course without being obliged to turn their bodies. Hence they possess great advantages both in chasing other insects, and in evading the pursuit of birds. *Bees*, which are hymenopterous insects, have often been observed to fly to great distances from their hive in search of food. The humble bee adopts a very peculiar mode of flight, describing, in its aerial course, segments of circles, alternately to

352 THE MECHANICAL FUNCTIONS.

the right and to the left. The velocity with which these insects move through the air in general much exceeds that of a bird, if estimated with reference to the comparative size of these animals.*

* I have been favoured by Mr. George Newport with the following account of the structure of the sting of the Wild Bee, (*Anthophora retusa*, Kirby) which he has lately carefully examined, and from whose drawings of the dissected parts the annexed figures (163) have been engraved. " The sting of the bee, A, is formed of two portions placed laterally together, but capable of being separated. The point, P, is directed a little upwards, and is a little curved: the barbs, seen still more highly magnified at Q, are about six in number, and are placed on the under surface, and their points directed backwards. At the base of the sting, E, there is a semicircular dilatation apparently intended to prevent the instrument from being thrust too far out of the sheath (seen separately at V), in which it moves: it has also a long tendon to which the muscles are attached. It is between these plates, when approximated, that the poison flows from the orifice of the somewhat dilated extremity of the poison duct, D, which comes from the anterior part of the poison bag, B. This bag is of an oval shape, and is not the organ which secretes the poison, but merely a receptacle for containing it: for it is

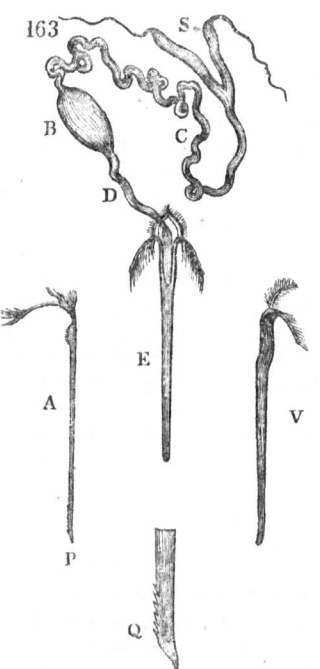

Although the greater number of insects have four wings, there are many, such as the common house fly, and the gnat, which have only two. These compose the order *Diptera* (Fig. 162). In these insects we meet with two organs, consisting of cylindrical filaments, terminated in a clubbed extremity; one arising from each side of the thorax (as seen in the above figure), in the situation in which the second pair of wings originate in those insects that have four wings. They are named the *halteres*, or poisers, from their supposed use in balancing the body, or adjusting with exactness the centre of gravity when the insect is flying. Whatever may be their real utility, they may still be regarded as rudiments of a second pair of wings; and they afford, therefore, when thus viewed, a striking instance of the operation of the tendency which

conveyed into this bladder by means of a long convoluted vessel, c, which receives it from the secreting organs, s. These organs consist of two somewhat dilated vessels resembling *cæca*, but which have each a slender secretory vessel extending from them. The sting moves in a tubular sheath, V; which is open at its base, and along its upper surface, as far as the part where the sting is prevented from being thrust out any farther. The muscles which move the sheath are distinct from those of the sting, and are attached to an elongated and curved part on each side of its base, and to an arched and moveable part which is apparently articulated with it. Swammerdam has delineated these parts as cæca in his dissection of the common hive bee, but has not noticed the secretory vessels. The sting of the hive bee resembles that of the *Anthophora retusa*."

prevails universally in the animal kingdom, and modifies the structure of each individual part so as to preserve its conformity to one general type.

The innumerable tribes of butterflies, sphinxes, and moths, are all comprehended in the order *Lepidoptera*, and are distinguished by having wings covered with minute plumes, or scales. These scales are attached so slightly to the membrane of the wing as to come off when touched with the fingers, to which they adhere like fine dust. When examined with the microscope, their construction and arrangement appear to be exceedingly beautiful, being marked with parallel and equidistant striæ, often crossed by still finer lines, the distinct visibility of which in many kinds of scales, as those of *Pontia brassica*, or cabbage butterfly, and the *Morpho Menelaus* of America, constitutes a good criterion of the excellence of the instrument. The beautiful colours which these scales possess may perhaps generally be owing to the presence of some colouring material: but the more delicate hues are probably the result of the optical effect of the striæ on the surface; and in some cases they result from the thinness of the transparent plate of which they consist; for I have observed in several detached scales that the colours they exhibit by transmitted light are the complementary colours to

FLIGHT OF INSECTS.   355

those which they display when seen by reflected light.

The forms of these scales are exceedingly diversified, not only in different species, but also in different parts of the wings and body of the same insect; for the surface of the body, generally, as well as the limbs, and even in some species the antennæ are more or less covered with these scales.* Fig. 164 exhibits some of

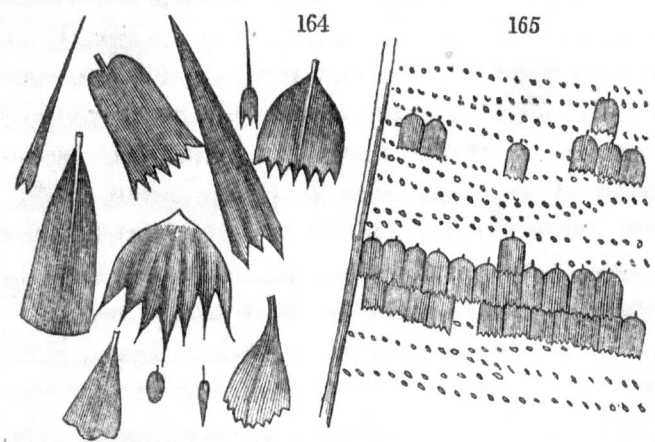

the more usual shapes as they appear when viewed with high magnifying powers.

Each scale is inserted into the membrane of the wing by a short pedicle, or root, and over-

---

* In the posthumous work of Lyonet, which has lately appeared, nearly the whole of six quarto plates are crowded with the delineations of the different forms of the scales found in the *Bombyx Cossus.*

laps the adjoining scales: and the whole are disposed in rows with more or less regularity; one row covering the next, like tiles on the roof of a house.* This imbricated arrangement, together with the marks that are left on the membrane of the wing where the scales have been rubbed off, are shown in Fig. 165, which is a faithful delineation of the appearance of the wing of the *Hesperia Sloanus*, seen through a powerful microscope. The membrane of the wing itself, when stripped of its scales, is as perfectly transparent as that of the bee, and is, in like manner, supported by diverging nervures. Many butterflies exhibit in some parts of the wing smooth pearly spots, called by entomologists, *ocelli*, or *eyes*, which arise from those parts being naturally destitute of scales. The number of these scales necessary to cover the surface of the wings must, from their minuteness, be exceedingly great. The moth of the silk worm (*Bombyx mori*, Fig. 148), which has but a small wing, contains, according to Lewenhoeck, more than two hundred thousand of these scales in each wing.

These scales doubtless contribute to the protection of the wing; but they at the same time

* The scales on the wing of the *Lepisma* are of two kinds; one set being arranged in rows, as usual, and the others, which are of a different shape, being inserted between and over the former, so as to fasten each firmly in its place.

add considerably to their weight, and impede the velocity of their action. This inconvenience appears to have been in a great measure compensated by the greater size of the wings, and by the extent of the surface with which they strike the air. Still, however, it is sufficiently obvious that insects of this order fly with less rapidity and steadiness than most others. But this unsteadiness, again, is turned to good account; for the butterfly, by its irregular and apparently capricious movements, alternately dipping and rising in the air, so as to describe a series of zigzag lines, more easily eludes capture when pursued, not only by naturalists, but also by birds that are eagerly seeking to secure them. It is astonishing to what a distance the silk worm moths will fly: some have been known to travel more than a hundred miles in a short time. The *Papilio Iris* often rises to so great a height in the air as to be quite invisible.

A mechanical contrivance is adopted in many of the Lepidoptera for keeping their wings steady during flight, consisting of a hook covered with hair and scales, attached to the under side of the upper wings near their base, and connected also by means of bristles to the base of the lower wing: by this attachment all the wings are locked together and brought into action at the same time. Insects of the Sphinx tribe are also provided with a kind of rudder formed by the expansion of the tail, enabling them to steer their course with more certainty. The Lepidoptera in general fly with the body nearly upright, contrary to the habits of most other winged insects, whose bodies, while flying, are nearly in a horizontal position.

The feats of agility and strength exhibited by insects have often been the theme of admiration with writers on natural history; and have been considered as affording incontrovertible proofs of the enormous power with which their muscles must be endowed. We have already had occasion to notice a remarkable instance of the force and permanence of muscular contraction in those caterpillars which frequently remain for hours together in a fixed attitude, with their bodies extended from a twig, to which they cling by their hind feet alone.* Ants will carry loads which are forty or fifty times heavier than their own bodies: and the distances to which many species, such as the *Elater*, the *Locust*, the *Lepisma*, and above all the *Pulex*, are capable of leaping, compared with the size of the insects themselves, appear still more astonishing. Linnæus has computed that the *Melolontha*, or chaffer, is, in proportion to its bulk, more than six times stronger than the horse: and has asserted that if the same proportional strength as is pos-

* See Fig. 148*, p. 315.

sessed by the *Lucanus*, or stag-beetle, had been given to the elephant, that animal would have been capable of tearing up by the roots the largest trees, and of hurling huge rocks against his assailants, like the giants of ancient mythology.

But while we must admit that all these facts indicate a remarkable degree of energy in the contractile power of the muscular fibres of insects, we should at the same time recollect that the diminutive size of the beings which display those powers is itself the source of a mechanical advantage not possessed by larger animals. The efficacy of all mechanical arrangements must ultimately depend on a due proportion between the moving and the resisting forces: hence mechanism of every kind must be adjusted with reference not merely to the relative, but to the absolute dimensions of the structures themselves. This will be evident when we consider that the forces which are called into action are resisted by the cohesion of the particles composing the solid parts of the machine: and this cohesion, being not a variable, but a constant and definite force, must necessarily limit the dimensions of every mechanical structure, whether intended for stability or for action. An edifice raised beyond a certain magnitude, will not support itself, because the weight of the materials increases more rapidly than the strength. How often has it been found that a machine which works admirably in a small model, will totally fail in its performance when constructed on a larger scale? Any lever, of whatever form, may be increased in its dimensions until the force of gravity becomes superior to the cohesion of its own particles: and consequently any structure, like a vegetable or animal body, composed of a combination of levers, would, if its size were to exceed a certain limit, fall to pieces merely by its own weight. This can be prevented either by employing materials of greater cohesive strength, or by increasing, at the points where the strains are greatest, the thickness of the parts compared with their length: but the choice of materials is necessarily restricted within narrow limits, and the latter expedient would entirely alter the relative proportions of the parts, and would require a complete change in the plan of their construction. In passing from the smaller to the larger animals, we find, accordingly, that new models are adopted, a new order of architecture introduced, and new laws of developement observed. We have, next, then, to direct our attention to the procedure of nature in the execution of this more enlarged and comprehensive scheme of animal organization.

Chapter VI.

VERTEBRATA.

§ 1. *Vertebrated Animals in general.*

If it be pleasing to trace the footsteps of nature in constructions so infinitely varied as those of the lower animals, and to follow the gradations of ascent from the zoophyte to the winged insect, which exhibits the greatest perfection compatible with the restricted dimensions of that class of beings, still more interesting must be the study of those more elaborate efforts of creative power which are displayed on a wider field in the higher orders of the animal kingdom. In the various tribes of beings which are now to come before us, we find nature proceeding to display more refined developements in her system of organization, resorting to new models of structure on a scale of greater magnitude than before, devising new plans of economy, calculated for more extended periods of duration, and adopting new arrangements of organs, fitted for the exercise of a higher order of faculties. The result of these more elaborate constructions is seen in the vast series of *Vertebrated Animals,* which comprises a well-marked division of Zoology, comprehending all the larger species that exist on the globe, in whatever climate or element they may be found; and including man himself, placed, as he unquestionably is, at the summit of the scale;—the undisputed Lord of the Creation.

A remarkable affinity of structure prevails throughout the whole of this extensive assemblage of beings. Whatever may be the size or external form of these animals, whatever the activity or sluggishness of their movements, whether they be inhabitants of the land, the waters, or the air, a striking similitude may be traced both in the disposition of their vital organs, and in the construction of the solid frame-work, or skeleton, which sustains and protects their fabric. The quadruped, the bird, the tortoise, the serpent, and the fish, however they may differ in subordinate details of organization, are yet constructed upon one uniform principle, and appear like varied copies from the same original model. In no instance do they present structures which are altogether isolated, or can be regarded as the results of separate and independent formations.

In proceeding from the contemplation of the structures of articulated to those of vertebrated animals, we appear to pass by a rapid excursive flight, from one great continent to another, separated by an immense gulf, containing no intermediate islands from which we might gather indications of these tracts of land having been originally connected. At the very first sight indeed, the general fabrics of these two descriptions of animals appear to have been constructed upon opposite principles; for in the one, as we have already seen, the softer parts are internal, and are enclosed in a solid crust, or shell, or horny covering, answering at once the purposes of protection and mechanical support, and furnishing extensive surfaces for the attachment of the organs of motion. But in the Vertebrata, the solid frame work which serves these purposes occupies, for the most part, an internal situation, constituting a true jointed skeleton, which is surrounded by the softer organs, and to which the muscles, destined to move their several parts, are attached. The office of external defence is entrusted solely to the integuments, and their different appendages. Such is the general character of the arrangements which nature has here adopted; from which, however, she has occasionally deviated with respect to some important organs of extremely delicate texture, and which require to be shielded from the slightest pressure. This occurs with regard to the brain, and the spinal marrow, which we shall presently find are specially guarded by a bony structure, enclosing them on every side, and forming an impenetrable case for their protection. The solid mass of bone, thus provided to defend the brain, gives also the opportunity of lodging safely the delicate apparatus subservient to the finer senses, namely, those of sight, of hearing, and of smell. The security which these organs derive from this protection allows of their being carried to a higher degree of improvement than could be attained in the lower orders.

There is also another advantage, of considerable moment, which results from the internal situation of the skeleton, namely, that it admits of an indefinite extension by growth, without interfering with the corresponding enlargement of the softer organs; for we have seen that in all the instances in which this arrangement is reversed, that is, whenever the enclosing surfaces become solid, and can no longer yield to the dilatation of the contained organs, no alternative remains but that of breaking up the exterior case, and wholly casting it off, to make room for the farther growth of the animal; after which operation, it has to be replaced by another covering of larger dimensions. This operation is generally required to be performed a great number of times, before the animal can acquire the size it is destined to attain. Hence the perpetual moultings of the caterpillar; hence the repeated castings of the shells of the crustacea; and hence also the successive metamorphoses of the insect. Nothing of this kind takes place among the Vertebrata; where all the organs are developed in regular and harmonious succession, without the slightest mutual interference, and without those vicissitudes of action and of torpidity, which we witness in the chequered existence of the insect.

§ 2. *Structure and Composition of the Osseous Fabric.*

THE process employed for the formation and extension of the solid frame work of the Vertebrata differs totally from that which we have seen exemplified in the growth of shells, or of the hard coverings of insects and of crustaceous animals. These latter structures, and the modes adopted for their increase, are suited only to animals in which the functions of the economy have not reached that perfection to which they are carried in the higher classes. In the more elaborate system of the vertebrata, the skeleton is composed of true *bones;* that is, of solid pieces, which, although they are dense calcareous structures, yet continue organized during the whole period of developement, and form as much a part of the living system as any other organ of the body. We have formerly seen that the membrane, in which the calcareous matter of the shell is deposited, should properly be classed among the integuments; being analogous to them not only in being situated externally, but also in their structure and in their function. It is not so with bone, which is essentially an internal structure.*

In their chemical composition, likewise, bones are strikingly contrasted with the calcareous products of the Mollusca: for in the former, the earthy portion consists almost wholly of phosphate of lime: a material which appears to have

---

* De Blainville regards the hard coverings of insects, together with the shells of the crustacea, as structures derived altogether from the integuments, and as perfectly analogous, in this respect, to the scales, hoofs, or other horny productions of the skin in vertebrated animals. Geoffrey St. Hilaire contends, on the contrary, that the former constitute the true skeleton of the lower classes, and that a perfect analogy may be traced between the rings, which are the essential constituents of the frame-work of annulose animals, and the vertebræ, which enclose the spinal cord of the higher classes. Professor Carus appears, in his system of organic formations, to have kept in view both these analogies; giving to the former class of structures the denomination of *Dermo-skeleton*, and to the latter that of *Neuro-skeleton* (See his Tabulæ Anatomiam Comparativam illustrantes, edited by Thienemann). Analogies have also been imagined to exist between the external and internal situations of the woody fibres of plants belonging respectively to the endogenous and exogenous classes, and that of the corresponding relative situations of the skeletons of invertebrated and vertebrated animals. (See a Memoir by Dumortier, in the Nova Acta Physico-Medica Acad. Cæsar. Leopold. Carolinæ Natur. Curios. XVI., 219).

been selected for this purpose from its forming much harder compounds with animal membrane than the carbonate. Wherever great strength and rigidity are required, this is the material depended on for imparting these qualities; and it has accordingly been employed for the osseous structures, which are among the most elaborate results of organization. The densest and hardest of these structures are those in which the proportion of phosphate of lime is the greatest, when compared with that of the animal substance which cements them together; the force of mutual cohesion among its own particles being much greater than that imparted by the cementing ingredient. The internal bony portions of the ear, where, in order perfectly to transmit the sonorous vibrations, the greatest solidity is required, are the densest parts of the skeleton; and phosphate of lime enters most largely into the composition of these bones. The tympanic portions of the temporal bone of the whale and the cachalot, where the great size of the organ gives us advantages in examining them, are as dense and as hard as marble. The bony portions of the teeth, likewise, afford instances of very hard calcareous formations; but the enamel, which consists almost wholly of phosphate of lime, is harder still, and resembles the siliceous stones, being, like flint, capable of striking fire with steel. It is scarcely necessary to point out the obvious intentions which are fulfilled by this peculiarity of structure, conferring extraordinary hardness on a part of which the appropriate office is that of breaking down hard bodies subjected to their mechanical action. But this extreme degree of crystalline hardness would be ill suited to other parts of the frame. In ordinary bones, absolute rigidity is not the quality which is alone wanted; for, in general, the hardest bodies are also the most fragile. An excess of rigidity, therefore, would have been attended with brittleness, and been productive of the worst consequences to parts exposed to sudden and violent concussions. It is in order to guard against this evil that an elastic animal matter is employed as the basis of the structure, acting as a strong cement interposed between the calcareous particles.

This composition of bone is rendered evident by subjecting it to certain chemical processes. On exposure to heat, we find it first becoming black, from the developement of the charcoal attendant upon the destruction of the animal membrane. The oil contained in the cavities exudes, and, taking fire, is soon totally consumed. The bone then recovers its whiteness, and undergoes no further change by the action of the fire. If it be now examined, it will be found to have lost nearly half its original

CHEMICAL COMPOSITION OF BONE.

weight, and to have become exceedingly brittle; this, as already mentioned, being the natural property of phosphate of lime, when deprived of its animal cement. We may perceive on the surface of a bone so treated, a number of minute crevices, showing where this animal substance had been situated in its original state. On breaking the bone across, we may also discover the size and shape of the cavities which contained the marrow, or oily fluid above-mentioned.

It is easy to reverse this process by steeping the bone in an acid sufficiently diluted to prevent its injuring the animal membrane, but yet sufficiently powerful to dissolve the phosphate and carbonate of lime. Diluted nitric or muriatic acids may be used for this purpose, and will, in this way, gradually separate the earthy particles from the membranous portion of the bone. During the action of the acid a few bubbles of carbonic acid gas make their appearance, indicating the presence of a small quantity of carbonate of lime, which always exists in bones, intermixed with the phosphate. The phosphate may be recovered from its solution in the acid by precipitation with a pure alkali, such as a solution of ammonia. This precipitate is readily dissolved, without effervescence, by nitric, muriatic, or acetic acids. A small quantity of sulphuric acid may also be detected in the fluid by the addition of nitrate of barytes. Iron, in small quantity, is also found in the composition of human bones.

The substance which remains, after the earth has been thus abstracted, retains the exact figure and dimensions of the original bone, but has lost all its other mechanical properties. It is soft, flexible, and elastic: resembling in every respect the muscular or fibrous structures, and being, like them, resolvable into gelatin and albumen by long boiling in water. This substance has sometimes, but erroneously, been considered as identical with cartilage; for it has neither the whiteness, nor the elasticity, nor the texture of cartilage, nor is it at all similar to that substance in its chemical composition: for while cartilage is formed almost wholly of albumen, the animal basis of bone is almost entirely resolvable into gelatin.

Thus may a bone be analysed into its two constituent parts: by the process first described we obtain its earth deprived of its animal constituent; by the second, we obtain its membranous basis free from earth. The first of these gives it hardness; the second, tenacity: and thus, by the intimate combination of these elements, two qualities, which, in masses of homogeneous and unorganized matter, are scarcely compatible with one another, are skilfully united.

The mechanical structure of bone is no less

worthy of admiration, as evincing the skill with which every part is adapted to its destined uses. The animal membrane, which, as we have seen, is the bed in which the calcareous phosphate is deposited, partakes of the reticular structure belonging to the ordinary cellular texture; and a bone, when minutely examined, exhibits also the same appearance of plates intermixed with fibres. In the outer compact portion, indeed, the fibrous arrangement of the particles is not so easily distinguished: but it may be detected in young bones while they are becoming ossified: and also in bones that have been long exposed to the weather, or long macerated in water. The interior of most bones, in the higher classes of animals, presents distinctly the appearance of irregular cavities, resulting from the partial separation of the plates, and their mutual crossings, and fibrous connexions.

The different mechanical purposes for which bones are employed in the animal economy require them to be of different forms. Where a part is intended to have compactness and strength, with a very limited degree of motion, it is divided into a great number of small pieces, united together by ligaments, and the separate bones are short and compressed, approaching more or less to a cubical shape. Of such is the column of the spine composed, as also the joints of the wrist and ankle. Where the principal object is either extensive protection, or the provision of broad surfaces for the attachment of muscles, we find the osseous structure expanded into flat plates; as is exemplified in the bones of the skull, in the shoulder blade, and still more remarkably in the bony shield which surrounds the body of the tortoise. On the other hand, where a system of levers is wanted, as in the limbs, which have to sustain the weight of the trunk, and to confer extensive powers of locomotion, the bones are modelled into lengthened cylinders, generally somewhat expanded at the extremities, for greater convenience of mutual connexion.

In the form, the structure, and the arrangement of these levers, which allow of the regular and accurate application of the moving power, and are calculated, in circumstances so various, to give effectual support to the fabric, and also to execute a great diversity of movements, we discern most palpable manifestations of profound design, and the most exquisite refinements of mechanic skill. All the scientific principles of architecture and of dynamics are more or less exemplified in the construction of this part of the animal fabric. Levers of various kinds are most artificially combined in the formation of the fins of fishes, the wings of birds, and the limbs of quadrupeds. The power of the arch in resisting superincumbent pressure is exhibited

STRUCTURE OF BONE.

in various parts of the osseous systems of vertebrated animals; such as the human foot, the spine, the pelvis, and more especially in the vaulted roof of the skull, and in the carapace, or upper shell, of the tortoise.

The construction of these levers evinces that a minute attention has been bestowed on every condition by which mechanical advantage could be gained. In the more perfect developements of structures, such as those which obtain in the higher orders of mammalia, and also in the class of birds, all the long bones are hollow cylinders; and their cavity is largest in the middle of their length. This is shown in Fig. 172, which represents a longitudinal section of a human thigh bone, and in Fig. 173, which is a similar section of the humerus, or bone of the arm. The walls of these bones consist of a dense and compact substance, formed by the close cohesion of the osseous plates. These walls are of greater thickness in the middle of the shank or shaft of the column, and become thinner as we follow them towards either of the ends. This gradual diminution in the thickness of the walls

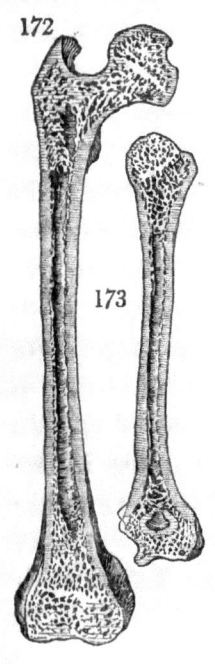

arises from the continual separation of the plates, which bend inwards, and crossing each other, leave a multitude of irregular spaces or cells, which are called *cancelli*. The plates, proceeding from each side obliquely inwards, at length meet each other in the axis of the cylinder, so as to close the middle cavity near the extremities of the bone, where this spongy or cancellated structure is found to occupy its whole diameter.

Now if we consider that the principal mechanical property required in every cylindrical lever is rigidity, and more especially the power of resisting forces applied transversely, that is, tending to break the cylinder across, we shall soon perceive, that a given quantity of materials could not possibly have been disposed in a manner better calculated for such resistance than when in the form of a tube, or hollow cylinder.* To this mechanical principle I have already had occasion to advert, when speaking of the hollow stems of vegetables, which derive their chief strength from their possessing this form;† and we now find it again applied in the structure of bones, which by having been made

---

* An elaborate mathematical demonstration of this proposition was long ago given by Dr. Porterfield, in a paper contained in the first volume of Medical Essays and Observations, published by a Society in Edinburgh, p. 95.

† P. 81.

hollow, are rendered considerably stronger than if the same materials had been collected into a solid cylinder of the same length. We may farther remark, that as it is in the middle of the shaft that the strain is greatest, so it is here that the cavity is largest, and the resistance most effectual.

§ 3. *Formation and Developement of Bone.*

BUT it is not enough to contemplate the purposes so admirably answered by these arrangements. Our curiosity cannot but be powerfully excited to learn what processes and refined series of means are employed by nature to raise and to perfect all these artificially contrived structures. It fortunately happens that in this instance we are permitted to penetrate a little farther than usual into the secrets of organic evolution: for the succession of changes can be better followed by the eye in the slow developement of the harder parts, than in the quicker growth of mere yielding and expansible textures. The peculiar material also, of which bone is formed, is easily distinguished by its hardness, its whiteness, and its opacity from the softer and more transparent animal substance with which it is intermixed. Hence we are allowed an opportunity of observing the earliest stages of its deposition, and of accurately following the subsequent changes it undergoes.

The parts of the embryo animal, which are destined to become bone, partake of the soft and gelatinous consistence, which, at that early period, characterises all the textures of the body; and they can hardly, indeed, be distinguished from the semi-fluid portions which surround them. In process of time, when the vascular circulation of the blood has been established, and the newly formed arteries have extended their branches over every part of the nascent organization, those vessels which are appropriated to the task of forming the bones, arrive at the pulpy masses where their work is to commence. As sculptors, before working upon the marble, first execute a model of a coarser and more plastic material, so the first business of these arteries is to prepare a model of the future bone, constructed, not with the same material of which it is afterwards to consist, but with another of a simpler and softer nature, namely cartilage. In every case, then, cartilage is first formed, and becomes visible by its greater opacity when compared with the adjacent jelly. It is an exact representation, in miniature, of the bone, which is, in due course, to take its place. It is evident that until the other parts of the fabric have proceeded so far in their developement as to have acquired a certain degree of solidity and firmness, and to bear, as well as to require, the support of more massive and rigid structures, this flexible and elastic cartilage may be employed with great advantage as its substitute. A hard and unyielding structure would, in the early stages of its formation, have even been injurious. But in proportion as the fabric is enlarged, the necessity for mechanical support increases, and further provision must be made for resistance to external violence.

When, at length, all is prepared for the construction of the bone, the next step to be taken is the removal of the cartilage, which had been erected as the scaffolding for the intended building. But in taking down this scaffolding, the whole must not be removed at once; each part must be carried away, piece by piece, while the operation of fixing in their position the beams and pillars of the edifice proceeds. The way is cleared at first by the absorption of the central part of the cartilage, and a few particles of ossific matter are deposited in its room. While this process is going on, greater activity is displayed in the arteries; they rapidly enlarge in diameter, so as to admit the colouring globules of the blood; and they thus become visible to the eye, which can now follow their course without difficulty. From being at first red points, they soon spread out into lines, of which we trace the branches to a certain extent, although we cannot pursue them to their minuter ramifications. They now assume more active functions, and hasten to execute their task by depositing granules of calcareous phosphate: these are laid down, particle by particle, in a certain determinate order, and in regular lines, so as to form continuous fibres. When a great number of these delicate fibres are gathered together, and connected by other fibres, which shoot in various directions across them, a texture composed of an assemblage of long spicula, or thin plates, is constituted.

In the cylindrical bones, the spicula prevail, and they are arranged longitudinally, and parallel to one another, and to the axis of the bone. They first constitute a ring in the middle of its length: this ring enlarges in all its dimensions, but principally in its length; the spicula becoming larger, not by the stretching of their parts, in consequence of the insinuation of fresh materials between those already deposited, but by the addition of new particles at both their extremities. In like manner, the ring increases in thickness, not by the deposition of phosphate of lime between the original layers, but by the application of fresh layers on the outside of those already existing.

In the flat bones, the process of ossification is very similar to what I have just described; only

OSSIFICATION. 379

the fibres have a radiated arrangement, shooting out from the spot where the first deposit took place, as from a common centre. This is seen in Fig. 174, which represents the parietal bone of

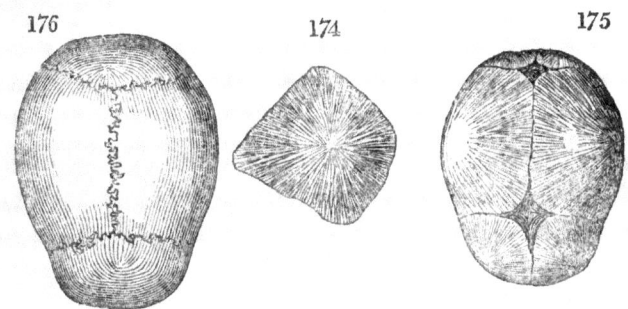

the human skull, in an early stage of its ossification, and shows the radiating fibres very distinctly. In the cubical, and more irregularly shaped bones, the process is, doubtless, conducted with the same order and regularity, although it cannot so readily be followed by the eye.

The same process is repeated in different parts of the bone, wherever nature has, in conformity with determinate laws of developement, appointed particular centres of ossification. The bone continues to extend from each of these centres, proceeding gradually towards the circumference, or the remoter parts of the cartilage, on which the ossific materials are moulded, and by the form of which that of the future bone is regulated. The process of ossification has, however, this peculiarity, that the cartilage is progressively absorbed to make room for the deposits of bony substance. When the bone is long, separate points of ossification appear in the extremities, before the central portions are ossified; and the ends, thus formed into bone, are afterwards united to the shaft, so that the whole shall form a continuous bony mass. In the flat bones, also, if the surface be extensive, an additional number of arteries are engaged to perform the work, which is begun from several auxiliary centres of ossification, and the completion of which is materially accelerated by their co-operation.

This mode of increase often gives rise to a curious result, of which a striking example is presented in the bones of the skull. The brain, which these bones are designed to protect, requires their protection at a very early period of life. The growth of so large a surface of bone, as would be required for covering the brain, could not have proceeded with sufficient quickness for the exigencies of the occasion, if it had originated from a single point. Therefore it is that, besides being commenced at a very early age, the process goes on from a great number of separate points at the same time. The ossification is evidently hurried on in order to complete the roofing in of the edifice by the time at which the animal is to be ushered into the world, and exposed to dangers from the contact of external bodies. The divergent fibres shoot out rapidly, coalescing with those in their immediate neighbourhood, which co-operate to form an extensive bony plate. When they have reached the prescribed line, they have become so much expanded as to have lost the power of coalescing with the fibres which have originated from other centres, and are proceeding in a contrary direction. Yet the arteries still continuing to deposit ossific matter, each set of fibres insinuate themselves between those of the opposite set, for some little distance, and until their further progress is stopped by the increasing resistance they encounter. The consequence is that the edges of the bones, which have thus met, are irregularly jagged, like the teeth of a saw, presenting externally the zig-zag line of junction which is called a *suture*. This is seen in Figures 175 and 176, the former of which represents the upper side of the skull of an infant; and the latter, the same bones when completely ossified.

The union of bony fibres proceeding from different centres of ossification is not indiscriminate, but is found to be regulated by definite laws, and to have certain relations to the general plan of conformation originally established. Each distinct bone is formed from a certain number of ossific centres, which altogether constitute a system appertaining to that bone only, and not extending to the adjacent bones. These pieces unite together, as if by a natural affinity; and they refuse to unite with the bony fibres proceeding from neighbouring centres, and belonging to other groups. The groups themselves are not arbitrary, but are pre-established parts of the original design. Circumstances occasionally, indeed, arise, which may overrule this inherent tendency to preserve the line of separation between two bones; and we then find them coalescing to form a single piece. Such unions are technically called *anchyloses*.

Were this the whole of what takes place in the formation of a bone, the process would not, perhaps, differ very materially from that by which a shell is produced; for a shell, as we have seen, is the result of successive depositions of calcareous matter, forming one layer after another, in union with a corresponding deposit of animal membrane. But the subsequent changes which occur, show that the constitution of bone is totally dissimilar to that of shell: for no portion of the shell that is once formed, and has not been removed, is subject to any farther alteration. It is a dead, though perhaps not wholly inorganic mass; appended, indeed, to the living system, but placed beyond the sphere of its influence. But a bone continues, during the whole of life, to be an integrant part of the system, partaking of its changes, modified by its powers, and undergoing continual alterations of shape, and even renewals of its substance, by the actions of the living vessels.

The form which had at first been rudely sketched, slowly advances towards perfection in the course of its growth; and the general proportions of the parts are still preserved; the finished bone exhibiting prominences and depressions in the same relative situation as at first; and not only having similar internal cavities, but being frequently excavated in parts which had before been solid. During all these gradual alterations of shape, however, there is no stretching of elastic parts; for all the osseous fibres and laminæ are rigid and unyielding, and in this respect retain an analogy with shell. The changes thus observed can have been effected in no other way than by the actual removal of such parts of the young bone as had occupid the situations where vacuities are found to exist in the old bone. We find, for instance, that in the early state of a bone there are no internal cavities, but the whole is a uniform solid mass. At a certain stage of ossification cells are excavated by the action of the absorbent vessels, which carry away portions of bony matter lying in the axis of the cylindrical, or in the middle layer of the flat bones.* Their place is supplied by an

* The bones of the lower classes of vertebrated animals, as of Fishes and Reptiles, seldom reach this stage of ossification, but remain solid throughout; corresponding to the bones of the higher classes at the early periods of their developement.

oily matter, which is the marrow. As the growth proceeds, while new layers are deposited on the outside of the bone, and at the ends of the long fibres, the internal layers near the centre are removed by the absorbent vessels, so that the cavity is farther enlarged. In this manner the outermost layer of the young bone gradually changes its relative situation, becoming more and more deeply buried by the new layers which are successively deposited, and which cover and surround it; until by the removal of all the layers situated nearer to the centre, it becomes the innermost layer; and is itself destined in its turn to disappear, leaving the new bone without a single particle which had entered into the composition of the original structure.

It has been found that by mixing certain colouring substances with the food of animals the bones will soon become deeply tinged by them. This fact was discovered accidentally by Mr. Belchier, who gives the following account of the circumstances that led him to notice it.* Happening to be dining with a calico printer on a leg of fresh pork, he was surprised to observe that the bones, instead of being white as usual, were of a deep red colour; and on inquiring into the circumstances, he learned that the

* Philosophical Transactions for 1736, vol. xxxix. 287 and 289.

pig had been fed upon the refuse of the dyeing-vats, which contained a large quantity of the colouring substance of madder. So curious a fact naturally attracted a good deal of attention among physiologists, and many experiments were undertaken to ascertain the time required to produce this change, and to determine whether the effect was permanent, or only temporary. The red tinge was found to be communicated much more quickly to the bones of growing animals than to those which had already attained their full size. Thus the bones of a young pigeon were tinged of a rose colour in twenty four hours, and of a deep scarlet in three days; while in the adult bird, fifteen days were required merely to produce the rose colour. The dye was more intense in the solid parts of those bones which were nearest to the centre of circulation, while in bones of equal solidity, but more remote from the heart, the tinge was fainter. The bone was of a deeper dye in proportion to the length of time the animal had been fed upon the madder. When this diet was discontinued, the colour became gradually more faint, till it entirely disappeared. I shall have occasion, in the sequel, to discuss the inferences which have been drawn from these curious facts.

§ 4. *Skeleton of the Vertebrata.*

THE purposes to be answered by the Skeleton, in vertebrated animals, resolve themselves into the three following; first, the affording mechanical support to the body generally, and also to different portions of the body; secondly, the providing a solid basis for the attachments of the muscles which are to effect their movements; and thirdly, the giving protection to the vital organs, but more particularly to the central parts of the nervous system. Of these the last is the circumstance that has the greatest influence in determining the principles on which the osseous frame-work has been constructed. In the nervous system of all the animals coming under the denomination of vertebrata, the spinal marrow, together with the brain, which may, indeed, be considered as the anterior extremity of the spinal marrow, only much enlarged by an additional mass of nervous substance, are the most important parts of that system, and the organs which stand most in need of protection from every kind of injury. These two portions of the nervous system, when viewed as composing a single organ, have been denominated the *spino-cerebral axis,* in contradistinction to the analogous parts of the nervous system of articulated animals: for amidst great differences of structure and of functions, an analogy is still retained among the several forms of the nervous system, characterising these two great divisions of the animal kingdom. In the embryo state of the vertebrata the central parts of that system consist of two separate filaments running parallel to each other the whole length of the body: but in process of time these two filaments unite, and constitute a single spinal cord: and the primary type of the skeleton is determined by the peculiar form of this, the central organ of the nervous system.

In laying the foundations of the skeleton, then, the first object is to provide for the security of the spinal cord: and this is accomplished by enclosing it within a series of cartilaginous rings, which are destined to shield it during its growth, and by their subsequent ossification, to protect it most effectually from all injurious pressure. It is this part of the skeleton, accordingly, of which the rudiments appear the earliest in the embryo animal. These rings form a column extending in a longitudinal direction along the trunk; retracing to us the series of horny rings, in which the bodies of worms, of insects, and indeed of all the *Articulata*, are encased. When ossified, these several rings are termed *vertebræ*; and the entire column which they compose is the *Spine*. Fig. 177 shows the form of one of the vertebræ of the back in the human skeleton. Fig. 178 is a side view of four vertebræ joined together, and Fig. 179 is a vertical section

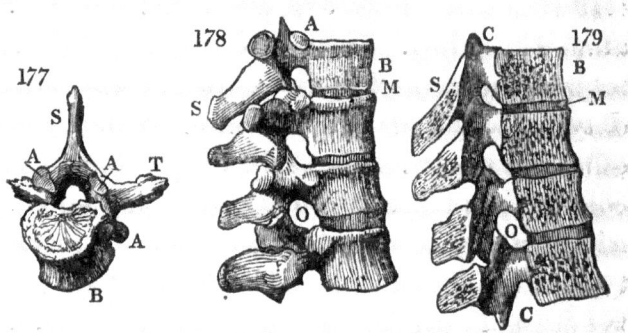

of the same part of the spine, showing the canal formed by the rings. From the constancy with which the spinal column is found in all animals of this type, and from the uniformity of the plan on which, amidst endless variations, it is modelled, it has been chosen as the distinctive character of this great assemblage of animals, which have accordingly been denominated the *Vertebrata*, or *Vertebrated Animals*.

Nor is the spine of less importance when viewed in its mechanical relations to the rest of the skeleton. It is the great central beam of the fabric; establishing points of union between all its parts, and combining them into one continuous frame-work: it is the general axis of all their motions, the common fulcrum on which the principal bones of the extremities are made to turn: it furnishes fixed points of attachment to all the large muscles which act upon these bones as levers, and also to those which move the trunk itself.

If this column had been perfectly rigid, the whole frame-work would have been exposed to inconvenience and even danger, amidst the shocks it must encounter during all the quick and sudden movements of the body. Not only must its mechanism be framed to sustain these shocks, but also to accommodate itself to various kinds of flexions, and twistings of the trunk. While these objects are provided for, care must at the same time be taken that the spinal marrow it encloses shall, amidst all these motions, remain secure from pressure; for so delicate is its structure that the least degree of compression would at once interrupt its functions, and lead to the most fatal consequences. A safe passage is likewise to be afforded to the nerves, which issue from the spinal marrow, at certain intervals, on each side throughout its whole length.

No where has mechanical art been more conspicuously displayed than in the construction of a fabric capable of fulfilling these opposite, and apparently incompatible functions. The principal difficulty was to combine great strength with sufficient flexibility. This we find accomplished, first, by the division of the column into a great number of pieces, each of which being locked in with the two adjoining pieces, and tightly braced by connecting ligaments, is allowed but a very small degree of flexion at the point of junction. This slight flexion at each single joint, however, by becoming multiplied along the series, amounts to a considerable degree of motion in the whole column.

The broad basis of each bone is connected with the next, not by a joint, but by a plate of equal breadth (M, M, Figures 178 and 179), composed of a peculiar substance, intermediate in its texture to ligament and cartilage, and possessing in a remarkable degree the qualities of toughness and adhesion, united with compressibility and elasticity. By yielding for a certain extent to a force tending to bend it to either side, it diminishes the quantity of motion which would otherwise have been required in each individual joint; and by acting at the same time as a spring, it softens all the jars and concussions incident to violent action: for we find that however the spine may be bent, no chasm is left by the flexions of the vertebræ upon one another, nor is the continuity of the column in the smallest degree interrupted.

The motions of the vertebræ upon each other are further regulated by the mode in which their articular processes, which are the pieces that project obliquely on each side, play upon each other. These processes, which are seen at A, A, in the preceding figures (177 and 178), are of

VERTEBRAL COLUMN. 391

great use in preventing the sudden displacement of the vertebræ; for this effect cannot be produced by any force short of that which would occasion fracture. Any one who will try to dislocate, by sheer force, the spine of a hare or rabbit will find reason to admire the art with which its bones have been locked together, and the skill displayed in combining great flexibility with such powerful resistance to every effort that can be made to separate them.

For the purpose of allowing a passage to the spinal marrow, the bodies of the vertebræ (B, Fig. 177 and 178), are hollowed out behind, into a groove, over which a broad plate of bone is thrown from the sides of the vertebræ, like the arch of a bridge. The succession of arches, when the vertebræ are joined together, forms a continuous canal, which is occupied by the spinal marrow. Notches, corresponding to each other, are left in the sides of each of the arches, forming apertures for the secure passage of the nerves as they issue from the spinal marrow. All these circumstances are visible in the figures, particularly in the section, Fig. 179, where c, c, is the canal for the spinal marrow, and in which the apertures just mentioned are distinctly seen, at o, o.

In order to give an advantageous purchase to the muscles which are attached to the spine, each vertebra has, besides the parts above described, a projecting piece of bone, extending upwards from the crown of the arch, and denominated the *spinous process* (s, s). The sharp ridge that runs along the middle of the back of a quadruped, is formed by the continued series of these processes. There are also, on the sides of the vertebræ, two other projecting pieces, which are denominated the *transverse processes* (T), and which serve as levers for bending the column laterally, that is, either to the right or to the left. All these component parts of the spine are subject to considerable modifications, in different tribes of animals, according to the particular mechanical circumstances of the system, and to the particular intentions of their formation.

There is scarcely any part of the osseous fabric of which the variations better illustrate the strict unity of plan and the beautiful law of gradation observed by nature in all her operations, than the spine. In studying the various modifications which this part of the skeleton undergoes, it will be useful to bear in mind the principles, which appear to regulate its formation, and which Geoffroy St. Hilaire has deduced by following the history of its early growth, and noticing the order in which its several parts are developed.* In common with

---

* Mémoires du Muséum, ix. 79 and 89.

STRUCTURE OF VERTEBRÆ.

all bones, the vertebræ take their rise from certain determinate points, or centres of ossification, where, at first, detached pieces of bone are formed, destined to unite together so as to compose the entire bone. An accurate knowledge of the general forms and relative situations of these elementary pieces is of much importance, because we find that particular circumstances determine the developement of some of these parts much earlier, and to a greater extent than other parts; and thus lead to great differences in the shapes and proportions of various bones, at different periods of their growth, although their origin and composition are essentially the same.

The number of elements which enter into the composition of a vertebra has been differently estimated by different physiologists: but the following are certainly entitled to that character. They are represented in their relative situations in Fig. 180. The first is the part which forms the *nucleus*, or *body* (B) of the vertebra; and its ossification begins at the centre. Next in importance are the two bony plates, or *leaves*, as they may be called (L, L), which proceed from the sides of the body, and embrace the spinal marrow which is si-

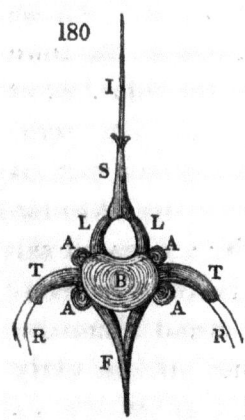

tuated between them. The fourth essential element is the *spinous process* (s), which unites the two leaves, and thus completes the superior arch, of which it may be regarded as the key stone, for the protection of the spinal marrow. Then come the two *transverse processes* (T, T) which extend outwards from the sides, and with which the arches of bone, that constitute the ribs (R, R) are generally connected. These are the six parts which may be considered as the elements that are most essential, and most constantly present in the composition of the vertebræ. But some other parts may also be noticed as of very frequent occurrence: such are the bony plates which cover the two flat portions of the bodies of the vertebræ, forming the surfaces immediately contiguous to the intervertebral ligament; which surfaces, in some of the lower orders of the vertebrata become articular. There is frequently, also, a developement of processes (F), forming arches and spines at the lower surface of the vertebræ, or the one opposite to that which gives rise to the superior arches already mentioned. This structure is very generally met with in fishes, and it is observed also in the cetacea. The arches thus formed enclose a large artery, which is the continuation of the aorta, or the main artery running along the back, immediately under the spinal column.

There are still other processes, less constantly

present and more variable in their shape. They form articular surfaces for the purpose of being connected with the surfaces of corresponding processes in the contiguous vertebra. Of these there are four (A, A, A, A) belonging to each vertebra, two in front, and two behind. These, however, should not be included among the primary elements of the vertebræ, because we find them, in different instances, occupying different positions, and formed sometimes by extensions of the bodies, and at other times of the leaves. In following them through the several tribes of animals, we observe them shifting their places, in various ways, and not even preserving any constancy in their number. They are wholly absent in fishes: in the crocodile, and other reptiles, they approximate so as to form three articular surfaces, namely, two close to one another, and a third posterior to these. In the Ornithorhyncus, while the latter retains its situation in the middle, the other surfaces have separated from each other, and have travelled outwards, taking their stations upon the leaves. In the Mammalia, the middle surface has wholly disappeared, and the outer surfaces have risen into what are termed the *oblique processes*.

In addition to these, accessory bones are often developed to suit particular occasions. Thus in fishes, we see that one or two additional pieces

(1) are affixed to the ends of each spinous process. In many cases, instead of being thus placed in a line with these processes, they appear at a little distance, as if they had slipped from their proper situations; they are then found between the spinous processes, and receive the name of *interspinous bones*.

The spinous processes have a tendency, when their developement proceeds, to divide into two branches, and this bifurcation frequently takes place also in the interspinous bones. The transverse processes likewise occasionally develope accessory pieces, as is found to be the case in some reptiles; but in other instances they undergo a gradual change of position, as we follow them backwards along the spinal column, where they descend towards the abdominal region.

The flexibility of particular portions of the spinal column is regulated by the size and form of its processes. When these are much developed, they necessarily obstruct the flexion of the vertebræ in the directions in which they are situated: when they are small, no such hindrance arises, and the spine is free to move in all directions. Thus, when we see the spinous processes much enlarged, while the transverse processes are small, we may infer that the spine is incapable of any bending in that direction; but that it has the power of free lateral flexion. This is the condition of the spine of fishes, where this latter kind of motion is the one principally wanted. In dolphins, and other cetacea, on the contrary, where the actions are required to be vertically upwards and downwards, the spinous processes are small, and the transverse processes very long and broad.

Every instance of variation in the forms of these important parts of the osseous system, will, in like manner, be found to have a relation to some particular circumstance in the living habits of the animal, and to be subordinate to the general plan of its economy. But in order to understand the mode in which nature has effected these changes, it is necessary to study the elements of each part of the osseous system ; for these constitute the alphabet by which the combinations she presents to us become legible, and their origin and progress are unfolded to our comprehension. According as each of these elements of ossification receives different degrees of developement, so do the different bones they compose acquire their particular shapes and relative dimensions. Sometimes, indeed, we find that one or other of these elements has disappeared; or at least we can discover no trace of its developement ; in other cases, we see it exceedingly expanded, and appearing under forms of greater complication, so as to be with difficulty identified: on some occasions, as we have just seen in the spinous bones of fishes, its accessory structures are multiplied, as if continued efforts were made by the system to repeat the same structures. Amidst all these modifications, the parts that preserve the greatest constancy of form are those which are of most importance, and which are constituent parts of the primordial type of the class to which the individual animal belongs.

The spinal column is generally prolonged at its posterior extremity into a series of vertebræ, which are sometimes exceedingly numerous; decreasing in their size as they extend backwards, and having continually smaller processes, the one disappearing after the other, till all of them are lost, and nothing remains in those at the extremity of the series but the cylindrical bodies of the vertebræ. Even these become stinted in their growth and ossification, until we find the terminal pieces generally remaining in the state of cartilage. Such is the structure of the osseous support of the tail, as seen in many quadrupeds in its most developed forms. It illustrates the law, that when in any system there occurs a frequent repetition of the same structure, the evolution, in the latest of those repetitions, becomes less perfect, and ends by being abortive. In the present instance, the consequences of this law are highly advantageous, since it provides for the flexibility of the tail, and qualifies it for being applied to a great variety of useful purposes, as we find more especially exemplified in the *Ateles*, or spider monkey, and in the *Kanguroo*.

Next in importance to the spine is the *cranium*, or osseous covering of the brain; together with the bones of the face, which protect the organs of the finer senses. An accurate investigation of the mode in which these bones are formed has led many modern anatomists to the opinion that they were originally parts of the spinal column, and that they are in fact developements of vertebræ, much altered, indeed, in shape, in consequence of the new conditions to which they have been subjected; but still possessing all the essential elements of vertebræ. In the embryo condition of these organs, and while the brain is yet undeveloped, the resemblance of the bony circles which enclose it to vertebræ is certainly very striking; but in proportion as the brain becomes expanded, the similarity diminishes; for the rapid growth of the brain in the higher orders of animals is necessarily attended with an equally sudden expansion of the bones of the skull. Hence their several elements are thrown into unusual positions, and being variously distorted and disfigured, can hardly be recognised under the strange disguises they assume.

The extensive researches that have been recently made in this branch of comparative anatomy, have supplied many facts which tend to support the hypothesis that the bony coverings of the brain are the result of the developement of three vertebræ. According to this theory, the first of these supposed *cranial vertebræ,* beginning our enumeration from the neck, is the origin of the occipital bone, of which the lower part, or that which immediately supports the cerebellum, corresponds to the body of the vertebra; the two lateral portions, to the leaves; and the upper flat plate to the spinous process. The body of the second cranial vertebra becomes, in process of time, the posterior half of the sphenoid bone, which lies in the middle of the basis of the skull; the temporal bones being formed by its leaves, and the parietal bones by the lateral halves of its spinous process. The third cranial vertebra is constituted by the anterior half of the sphenoid bone, which is its body, and the frontal bones, which are its leaves. This theory, which originated with Oken, has been further extended to the bones of the face, by Geoffroy St. Hilaire, who conceives them to be likewise developements of several other supposed cranial vertebræ;[*] but the analogies by which the hypothesis is supported become more feeble

[*] In this theory of G. St. Hilaire the number of cranial vertebræ is seven, each composed of nine elementary pieces.

and confused as we recede from the middle of the spinal column.

All the other parts of the skeleton may be regarded as accessory to the spine: and they are far from exhibiting the same constancy either in form or number, as the vertebral column. In some instances, as in serpents, these accessory parts are altogether wanting; in others, they exist only in rudimental states; and it is but in a few that they can be considered as having reached their full developement. In order to obtain a standard of comparison by which to estimate all their gradations of evolution, it will be best to consider them first in their more perfectly developed forms, as they are presented in the higher classes of quadrupeds. In the following descriptions, the skeleton of the Hog (Fig. 181) will be taken for the purpose of reference.

The ribs consist of arches of bone affixed at their upper ends to the bodies of the vertebræ, and also, by a separate articulation, to their transverse processes; where, in general, they are allowed a slight degree of motion. Their primary use is to defend the vital organs situated in the region of the chest, or *thorax* (namely, the heart and the lungs); but they are subservient also to the function of respiration, by the alternate movements that are given to them by their muscles. The two parts, of which they are composed, often form an angle by their junction, and at this angle a process

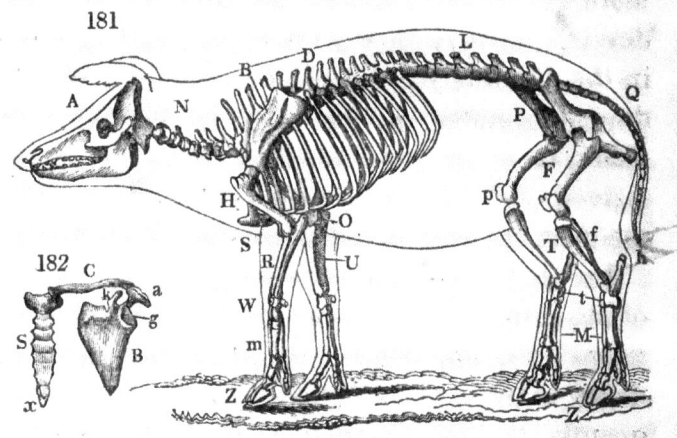

occasionally extends, for the purpose of forming connexions with the neighbouring ribs.

The ribs are connected in front with the breast bone, or *sternum* (s), often by the intervention of cartilages, which, from their similarity of form to the ribs, appear as continuations of them, and are provided apparently to eke out the remainder of the semicircle. These cartilages, which have been termed the *sterno-costal appendices*, often become ossified, either wholly or in part.

The sternum is formed of nine elementary pieces, each proceeding from a separate centre of ossification. Two of these occupy the end which is nearest to the head, four are lateral, and two are situated at the opposite extremity:

one only being central and surrounded by the rest. Few subjects in comparative osteology are more curious and instructive than to trace the developement of these several elementary parts in the different classes of animals, from the rudimental states of this bone as it occurs in fishes, to its greatly expanded conditions in the tortoise and the bird, which severally exhibit the most opposite proportions of these elements.

Last in the order of constancy come the bones of the extremities. As we ascend in the scale of animals we may observe the prevalence of a tendency to the concentration of organs, and consequently to the diminution of their number. While in animals of the inferior orders, which are possessed of extremities, we find a considerable number of legs; in all the animals comprised in the class of true insects nature has limited the number to six; and in the vertebrata it never exceeds four. As in insects we observed that all the legs are divided into the same number of parts; so we find among quadrupeds a striking correspondence in the bones of the fore and the hind extremities. Both the one and the other are connected with the spine by the intermedium of large and broad bones, which are intended to serve as a basis for their more secure attachment, and for giving, at the same time, extensive and advantageous purchase to the muscles, which are to move the limbs.

The two bones by which the anterior extremity is connected with the trunk are the *blade-bone*, or *Scapula* (B), which sends out a process called the *coracoid bone;* and the *collar-bone*, or the *Clavicle*,* which extends from the scapula to the sternum. The corresponding connecting bones of the posterior extremity are three in number, and constitute, together with the part of the spine to which they are attached, what is called *the Pelvis* (P). The part of the spine which is thus included in the pelvis, is termed the *Sacrum*. In its complete state of ossification it is a single bone; but it was originally composed of a number of separate vertebræ, which have afterwards become consolidated into a single bone, and which bear the marks of having been compressed from behind forwards during their growth, so that they could only expand laterally. The vertebræ which succeed to these, and which are not consolidated with the sacrum, compose what is called the *os coccygis*, (Q), or more properly the *coccygeal vertebræ:* when they are sufficiently numerous to compose a tail, they come under the denomination of *caudal vertebræ*. The three

---

* This bone does not exist in the skeleton of the hog; but its form and connexions with the sternum and scapula in the human skeleton are shown in Fig. 182, where s is the sternum; c, the clavicle; B, the scapula; a, the acromion; k, the coracoid process; and g, the glenoid cavity for the articulation of the humerus.

bones of the pelvis, are the *ilium*, the *ischium*, and the *pubis*. They all concur in the formation of a large cup-like cavity, called the *acetabulum*, which receives the head of the thigh bone (F), constituting generally the largest joint in the body.

A single bone composes the first division of each limb, both in the fore and hind extremities. In the fore leg it is termed the *humerus* (H), in the hind leg, the *femur* (F). The next division contains two bones, placed parallel to each other; they are in the former, the *radius* (R), and the *ulna* (U); in the latter, the *tibia* (T), and *fibula* (f). These are followed by a number of small, rounded or cubical bones, collected together in a group, which constitutes the *Carpus* (w), in the fore leg, and the *Tarsus* (t), in the hind leg. Next come a set of long cylindrical bones, composing the *metacarpus* (m), in the former, and the *metatarsus* (M), in the latter case. In the most complete forms of developement these are always five in number in each limb; they are placed generally parallel to each other, but are enveloped in one common covering of integument. The *Phalanges*, or toes (z), are cylindrical bones, continued in a line from each of the former: they are generally three in number in each toe. To the last joint, which is often termed the *ungual bone*, there is usually attached either a nail, a claw, or a hoof. Small detached bones are frequently found at the exterior part of the angles which they form by their junction, serving the purpose of giving a more advantageous position to the tendons of the muscles which extend those joints. The *patella*, or knee pan, (K), is the largest of these, and is pretty constantly present. Smaller bones of this description are met with on the joints of the fingers, and are termed *sesamoid bones*.

On comparing these divisions of the limbs of quadrupeds with those of insects we cannot fail to perceive that there exists between them a marked analogy: and that naturalists were not led away by mere fancy when they applied to the latter the same names as those borne by the former. This, however, is not the only instance of analogy that may be discovered between the structures of articulated and of vertebrated animals, however strong may be the contrast which they offer in all the essential features of their conformation. The rings which compose the skeleton of the insect, and which enclose its principal nervous chords, have been supposed to have an analogy with the circles of bone which constitute the primary forms of the vertebræ, and which contain the spinal chord; although in the first case, it is true, other viscera are included within the arches, whereas none are contained in the last case. They agree, also, in having the head placed at one extremity, distinct from the trunk, and containing the principal organs of the senses. Further correspondences have been likewise traced in the minuter anatomy of these parts, which it would here occupy too much space to examine in detail.

An approximation is evidently made towards an internal skeleton in the cephalopodous mollusca; where we find a central body, cartilaginous in some species, calcareous in others. In the Loligo it has a long and slender shape, and is pointed at the end like the blade of a sword; it bears, as we shall hereafter notice, some resemblance to the cartilaginous spine of the fish called the *Myxine*, or *Gastrobranchus*, which does not enclose the spinal marrow, but only admits it to pass along a groove in its upper edge.

All these multiplied instances, when weighed together, and united in a comprehensive view, are sufficient to prove, that there exist very perceptible links of connexion among all the classes of created beings, even in those apparently the most remote from one another. They render it clear to the discerning eye of the philosophic naturalist, that all the races of animated beings are members of one family, and the offspring of the same provident parent, who has matured all his plans on a deeply premeditated system, and who dispenses all his gifts with the most salutary regard to the general welfare of his creatures.

Chapter VIII.

FISHES.

In reviewing the series of animals which compose each great division of this kingdom of nature, we constantly find that the simplest structures and modes of progression are those belonging to the aquatic tribes. Among vertebrated animals, the lowest rank is occupied by *Fishes*, a class comprehending an immense number of species, which are all inhabitants of the water, which exhibit an endless variety of forms, and open to the physiologist a wide field of interesting research. We cannot fail to perceive, on the most cursory glance, the beautiful adaptation of the form and structure of all these animals to the properties of the element in which they are destined to reside. In order that the fish might glide through the fluid with the least resistance, all its vital organs have been collected into a small compass, and the body has been reduced into the shape of a compact oval, compressed laterally, and tapering to a thin edge, both before and behind, for the purpose of readily cleaving the water as the fish darts forward, and also of obviating the retardation that might arise from the reflux of the water collected behind. With a view to diminish friction as much as possible, the surface of the body has been rendered smooth, and the skin impregnated with oil, which defends it from injurious impressions, and at the same time prevents the water from penetrating into its substance.

The body of a fish is nearly of the same specific gravity as the water it inhabits; and the effect of gravity is therefore almost wholly counterbalanced by the buoyant force of that fluid: for the weight of a mass of water, equal in bulk to the body itself, is the exact measure of this buoyant force. If this weight were precisely the same as that of the fish, the animal would be able to remain suspended in any part of the fluid without the necessity of employing any voluntary motion or exertion for that purpose: but as the body of a fish is generally a little heavier than the fluid medium, especially if it be fresh water, it is necessary for the animal to give its body some degree of motion, in order to prevent its sinking.

In land quadrupeds, the limbs have to perform the double office of supporting the body, and of effecting at the same time its locomotion: but as nearly the whole of the weight of a fish is already sustained by the element in which it is immersed, its instruments of motion may be employed exclusively for progression; and the powerful hydrostatic pressure, which supports the body on all sides, supersedes the necessity of that cohesive rigidity of frame, which is essential to the safety of terrestrial animals. Hence we find that in one whole tribe of fishes, the skeleton is composed merely of cartilage; and, in all, it exhibits much less of the osseous character than in the higher classes. The frame-work of the skeleton, even of osseous fishes, has not the compactness possessed by that of quadrupeds or reptiles: the pieces which compose it are joined together less firmly; many of them, indeed, remain in an imperfectly ossified condition, their elementary pieces being detached from one another, as if the usual process of consolidation had been arrested at an early stage. The texture of the bones of cartilaginous fishes corresponds to this primeval condition; for it is composed merely of granules of calcareous phosphate, interspersed amidst the cartilaginous substance in detached masses, or presenting the appearance of coarse fibres, thinly scattered through the semitransparent bone. Compared with the quantity of gelatin which enters into their composition, the bones of fishes contain but a small proportion of earthy ingredient; a circumstance which explains the pellucidity of the mass, and the readiness with which the osseous fibres it contains can be distinguished. Another consequence of the want of density in the bones of fishes is, that their articulations are less regular and perfect than the corresponding joints of terrestrial animals; for it is evident that where the parts are soft and flexible, joints are not required.

In the osseous fishes, the bony structures are more finished; and they even arrive at a degree of hardness equal to that of the higher classes. But this developement is not uniform in all the bones; in the head of the pike, for instance, while some of the bones have acquired a great hardness, others remain wholly and permanently in a cartilaginous condition. The bones of fishes, however advanced in their ossification, never reach that stage of the process in which cavities are formed; thus there is no space for marrow, nor even for the cellular or cancellated structure which we have noticed in the more perfect bones.*

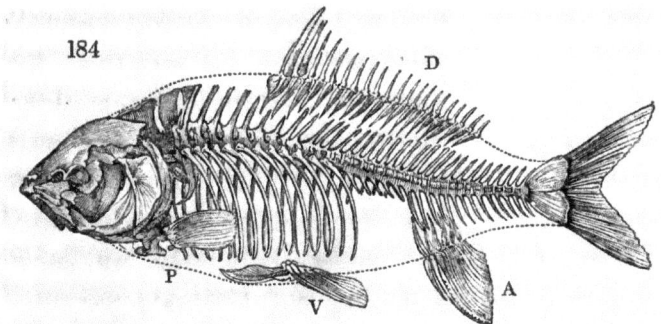

The general disposition of the bones which compose the entire skeleton will be understood from Fig. 184, which represents that of the *Cyprinus*

* Cuvier, sur les Poissons. Tom. i. p. 218.

THE MECHANICAL FUNCTIONS.

carpio, or carp. The muscular flesh of fishes is likewise softer than that of the higher classes; and the cellular substance more attenuated and more gelatinous; so that the membranes which it forms are of a looser and more pulpy texture.

Progressive motion in fishes is effected by the simplest means, the principal instrument employed for this purpose being the tail; for the fins, as we shall presently find, are merely auxiliary organs, serving chiefly to balance the body while it receives its propulsion from the tail. A fish moves in the water upon the same principle as a boat is impelled in sculling; for the action of the tail upon the water is lateral, like that of an oar, which it resembles in the vertical position of its plane; and the effect is transferred

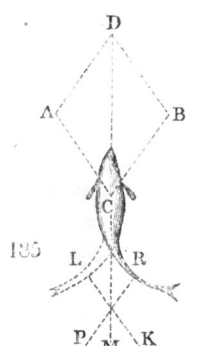

by the resistance of the water to the body where the impulse originates. Let us suppose, for example, that the tail is slightly inclined to the right, as shown in Fig 185. If, in this situation, the muscles on the left side, tending to bring the tail in a right line with the body, are suddenly thrown into action, the resistance of the water, by reacting against the broad surface of the tail in the direction P R, perpendicular to that surface, will cause the muscular action to give the whole body an impulse in that direction; and the centre of gravity, c, will move onwards in the direction c b, parallel to p r. This impulse is not destroyed by the farther flexion of the tail towards the left side, because the principal force exerted by the muscles has already been expended in the motion from r to m, in bringing it to a straight line with the body; and the force which carries it on to l is much weaker, and therefore occasions a more feeble reaction. When the tail has arrived at the position l, indicated by the dotted outline, a similar action of the muscles on the right side will create a resistance and an impulse in the direction of k l, and a motion of the whole body in the same direction, c a. These impulses being repeated in quick succession, the fish moves forwards in the diagonal c d, intermediate between the directions of the two forces. By bending the whole body almost in a circle, and then suddenly straightening it, fishes are often able to leap to the top of a high cataract, in ascending against the stream of a river.

Such being the plan upon which progression is to be effected, we find that every part of the mechanism of the fish is calculated to promote its execution. The principal muscular strength is bestowed upon the movements of the tail; and the largest assemblage of muscles consists of those which give it the lateral flexions that have been just described. For this purpose all the important viscera are placed forwards, and crowded towards the head. No room is allowed for a neck; and the abdomen may be almost regarded as continuous with the head, there being properly no intervening thorax; for the respiratory organs are situated rather beneath than behind the head. All this has been done with a view to leave ample scope for the prolonged expansion of the coccygeal vertebræ, and of their muscles, which compose more than half the bulk of the animal.

Having seen how all impediments to the free motion of the tail have been carefully removed, let us next inquire into the mechanism by which mobility has been given to that organ. The first peculiarity we meet with in the structure of the spine of fishes is the mode in which the vertebræ are connected together. The bodies of

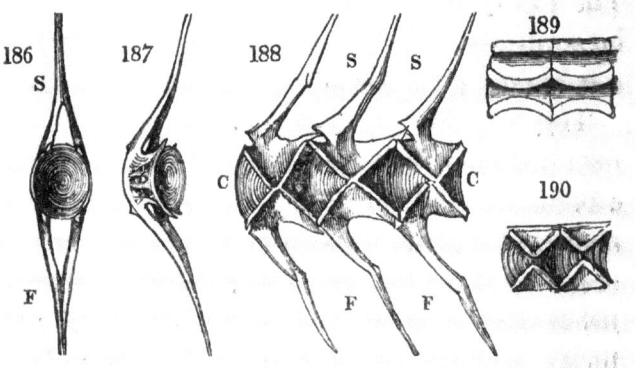

each vertebra, as may be seen in Figures 186 and 187, are hollowed out, both before and behind, (considering the spinal column as extended horizontally), so as to form cup-like hollows: by which means, where the concave surfaces of two adjacent vertebræ are applied to one another, a cavity, having the shape of a double cone, is formed by the junction of the margins of these conical hollows. These cavities are distinctly seen laid open in Fig. 188, which represents a vertical section of three adjacent vertebræ of a cod. The edges that are in contact, are united all round by an elastic ligament, which readily yields to the bending of the vertebræ upon one another by the application of any force to one side of the spine, and restores it to its former state when the force has ceased to act. The extent of motion in each joint is but small; but being multiplied in the whole series, the resulting effect is considerable. The cavity itself is filled with a gelatinous, but incompressible fluid substance, which constitutes a spherical pivot for all the motions of the joint.

This singular kind of articulation would appear framed with a view to allow of motion in all directions. Here, however, the motions are restricted by the extension of the spinous processes (s, s, in the preceding figures), which in fishes are of great length; so that they effectually prevent all flexions either upwards or downwards, and limit it to those from side to side. It is precisely these latter kind of motions that are wanted in the fish, for striking the water laterally, with the broad vertical surface of the tail. Processes of a similar form and appearance, (F, F), and which impede any flexion downwards, are generally also met with in the lower surface of the spine, and more especially in the hinder portion of the column. These are the *inferior spinous processes*, and, like the superior, they also form an arch, through which there passes the continuation of the abdominal aorta, or great artery which proceeds down the back. The number of vertebræ is very various in different fishes: in some they are multiplied exceedingly, as in the shark, where there are more than two hundred.

There are few parts of the structure of animals that exhibit more remarkable instances of the law of gradation than the spine of fishes, in which we may trace a regular progress of developement from the simplest and almost rudimental condition in which it exists in the *Myxine* and the *Lamprey,* to that of the most perfect of the osseous tribes. Its condition, in the former of these animals, presents a close analogy with some structures that are met with in the molluscous, and even in annulose animals. So near is the resemblance of the spinal column of the myxine, more especially, to the annular condition of the frame-work of the vermes, that doubts have often arisen in the minds of naturalists whether that animal ought not properly to be ranked among this latter class. Its pretensions to be included among the vertebrata are, indeed, but slender and equivocal; for, in place of a series of bones composing the vertebral column, it has merely a soft and flexible tube of a homogeneous and cartilaginous substance, exhibiting scarcely any trace of division into separate rings, but appearing as if it were formed of a continuous hollow cylinder of intervertebral substance, usurping the place of the vertebræ, which it is the usual office of that substance to connect together, and having in its axis a continuous canal filled with gelatinous fluid. This, however, is not the channel intended for containing the spinal marrow, for that nervous cord is on the outside of this column. The cartilage, indeed, sends out no processes to bend round the spinal marrow, and forms no canal for its passage and protection. The nervous matter here consists merely of two slender cords, which run parallel to one another in a groove on the upper part of the spinal column; and these cords are covered only by a thin membrane, the presence of which it requires very minute attention to detect. The partial protection thus afforded to so important an organ is not greater than that given by the cartilaginous lamina of the cuttle-fish, which in form, texture, and situation is very analogous to the spine of the myxine.

As we ascend from this rudimental condition of the spine, we find it, in the lamprey, more distinctly divided into rounded portions, appearing like beads strung together. These rudimental bodies of vertebræ have not yet completed the cup-like hollows on their two ends, but are shaped like rings, being perforated in the centre, so as still to form a continuous canal throughout the whole column.

Proceeding to more advanced developements, we find, in the sturgeon and other cartilaginous fishes, a greater condensation of substance produced by the deposition of granules of osseous matter; the central canal becomes divided into lozenge-shaped compartments by the closing in of the sides of the body of each vertebra.* Frequently the sides do not quite meet, and the leaves, which are developed from the upper surfaces of the vertebræ, now form arches over the spinal cord, and are united above by spinous processes. Yet the whole skeleton in these

* A small aperture still remains, establishing a communication between the cavities the whole length of the spine. This is supposed to be designed to obviate the compression of the fluid in the different cells or cavities during the motions of the spine. The vertical sections, Fig. 189 and 190, of two contiguous vertebræ in different fishes, will convey an idea of this gradation of developement.

STRUCTURE OF FISHES.

fishes remains in the incipient stage of ossification, being more or less cartilaginous; and where the ossific process has begun, it has not advanced the length of producing union between the pieces formed from the separate centres of ossification. Where they meet without uniting, they form no sutures, but overlap one another. Thus the bony structures are detached, and often completely isolated; affording to the physiologist an opportunity of studying the earlier stages of this interesting process, and marking with distinctness the number of the elements of each bone, and the relative situations of their centres. This knowledge is more especially of importance towards understanding the formation and connections of the bones of the head, which are very numerous and complicated; and the investigation of which has been prosecuted with extraordinary diligence by Geoffroy St. Hilaire and other continental zootomists.

It is here, more especially, that we obtain the clearest evidence of the derivation of the cranial bones from vertebræ analogous to those of the spine. The occipital bone, in particular, corresponds to a spinal vertebra in all its essential elements. In many fishes, the body of this bone, being lengthened out to form the posterior part of the basis of the skull, becomes the basilar portion. We find, on its posterior surface, the same cup-like cavity as in the true vertebræ; and it is joined to the next vertebra in the same manner as the spinal vertebræ are joined to each other. Its crest has the exact shape of a spinous process. In front the basilar bone is united to the spenoid bone, which, with the vaulted roof that springs from the sides of both these bones, like the leaves and spinous processes of the vertebræ, form together a long cranial cavity. This cavity is placed in a direct line with the spinal canal, and contains the nervous tubercles which constitute the brain. Yet the brain does not completely fill this cavity; for a space is still left, which is occupied by a pulpy substance. In like manner, the accordance of the other cranial bones with vertebræ, has been attempted to be traced; but in proportion as we recede from the central parts of the spine, this correspondence is less distinct, in consequence of the various degrees of developement which these several elements have received, in order to adapt them to particular purposes relating to sensation, to the prehension and deglutition of the food, and also to aquatic respiration. It is impossible, however, without exceeding the limits within which I must here confine myself, to enter into the details of structure which would be requisite in order to render this subject sufficiently intelligible.

The rest of the skeleton of fishes is extremely simple. In many, as in the *Ray* and *Tetrodon*, there are no ribs. Where these bones exist, they are articulated with the extremities of the transverse processes of the vertebræ, of which they appear to be merely continuations, or appendices. There is generally no sternum to which they can be attached below: in a few fishes only, such as the *herring* and the *dory*, we find rudiments of this bone, consisting of a few pieces placed in a line on the lower part of the trunk.*

The parts of the skeleton of fishes, which correspond to the arms and legs of quadrupeds, are the pectoral and ventral fins (marked respectively by the letters p and v in Fig. 184). The former are met with, with but few exceptions, in all fishes; and they consist of a series of osseous pieces, in which we may often recognise with tolerable precision the analogous bones composing the anterior extremities of a quadruped; such as the scapula, clavicle, humerus, ulna, and radius.†
These two latter bones are very distinctly marked

---

* The bony arches arising from the skull, which support the branchiæ, or gills, have been considered as the bones corresponding to the ribs of terrestrial quadrupeds; and if this view were taken of them, it would tend to confirm the analogy of the cranial bones to the spinal vertebræ.

† Those anatomists who are fond of pursuing the theory of analogies, maintain that all these bones are merely developements of certain ribs, proceeding from the spine in its anterior parts. A similar origin has been assigned to the pieces of bone to which the ventral fins are attached: but it is difficult to reconcile this

in the *Lophius piscatorius,* or Angler, as may be seen in Fig. 191, where B is the scapula; C, the clavicle; U, the ulna; and R, the radius. The

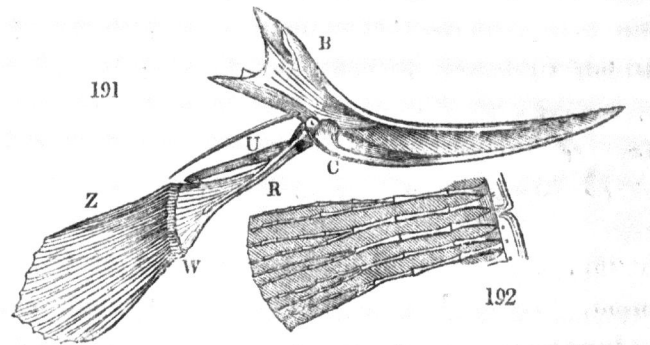

carpus may also be recognised in a chain of small bones, w, interposed between the radius and the Phalanges, z. In the *Ray* these phalanges are very numerous, and each is divided into several pieces by regular articulations: these are shown in Fig. 192: they are arranged close to one another in one plane, and form an effectual base of support to the integument which covers them. The scapula, according to Cuvier, is sometimes detached from the rest of the skeleton, and at other times connected with the spine: in most cases, however, it is suspended

theory with the fact that these bones do not proceed from the spine, and are quite detached from the rest of the skeleton. It is evident, therefore, that if they are to be considered as analogous to the bones of the hinder extremities in the mammalia, they are in a condition of very imperfect developement.

STRUCTURE OF FISHES.

from the cranium; a fact which may be cited in further corroboration of the analogy which the cranial bones have to vertebræ.

In the ray and the shark tribes, both the anterior and posterior extremities are supported by arches of bones, forming a sort of belt. This

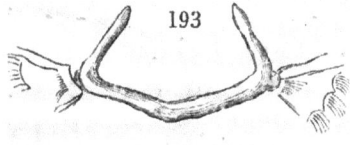

structure is an approach to that which obtains in many reptiles, and indicates a further step in the regular progress of developement. This belt in the ray is shown in Fig. 193.

In examining that part of the skeleton of fishes which corresponds to the posterior extremity, we observe the total absence of both femur and tibia; but the bones of the toes are attached to a set of small bones, which appear to act the part of a pelvis, but which, in consequence of their not being connected with the spine, have no determinate situation, and are found at various distances from the head in different fishes. They appear emancipated from the restraints to which they would have been subjected had they been fixed to a sacrum, or to any particular part of the spine: and we find them, accordingly, often placed considerably forwards; and in some instances, as in the *Subbrachieni*, even anteriorly to the pectoral fins, which are the true arms of the animal. But in one whole order of fishes, the *Apodes*, there is not even a vestige of ventral fins, nor are any pelvic bones provided for their support. This is the case with the *Eel*, the *Gymnotus*, &c. In a few species there is also a total absence of pectoral as well as ventral fins.

The dorsal fins are supported by a series of slender bones (D Fig. 184), which are joined to the spinous processes of the vertebræ, and are formed from distinct centres of ossification. These *rays*, as they are called, are sometimes destined to grow to so considerable a length, as to require being subdivided into many pieces, in order to lessen the danger of fracture, to which a very long filament of bone would have been exposed, and also to allow of a greater degree of flexibility. These rays assume branched forms from the further subdivision of their parts, and when, for the purpose of adding strength to the fin, it becomes necessary to multiply the points of support, intermediate bones are developed, serving as the basis of the rays. Convenience requires that they should be detached from the ends of the spinous processes, which is their usual position, and placed between them: when in this situation, they bear the name of *interspinous bones;* and when a still greater length of osseous support is wanted, new centres of ossification are developed at their extremities, giving rise to a series of additional pieces, joined end to end, and carrying out the interspinous

MUSCULAR SYSTEM OF FISHES. 425

bone, and the ray which terminates it, to a considerable distance. This structure is distinctly seen in the small dorsal fins of the *Mackarel*. The anal fins, which are situated on the lower side of the body, in the vertical plane, and next to the tail, are, in like manner, supported by rays, having the same parallel, or fan-like arrangement as the preceding. The caudal fin, or terminal expansion of the tail has also a similar structure.

The muscles of fishes compose a large portion of the bulk of the body, but they are arranged in a less complex manner than those of the animals of the higher classes. Those which appear immediately underneath the integuments are shown in Fig. 194, where M, M are the great

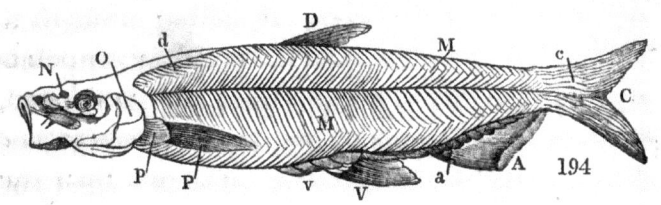

lateral muscles, producing the flexion of the body and tail: D is the dorsal fin, which is raised by the muscle d; P, the pectoral fin, expanded by the muscle p: V, the ventral fin, moved by the muscles situated at v: A, the anal fin, in like manner moved by muscles at its base a: and c, the caudal fin, the muscles for moving which are seen at c: o is the operculum, or flap, which covers the gills: and N, the nasal cavities, or organs of smell. The form of the body, and disposition of the skeleton, allow of their being inserted immediately on the parts which they are intended to approximate. Hence the use of long tendinous chords is dispensed with.*

The actions of the muscles are easily understood from the nature of their insertions. In general, the direction of the fibres is in some degree oblique, with reference to the motion performed. Two series of muscles are provided for the movements of the tail, which consist almost exclusively of lateral flexion, the whole spine in some degree participating in this motion. These muscles occupy the upper and lower portions of the trunk; their limits being strongly marked by a line running longitudinally the whole length of the body on each side. The inclination of their fibres is somewhat different in each. The advantage in point of velocity of action which results from this obliquity has already been pointed out.

Those fins which are in pairs are capable of four motions; namely, those of flexion and ex-

---

* Between the layers of flesh, however, there occur slender semi-transparent tendons, which give attachment to a series of short muscular fibres, passing nearly at right angles between the surfaces of the adjoining plates. See Sir A. Carlisle's account of this structure in the Philosophical Transactions for 1806.

tension, and also those of expanding and closing the rays; for each of which motions appropriate muscles are provided: and indeed each ray is furnished with a distinct muscular apparatus for its separate motion; and these smaller muscles regulate with great nicety all the movements of the fins, expanding or closing them like a fan, according as their action is to be strengthened or relaxed. This feathering of the fin, as it may be called, takes place in most fishes, and is particularly observable in the tail of the *Esox*, or pike tribe. Each ray of these fins, indeed, is furnished with a distinct muscular apparatus, for its separate motion.

Whatever analogy may exist in the structure of the fins of fishes and the feet of quadrupeds, there is none in the manner in which they are instrumental in effecting progressive motion. The great agent by which the fish is impelled forwards is the tail: the fins, which correspond to the extremities of land animals, are useful chiefly for the purposes of turning, stopping, or inclining the body, and for retaining it in its proper position. The single fins, or those which are situated in a vertical plane, passing through the axis of the body (the mesial plane), prevent the rolling of the body, while the fish darts forwards in its course. The fins that are in pairs (that is the pectoral and the ventral fins), by their alternate flexions and extensions, act like oars; while they are capable, at the same time, of expanding and of closing the rays, like the opening and shutting of a fan, according as their action is required to be effective or the contrary. All these auxiliary instruments are chiefly serviceable in modifying the direction, and adjusting the variations of force derived from the impulse of the tail. They are employed also in suddenly checking or stopping the motion, and giving it a more rapid acceleration. But still the tail is the most powerful of the instruments for progression, being at once a vigorous oar, an accurate rudder, and a formidable weapon of offence.

Independently of these external instruments of progression, most fishes are provided with internal means of changing their situation in the water. The structure by which this effect is accomplished is one of the most remarkable instances that is met with of an express contrivance for a specific purpose, and of the employment of an agency of a class different from that of the mechanical powers usually resorted to for effecting the same object. We have seen that if the body of a fish were heavier than an equal bulk of water, and if no muscular exertions were made, it must necessarily descend in that fluid. If, on the contrary, it were specifically lighter, it would as necessarily rise to the surface. Were the animal to acquire the power of altering at pleasure its specific gravity, it would then pos-

SWIMMING BLADDER OF FISHES. 429

sess the means of rising or sinking, without calling into action either the fins or the tail. Such is precisely the object of a peculiar mechanism, which nature has provided in the interior of the body of the fish. A large bladder, filled with air, has been placed immediately under the spine, in the middle of the back, and above the centre of gravity. This is known by the name of the *air-bladder*, or the *swimming bladder*, and in the cod-fish it is called the *sound*. It frequently, as in the Carp, consists of two bladders (A, B, Fig. 195) joined endwise, and

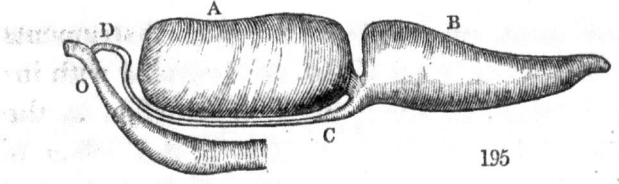

communicating with each other by a narrow neck.* When distended with air, it renders the whole fish specifically lighter than the surrounding water; and the fish is thus buoyed up, and remains at the surface without any effort of its own. On compressing the bladder, by the action of the surrounding muscles, the included air is

---

* There is great variety in the form and structure of the air-bladder in different fishes. Sometimes it contains a large glandular body of a peculiar structure, which has been conjectured to be an apparatus for secreting air from the blood: but it is by no means very generally met with.

condensed, the specific gravity of the whole body is increased, and the fish sinks to the bottom. On relaxing the same muscles, the air recovers its former dimensions, and the fish is again rendered buoyant. Can there be stronger evidence of design than the placing of this hydrostatic apparatus, acting upon philosophical principles, in the interior of the organization, for a purpose so definite and unequivocal?

In several tribes of fishes there is a canal (C D) establishing a communication between this bladder and the stomach, or the gullet (o); so that by compressing the bladder, a quantity of air may be forced out, and a very sudden increase of specific gravity produced; followed, of course, by a quick descent. When, by any accident, the air bladder has been opened, or has burst, so that all the air has escaped, the fish is seen to grovel at the bottom, lying on its back, and can never afterwards rise to the surface. On the other hand, it occasionally happens that a fish which has remained too long at the surface of the sea, exposed to the scorching rays of a tropical sun, suddenly finds itself retained against its will at the surface, because the bladder has become over distended by the heat, and resists all the efforts which the animal can make to compress it. It thus continues floating, until the coolness of the night has again condensed the air in the bladder to its former bulk, and restored the power of descending.

Some tribes of fish are totally unprovided with an air-bladder. This is the case with the flounder, the sole, and other genera of a flat shape, forming the family of *Pleuroncetes*. They are chiefly inhabitants of sand-banks, or other situations where they are comparatively stationary, seldom moving to a distance, or rising much in the water; and when they do so, it is with manifest effort, for their ascent must be accomplished entirely by the continued beating and flapping of the water with their expanded pectoral fins. It is only the larger fish of this form, such as rays, which have very voluminous and powerful pectoral fins for striking the water downwards with considerable force, that can rise with facility without the assistance of an air-bladder. In these, the lateral fins, which are enormous expansions of the pectoral fins, may be compared to wings, their vertical action on the water being similar in effect to the corresponding movements of a bird, when it rises vertically in the air. Those fishes which swim rapidly, and frequently ascend and descend in the water, are in general provided with the largest air-bladders.

In studying the varieties presented by the forms of the fins in different tribes of fishes, we find the same constant relation preserved with the particular situations and circumstances in which they are placed. The dorsal fins, which are more especially useful for steadying the body, are longest in those fishes which inhabit the most stormy seas. The most voracious tribes, which incessantly pursue their prey, are furnished with most powerful muscles, and possess the greatest means of rapid progression. On the other hand, many of the more pacific, and weaker species are studiously guarded by a dense and hard integument, serving as a shield against the attacks of enemies, and often armed with sharp points, which are sufficient to repel the most daring assailant. The *Balistes* is covered with scales of singular hardness closely set together, and frequently having rough edges. The *Ostracion*, or trunk fish, instead of these scales, is provided with a kind of coat of mail, composed of osseous plates, curiously joined together, like a tesselated pavement, and reminding us of the arrangements we have seen adopted in the calcareous coverings of the echinida.

Some of the cartilaginous fishes are in like manner protected by calcareous plates, appended to the integuments. There is a row of plates of this kind, of a quadrangular shape, which pass along the middle of the back in the sturgeon: and the whole body of the *Ostracion*, or Trunk-fish, is covered with osseous scales. All these have no immediate relation to the skeleton, but are apparently remnants of inferior types, of which one of the prevailing characters is the external situation of the protecting organs.

Diodons and *Tetrodons* are remarkable for being provided with the means of suddenly assuming a globular form by swallowing air, which, passing into the crop, or first stomach, blows up the whole animal like a balloon. The abdominal region being thus rendered the lightest, the body turns over, the stomach becoming the uppermost part; and the fish floats upon its back, without having the power of directing itself during this state of forced distension. But it is while lying thus bloated and passive at the mercy of the waves, that this animal is really most secure; for the numerous spines, with which the surface of the body is universally beset, are raised and erected by the stretching out of the skin, thus presenting an armed front to the enemy, on whatever side he may venture to begin the attack.

There is a numerous family of fishes, found in the seas of India, so constructed as to be able to crawl on land to some distance from the shore. One of these, the *Perca scandens*, is even capable of climbing on the trees which grow on the coast.*

* See the account given by Lieutenant Daldorff; Linnean Transactions, III. 62. I shall have occasion to notice, in the

If we consider the density of the medium which fishes have to traverse, the velocity with which they move will appear surprising. They dart through the water with apparently as much ease and rapidity as a bird flies through the air. Although this may partly be accounted for by the size of their muscles, and the advantageous mode of their insertion, yet these advantages would avail but little, were it not for the sudden manner in which their power is exerted. Where the great length and flexibility of the spine tend to impair the force with which the tail strikes the water, the resulting motion is slow and desultory, as is the case with eels, and other fishes of the same elongated construction.* Most fishes, however, move with the utmost rapidity, and with scarcely any visible effort; and perform long journeys without apparent fatigue. The Salmon has been known to travel at the rate of sixteen miles an hour for many days together. Sharks often follow ships across the Atlantic, not only outstripping them in their swiftest sailing, but playing round them on every side, just as if the vessel were at rest.

---

sequel, the remarkable conformation of the respiratory organs of these and other fishes, which enable them to live for a time out of their natural element.

* Carlisle, Phil. Trans. for 1806, p. 9.

Chapter VIII.

REPTILIA.

§ 1. *Terrestrial Vertebrata in general.*

THE numerous tribes of vertebrated animals which are strictly terrestrial, or destined to move on land, differ widely in their modes of progression, and in the mechanical advantages of their formation. The greater number are quadrupeds; some formed for climbing trees, others, for burrowing in the earth; some for treading on sandy plains, some for scaling precipices. A few seem scarcely capable of advancing; others outstrip the winds in fleetness. Some families of reptiles are entirely destitute of any external organs of motion, the whole trunk of the body resting on the ground: while man occupies a place where he stands alone, being distinguished by the exclusive faculty of permanently sustaining himself on the lower extremities.

In reviewing the developements and the mechanical functions exhibited by so great a diversity of structures, I shall commence with an examination of those amphibious reptiles which appear to form an intermediate link in the chain connecting the strictly aquatic, with the terrestrial vertebrated animals: then, taking up this latter series, I shall consider the more simple conformation, and less perfect motions of terrestrial animals destitute of limbs; and gradually ascend to those in which the support and progression of the body is effected by extremities, more and more artificially formed: concluding with the human structure, which terminates this extensive series.

§ 2. *Batrachia*.

THE order of *Batrachia*, or Amphibious Reptiles, constitutes the first step in the transition from aquatic to terrestrial vertebrata. It is more particularly the function of respiration that requires to be modified in consequence of the change of element in which the animal is to reside; and as if it had been necessary, conformably to the laws of animal creation, that this change should not be abruptly made, we find that Batrachian reptiles, with which this series commences, are constructed at first on the model of fishes; breathing the atmospheric air contained in the water by means of gills, and moving through the fluid by the same instruments of progression as fishes, which indeed they exactly

BATRACHIA. 437

resemble in every part of their mechanical conformation. The tadpole, which is the young of the frog, is at first not distinguishable in any circumstance of its internal skeleton, or in the disposition of its vital organs from the class of fishes. The head, indeed, is enlarged, but the

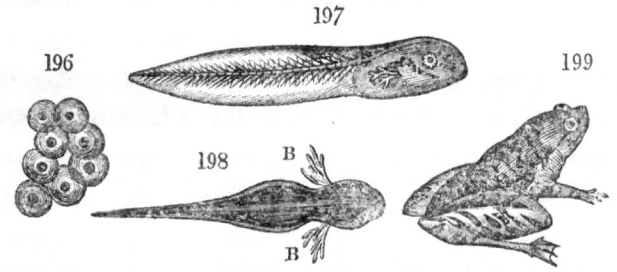

body immediately tapers to form a lengthened tail, by the prolongation of the spinal column, which presents a numerous series of coccygeal vertebræ, furnished with a vertical expansion of membrane to serve as a caudal fin, and with appropriate muscles for executing all the motions required in swimming. The appearance of the tadpole in its early stage of developement is seen in Fig. 197 and 198, the former being a side, and the latter an upper view of that animal.

Yet with all this apparent conformity to the structure of a strictly aquatic animal, the tadpole contains within its organization the germs of a higher developement. Preparations are silently making for a change of habitation, for the animal's emerging from the waters, for the reception of atmospheric air into new cavities, for the acquisition of limbs suited to new modes of progression; in a word, for a terrestrial life, and for all the attributes and powers which belong to quadrupeds. The succession of forms, which these metamorphoses present, are in themselves exceedingly curious, and bear a remarkable analogy with the progress of the transformations of those insects, which in the first stages of their existence are aquatic. To the philosophic inquirer into the marvellous plans of creation, the series of changes which mark these singular transitions cannot fail to be deeply interesting; and occurring, as we here find them, among a tribe of animals allied to the more perfect forms of organization, they afford us a better opportunity of exploring the secrets of their developement by tracing them from the earlier stages of this complicated process so full of mystery and of wonder.

The egg of the frog (Fig. 196) is a round mass of transparent nutritive gelly, in the centre of which appears a small black globule. By degrees this shapeless globule exhibits the appearance of a head and tail, and in this form it emerges from its prison, and moves briskly in the water. From the sides of the neck there grow out feathery tufts (Fig. 198, B, B), which float loosely, and without protection, in the surrounding fluid. These, however, are mere temporary organs, for they serve the purposes of respiration only until the proper gills are formed, and they then shrink and become obliterated. The true gills, or *branchiæ*, are contained within the body, and are four in number on each side, constructed on a plan very similar to those of fishes. Retaining this aquatic constitution, the tadpole rapidly increases in size and in activity for several weeks. In the mean time the legs, of which no trace was at first apparent, have commenced their growth. The hind legs are the first to make their appearance, showing their embryo forms within the transparent coverings of the hinder part of the trunk, just at the origin of the tail. These are soon succeeded by the fore legs, which exactly follow the hind legs in all the stages of their developement, until they have acquired their due proportion to the size of the trunk. The animal at this period wears a very ambiguous appearance, partaking of the forms both of the frog and of the lizard, and swimming both by the inflexions of the tail, and the irregular impulses given by the feet. This interval is also employed by this amphibious being, in acquiring the faculty of respiring atmospheric air. We observe it rising every now and then to the surface, and cultivating its acquaintance with that element, into which it is soon to be raised; occasionally taking in a mouthful of air, which is received into its newly developed lungs, and afterwards discharging it in the form of a small bubble. When the necessary internal changes are at length completed, preparations are made for getting rid of the tail, which is now a useless member, and which, ceasing to be nourished, diminishes by degrees, leaving only a short stump, which is soon removed. The gills are by this time shrunk, and rapidly disappear, their function being superseded by the lungs, which have been called into play; and the animal now emerges from the water and begins a new mode of existence, having become a perfect frog (Fig. 199). It still, however, retains its aquatic habits, and swims with great ease in the water by means of its hind feet, which are very long and muscular, and of which the toes are furnished with a broad web derived from a thin extension of the integuments.

No less curious are the changes which take place in all the other organs, for the purpose of effecting the transformations rendered necessary by this entire alteration in all the external circumstances of that animal,—this total reversal of its wants, of its habits, of its functions, and of its very constitution. I shall have occasion to notice several of these transitions when reviewing the other functions of the animal economy: but at present our concern is chiefly with the structure of the frame in its mechanical relations to progressive motion. In order to form a correct idea of these relations it will be necessary

SKELETON OF THE BATRACHIA. 441

to notice the leading peculiarities of the skeletons of this tribe of animals.

The skeleton of the adult frog is shown in Fig. 200; from which it will be seen that the spinal

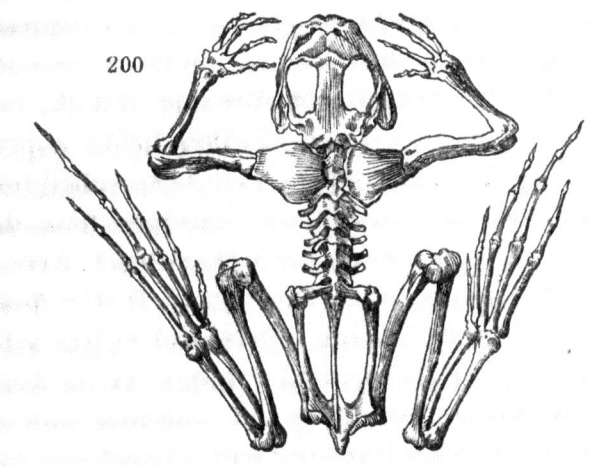

column is comparatively much shorter than that of fishes, or indeed of any other class of animals; for it consists of only eight vertebræ, exclusive of those which have united to form the os coccygis. It was evidently the intention of nature to consolidate the frame-work of the trunk, in which flexibility was not required for progressive motion: the performance of that function being transferred to the hind extremities, which are exceedingly large in proportion to the rest of the body. There is a tendency in every part of the skeleton to develope itself in a transverse direction, while the trunk is shortened as much as possible.

The mode in which the vertebræ are articulated together differs widely from what we have seen in fishes, and approaches to the structure of the higher classes of vertebrata. The body of each vertebra, instead of having at its posterior surface a cup-like cavity, terminates by a projecting ball, which is received into the cavity in the anterior surface of the next vertebra, so as to compose a true ball and socket joint, capable, when other circumstances permit, of a rotatory motion. But the vertebræ of the tadpole, as we have seen, are constructed on the model of those of a fish; that is, have cup-like cavities on both their surfaces, which play on balls of soft elastic matter interposed between them. We should naturally be curious to learn the mode in which the transition from this structure to that of the frog is accomplished. By carefully watching the progress of ossification, while this change is taking place, Dutrochet found that the gelatinous ball, on which both the adjacent vertebræ play in the tadpole, becomes gradually more solid, and is converted into cartilage. This cartilage afterwards becomes united by its anterior surface to the vertebra which is in front of it; and the whole then becomes ossified, so as to compose only one bone, its posterior surface remaining distinct, and continuing to play within the cup-like hollow of the vertebra which is behind it. The cartilaginous coccygeal vertebræ of the tadpole are lost long before there is time for their being ossified; but those nearest to the body are consolidated into one long and straight os coccygis, which being joined to the sacrum at an angle, gives rise to the strange deformity observable at that part of the back of a frog; for it here looks as if it had been broken. The spinal cavity is at the same time obliterated, that portion of the spinal marrow which had passed through it in the aquatic life of the animal being now withdrawn.

The theory of the spinal origin of the cranial bones receives considerable support from their structure and relative position in the skeleton of the frog. The cavity for the lodgement of the brain, which is enclosed by these vertebræ, is perfectly continuous in the same line with the spinal canal, which, indeed, it scarcely exceeds in its diameter. The bones of the face are, at the same time, expanded laterally, so as to bear no proportion to the cranial cavity. The head plays on the vertebral column by two lateral articular surfaces, formed upon the root of each leaf of the occipital bone, while its body, or basilar portion, is scarcely connected with the first cervical vertebra, and has no articular surface.

In place of ribs, we find only small slender detached bones, or rather cartilages, affixed to the extremities of the transverse processes of some of the vertebræ. They may be regarded as rudimental ribs.*

The pelvis consists of two slender and elongated iliac bones, which are extended backwards, and which, at their anterior extremities, merely touch the points of the transverse processes of the last vertebra of the back. This vertebra is much broader than the rest, and although it consists but of a single vertebra, must be considered as a sacrum. The two pubic and ischiatic bones are exceedingly small, but still contribute to form the acetabulum, or cavity for the reception of the thigh bone, at the hinder extremity of the slender bones above mentioned. This is the simplest possible form to which the pelvis can be reduced, while it preserves its attachments to the spine. It presents in this respect a more advanced stage of developement than that of fishes.

The connexion of the bones of the anterior extremities with the spine is analogous to that which takes place in rays and sharks: there being an osseous belt formed by the scapula, clavicle, and coracoid bone, with the latter of which the humerus is connected. The sternum

* The plan of reproduction in these animals requires that the ovary, or organ which contains the eggs, should be capable of enormous dilatation, in order to contain the immense bulk to which these eggs are expanded, previous to their being brought forth. It was probably in order to make room for this dilated ovary that the ribs have not been developed.

is large, and considerably developed; making some slight approach to the expansion it receives in the *Chelonia*. The radius and ulna are united into one bone: the bones of the arm and leg in general resemble in their figure and connexions those of the higher orders of *Mammalia*, to the type of which this order of reptiles is evidently making an approximation. There are five toes in the foot, with sometimes the rudiment of a sixth: the anterior extremity has only four toes, which are without claws.

The necessity of employing the same instruments for progression in the water and on land, is probably the cause which prevents their having the form best adapted for either function. The hind feet of the frog, being well constructed for striking the water backwards in swimming, are, in consequence, less capable of exerting a force sufficient to raise and support the weight of the body in walking: and this animal accordingly is exceedingly awkward in its attempt to walk. On a short level plane it can proceed only by leaps; an action which the length and great muscularity of the hind legs particularly fit them for performing. The toad, on the other hand, whose hind legs are short and feeble, walks better, but does not jump or swim so well as the frog.* The Hyla, or tree-frog, has the extremities

* It is singular that the frog, though so low in the scale of vertebrated animals, should bear a striking resemblance to the

of each of its toes expanded into a fleshy tubercle, approaching in the form of its concave surface to that of a sucker, and by the aid of which it fastens itself readily to the branches of trees, which it chiefly inhabits, and along which it runs with great agility.

The *Salamander* is an animal of the same class as the frog, undergoing the same metamorphoses from the tadpole state. It differs much, however, in respect to the developement of particular parts of the skeleton. The anterior extremities of the salamander make their appearance earlier than the hind legs, and the tail remains as a permanent part of the structure. The rudimental ribs are exceedingly small, and the sternum continues cartilaginous. The pelvis has no osseous connexion with the spine, but is merely suspended to it by ligaments. The land salamanders have a rounded tail, but the aquatic species, or *Tritons*, have it compressed vertically; thus retaining the fish-like form of the tadpole, and the same radiated disposition of the muscles.

---

human conformation in its organs of progressive motion. This arises from the exertions which it makes in swimming being similar to those of man in walking, in as far as they both result from the strong action of the extensors of the feet. Hence we find a distinct calf in the legs of both, produced by the swelling of similar muscles. The muscles of the thigh present, also, many analogies with those of man; particularly in the presence of the long muscle called the *sartorius*, the use of which is to turn the foot outwards, both in stepping and in swimming.

§ 3. *Ophidia*.

IN the class of serpents we see exemplified the greatest possible state of simplicity to which a vertebrated skeleton can be reduced; for, as may be seen in Fig. 201, which shows the skeleton

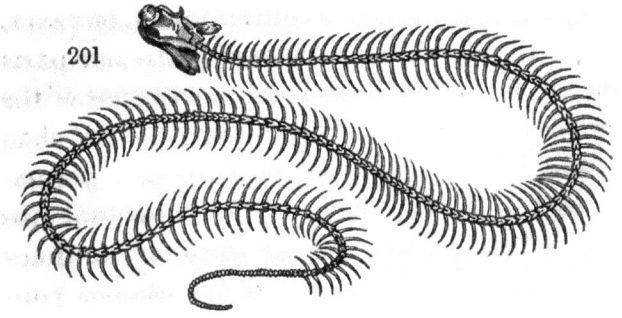

of a viper, it consists merely of a lengthened spinal column, with a head but little developed, and a series of ribs; but apparently destitute of limbs, and of the bones which usually connect those limbs with the trunk; there being neither sternum, nor scapula, nor pelvis.* In the con-

* Professor Mayer has, however, traced obscure rudiments of pelvic bones in the *Anguis fragilis*, the *Anguis ventralis*, and the *Typhlops crocotatus*, and is of opinion that they exist much more generally in this order of reptiles, than has been commonly imagined. Some serpents, as the *Boa*, *Python*, *Tortryx* and *Eryx*, have claws, which may be considered as rudiments of feet, visible externally. In others, as the *Anguis*, *Typhlops*, and *Amphisbœna*, they exist concealed under the skin.

formation of the skull and bones of the face, they present strong analogies with batrachian reptiles, and also with fishes, one tribe of which, namely, the apodous or anguilliform fishes, they greatly resemble by the length and flexibility of the spine. These peculiarities of conformation may be in a great measure traced to the mode of life for which they are destined.

In others, he has discovered cartilaginous filaments, which he conceives to correspond to these parts. (Annales des Sciences Naturelles, VII. 170.) Some of these are represented in the following figures. Fig. 203 exhibits the claw of the *Boa con-*

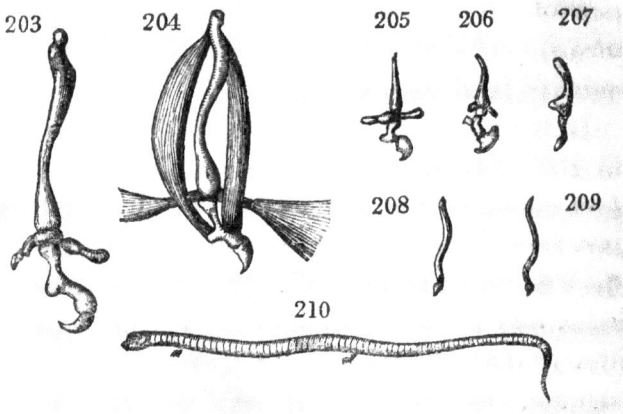

strictor, placed at the termination of a series of bones, representing very imperfectly the bones of the lower extremities. Fig. 204 shows the muscles attached to these small bones. The three following figures, 205, 206, and 207, represent the claws and rudimental bones of the *Tortrix scytale, Tortrix corallinus*, and *Anguis fragilis*, respectively. Those of the *Amphisbœna alba*, Fig. 208, and the *Coluber pullatus*, Fig. 209, are still less developed. The *Chalcides*, or snake lizard, which has four minute feet, is represented in Fig. 210.

The food assigned to them is living prey, which they must attack and vanquish before they can convert it into nourishment. The usual mode in which the boa seizes and destroys its victims is by coiling the hinder part of its body round the trunk or branch of a tree, keeping the head and anterior half of the body disengaged; and then, by a sudden spring, fastening upon the defenceless object of its attack, and twining round its body, so as to compress its chest, and put a stop to its respiration. Venomous serpents, on the other hand, coil themselves into the smallest possible space, and suddenly darting upon the unsuspecting or fascinated straggler, inflict the quickly fatal wound.*

It is evident, from these considerations, that, in the absence of all external instruments of prehension and of progressive motion, it is necessary that the spine should be rendered extremely flexible, so as to adapt itself to a great variety of movements. This extraordinary flexibility is given, first, by the subdivision of the spinal column into a great number of small pieces; secondly, by the great freedom of their articulations; and thirdly, by the peculiar mobility and connexions of the ribs.

* Their prey is swallowed entire; and therefore, as we shall afterwards find, the bones of the jaws and face are formed to admit of great expansion, and of great freedom of motion upon one another.

Numerous as are the vertebræ of the eel, the spine of which consists of above a hundred, that of serpents is in general formed of a still greater number. In the rattle-snake *(Crotalus horridus)* there are about two hundred; and above three hundred have been counted in the spine of the *Coluber natrix*. These vertebræ are all united by ball and socket joints, as in the adult batrachia; the posterior rounded eminence of each vertebra being received into the anterior surface of the next. Fig. 202 is a view of this portion of the skeleton in the *Boa constrictor*, showing the articulation of the ribs with the vertebræ.

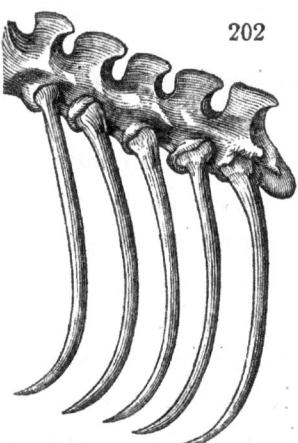

While provision has thus been made for extent of motion, extraordinary care has at the same time been bestowed upon the security of the joints. Thus we find them effectually protected from dislocation by the locking in, above and below, of the articular processes, and by the close investment of the capsular ligaments. The direction of the surfaces of these processes, and the shape and length of the spinous processes, are such as to allow of free lateral flexion, but to limit the vertical and longitudinal motions: and whatever degree of freedom of motion may exist between the adjoining vertebræ, that motion being multiplied along the column, the flexibility of the whole becomes very great, and admits of its assuming every degree and variety of curvature. The presence of a sternum, restraining the motions of the ribs, would have impeded all these movements, and would have also been an insurmountable bar to the dilatation of the stomach, which is rendered necessary by the habit of the serpent of gorging its prey entire.

The mode in which the boa exerts a powerful pressure on the bodies of the animals it has seized, and which it has encircled within its folds, required the ribs to be moveable laterally, as well as backwards, in order to elude the force thus exerted. The broad convex surfaces on which they play give them, in this respect, an advantage which the ordinary mode of articulation would not have afforded. The spinous processes in this tribe of serpents are short and widely separated, so as to allow of flexion in every direction. In the rattle-snake, on the other hand, their length and oblique position are such as to limit the upward bending of the spinal column, although, in other respects, its motion is not restricted. The vertebræ at the end of the tail are furnished with broad transverse processes for the attachment of the first joints of the rattle.

But of whatever variety of flexions we may

suppose the lengthened body of a serpent to be capable, it will, at first view, be difficult to conceive how these simple actions can be rendered subservient to the purposes of progression on land: and yet experience teaches us that few animals advance with more celerity on the surface of the ground, or dart upon their prey with greater promptitude and precision. They raise themselves without difficulty to the tops of the highest trees, and escape to their hiding places with a quickness which eludes observation and baffles the efforts of their pursuers.

The solution of this enigma is to be sought for partly in the structure of the skin, which, in almost every species, is covered with numerous scales: and partly in the peculiar conformation of the ribs. The edges of the scales form rough projections, which are directed backwards, so as to catch the surfaces of the bodies to which they are applied, and to prevent any retrograde motion. In some species, the integument is formed into annular plates, reminding us of the structures so prevalent among worms and myriapode animals. Each scale is connected with a particular set of muscular fibres, capable of raising or depressing it, so that in this way it is converted into a kind of toe; and thus the body rests upon the ground by numerous fixed points of support.

This support is further strengthened by the

connexion of the ribs with the abdominal *scuta*, or the scales on the under side of the body. The mode in which the ribs become auxiliary instruments of progressive motion was first noticed by Sir Joseph Banks.* Whilst he was watching the movements of a *Coluber* of unusual size which was exhibited in London, and was moving briskly along the carpet, he thought he saw the ribs come forward in succession, like the feet of a caterpillar. Sir Everard Home, to whom Sir Joseph Banks pointed out this circumstance, verified the fact by applying his hand below the serpent, and he then distinctly felt the ends of the ribs moving upon the palm, as the animal passed over it. The mode in which the ribs are articulated with the spine is peculiar, and has evidently been employed with reference to this particular function of the ribs, which here stand in place of the anterior and posterior extremities, possessed by most vertebrated animals, and characterising the type of their osseous fabric. In the ordinary structure, the head of each rib has a convex surface, that plays either on the body of a single vertebra with which it is connected, or upon the two bodies of adjacent vertebræ : but in serpents the extremity of the head of the rib has two slightly concave articular surfaces, which play on a

* Philos. Trans. for 1812, p. 163.

convex protuberance of the vertebra. This structure is attended with the advantage of preventing the ribs from interfering with the motions of the vertebræ upon one another. At their lower ends the ribs of one side have no connexion with those of the other, nor are they joined to any bone analogous to a sternum: for, except in the *Ophiosaurus* and the Blindworm *(Auguis fragilis)*, there is no vestige either of a sternum or scapula, in any animal of this class. Each rib terminates in a slender cartilage, tapering to a point, which rests, for its whole length, upon the upper surface of one of the *scuta*, or broad scales on the lower side of the body. These scuta, which are thus connected with the ends of the ribs, and which are moved by means of short muscles, may be compared to hoofs, while the ribs themselves may be considered as performing the office of legs. The ribs move in pairs; and the scutum under each pair, being carried along with it in all its motions, and laying hold of the ground by its projecting edge, becomes a fixed point for the advance of the body. This motion, Sir E. Home observes, is beautifully seen when a snake is climbing over an angle to get upon a flat surface. When the animal is moving on a plane, it alters its shape from a circular or oval form, to one that approaches to a triangle, of which the surface applied to the ground forms the base. Five sets of muscles are provided for the purpose of giving to the ribs the motions backwards and forwards, by which, as levers, they effect this species of progression. These muscles are disposed in regular layers; some passing over one or two ribs to be attached to the succeeding rib. In all snakes the ribs are continued backwards much beyond the region occupied by the lungs; and although the anterior set are subservient to respiration, as well as to progressive motion, it is evident that all those posterior to the lungs must be employed solely for the latter of these purposes.

It is easy to understand how the serpent can slowly advance, by this creeping, or vermicular motion, consisting in reality of a succession of very short steps. But its progress is accelerated by the curvatures into which it throws its body; the fore part being fixed, and the hind part brought near to it; then, by a reverse process, the hind part is fixed, and the head projected forwards. By an alternation of these movements, assisted by the actions of the ribs, the serpent is enabled to glide onwards with considerable rapidity, and without attracting observation. But where greater expedition is necessary, they employ a more hurried kind of pace, although one which exposes them more to immediate view. The body, instead of being bent from side to side, is raised in one great arch, of which the two extremities alone touch the ground; and these being alternately employed as points of support, are made successively to approach and to separate from each other, the body being propelled by bringing it from a curved to a straight line.

There is yet a third kind of motion, which serpents occasionally resort to, when springing upon their prey, or when desirous of making a sudden escape from danger. They coil themselves into a spiral, by contracting all the muscles on one side of the body, and then, suddenly throwing into violent action all the muscles on the opposite side, the whole body is propelled, as if by the release and unwinding of a powerful spring, with an impulse which raises it to some height from the ground, and projects it to a considerable distance.

Thus these animals, to which Nature has denied all external members, are yet capable, by the substitution of a different kind of mechanism, still constructed from the elements belonging to the primitive type of vertebrated animals, of silently gliding along the surface of the earth, of creeping up trees, of striding rapidly across the plain, and of executing leaps with a vigour and agility which astonish the beholder, and which, in ages of ignorance and superstition, were easily ascribed to supernatural agency.

§ 4. *Sauria*.

THE conformation of those parts of the frame which are subservient to progressive motion becomes more perfect in the class of Saurian reptiles, which includes all the Lizard tribes. Several links of connexion with the preceding class may still be noticed, marking the progress of developement, as we follow the ascending series of animals. Rudiments of the bones of the extremities, and also of the sternum make their appearance very visibly in the *Ophiosaurus*, and in the blind worm *(Anguis fragilis)*. The *Siren lacertina* has two diminutive fore feet, placed close to the head. The *Lacerta lumbricoides* of Linneus, or the *Bipes canaliculatus* of Lacepede, which is found in Mexico, and of which a specimen is preserved in the collection at Paris, has a pair of very short feet, also placed near the head, and divided into four toes, with the rudiment of a fifth. The *Lacerta bipes* (Linn), or *Sheltopusic* of Pallas, has, on the other hand, a pair of hind feet only, but extremely small, together with rudiments of a scapula and clavicle concealed under the skin. Next in order must be placed the *Chalcides*, or Snake-lizard (Fig. 210), and the *Lacerta seps*, animals frequently met with in the South of France, and which have four minute feet, totally inefficient for the support of the body, and only remotely useful in contributing to its progressive undulations.

Ascending from these, we may form a series of reptiles, in which the developement of the limbs becomes more and more extended, till we arrive at Crocodiles, in which they attain a considerable degree of perfection. As a consequence of this greater developement of the skeleton, we find the trunk divisible into separate regions. We now, for the first time, meet with a distinct neck, separating the head from the thorax, which is itself distinguishable from the abdomen; and a distinct sacrum is interposed between the lumbar and the caudal vertebræ.

A further approach to the higher classes, is observable in the number of cervical vertebræ, which is almost constantly seven; as we shall find it to be in the mammalia. The articulations of the vertebræ are similar to those of serpents, inasmuch as they consist of ball and socket joints. In that of the occipital bone with the first vertebra of the neck, we find that nature again reverts to the simpler form of a single condyle projecting from the body of the occipital bone, instead of lateral condyles proceeding from its leaves, as we noticed was the structure in the batrachia. The caudal vertebræ are always numerous, and the tail is compressed vertically, which is the form most favourable for progression in water. They are remarkable also for having inferior spinous processes attached to the bodies by cartilages; a structure analogous to that which we have seen in fishes.

The number of ribs differs in different species of Sauria: they are always articulated to the extremities of the transverse processes of the vertebræ, of which they appear to be continuations. Processes of this description also occur in the neck, attached to the transverse processes of the cervical vertebræ; and these have been regarded as *cervical ribs*. Their presence are impediments to the flexions of the neck; whence arises the difficulty which the crocodile appears to have in bending the neck while turning round upon the animal he is pursuing. In the thorax, the ribs are connected with a broad sternum; but there are other ribs, both before and behind, which have no such termination, and therefore bear the name of *false ribs*.

The pelvis consists chiefly of the iliac bones, which, as in the batrachia, pass backwards to form the articular cavity for the thigh bone. Two small and slender bones extend forwards from the pubic bones, on the under side of the body, apparently for the purpose of supporting the abdominal viscera.* The bones of the extremities are very perfectly formed, approaching in their shape and arrangement very nearly to the corresponding parts of the skeleton of the higher orders of quadrupeds. The toes are usually provided with membranes spread between them, to assist in swimming. The form of the tail, which is generally compressed vertically, like that of fishes, though perhaps not to an equal degree, is another indication of their being formed for an aquatic life: for where the tail has this shape, we always find that the chief muscular power is bestowed upon it as an instrument of aquatic progression, producing, by its lateral flexions, a horizontal movement of the body. Crocodiles and alligators, for instance, which have this conformation, are comparatively weak when on land, and as soon as they have seized their prey, their efforts are always directed to drag it with them into the water; knowing that when in their own element they can readily master its struggles, and dispose of it as they please.

In the *Gecko* tribe, we find a particular mechanism provided for effecting the adhesion of the feet to the objects to which they are applied.

* They appear to be analogous to the marsupial bones peculiar to a family of mammalia.

FEET OF THE GECKO.

It is somewhat analogous to that employed in the case of the house-fly, already mentioned. Each foot has five toes; all, except the thumb, terminated by a sharp curved claw. On the under surface of each toe (represented in Fig. 211) there are as many as sixteen transverse slits, leading to the same number of cavities, or sacs; these open forwards, and their external edge is serrated appearing like the teeth of a small-toothed comb. A section of the foot, showing these cavities, is seen in Fig. 212. All these parts, together with the cavities, are covered or lined with cuticle. Below them are large muscles which draw down the claw; and from the tendons of these muscles arise two sets of smaller muscles, situated so as to be put upon the stretch, when the former are in action. By the contractions of these muscles, the orifices of the cavities, or sacs, to which they belong, are opened, and the serrated edges applied accurately to the surfaces with which the feet are in contact. Sir Everard Home, in his account of this structure, compares it to the sucking disk

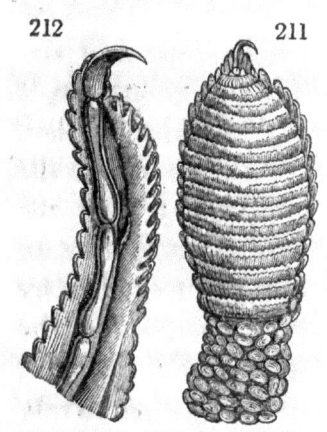

of the *Remora*.* By its means the animal is enabled to walk securely upon the smoothest surfaces, even in opposition to the tendency of gravity. It can run very quickly along the walls or ceiling of a building, in situations where it cannot be supported by the feet, but must depend altogether upon the suspension derived from a succession of rapid and momentary adhesions.

Although the Sauria are better formed for progressive motion than any of the other orders of reptiles, yet the greater shortness and oblique position of their limbs, compared with those of mammiferous quadrupeds, obliges them in general to rest the weight of the trunk of the body on the ground, when they are not actually moving. None of these reptiles have any other kind of pace than that of walking, or jumping; being incapable of performing either a trot or a gallop, in consequence of the obliquity of the plane in which their limbs move. The *Chamelion* walks with great slowness and apparent difficulty; and we have seen that, in consequence of the structure of the bones of its neck, the *Crocodile*, though capable of swift motion in a straight line, is unable to turn itself round quickly. The general type of these reptiles, having reference to an amphibious life, has

---

* Philosophical Transactions for 1816, p. 151, and 323.

not attained that exclusive adaptation to a terrestrial existence, which we find in the higher orders of the Mammalia. But before proceeding to consider these, we have to notice a singular group of animals, whose conformation appears to be exceedingly anomalous, and as if it interrupted the regularity of the ascending series, of which it seems to be a collateral ramification.

§ 5. *Chelonia.*

THE order of *Chelonian Reptiles*, which comprises all the tribes of *Tortoises* and *Turtles*, appears to constitute an exception to the general laws of conformation, which prevail among Vertebrated Animals: for instead of presenting a skeleton wholly internal, the trunk of the body is found to be enclosed on every side in a bony case, which leaves openings only for the head, the tail, and the fore and hind extremities. That portion of this osseous expansion which covers the back is termed the *Carapace;* and the flat plate which defends the lower part of the body is termed the *plastron.* It is a form of structure that reminds us of the defence provided for animals very low in the scale of organization, such as the echinus, the crustacea, and the bivalve mollusca. Yet the substance which forms these strong bucklers, both above and below, is a real osseous structure, developed in the same manner as other bones, subject to all the changes, and having all the properties of these structures. The great purpose which nature seems to have had in view in the formation of the Chelonia is security; and for the attainment of this object she has constructed a vaulted and impenetrable roof, capable of resisting enormous pressures from without, and proof against any ordinary measures of assault. It is to the animal a strong castle, into which he can retire on the least alarm, and defy the efforts of his enemies to dislodge or annoy him.

These considerations supply us with a key to many of those apparent anomalies, which cannot fail to strike us in viewing the dispositions of the parts of the skeleton (Fig. 213), and the remarkable inversion they appear to have undergone, when compared with the usual arrangement. We find, however, on a more attentive examination, that all the bones composing the skeleton in other vertebrated animals exist also in the tortoise; and that the bony case which envelopes all the other parts is really formed by an extension of the spinous processes of the vertebræ and ribs on the one side, and of the usual pieces which compose the sternum on the other. The upper and lower plates thus formed are united at their edges by expansions of the sterno-costal appendices, which become ossified. Thus no new element has been created; but advantage has been taken of those already existing in the general type of the vertebrata, to modify their

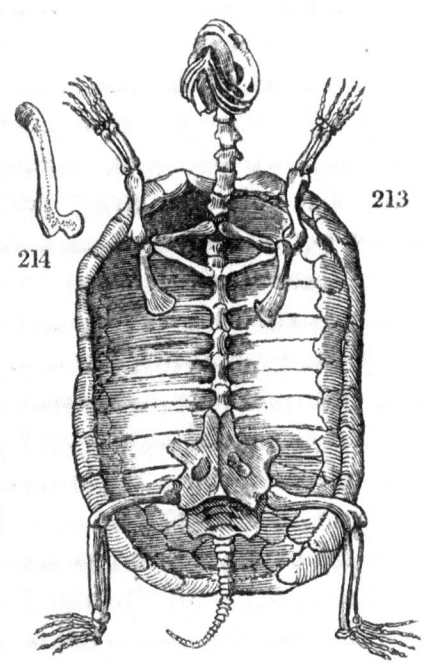

forms, by giving them different degrees of relative developement, and converting them, by these transformations, into a mechanism of a very different kind, and subservient to other objects than those to which they are usually applied. It is scarcely possible to have stronger proofs, if such were wanting, of the unity of plan which has regulated the formation of all animal structures, than those afforded by the skeleton of the tortoise.

The first step taken to secure the relative immobility of the trunk, is to unite in one rigid bony column all its vertebræ, and to allow of motion only in those of the neck, and of the tail. The former, accordingly, are all anchylosed together, leaving, indeed, traces of their original forms as separate vertebræ, but exhibiting no sutures at the place of junction. The canal for the spinal marrow is preserved, as usual, above the bodies of these coalesced vertebræ, and is formed by their united leaves; the arches being completed by the spinous processes. But these processes do not terminate in a crest as usual; they are further expanded in a lateral direction, forming flat pieces along the back, which are united to one another by sutures, and which are also joined to the expanded ribs, so as to form the continuous plane surface of the carapace. The transverse processes of the vertebræ are well marked, but, though firmly united to the ribs, do not give rise to them; for the ribs, which are flattened and expanded, so as to touch one another along their whole length, are inserted below, between the bodies of every two adjoining vertebræ; while above, they are united by suture with the plates of the spinous processes. This change in the situation of the ribs is the consequence of the change in their office. When designed to be very moveable, we find them attached either to the extremities of the transverse processes, or to the articular surfaces of a single vertebra; but where solidity and security are aimed at, they are always inserted between the bodies of two vertebræ. This we shall find to be the case also in birds, where the bones of the thorax are required to be immovable. It is remarkable, indeed, that a great number of the peculiarities which distinguish the conformation of the chelonia from that of other reptiles, indicate an approach to the structure of birds; as if nature had intended this small group of animals to be an intermediate link of gradation to that new and important type of animals destined for a very different mode of existence.

The sterno-costal appendages, which connect the ribs to the sternum, are, in most animals, cartilaginous; though occasionally we find them partially ossified. In the tortoise, however, their ossification is not only complete, but has been expanded laterally, so as to form a continuous surface with the extremities of the ribs and with the edges of the plastron, and completely to fill up the vacancy between them; constituting a dense and solid wall, which entirely closes the sides of the general bony case. So strong is the tendency to ossification in all these pieces, that the sutures at first formed between them are often, in process of time, obliterated; and the bony fibres are continuous throughout a great extent of surface.

The most remarkable metamorphosis in the osseous system of this new type is that which occurs in the sternum. So expanded are all its parts, that it is difficult to recognise this bone under the disguised form in which it constitutes the plastron, or broad plate, which, as we have seen, covers the whole of the under side of the body. Yet, by a careful examination of its structure, both in the young animal, and also in the adult, when the sutures are not obliterated, we may easily recognise the nine elements of the sternum; namely, the one in the middle and fore part, and the four pair of lateral pieces; each having been formed from its respective centre of ossification. In form and relative proportion, indeed, they are widely different from the same parts as they are presented in the skeletons of other animals: yet in number and in relative situations they preserve that constancy and uniformity so characteristic of the beautiful harmony which pervades all animal structures.

It is to be noticed, also, that as the plates, which form this investing case, are bony structures, they could not with any safety have been exposed to the action of the atmosphere. Hence we find them covered throughout with a thin horny plate, originally a production of the integument. It is this substance which is commonly known by the name of *tortoise shell.**

The immobility of the trunk is compensated, as far as regards the safety of the head, by the great flexibility of the neck ; which is composed of seven vertebræ, unencumbered by processes, and capable of taking a double curvature like the letter S, when the head is to be retracted within the carapace. These vertebræ are joined by the ball and socket articulation common to all the *existing* species of reptiles.† The articulation of the head with the neck is effected in the same manner ; but it is interesting to remark that the occipital condyle, which is situated at the lower margin of the great aperture, though presenting a single convex surface, yet has that

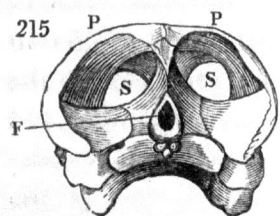

surface evidently divided into three parts; the two upper portions being lateral, and the lower portion in the middle. These three articular surfaces are seen immediately below the central aperture, F, in Fig.

* It should be observed, that the divisions of these plates, which appear externally, bear no relation to the sutures which separate the subjacent bones, so that it is not possible to draw inferences respecting the form of the latter from the mere inspection of the external shell.

† The expression of this fact is thus qualified, because it does not apply to many fossil or extinct species, such as the *Ichthyosaurus*.

215, which exhibits the skull of the *Testudo mydas,* viewed from behind. Although closely approximated, a faint line of demarcation, which divides their surface, indicates an incipient tendency to separate; we shall find that in the further steps of developement which occur in the higher classes, this separation actually takes place by the obliteration of the lower articular surface, and the transfer of the two lateral surfaces to the condyloid processes arising from the developement of the leaves of the occipital bone.

The singular conformation of the bones of the head in the turtle affords fresh evidence in support of the theory that these bones were originally vertebræ. The brain of the tortoise is exceedingly small; and yet the skull, when viewed from above, presents an appearance of great breadth, as if it enclosed a cavity of large dimensions. But if we look upon it from behind, as is shown in Fig. 215, we soon discover that the real cavity in which the brain is lodged, and to which the aperture at F leads, is very small, only just admitting the end of the finger, and that the broad plates of bone, P, P, which form the upper surface of the skull, have no relation to this cavity, and are merely extended over the temporal muscles, which are of very large size, occupying the whole of the spaces, s, s; which spaces are completely surrounded by these bones. It would appear that the same tendency to lateral expansion, which exists in the spinous processes of the dorsal vertebræ, prevails also among those which contribute to form the skull. The parietal bones, which represent the spinous processes of the second cranial vertebra, after having performed their primary office of protecting the hemispheres of the brain by closing over them, still proceed in their developement, forming first a crest on the upper part of the real cranium, and then separating to the right and left, and expanding horizontally into the upper roof (P, P) already mentioned, for the protection of the temporal muscles. This great breadth of the head in the turtle gives the animal an aspect of superior intelligence, to which character, from the really diminutive size of its brain, it is in no respect entitled. As the turtle is unable to withdraw its head within the carapace, such extraordinary protection appears to have been necessary: for it is not met with in the tortoise, which has a carapace sufficiently capacious to give shelter to the head whenever occasion may require.*

This arrangement of the expanded spinous processes and ribs gives rise to a singular inversion in the position of the scapula; for it is here

* The analogy of the spine of the occipital bone with that of a vertebra is further shown by this bone extending backwards to a considerable length, exactly in the manner of the spinous processes of the cervical vertebræ in other animals.

placed on the inside of the ribs and sternum, that is, between the carapace and plastron.* The humerus is remarkably curved, especially in the tortoise, where it has the form nearly of a semi-circle. The radius and ulna are distinct from each other; the carpus and phalanges are short and stunted, forming a compressed kind of hand.

The pelvis, like the scapula and clavicle, is enclosed within the bony shell which protects the trunk. The sacrum is moveable upon the last dorsal vertebra; and the coccygeal vertebræ are continued from it, forming a short tail. The femur is short and powerful, and somewhat bent, but less so than the humerus; and the rest of the bones of the hind extremity are similar to those of the fore leg.† All the feet are joined obliquely to the limbs which support them, giving the animal an apparent awkwardness of gait, as if it were obliged to walk upon club

---

* The anomalous situation of these bones, and the strangely disguised forms which their several parts assume, render it very difficult to recognise in the skeleton the several pieces which correspond to the normal type of the scapula, acromion, coracoid bone, and clavicle; and anatomists are not yet agreed as to the proper designations which are applicable to these bones in the Chelonia.

† The cylindrical bones of the tortoise are solid throughout, and have no cavity for containing marrow, as in the more highly developed bones of the mammalia. This is seen in the section of the femur, Fig. 214.

feet. The impulse which they give being lateral and oblique renders them more efficacious for progression in the water than on land: this circumstance, in conjunction with the constitutional torpor of the animal, sufficiently accounts for the excessive, and indeed proverbial tardiness of its movements.

Security appears still to be the object aimed at in the mechanism of all the other parts of the skeleton. The articulations at the shoulders and the hips are such as facilitate the complete retraction of the limbs within the carapace. After the head has been drawn in by the double, or serpentine flexion of the neck, the knees are brought together, and the whole limb withdrawn within the shell, the fore legs folding completely over the head, so as to cover and protect it most effectually. For this purpose, the carpus and metacarpus are exceedingly flattened, and approximate to the fin-like form which we shall presently see exemplified in the cetaceous tribes. The phalanges are also large and lengthened, forming a kind of oval hand, or rather paddle, the functions of which it is well calculated to perform. The curvature of the humerus is of great advantage to the tortoise in assisting it to turn itself, when, by any accident, it has been laid on its back.

Considerable differences may be noticed in the structure of the several species of Chelonia, according to the diversity of their habits. Tortoises which live on land, require more complete protection by means of their shell than turtles, or *Emydes*, which dwell only in the water: hence the convexity of their carapace, the solidity of its ossification, its immoveable connexion with the plastron, and the complete shelter it affords to the head and limbs. Turtles, on the other hand, receiving support from the element in which they reside, require less provision to be made for these objects. Their carapace is smaller, has a more flattened form, and cannot afford protection to the head and limbs. These latter organs are proportionally larger, present a greater developement of the radius and ulna, and are compressed into a flat expanded surface. Previously to the retraction of the head and limbs within the shell, the air is expelled from the large cavities of the lungs, by the vigorous actions of the abdominal muscles, which exist in these animals as well as in all the vertebrata, although here they are covered by the bones, and compress the lungs by pushing the abdominal viscera against them. This sudden expulsion of air is the cause of the long continued hissing sound which the tortoise emits while preparing to retreat into its strong hold.

The ribs, though they at first assume the form of broad plates immoveably united to the spine, when they have proceeded a certain distance, separate from each other, and resume their usual form; the intervening spaces between two adjacent ribs being here filled up by membrane. The plastron is united with the carapace by membrane likewise; and the sternum, instead of forming one broad plate of bone, has the intervals between its imperfectly developed elements also membranous. All this renders the whole shell less compact, more flexible, and more feeble: but the movements of the animal are quicker and more energetic.

These characteristic differences between the aquatic Chelonia and those that live on land are still more strongly marked in the genus *Trionyx*, or soft tortoise; which is destitute of scales, and in which many of the pieces that are bony in the tortoise are replaced by simple cartilage or membrane.

The enormous weight of the shell of the turtle would be a serious impediment to the motion of this animal in the water, were there not some provision made for diminishing the specific gravity in the body. This purpose is answered by the great capacity of the lungs, which, when inflated with air, nearly fill the thorax, and give great buoyancy to the whole mass. Thus, wherever there exists a supposed inconvenience, dependent on the fulfilment of one condition, we are certain to meet with a compensation in the structure of some other part, and in the mode of executing some other function. An express provision for giving buoyancy has been made in the construction of the shell of a species of tortoise inhabiting the coasts of the Scychelle Islands. The under surface of the shell, instead of being gently concave, as in land tortoises, has a deep circular concavity in the centre, above four inches in depth, which, when the animal goes into the water, retains a large volume of air, buoying up the whole mass while it remains in that element.* The greater size of turtles, when compared with tortoises, is a farther instance of the superior facility with which organic growth proceeds in aquatic than in land animals formed on the same model of construction.

* Home's Lectures, vi. 37.

Chapter IX.

MAMMALIA.

§ 1. *Mammalia in general.*

THE singular animals, so remarkable for their anomalous shapes, their torpid vitality, and their amphibious constitution, which have lately occupied our attention, appear placed by nature as forms of transition, in the passage from those vertebrated animals which dwell in the water, to those which inhabit the land. The class of *Mammifera*, or *Mammalia*, comprehends all the animals which possess a spinal column, breathe air by means of lungs, and are also warm blooded, and viviparous, conditions which render it necessary that they should possess organs, called *mammæ*, endowed with the power of preparing milk for the nourishment of their young; a peculiarity from which the name of the class is derived. But they are not exclusively land animals; for among the mammalia must be ranked several amphibious and aquatic tribes, such as the seal, the walrus, the porpus, the dolphin, the narwal, the cachalot, and the whale; animals which, however widely they may differ in their habits and external conformation from terrestrial quadrupeds, possess, in common with the latter, all the essential characters of internal structure and of functions above enumerated. These characters belong also to the human species, which must consequently, in its zoological relations, be ranked as a genus of the class mammalia. So numerous, indeed, are the analogies which connect the natural families of this class with our own race, that we must ever feel a deep interest in the accurate investigation of their comparative anatomy and physiology; and it has been found, accordingly, that the progress which has, of late years, been made in this branch of science has materially enlarged our knowledge of the structure, the functions, and the physical history of man: subjects with which our welfare has obviously the closest and most intimate relation.

The principle of analogy, which prevails so generally in the inferior departments of the animal creation, may be also traced in the class mammalia; for we always find its influence more conspicuous in proportion as the objects comprehended in the natural series of beings are more numerous and more diversified. Scarcely any of the great natural assemblages of animals exhibit more variety in their habits and modes of existence, than the one we are now examining. Each race has its peculiar destination with regard to the kind of food by which it is nourished, and the means by which that food is obtained. The carnivorous tribes wage war with the larger animals, whom they either spring upon unawares, or openly pursue and overpower, displaying the savage energies of their nature, in practising all the arts of ferocious and sanguinary destruction. Others, intent on meaner prey, resort to divers stratagems for its possession; some are designed to feed chiefly on the mollusca, and others swallow insects only. The numerous tribes which are formed to subsist on vegetable food exhibit, in like manner, a great diversity of constructions, adapted to the particular nature of that subsistence, whether it be herbage, or the leaves of trees, or fruits, or seeds, or the coarse fibres of the wood and bark. While all are gifted with powers to obtain the nourishment they require, those that have not been armed with weapons of attack, are still provided with instruments of defence, or with means of flight. Each has its respective sphere of operation; and to each has its appropriate soil, habitation, climate, and element been assigned.

It is easy to conceive that all these various circumstances must lead to great diversities in the apparatus for mastication and for digestion, in the organization of the senses, in the construction of the instruments of locomotion and of prehension, and in the general form of the body to which these various parts are to be adapted. Yet, amidst all these variations, we may perceive the same laws of analogy connecting the whole into one series, and assimilating all these multiform structures to one common standard. The same organ, however modified in its shape and size, however stinted in one, or developed in another, is ever found in its appropriate place, and retains the same connexions with adjacent organs, whether we seek it in the carnivorous or the herbivorous quadruped, in the inhabitant of the land or of the water, in the denizen of the frigid or of the torrid zone; or in animals of the most diminutive or most colossal statures.

As an example, we may take the vertebræ of the neck. It is a universal law, that this part of the spinal column shall, in every animal of the class mammalia, consist of neither more nor less than seven vertebræ. Whatever be the length or shortness of the neck, whether it be compressed into a small space, as in the elephant and the mole, whether it be lengthened to allow the head to reach the ground, as in the horse and the ox, or whether it be excessively prolonged, to allow the animal to reach the tops of trees, as in the cameleopard, still this same constant number is preserved in the vertebræ which it contains. When the neck is long, each individual vertebra must necessarily be lengthened in the same proportion. Thus in the *Cameleopard*, the vertebræ of the neck consist of seven very long tubes, joined together endwise, with scarcely any developement of spinous processes, lest they should impede the bending of the neck. The greatest contrast to this structure is met with in the *Dolphin*, and other *Cetacea*, which present externally no appearance whatever of a neck, but whose skeleton exhibits cervical vertebræ, closely compressed together, and exceedingly thin, and most of them united together;* every bone, thus formed, however, retains the marks of having originally consisted of separate vertebræ; and still, in this extreme case, the number of primary pieces is constantly seven.†

* In the cachalot, the whole of these seven vertebræ are usually anchylosed into one bone.

† The *Bradypus tridactylus*, or three toed sloth, was, till very lately, thought to constitute a notable exception to this law, being described as having nine, instead of seven, cervical vertebræ. It is now found, however, that the two last of these vertebræ, which appeared to be supernumerary, ought properly to be classed among the dorsal vertebræ, of which they possess the distinctive characters, not only from the form and size of their transverse processes, but also from their having small bony appendices, articulated with them by a regular joint at their extremities, and corresponding exactly, both in shape and situation, to the ribs, of which they may, in fact, be considered as

§ 2. *Cetacea.*

REMARKABLE exemplifications of the law of uniformity of organic structure are furnished by the family of the *Cetacea*, which includes the whale, the cachalot, the dolphin, and the porpus, and exhibits the most elementary forms of the type of the mammalia, of which they represent the early, or rudimental stage of developement. Here, as before, we have to seek these first elements among the inhabitants of the water: for whenever, in our progress through the animal kingdom, we enter upon a new division, aquatic tribes are always found to compose the lowest links of the ascending chain. Here, also, we observe organic developement proceeding with more rapidity, and raising structures of greater dimensions in aquatic than in terrestrial animals. The order Cetacea comprises by far the largest

rudiments. These small bones have been observed, both by Meckel and by Cuvier, attached to the ninth vertebra: and Mr. T. Bell has recently not only confirmed the observations of these anatomists, but has farther discovered, that similar rudimental ribs are attached also to the eighth vertebra. (See Philosophical Magazine, third series, iii. 376). The *Bradypus torquatus*, which has been said to possess eight cervical vertebræ, will, perhaps, on closer examination, be hereafter found not to deviate, any more than the three-toed sloth, from the normal type, as regards the number of these vertebræ. Instances have occurred of supernumerary cervical processes, or ribs in the human skeleton. (See Edinburgh Medical and Surgical Journal, xl. 304.)

animals which inhabit the globe. Whatever may have been the magnitude of those huge monsters which once moved in the bosom of the primeval ocean, or stalked with gigantic strides across antediluvian plains, and whose scattered remains bear fearful testimony of the convulsions of a former world, certain it is that, at the present day, the whales of the northern seas are the most colossal of the living animal structures existing on the surface of this planet.

A cursory survey of the organization of the tribes belonging to this semi-amphibious family, will impress us with the resemblance they bear to fishes; for they present the same oval outline of the body, the same compact form of the trunk, which is united with the head without an intervening neck; the same fin-like shape of the external instruments of motion, and the same enormous expansion and prolongation of the tail, which is here also, as in fishes, the chief agent in progression. With all this agreement in external characters, their internal economy is conducted upon a totally different plan; for although constantly inhabiting the ocean, their vital organs are so constructed as to admit of their breathing only the air of the atmosphere, and the consequences which flow from this difference are of great importance. The necessity of aerial respiration compels them to rise, at short intervals, to the surface of the water; and this air, with which they fill their lungs in respiration, gives their bodies the buoyant force that is required to facilitate their ascent, and supersedes the necessity of a swimming bladder, an organ which is so useful to the fish.

With the intent of diminishing still farther their specific gravity, nature has provided that a large quantity of oily fluid shall be collected under the skin, a provision which answers also the purpose of preserving the vital warmth of the body. A great accumulation of this lighter substance is formed on the upper part of the head, apparently with a view to facilitate the elevation to the surface of the blowing hole, or orifice of the nostrils, which is placed there.*

Another peculiarity of conformation, in which the cetacea differ from fishes, and which has also an obvious relation to their peculiar mode of breathing, is in the form of the tail, which, instead of being compressed laterally, and inflected from side to side, as in fishes, is flattened horizontally, and strikes the water in a vertical direction, thereby giving the body a powerful impulsion, either towards the surface, when the animal is constrained to rise, or downwards, when, by diving, it hastens to escape from danger.

All the essential and permanent parts of the skeleton of vertebrated animals, that is, the spinal column, and its immediate dependencies, the

* The substance called *Spermaceti* is lodged in cells, formed of a cartilaginous substance, situated on the upper part of the head of the *Cachalot*.

skull, the caudal prolongation, and the ribs, are found in that of the Cetacea. The thorax is carried very much forwards, especially in the whale, and the neck is so short as to be scarcely recognisable : for the object of the conformation is here, as in that of the fish, to allow free scope for the movements of the tail, and ample space for the lodgement of its muscles. For the purpose of giving greater power and more extensive attachment to these muscles, the transverse processes of the dorsal and lumbar vertebræ are expanded both in length and breadth, and being situated horizontally, offer no impediment to the vertical flexure of the spine. For the same reason the ribs are continued in a line with the transverse processes, and articulated with their extremities, thus giving still farther breadth to the trunk.

As there is a total absence of hinder extremities, so there is no enlargement of any of the vertebræ corresponding to a sacrum, and the caudal vertebræ are uninterrupted continuations of those of the trunk. They develope, however, parts which are met with only among fishes and reptiles, namely, arches composed of inferior leaves* and spinous processes, enclosing and giving protection to a large artery. Although the bones of the legs do not exist,

* These leaves being formed of cartilage, are generally lost when the bones are macerated for the purpose of preparing the skeleton.

yet there are found, in the hinder and lower part of the trunk, concealed in the flesh, and quite detached from the spine, two small bones, apparently corresponding to pelvic bones, for the presence of which no more probable reason can be assigned than the tendency to preserve an analogy with the more developed structures of the same type.

A similar adherence to the law of uniformity in the plan of construction of all the animals belonging to the same class, is strikingly shown in the conformation of the bones of the anterior extremities of the cetacea; for although they present, externally, no resemblance to the leg and foot of a quadruped, being fashioned into fin-like members, with a flat oval surface for striking the water, yet when the bones are stripped of the thick integument which covers them and conceals their real form, we find them (as may be seen in Fig. 216) exhibiting the same divisions into carpal and metacarpal bones, and phalanges of fingers, as exist in the most highly developed organization, not merely of a quadruped, but also of a monkey, and even of man.

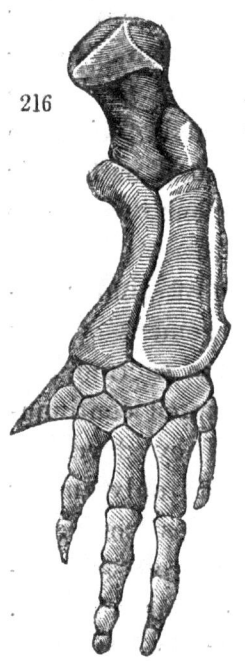

§ 3. *Amphibia.*

In the small tribe denominated by Cuvier *Amphibia*, and consisting of the *Phoca*, or Seal, and the *Trichecus*, or Walrus, we perceive that an advance is made towards a fuller developement of the limbs: these animals having a distinct neck and pelvis, and both hind and fore extremities. In the seal the hind legs are drawn out posteriorly to a considerable length, and placed parallel to each other: when united and alternately raised and depressed, they perform the same office as the tail of the cetacea, and propel the animal forwards: but when employed separately, they are more qualified to act as oars. The walrus has feet still more developed, and distinctly divided into toes, which are disposed so as to strike backwards against the water.

§ 4. *Mammiferous Quadrupeds in general.*

From the imperfectly developed aquatic and amphibious tribes we gradually ascend to the more finished structures of mammiferous quadrupeds, which are expressly fitted for progression on land. In these the powers of developement, not being expended in the mere effort of giving expansion to the several textures, and of swelling the bulk of the frame, sometimes to inordinate dimensions, are employed rather in reducing the elements of the organization into compact forms, and in concentrating their energies, so as ultimately to attain the extent of power and harmony of action, which are displayed in the higher orders of warm-blooded quadrupeds.

It is to these favoured tribes that we must look for examples of the most complete developement of the skeleton, and the most advantageous disposition of mechanic force. We have seen that reptiles, from the comparative shortness of their limbs, and the torpidity of their muscular powers, are but ill adapted for rapid progression. In all the more perfectly formed quadrupeds of the class mammalia, the trunk of the body, being raised high upon the limbs, possesses great range of motion, and can traverse with fewer steps a given space.

The office of the limbs, as far as they are concerned in progressive motion, is two-fold. They have, first, to sustain the weight of the body, which they must do by acting in opposition to the force of gravity; and they must, secondly, give the body an impulse forwards. Let us consider more particularly the relations which the structures bear to each of these two functions.

The limbs of quadrupeds constitute four

columns of support to the trunk, which is placed horizontally above them; but the whole weight of the body, together with that of the head and neck, does not bear equally upon them; the fore extremities almost always sustain the greater part of that weight, both because the fore part of the trunk is itself heavier than the hind part, and because it is loaded with the additional weight of the head and neck. Hence, in the usual attitude of standing, the pieces of which the fore limbs are composed are required to be placed more in a straight line than those of the hinder limb: for the power of a column to support a weight is the greater in proportion as it approaches to the perpendicular position. The hind limbs are composed of exactly the same number of divisions; but the separate portions are usually longer than those of the fore extremity, and consequently if they had been disposed vertically in a straight line, they would have elevated the hinder part of the trunk to too great a height compared with the fore part. This is obviated by their forming alternate angles with one another. As the pelvis connects the spine with the joint of the hip, and even extends farther backwards, the thigh bone must necessarily be brought forwards; then the tibia and fibula, which compose the bones of the leg must be carried backwards to their junction with the bones of the foot; and again the foot must be turned forwards in its whole length from the heel to the extremities of the toes. On comparing the positions of the corresponding divisions of the anterior and posterior extremities, we observe that they incline, when bent, in opposite directions; for in the former we find, in following the series of bones from the spine, that the scapula proceeds forwards, the humerus backwards; the radius and ulna again forwards, and the fore foot backwards, positions which are exactly the reverse of the corresponding bones of the hind limb. (See Fig. 218, page 507.)

The weight of the body, in consequence of this alternate direction of the angles at the successive joints, must always tend, while the quadruped is on its legs, to bend each limb: a tendency which is required to be counteracted by the actions of the muscles which are situated on the external side of each of those angles. These muscles are the *extensors* of the joints; that is, the muscles which tend to bring their parts into a straight line. It is, in fact, by this muscular action, much more than by simple rigidity, that the limb supports the superincumbent weight of the body. It is evident that greater muscular force is necessary for this purpose when the joints are bent, than when they are already extended; and the portions of the fore legs being naturally in this condition, require less power than those of the hinder legs to retain them in their proper relative positions.

The most complete instance of a vertical arrangement of the bones of the extremities is seen in the *Elephant;* where in order to sustain the enormous weight of the body, the limbs are shaped into four massive columns, of which the several bones are disposed nearly in perpendicular lines. By this means the body is supported with scarcely any muscular effort, and the attitude of standing is, in this animal, a state of such complete repose, that it often sleeps in that position. The elephant which was kept some years ago at the Menagerie at Paris, although much enfeebled by a lingering disorder, was never seen to lie down till the day on which he died. When he was in the last stage of debility, what seemed to give him most distress was the effort requisite to support his head: and in order to relieve the muscles of the neck which were strained in that exertion, he was in the habit of extending his trunk perpendicularly to the ground, by contracting all the muscular fibres which run transversely in that organ, and thus formed a vertical prop for the head. But in almost all other quadrupeds the mere act of standing, though a state of comparative rest, implies, for the reasons already given, a degree of muscular exertion, and they can enjoy complete repose only by letting the body recline upon the ground.

The conformation of the hind extremities, which, as we have seen, is not so well calculated for the simple support of the trunk, is, on the other hand, better adapted to give it those impulses which are to effect its progressive movements. The nature of those movements, and the order in which they succeed each other, are different according to the peculiar mode of progression which the animal practises, the degree of speed it is desirous of exerting, and the particular end it has in view. The paces of a quadruped usually distinguished, are the walk, the trot, the gallop, the amble, and the bound.

In slow walking, only one foot is raised from the ground at the same moment, so that three points of support always exist for sustaining the weight of the body. If the centre of gravity be situated, as it generally is, nearly over the middle of the quadrangular base formed by the feet, while they rest upon the ground, the first effect to advance which the quadruped makes, propels the centre of gravity forwards. This it accomplishes by pressing one of its hind legs against the ground; which leg being thus fixed by the resistance it there meets with, becomes the fulcrum of the first movements. The extensor muscles of the limb are now exerted in giving the body an impulse forwards. As soon as this impulse has been given, the muscles which had been in action are relaxed, and the leg is raised from the ground, brought forwards, and laid down close to the fore foot of the same side. This fore foot is next raised and advanced: and then the same succession of actions takes place with the hind and the fore foot of the other side.

An attentive examination of the conditions of these successive positions will show that, amidst all the changes which take place in the points of support, the stability of the body is constantly preserved. It is an elementary proposition in mechanics that all that is necessary for ensuring the support of a body on any given base, is that the vertical line drawn from the centre of gravity shall fall within that base. When the animal is standing, the feet form a quadrilateral base, and the centre of gravity is in a vertical line passing either through the centre of the base, or, as, for the reasons already mentioned, more frequently happens, through a point a little in front of the exact centre. At the time when the hind foot which began the action is raised from the ground, the centre of gravity, having been, by that action, impelled forwards, still remains above the base formed by the other three feet, and which is now reduced to a triangle. That hind foot being set down, while the corresponding fore foot is raised, a new triangular base is formed by the same hind foot, together with the two of the other side, which have not yet been raised. The centre of gravity is still situated above this new triangle, and the body is consequently still supported on these three feet. The fore foot may now be advanced without endangering the stability of the body: and by the time this foot is set down, and has thereby formed a new quadrilateral basis with the other feet, the centre of gravity has arrived above the centre of this new base. But at this moment the centre of gravity is again urged forwards by the other hind foot, which now comes into action, and repeats on the other side the same succession of actions, which are attended with the same consequences as before. Thus, during its whole progress, the animal is never for an instant in danger of falling; for whichever of the feet may be raised from the ground, the other three feet are always so placed as to form a stable base of support.

In quick walking it often happens that quadrupeds raise their fore foot on either side a little before the hind foot comes to the ground. This is shown by the impression made by the latter being in the same spot, or even rather in advance of the impression made by the former. But the time during which the body is thus supported only by two feet is so short as not sensibly to influence the results.

In consequence of the obliquity of the alternate impulses given to the centre of gravity by the successive actions of both the hind legs, a slight degree of undulation is occasioned; but these undulations are only lateral. A trot may be considered as a succession of short leaps made by each set of feet taken diagonally; that is, by the right fore foot, and the left hind foot; or, vice versa, the one set being raised together a short time before the others have reached the ground: so that during that minute interval of time all the feet are in the air at the same moment; and during the remaining portion of the time, the body is resting upon the two feet placed diagonally with regard to each other. The undulations are here chiefly vertical, instead of lateral, as they are in the walking pace.

A gallop is a continued succession of longer leaps made by the two hind feet in conjunction. In this case, the centre of gravity is lifted higher from the ground, and is projected in a wide arch, and with great velocity.

In the amble, both the legs on one side are raised together; so that the impulsions given are directed much more laterally than in any other pace, and the body is thrown into a strong undulatory motion from side to side.

Another kind of pace is the bound, which is often practised by deer, and is performed by striking the ground with all the legs at the same moment. It consists, therefore, like the gallop, of a series of leaps; but their direction is more uniformly upwards, from the concurrence of all the legs in the same action.

Nature has purposely endowed different tribes with very different capacities to execute progressive movements, by the variations she has introduced into the comparative lengths of the several parts of the trunk, and the size and mobility of the extremities. Of all the large animals, the *Lion* has been constructed with the finest proportions for conferring both strength and activity. The mass of his body is supported more by the fore than by the hind extremities. In walking, the lion takes long strides, and exhibits strongly the lateral undulations of the trunk.

Quadrupeds having a very long, or a very massive body, or whose limbs are short, and nearly of equal height, are incapable of advancing by a gallop, or at least cannot sustain this pace without a painful effort, and never but for a short time. The *Tiger*, which has a longer body than the lion, gallops with less facility; and runs chiefly by an acceleration of its walking pace. It excels principally in the vigour and extent of its bounds; for which it is admirably qualified by prodigious power of its muscles, enabling it to spring forwards upon its victim with an impetus which nothing can resist.

The speed with which a quadruped is capable of advancing depends more on the disposition of the muscles and the extent of the articulations, and more especially on the power of the extensors of the hind extremities, than on the form of the body. Great length and muscularity in the hind legs are generally attended with considerable power of leaping. This is exemplified in the *Jerboa* and the *Kanguroo*, animals, which, from the disproportionate shortness of their fore legs, are totally incapacitated from walking; and for the same reason, they cannot run with any degree of swiftness. It is only in climbing up a steep acclivity that the jerboa is enabled to employ all its limbs: in a descent, on the contrary, it uses only its fore legs, the hinder being dragged after them. But, when pursued, these animals are capable, for a long continuance, of taking leaps of nine feet distance, and of repeating these leaps so quickly, that the Cossacks, though mounted on the swiftest horses, are unable to overtake them.

The *Kanguroo*, in almost all his movements, brings into action his powerful tail, which is furnished with very strong muscles, and may be considered as constituting a fifth limb. It is of great assistance to the animal in taking leaps, and during its repose, contributes, together with the hind feet, to support the weight of the body, as on a tripod, and to leave at liberty the fore legs, which may then be employed as arms.

The *Hare* and the *Rabbit* furnish other instances of an extraordinary length of the hinder legs depriving the animal of the power of walking, and obliging it to move forwards only by a succession of leaps. The hare may be said, indeed, to walk with its fore legs only, while it gallops with the hinder: but this disadvantage is amply compensated by its amazing swiftness when running at full speed.

Animals like the hare, in which, from the great length of the hinder limbs, the posterior half of the body is higher than the anterior, run much better up a declivity than on level ground. In a descent, on the contrary, they are obliged to pursue an oblique and zig-zag course, otherwise they would be in danger of oversetting, as happens occasionally to the *Agouti* and the *Guinea pig*, when these animals attempt to run down hill.

The *Sloth*, which is formed for clinging with great tenacity to the boughs of trees, presents a remarkable contrast to the animals we have just noticed; its fore legs being much longer than the hinder, and its movements being proverbially slow. The peculiar modifications of its muscular powers are probably consequences of the singular mode in which, as I shall afterwards have occasion to notice, its arteries are distributed.

The *Cameleopard*, likewise, has the fore legs much longer than the hinder. The object of this conformation was probably to elevate the anterior part of the spine, so as to raise the head as much as possible, and also to give a considerable inclination to the whole column, for the purpose of distributing more equally the weight of the head and of the very long neck upon all the legs; for the length of the neck is fully equal to that of the trunk. It is evident that if the body had been placed in the usual horizontal position, the anterior extremities would have had to support the whole of the enormous weight of this neck and head. This peculiarity of structure, however, introduces considerable modifications in the mode of progression of the animal. The ordinary pace of the cameleopard is the amble; but it has also a slower walking pace, and occasionally a gallop. In the amble, its undulation is so considerable as to give it the appearance of being lame. A similar kind of limping gait, arising from the same cause, namely, the disproportionate elevation of the fore part of the spine, has been observed in the *Hyæna*.

§ 5. *Ruminantia*.

IN following the series of Mammalia in the order which best exhibits their successive stages of developement, I shall commence with those whose digestive apparatus is formed to extract nourishment exclusively from the vegetable kingdom. The first assemblage that presents itself to our notice is the remarkable family of *Ruminants*, which feed principally on herbage. Wherever the earth is cloathed with vegetation, it requires neither skill nor exertion on their part to seek and to devour the rich repast which is profusely spread under their feet. To remove from one pasture to another, to browse, and to repose, constitute the peaceful employments of their lives, and satisfy the chief conditions of their existence. To these purposes the whole conformation of their skeleton, and especially of those parts which constitute the limbs, is adapted. The anterior extremities having only to support the weight of the fore part of the trunk, and to assist in progressive motion, have a less complicated arrangement of joints, and exhibit many of those consolidations of the bones, which tend to simplify the structure, and to contribute to its strength.

But though never incited by the calls of appetite to engage in sanguinary warfare, they are yet liable to the assaults of many ferocious and well armed adversaries, and often unprovided with any adequate means of defence; their only resource, therefore, is to avoid the dangers of the encounter by a rapid and precipitate flight. To confer this power appears to have been the object aimed at by nature in every part of the conformation of these animals. It is among the ruminant tribes that the fleetest of quadrupeds are to be found, such as the gazelle, the antelope, and the deer, animals which exhibit the

RUMINANT QUADRUPEDS. 501

highest perfection of structure belonging to this type. We may observe that the parts composing the hind legs are longer, and inclined to one another at angles more acute in these animals than in other tribes of mammalia, so that they are always ready for instantly commencing their flight, and springing forwards on the slightest notice of danger. (See Fig. 218, page 507).

As it was necessary, from the situation of their food, that their heads should reach the ground in grazing, we find that the neck has been much elongated, that the muscles which raise the head have been enlarged and strengthened, and that the spinous processes of the back and neck have been much expanded in order to allow of sufficient surface for the attachments of these muscles. The effort requisite to raise, and even support the head is very considerable; as will appear when we reflect that its weight acts by means of an extremely long lever; for such is the mechanical office of the elongated neck. But in order to economize the muscular power, an elastic ligament is employed to sustain the weight of the head. This, which is termed the *ligamentum nuchæ*, and is represented at N, in Fig. 217, is formed of a great number of bands which connect the hinder part of the cranium, at the ridge of the occipital bone, and all the spinous processes of the neck, with those of the back, the separate slips from each being successively joined together, and composing a ligament of great length and power. It differs in its structure from ordinary ligaments, being highly elastic, so that it yields to the extension of the neck when the animal lowers its head, and gives considerable assistance to the muscles in raising it. In

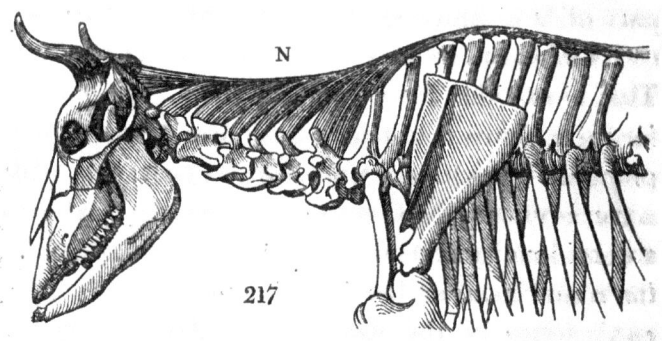

the deer and the ox, which toss their heads with force, and especially in the males, which are armed with antlers or horns, the muscles performing those motions are remarkably strong, and the spinous processes of the back particularly prominent. In the loins, on the contrary, we find the transverse processes more enlarged, for the purpose of giving a powerful mechanical purchase to the muscles which are inserted into them.

The chest of ruminant quadrupeds is compressed laterally in order to allow room for the unrestrained motions of the anterior extremity; and the sternum projects so as to resemble the keel of a ship. The bones of the anterior extremity are not joined to the rest of the skeleton by means of any bone corresponding to a clavicle; but they are connected with the spine and ribs only by ligaments and muscles; so that the fore part of the trunk is in fact suspended between the limbs by its muscular attachments alone. This is not the case with the hind extremities; for their bones commence with the pelvis, which proceeds backwards from the sacrum, but with a considerable inclination downwards, and has a deep hemispherical cavity for the lodgment of the round head of the thigh bone. The lengthened forms of the iliac bones, and also of the scapula, provide for the application of muscles of considerable length, which are consequently capable of communicating to the parts they move a greater velocity than could have been effected by muscles of equal strength, but with shorter fibres.

Both the humerus in front, and the femur behind, are so short as to appear, on a superficial view, to form part of the trunk, being entirely enveloped and concealed by the large muscles connecting them with the body. The heads of the two humeri, in consequence of the absence of the clavicle, are brought very near each other, so as to occupy a situation as nearly as possible underneath the weight which the limb has to support.

The radius and ulna, which are the two bones of the fore arm, although completely separate at an early period of growth, soon unite to form but one bone. This union begins at their lower end, and proceeds upwards to within a short distance from the top, where a separation may still be observed in the processes which project from that end, forming for some way down a distinct suture. This union of the two bones must, of course, preclude all rotatory motion; but it is calculated to give the joint great security: and this appears to have been the main object in the conformation of the whole limb. The same process of consolidation takes place in the hind leg, between the tibia and the fibula, which are so completely united, as to afford scarcely any trace of their having been originally separate.

The carpus and the tarsus are both of very limited extent, and consist of a smaller number of pieces than usually occur in these joints. The consolidation of parts is most conspicuous in the succeeding division of the limb, namely, that constituting the metacarpus in the anterior, and the metatarsus in the hind extremity. In either case we find it consisting, not of five bones, as in the more highly organized carnivorous mammalia, but of a single bone only, termed the *cannon bone*. In the early periods of ossification, however, they each consisted of two slender bones, lying close and parallel to each other; but afterwards united by an ossific deposition, which fills up the interval between them, and leaves behind no trace of suture.* In proportion as the young animal acquires strength, the union of these two bones becomes still more intimate by the absorption of the partition which separated their cavities; so that ultimately they constitute but one cylinder, with a single central cavity, which is occupied by marrow.

The cannon bone is much elongated, both in the fore and hind extremity; so that the carpus and tarsus, which are the commencements of the real feet, are raised considerably above the ground. It is a common mistake, arising from the height of these joints, and the names they bear in ordinary language, to consider them as the knees of the animal. The slightest inspection of the skeleton will be sufficient to show that what is called the knee in the fore leg is properly the wrist; and in the hind leg, the part so misnamed is really the heel. Thus the foot, especially in the posterior extremity, is of great length; a structure which is evidently intended

* The observations which establish this fact are detailed by G. St. Hilaire, in a paper in the "Mémoires du Muséum," x. 173.

to give greater velocity to the actions of the muscles, while it at the same time ensures the utmost steadiness and security of motion.

At the lower extremity of the cannon bone there are two articular surfaces, indicating the originally separate ends of its two component bones. They are for the articulation of the two following bones, which are also very long, and which correspond in situation to the first phalanges of the fingers and toes. These are followed by a second and third set of phalanges; the last of which terminate in hoofs. All ruminant quadrupeds have thus a double hoof; a character which is peculiar to this family.

Thus, then, has Nature moulded the organs of progressive motion in this remarkable tribe of animals to accommodate them to the peculiar conditions of their existence, while she has still preserved their relations to the primitive type of the class to which they belong. Thus has she bestowed upon them the slender and elegant forms, so pleasing to the eye, which characterise the fleetest racer, and has provided for the agile, yet firm and secure movements which they are to exercise in various ways in eluding the observation, and escaping from the pursuit of their stronger and more sagacious foes. This purpose they effect, at one time by rapid flight across extensive tracts of country; at another, by retirement into unfrequented forests, or mountains

RUMINANT QUADRUPEDS. 507

of difficult access, crossing their rugged surfaces in all directions, clambering their precipitous

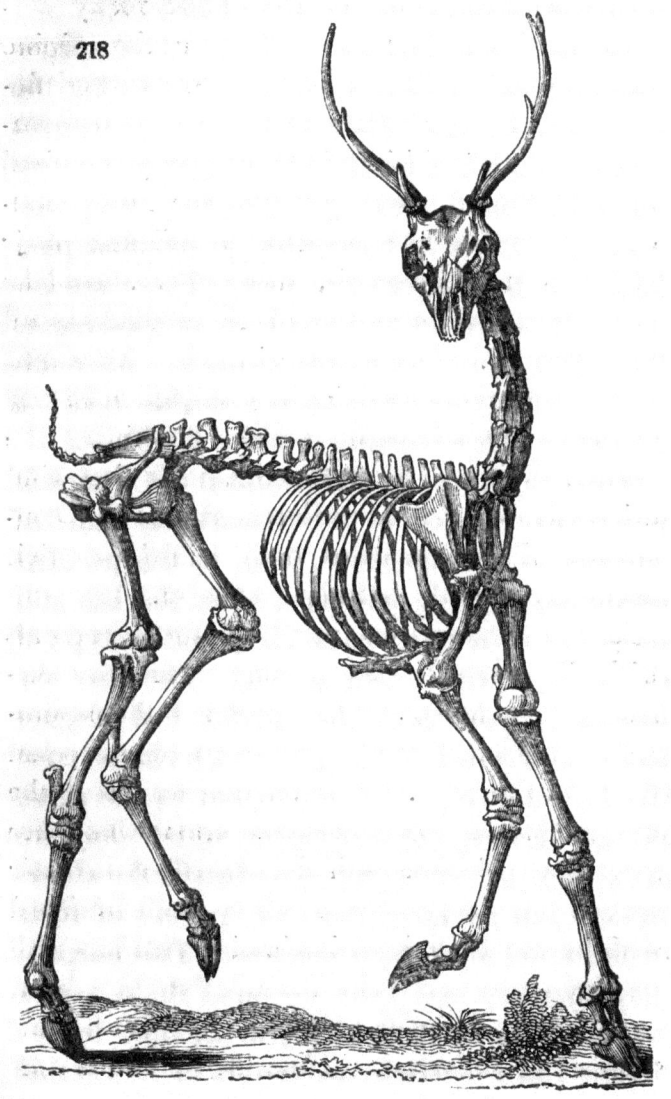

218

acclivities, and fearlessly bounding over intervening abysses, from point to point, till the place of safety is attained on some rocky eminence. From this secure station the Alpine chamois looks down upon its pursuers, and defies their further efforts at capture or molestation. The astonishing feats of agility practised by this animal, and by which the most experienced hunters are perpetually baffled in their attempts to approach it, sufficiently attest the perfection of its organization in reference to all these objects. The chamois has often been seen to leap down a perpendicular precipice of twenty or thirty feet in height, without sustaining the slightest injury. How the ligaments that bind the joints can resist the violent strains and concussions they must be exposed to in these quick and jarring efforts, is truly wonderful.

While Nature has provided these animals with the means of safety from their more formidable enemies, she has not left them altogether without defence against their more equal rivals in the field. It is on the head that she has implanted those powerful arms which are sometimes wielded with deadly effect in their mutual combats. Even when not furnished with horns, the animal instinctively strikes with its forehead, where the frontal bone has been expanded and fortified, apparently with a view to this mode of attack. Thus, the ram butts with its head without reference to the horns, which are coiled so as to be turned away from the object to be struck. In the deer and the ox tribes, however, the horns are formidable weapons of offence: and it will be interesting to inquire into the nature of these organs, and the phenomena of their production.

The antlers of the male stag are osseous structures, supported on short and solid tubercles of the frontal bone: after remaining nearly a year they are cast off, and soon replaced by a newly formed antler, which is of larger size than the one which was lost. Previously to the formation of this structure, those branches of the artery, termed the *carotid*, which supply blood to the frontal bone, are observed very rapidly to dilate, and to throb with unusual force; and all the blood-vessels of the skin of the part where the antler is to arise, soon become distended with blood, an effect which is accompanied by general heat and redness, like a part in a state of high inflammation.* Presently the skin is elevated by the growth of a tubercle from the subjacent bone: this tubercle is at first a cartilage, and after it has attained a certain size, becomes ossified, and grows like other osseous structures, first shooting into the form of a lengthened cylinder, and then dividing into branches.

* These phenomena are connected with periodical changes in the constitution relating to the reproductive functions.

It is followed in its elongation by the skin, which during the whole time that the antler is growing is extended over it in every part, forming what is called, from the delicate investment of hair, its *velvet coat*. The blood-vessels of the proper membrane of the antler, or *periosteum*, still continuing to supply it with the materials required for its growth and consolidation, deposit so great an abundance of bony matter, that its enlargement is exceedingly rapid. The whole antler, which often weighs nearly thirty pounds, has been known to be completely formed in ten weeks from the time of its first appearance. There is no other instance in the animal kingdom of so rapid a growth; which is the more remarkable from its occurring in a small part of the system, and in a bony structure.

After the antler has attained its full size, a deposition of osseous substance still continues at its base, around the trunks of the arteries which are proceeding along the investing membrane of the bone for the purpose of conveying nourishment. The accumulation of this substance raises a ring, called the *burr*, round that part of the antler: and by encroaching on the arteries themselves, it gradually diminishes their capacity of conveying blood, and they at length become entirely obliterated. The bone, no longer receiving a superabundant nourishment, ceases to grow; the integuments which covered it, decay, and becoming dry and shrivelled, are torn by rubbing against trees, and peel off in long shreds, leaving the antler exposed, which, by the continued effects of the same kind of friction, soon acquires a polished surface.

During many months the antler being sufficiently nourished by its own interior vessels, continues in a living state, and preserves its connexion with the system. But at length the arteries, whether from the effect of the progressive deposition of osseous matter, or from some change in the balance of the vital powers, shrink and become by degrees obliterated. The antler dies in consequence, and although it continues to adhere to the skull, it is only as a foreign body, and it is not long destined to remain thus attached; for the absorbent vessels are now actively employed in scooping out a groove of separation between the living and the decayed substance, at the place where the base of the antler is contiguous to the frontal bone. As soon as this has proceeded to a sufficient depth, the adhesion ceases, and the slightest concussion occasions the fall of the whole structure. After the separation of the antler, the eminence of the frontal bone on which it stood is left rough and uneven like that of a fractured part: but the surrounding integuments soon close over, and cover it completely; until the period arrives when it is to be replaced by a new antler, which exhibits the same succession of phenomena in its growth and decay as its predecessor, only that its developement is usually carried farther, the new stem being both thicker and longer, and the branches wider and more numerous. The antler of each successive year has, consequently, a different form from that of the preceding; and when the animal has attained a certain age, the extremities of the branches present broad expansions of bone, which the antlers of an earlier growth had never exhibited.

The short bony processes which extend in a perpendicular direction on the head of the cameleopard, are analogous, in some of the circumstances of their formation, to the antlers of the deer, being of an osseous nature, and continuous with the frontal bone: but in other respects they are very different; for instead of being annually shed, they remain through life, and continue to be covered with the integuments, which retain, at the extremities, a tuft of hair. The developement of these processes in the young animal takes place in the same manner as that of an antler, but it reaches only to a certain point, upon attaining which the growth is arrested, and never proceeds farther. The arteries cease to deposit superabundant nourishment, but continue to maintain an exact equilibrium between the expenditure and the supply; so that the horns of the cameleopard are never shed, and remain permanent bony structures.

A further modification of this process occurs

in the construction of the horns of the ox and of the sheep: for in these the bony processes arising from the frontal bones are invested with a covering composed of horn, the nature of which is totally different from bone. Two tubercles may be seen in the young calf, proceeding from the bones of the forehead: the skin covering these tubercles, unlike that which precedes the antlers of the deer, is unusually thick and hard. As the skull expands, this portion of integument becomes more and more callous, till it is converted, by the action of the subjacent vessels, into a solid, hard, elastic, and insensible fibrous substance, fitted to give effectual protection to the subjacent bony layers which are forming underneath it. The highly vascular membrane, from which these new structures chiefly arise, appears to have different powers of production at its two surfaces: for while the inner surface is forming the osseous portion of the horn, and supplying the phosphate of lime required for the construction of its plates and fibres, the exterior surface is adding successive layers of horny substance to the inner side of those portions which had been before deposited. These two operations, which offer a remarkable contrast, both as to the mode of their performance, and as to the nature of the resulting products, are carried on at the same time, and by the same organ, but on different sides. The bony basis of the horn is an organic structure, which continues to be nourished by vessels forming part of the general system: the horn is a mere excretion, which appears to be destitute of vessels, and is, consequently, removed from the influence of the living powers. Thus the growth of horn is somewhat analogous to that of shell; for the layers which compose it are deposited in succession; each new layer is agglutinated to the inner surface of the preceding; and each has the shape of a hollow cone, occupying the part towards the apex of the former cone, and extending farther towards the base. Hence a longitudinal section of the whole presents the appearance represented in the annexed figures (218*), where A is the section of the horn of an Ox, and B, a similar section of the horn of an Antelope. C is a magnified view of the extremity of the latter, together with a portion of the bone D, which occupies the axis of the horn.

In this process of the formation of horn, as happens in that of shells, there sometimes occur irregularities, or periodical intermissions and increase of action in the secreting organs, giving rise to transverse grooves, or ridges. These may be seen in the horns of the goat, in which the fibres are short, and laid one over another with the same regularity as the tiles of a house. The tendency in these horns to assume a spiral form is explicable on the same principles as those which regulate the growth of turbinated shells. The horns of the ox and of the an-

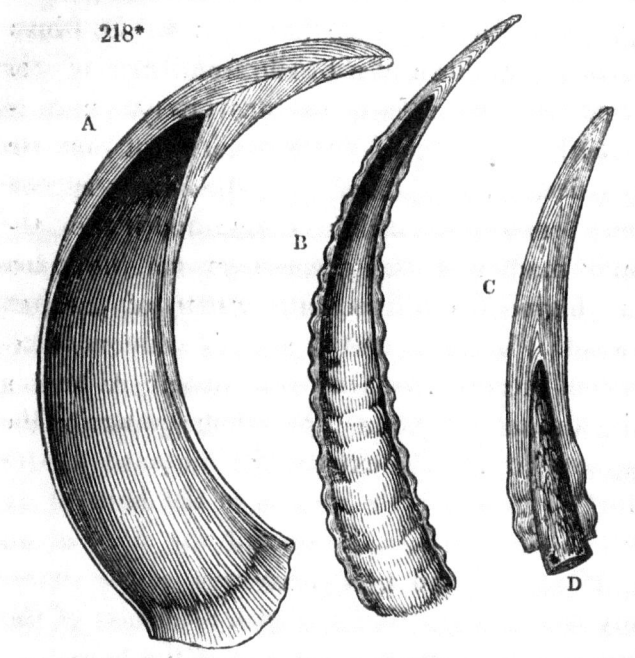

218*

telope tribes are formed of longer and more continuous fibres, which are closely compacted together, and exhibit very distinctly the series of hollow cones of which they are composed.

The horns of the *Rhinoceros*, both of the one and two horned species, grow from the integument covering the nose, to which they adhere without having any connexion with the subjacent bones. They have a pyramidal shape, and are composed of parallel fibres, resembling hairs, agglutinated together into a solid mass by a material which acts as a cement. This fibrous structure is most distinctly seen at the base of the horn, where the ends of the fibres project, like those of a brush, from the surface. When these horns are sawn transversely, and examined with a magnifying glass, a great number of orifices are seen, marking the empty spaces that intervene between the hairs; and if the section be made in a longitudinal direction, the same spaces give rise to the appearance of parallel grooves. These horns are not deciduous, like those of the stag: but continue to adhere to the skin, and to grow from the root, in proportion as they are worn at the extremity.

§ 6. *Solipeda.*

THE *Solipeda* form a natural family of quadrupeds, including the *Horse,* the *Ass,* the *Quagga,* the *Zebra,* &c. which are very nearly allied in their conformation to the ruminant tribe. To combine fleetness with strength has been the obvious design of nature in the construction of these animals. We find, accordingly, that the consolidation of the bones of the foot is carried still further than in the ruminant tribe; for in place of the two parallel phalanges, which are in the latter articulated with the cannon bone there is here only a single metatarsal bone. The three phalanges, of which that single finger consists, bear the names of the *pastern*, the *coronet*, and the *coffin bone;* and the hoof, of course, is single likewise; there is also a small bone, connected with the last, and called the *shuttle bone*. To the cannon bone are joined, behind, and on the side, two much shorter and very slender bones, which are rudiments of the other metacarpal bones. They have been termed the *styloid*, or *splint bones;* and are generally united by ossification with the cannon bone. The scapula of the horse is very narrow, and placed very nearly in a straight line with the humerus; which latter bone is very short, and scarcely descends below the line of the chest. The thigh-bone is also unusually short. The muscles, which extend the joint, and throw the thigh backwards in kicking, are particularly powerful. This is the natural defensive action of the horse: and its force is increased by a particular process with which the bone is furnished, and which has the form of a strong curved spine, situated on the outside, and opposite to the lesser trochanter,* giving to the muscles the advantage of a long lever. The cervical vertebræ have only short spinous processes that they might not interfere with the motions of

* This process has been termed the *processus recurvatus femoris*.

the neck. In the vertebræ of the back, on the other hand, these processes are remarkably long, especially at the part where the shoulder rests; their projection constituting what is called the *Withers*.

§ 7. *Pachydermata*.

FROM the horse we pass by a natural transition to the *Pachydermata*, a small group of animals interesting by their peculiarities, and by their being remnants of a very extensive tribe, which formerly inhabited the earth, but have now almost entirely disappeared. Although they feed upon grass, they do not ruminate, nor are they cloven-footed. They are for the most part huge and unwieldy animals, with thick integuments, rendered tough by a large mass of condensed cellular substance, which forms the chief defensive armour of those that are destitute of either tusk, proboscis, or nasal horn.

The most remarkable genus of this family is the *Elephant*, the colossal giant of quadrupeds. The many peculiarities that are observable in the conformation of this animal have all an obvious relation to the circumstances of its condition. Formed for feeding on a great variety of vegetable substances, and more especially on the tender shoots of trees, fruits, and grains, as well as on herbage, and succulent roots, its organs of mastication are powerful, and its teeth of great size. The whole of this apparatus requires an immense developement of bone to render it efficient; so that the head, with its huge tusks and grinders, is of enormous weight. Had this ponderous head been suspended at the end of a neck of such length as to admit of its being carried to the ground, as is the case in grazing animals, it would have destroyed the balance of the body, and would have required greater force to raise and retain it in a horizontal position than was competent to any degree of muscular power. Nature has accordingly abandoned this form of structure, and has at once curtailed the neck, bringing the head close to the trunk of the body, and supporting it by means of short, but powerful muscles, which are not implanted in any particular point of the skull, as they are in other quadrupeds, where the occipital bone forms a crest or ridge for that purpose; but the general surface of the cranium has been enlarged by an immense expansion given to its interior cellular structure, and thus the muscles are attached to a considerable extent of bone, instead of being affixed to a single process, which would have incurred great risk of being broken off by their action. These large cells are constructed with a view to combine strength with lightness; the plates which form their sides being disposed in a radiated manner towards the circumference, and arranged with great regularity; and the cells themselves, instead of containing marrow, are filled with air, by means of communications with the Eustachian tubes, which open into the nostrils: thus a great extent of surface is given to the skull, without any addition to its weight. The ligamentum nuchæ also comes in aid of the muscular power, being here of vast size and strength.

The head being limited in its range of motion by its approximation to the trunk, the mouth cannot be applied directly to seize the food: and some means were therefore to be provided for bringing the food to the mouth. For this purpose a new organ, the *proboscis*, has been constructed: it consists of a cylinder, perfectly flexible, and of a length sufficient to reach the ground, when the elephant is standing. The animal has the power of moving it in all possible directions by means of a prodigious number of muscular fibres, which are collected in small bands, some passing transversely, and radiating from the interior towards the circumference, others situated more obliquely, and a third set running longitudinally, and forming an exterior layer: but they are all variously interlaced together so as to compose a very complicated arrangement. The extremity of the proboscis, which is endowed with great sensibility, is furnished with an appendix, resembling a finger, most of the functions of which, indeed, it is capable of performing.

For the formation of this admirable member it has not been necessary to deviate from the ordinary laws of developement by the creation of a new organ; the same end being accomplished by the extension of a structure already belonging to the type of mammiferous animals. In several of the pachydermata the nostrils are already considerably advanced, so as to form a moveable snout: this is observable in a certain degree in the *Hog*; it is still more remarkably seen in the *Tapir*, which has a snout so lengthened and so moveable as very much to resemble, though on a far smaller scale, the proboscis of the elephant. This latter organ, then, may be considered as merely an elongation of the nostrils, which have been drawn out to suit a special purpose, very different from the function to which that part is usually subservient.*

While fleetness and elasticity are the results of the mechanical conformation of the horse, solidity and strength are the objects chiefly

---

* A defective developement of the bones of the nasal cavity, while the natural growth of the soft parts has continued, has often, in the case of the human fœtus, given rise to a monstrosity very much resembling the trunk of the tapir or of the elephant. (See Geoffroy St. Hilaire.)

aimed at in the construction of the pachydermata. The limbs have a great weight to sustain, in consequence of the huge size of the body; and hence the several bones which compose the pillars for its support are arranged nearly in vertical lines. The joints of the elbow and knee are placed low from the body; the ulna in the forelegs, and the fibula in the hinder, are fully developed, and are distinct from the radius and the tibia. The number of the toes, instead of being reduced to one, as in the horse, or to two, as in ruminants, is here increased to five: though, in consequence of their being very short, and of the skin which covers and surrounds them being very thick, they hardly appear externally, and are distinctly recognised only in the skeleton.

It would carry me far beyond the limits of the present work, were I to engage in a detailed examination of all the varieties of forms and structures that occur in the mechanism of the different tribes of mammalia, in reference to the purposes they are intended to serve, and to the peculiar circumstances of the animal to which they belong. I must necessarily pass over a multitude of instances of express adaptation, which are suited only to particular cases, and are, consequently, of minor importance as regards the general plans of organization. In the sort of bird's-eye view which I am taking of the endless modifications of structure that have been executed in conformity with those plans, I am able particularly to notice only such as are most remarkable.

§ 8. *Rodentia.*

As the tribes of mammalia we have hitherto examined employ the anterior extremities for the purposes of progression only, they are destitute of a clavicle. In most of those which follow, and where a greater developement of the limb confers more extensive and more varied powers of motion, applicable to a greater range of objects, this bone is found. In the greater number, however, it is merely in a rudimental state; that is, developed only to a certain extent, one portion being bony, and the rest cartilaginous; as if the ossification had been arrested at an early stage. These imperfect clavicles are too short to connect the scapula with the sternum; the rest of the space being eked out by cartilage, and by ligaments: but still they are of great use in affording points of attachment to the muscles of the limb, and giving them the advantage of acting by a rigid lever. The carnivorous tribes, which make considerable use of their fore paws in striking and seizing their prey, have clavicles of this description. Those quadrupeds which have to execute still more complex actions with their fore feet, have perfect clavicles, extending from the shoulder to the chest, and connecting the bones of the anterior extremity with the general frame-work of the skeleton. This is the case in a large proportion of the family of *Rodentia*, such as the *Squirrel*, which employs its paws for holding objects; and the *Beaver*,* which likewise makes great use of its feet for moving and arranging the materials of its habitation. Animals that dwell in trees, and require to grasp with force the branches in moving along them, such as the *Sloth*, have also distinct clavicles. Animals which rake or dig the ground, as the *Mole*, the *Ant-eater*, and the *Hedge-hog* are all provided with these bones, which, by keeping the shoulders at the same constant distance from the trunk, and affording a firm axis for the rotatory motions of the limb, materially assist them in the performance of these actions.

---

* The beaver presents a singular modification in the structure of the tail, which is expanded into a flattened oval disk, covered by a skin beset with scales: the whole forming a mechanical instrument, which may be compared to a trowel, exceedingly well adapted for the purposes to which it is applied by the animal in constructing its mud habitation.

§ 9. *Insectivora*.

In the tribe of *Insectivorous quadrupeds* we meet with several races which present singular conformations. In none are these anomalies more remarkable than in the *mole*, an animal which nature has formed for subterranean residence, and whose limbs are constructed with a view to the rapid excavation of passages under ground. The hands of the mole, for its fore paws almost deserve that appellation, are turned upwards and backwards for scooping the soil, while the feet are employed to throw it out with great quickness. These mining operations are aided by the motions of the head, which is lifted with great power, so as to loosen the ground above, and overcome the resistances that may be opposed to the progress of the animal. That no impediment might be offered to these motions of the head, the spinous processes of the cervical vertebræ have not been suffered to extend upwards. Large muscles are provided for bending the head backwards upon the neck; and they are assisted by a cervical ligament of great strength, which is generally in part ossified. The muscles of the fore extremities are also of extraordinary power. The scapula is a long and slender bone, more resembling a humerus in its shape than an ordinary scapula: the humerus, on the contrary, is thick and square, and the clavicle is short and broad. The radius and the ulna are distinct from each other; the hand is very large and expanded; the palms being turned outwards and backwards, and its lower margin being fashioned into a sharp cutting edge. The carpal bones and the phalanges of the fingers are very much compressed; but they are furnished with large nails, which compose more than half the hands; and they are expressly constructed for digging, being long, broad, and sharp at the extremities. The sternum has a large middle crest, and is prolonged at its extremity into a sharp process, having the figure of a ploughshare, thus affording an extensive surface of attachment for the large pectoral muscles, from which the limb derives its principal force. The head terminates in front by a pointed nose, which is armed at its extremity with a small bone, intended to assist in penetrating through the ground.

While all this attention has been paid to the developement of the anterior part of the body to which these instruments specially contrived for burrowing are affixed, the hinder part is comparatively feeble, and appears stinted in its growth, and curtailed of its fair proportions. The pelvis is exceedingly diminutive, being reduced to a slender sacrum; and it is thrown far back from the abdomen, to which it could give no effectual protection. Hence the animal, when above ground, walks very awkwardly, and is unable to advance but by an irregular and vacillating pace.*

We have seen that there is a tribe of fishes armed externally with sharp spines, which they are capable of erecting when in danger of attack. A similar kind of defensive armour is furnished to the *Porcupine* and the *Hedgehog*, which belong to the family of insectivorous quadrupeds. For the purpose of erecting these bristles, when the animal is irritated or alarmed, there is provided a peculiar set of muscular bands, which forms part of the usual subcutaneous layer, termed the *panniculus carnosus*. In the hedgehog these muscles are very complicated, and give the animal the power of rolling itself into a ball. A minute description of these muscles has been given by Cuvier, who found that the whole body is enveloped in a large muscular bag, or mantle, lying immediately under the integuments; and capable, by the contraction of different portions of its fibres, of carrying the

* The only quadrupeds which resemble the mole in the perfect adaptation of their structure to the purposes of burrowing, are the *Wombat* and the *Koala*, which are among the many extraordinary animals inhabiting the continent of Australia. Their hind legs are constructed in a manner very much resembling the human fore-arm. (See Home, Lectures, &c. i. 134.)

skin over a great extent of surface. In the usual state of the animal, this broad muscle appears on the back (as represented in Fig. 219), contracted

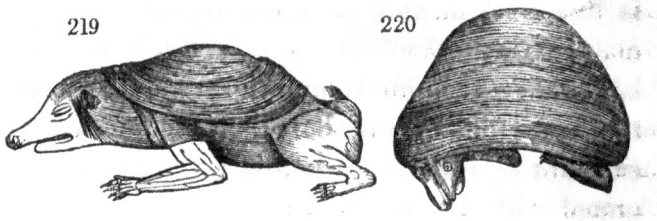

into a thick oval disk, of which the fibres are much accumulated at the circumference. From the edges of this disk there pass down auxiliary muscles towards the lower parts of the body; the action of which muscles tends to draw the skin downwards, and to coil it over the head and paws, in the manner shown in Fig. 220, like the closing of the mouth of a great bag.

§ 10. *Carnivora.*

THE type of the Mammalia may be considered as having attained its full developement in the carnivorous tribes, which comprehend the larger beasts of prey. As their food is animal, they require a less complicated apparatus for digestion than herbivorous quadrupeds, possess greater activity and strength, and enjoy a greater range of sensitive and intellectual faculties. In accordance with these conditions we may notice the greater expansion of their brain, the superior acuteness of their senses, and their enormous muscular power. The trunk of the body is lighter than that of vegetable feeders, especially in the abdominal region, and is compressed laterally: the spine is more pliant and elastic,* the limbs have greater freedom of motion, the extremities are more subdivided, and they are armed with formidable weapons of offence and destruction. Great mechanical power was required for raising the head, not only on account of the force to be exerted in tearing flesh, but also that these animals might be enabled to carry away their prey in their mouths. Hence we find that in the Lion, of which the skeleton is represented in its relations to the outline of the body, in Fig. 221, the first vertebra of the neck, or atlas, has very widely expanded transverse processes, while the second vertebra has a largely developed spinous process, for supplying levers for the muscles which have to perform these and other actions in which the head is concerned.

The whole of the remaining part of the skeleton of these animals is constructed with reference to their predatory nature. The sudden

---

* The suppleness of the spine might at once be inferred, on the simple inspection of the skeleton, from the circumstance that the vertebræ of the neck and loins have a comparatively small developement of their spinous processes.

springs with which they pounce upon their prey must impart to the whole osseous frame the most violent concussion. The first stroke with which they attempt the destruction of their victims is given with the fore leg: so that had the limb been rigidly connected with the sternum by means of an entire clavicle, its motions would have been too limited, and danger of fracture would have been incurred. The scapula is broad, and the humerus of great length, compared with the same bones in ruminants; and the latter has besides a large surface for its articulation with the former of these bones, thus allowing of a great range of motion: the radius and ulna are perfectly distinct, and play extensively on each other.

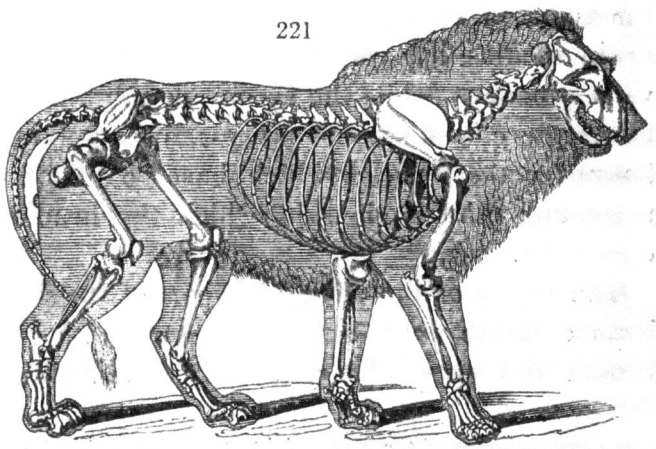

221

The fore feet rest on the ground by means of the second of the three joints of which each toe is composed. The last phalanges are raised at right angles to the former, for the purpose of supporting the claws in an erect position. It has been considered of such importance to preserve these formidable instruments constantly sharp, and in a condition fitted for immediate use, that an express contrivance has been resorted to for this purpose. It consists in a sheath, within which the claws, when not employed, are kept retracted, by means of an elastic ligament, which constantly tends to withdraw them within the sheath: and they are at the same time so connected with the tendons of the flexor muscles of the toes, that the moment these muscles are thrown into action, which is the case when the animal aims a stroke with its paw, the claws are instantly drawn out, and combine in inflicting the severest lacerations.*

Connected with the superior strength of the hind extremities, we find the pelvis extending farther backwards, and more in a perpendicular line with the femur. This latter bone is longer and more slender than in the horse, but it is more compact in its form, and its processes are more strongly developed: the fibula is a separate bone from the tibia. The muscles, in

* There exists, concealed in the tuft of hair, at the extremity of the lion's tail, a small conical and slightly curved claw, which is attached to the skin only, and not to the last caudal vertebra: it is difficult to conjecture what can be its use.

general, are more divided into portions, and are thus capable of greater diversity of action, at the same time that they have greater power than those of herbivorous quadrupeds. The articular surfaces are of greater extent, and are lubricated with a more copious supply of synovia; their ligaments are more delicate and more numerous; and the joints, in general, adapted to a greater variety of movements. All these provisions are evidently directed to confer great freedom and facility of motion, and to enlarge the sphere of action of the body generally, as well as of the limbs.

§ 11. *Quadrumana.*

WE may trace in the series of quadrupeds which have come under our review a gradual increase in the developement of the hind feet: beginning from the horse, which is single hoofed, or *solipede;* next to which rank the cloven-footed ruminants, a tribe which includes the camel, whose foot is widely expanded for the purpose of treading securely on sand; then come the Rhinoceros, which has three hoofed toes; the Hippopotamus, which has four, and the Elephant, which has five. To these succeed another series, where nails, or claws, are substituted for hoofs, as is the case with all the *Carnivora,* which, standing on the extremities of their toes, have been termed *Digitigrades*. Then follow the *Plantigrade* quadrupeds, such as the bear, the badger, the hedgehog, and the mole, which rest with the whole foot on the ground, and are in consequence able to make great use of their fore paws. These conduct us to the family of the *Quadrumana*, comprehending the Monkey and the Lemur tribes, which are characterised by having the inner toe quite distinct from the others, like the human thumb, and which appear, therefore, as if they had four hands.

The Quadrumana present the nearest approximation to the human structure: they are naturally inhabitants of the forest, and their conformation is adapted to the actions of climbing upon trees, of grasping the branches, and of springing from the one to the other, with precision and agility. It is here that they are at home; it is here that they gather the food which is most suited to their nature; it is here that they engage in successful combats with serpents and other enemies; retaining their positions in perfect security on the moving branches, or sportively swinging by their extremities in the air. Both the feet and the hands are formed for this species of prehension; and many are further provided with a strongly prehensile tail, which is an instrument admirably adapted for all these purposes. Hence the attitude most natural to these animals is neither the horizontal one of quadrupeds, nor the erect posture of man, but an intermediate or semi-erect position.

This view of the living habits of the quadrumana will afford the key to most of the peculiarities of structure they present to our observation. The head, being no longer suspended at the end of a horizontal, or recurved neck, is, in the usual attitude of the animal, supported chiefly by the cervical vertebræ. The greater developement of the brain, and more especially of its posterior lobes, creates a necessity for an extension of the occipital bone in that direction; a portion of the weight to be sustained by the atlas is accordingly thrown behind the centre of motion, which is at its articulation with the latter bone; and this weight tends, therefore, to balance that of the anterior part of the head; hence there is no need of the strong cervical ligament, which is so universally met with in quadrupeds, and although this ligament exists in the monkey, it is very slender, and of no very great extent.

Great mobility has been conferred on the spine by the form of its articulations; and the caudal vertebræ are generally greatly multiplied to form a tail of considerable length, which in the *Ateles*, or spider monkey of America, is moved by powerful muscles, and is an organ of great flexibility and strength. Monkeys possess a distinct clavicle, a lengthened humerus and femur, a radius and ulna moveable upon each other, and a hand nearly approaching to the human construction. But the thumb is less developed, and its muscles are much weaker than in man.

The bones of the pelvis, as well as those of the leg are elongated, for the purpose of giving greater length to the muscles which are to move their several parts; by this means, although the force with which they act may be somewhat lessened, yet the velocity of the motion they produce is increased in the same proportion. The fibula is here a bone of more importance than in quadrupeds; for it performs a motion of rotation round the tibia, analogous to that of the radius upon the ulna, giving a great extent of action to the foot, and converting the leg into an arm, as we have already seen that the foot itself is transformed into a hand. A small inclination is given to the articulation of the tarsus with these last mentioned bones, which imparts a degree of twist to the feet, throwing the sole inwards, and causing the monkey while walking to rest chiefly on its outer edge. This seeming defect gives a slight appearance of awkwardness to the gait; it is not, however, to be viewed as an imperfection, for it is evidently designed to assist the animal in climbing trees, which is its most usual action, the oblique position of the foot enabling it most effectually to lay hold of the branches. Monkeys are evidently not formed to excel in swiftness; for the heel, in these animals, presents no large projection, as in other orders of mammalia; nor are the muscles that are inserted into the heel particularly powerful; they hardly, indeed, can be said to compose a calf as in the human leg.

§ 12. *Man.*

THE series of structures modelled on the characteristic type of the Mammalia, after having exhibited the successive developement of all its elements, attains the highest perfection in the human fabric: for even independently of those prerogatives of intellect and of sensibility, by which Man is so far exalted above the level of the brute creation, both his physical structure and his physiological constitution place him incontestibly at the summit of the scale of terrestrial beings. Considered zoologically, indeed, the human species must rank among the Mammalia, and it even makes a near approach to the Quadrumana; yet there exist many peculiarities of structure, which entitle Man to be placed in a separate order, where disclaiming any close alliance with inferior creatures, he proudly stands alone, towering far above them all.

It is not, however, on a pre-eminence in any single physical quality or function that this title to superiority can be founded; for in each of these endowments man is excelled in turn by particular races of the lower animals; but the chief perfection of his frame consists in its general adaptation to an incomparably greater variety of objects, and an infinitely more expanded sphere of action. As the beauty of an edifice depends not on the elaborate finishing of any one portion, but results from the general suitableness of the whole to the purposes for which it was constructed, so the excellence of the human fabric is to be estimated by the exquisite proportion and harmony subsisting among all its parts, and pervading the whole system of its functions. The design of its structure and economy embraces widely different, and far higher aims than those contemplated in the organization of any of the inferior animals. Destined to an intellectual, a social, and a moral existence, Man has had every part of his organization modified with an express relation to these great objects of his formation. This will best appear when we come to examine the organs which are subservient to the sensitive and active faculties; but even here, where our views must, for the present, be limited to the mechanical circumstances of his structure, the proofs are sufficiently numerous to warrant this general conclusion.

Man presents the only instance among the mammalia of a conformation by which the erect posture can be permanently maintained, and in which the office of supporting the trunk of the body is consigned exclusively to the lower extremities. To this intention the form and arrangement of all the parts of the osseous fabric, and the position and adjustments of the organs of sense have a well marked reference.* The lower limbs are qualified to be the efficient instruments of progression by their greater length and muscularity, compared with the generality of quadrupeds. The only exceptions to this rule occur in those mammalia which are constructed expressly for leaping, such as the *Kanguroo* and *Jerboa*, where, however, the hind legs are employed almost solely for that mode of progression. The Quadrumana, which come nearer to the human form than any of the other tribes, have the lower limbs comparatively weak. In almost all other quadrupeds the disproportion is still greater, the thigh being short, and almost concealed by the muscles of the trunk, and the remainder of the limb being slender, and not surrounded by any considerable mass of muscles.

* In most quadrupeds, as we have seen, the thorax is deep in the direction from the sternum to the spine, but is compressed laterally, for the evident purpose of bringing the fore limbs nearer to each other, that they might more effectually support the anterior part of the trunk. In Man, on the contrary, the thorax is flattened anteriorly, and extends more in width than in depth; thus throwing out the shoulders, and allowing an extensive range of motion to the arms.

The articular surfaces of the knee joint are broader, and admit of greater extent of motion in man than in quadrupeds: hence the leg can be brought into the same line with the thigh, and form with it a straight and firm column of support to the trunk; and the long neck of the thigh bone allows of more complete rotation. The widely spread basin of the pelvis effectually sustains the weight of the digestive organs, and they rest more particularly upon the broad expansion of the iliac bones: in quadrupeds, these bones, having no such weight to support, are much narrower.

The base on which the whole body is supported in the erect position is constituted by the toes, and by the heel, the bone of which projects backwards at right angles to the leg. Between these points the sole of the foot has a concavity in two directions, the one longitudinal, the other transverse, constituting a double arch. This construction, besides conferring strength and elasticity, provides room for the convenient passage of the tendons of the toes, which proceed downwards from the larger muscles of the leg, and also for the lodgement of smaller muscles affixed to each individual joint, and for the protection of the various nerves and blood vessels distributed to all these parts. The concavity of the foot adapts it also to retain a firmer hold of the inequalities of the ground on which we tread. The muscles which raise the heel, and which compose the calf of the leg, are of great size and strength, and derive a considerable increase of power from the projection of the bone of the heel, into which their united tendons are inserted. In all these respects the human structure possesses decided advantages over that of the monkey, with reference to the specific objects of its formation.

It is impossible to doubt that nature intended man to assume the erect attitude, when we advert to the mode in which the head is placed on the spinal column. The enormous developement of the brain, and of the bones which invest it, increases so considerably the weight of that part of the head, which is situated behind its articulation with the vertebræ of the neck, that the balance of the whole is much more equal than it is in the monkey, where the weight of the fore part very greatly preponderates. The muscles which bend the head back upon the neck, and retain it in its natural position, are therefore not required to be so powerful as they must be in quadrupeds, especially in those which graze, and in which the mouth and eyes must frequently be directed downwards, for the purpose of procuring food. In man this attitude would, if continued, be extremely fatiguing, from the weakness of those muscles, and the absence of that strong ligament which sustains the weight of the head in the ordinary horizontal attitude of quadrupeds.

"Pronaque cum spectant animalia cætera terram,
Os homini sublime dedit, cælumque tueri
Jussit, et erectos ad sidera tollere vultus."---OVID.

The space comprehended by the two feet is extremely narrow, when compared with the extended base on which the quadruped is supported. Hence the stability of the body must be considerably less. The statue of an elephant placed upon a level surface, would stand without danger of oversetting: but the statue of a man resting on the feet, in the usual attitude of standing, would be thrown down by a very small impulse. It is evident, indeed, that in the living body, if the centre of gravity were at any moment to pass beyond the base, no muscular effort which could then be made would avail to prevent the body from falling. But the actions of the muscles are continually exerted to prevent the yielding of the joints under the weight of the body, which tends to bend them. In quadrupeds less exertion is requisite for that purpose; and standing is in them, as we have seen, a posture of comparative repose: in man it requires nearly as great an expenditure of muscular power as the act of walking. Soldiers on parade experience more fatigue by remaining in the attitude of standing, than they would by marching during an equal time. Strictly speaking, indeed, it is impossible for even the strongest man to remain on his legs, in precisely the same position, for any considerable length of time. The muscles in action soon become fatigued, and require to be relieved by varying the points of support, so as to bring other muscles into play. Hence the weight of the body is transferred alternately from one foot to the other. The action of standing consists in fact, of a series of small and imperceptible motions, by which the centre of gravity is perpetually shifted from one part of the base to another; the tendency to fall to any one side being quickly counteracted by an insensible movement in a contrary direction. Long habit has rendered us unconscious of these exertions, which we are, nevertheless, continually making; but a child learning to walk finds it difficult to accomplish them successfully. It is one among those arts which he has to acquire, and which costs him in the apprenticeship many painful efforts, and many discouraging falls. But whenever nature is the teacher, the scholar makes rapid progress in learning; and no sooner have the muscles acquired the necessary strength, than the child becomes an adept in balancing its body in various attitudes, and in a very short time is unconscious that these actions require exertion.

In walking, the first effort that is made consists in transferring the whole weight of the body upon one foot, with a view to fix it on the ground; and then the other foot, being at liberty, is brought forwards. By this action the centre of gravity is made to advance, till it passes beyond the base of the foot: in this situation the body, being unsupported, falls through a certain space, and would continue its descent, were it not that it is received on the other foot, which, by this time, has been set upon the ground. This falling of the body would, if not immediately checked, become very sensible; as happens when, on walking inattentively, the foot we had advanced comes down to a lower level than we were prepared for; in which case the body, having acquired a certain velocity by its greater descent, receives a sudden shock when that velocity is checked, and thus a disagreeable jar is given to the whole frame.

While the weight of the body is thus transferred alternately from one foot to the other, the centre of gravity not only rises and falls, so as to describe at every step a small arch, but also vibrates from side to side, so that the series of curves it describes are somewhat complicated in their form. This undulation of the body from one foot to the other would scarcely ever be performed with perfect equality on both sides, if we trusted wholly to the sensations communicated by the muscles, and if we were not guided by the sense of sight, or some other substitute. Thus a person blindfolded cannot walk far in a straight line; for, even on a level plane, he will incline unconsciously either to the right or to the left.

In all quadrupeds, and even also in the quadrumana, the fore extremities more or less contribute to the support and progression of the body: it is only in man that they are wholly exempted from these offices, and are at liberty to be applied to other purposes, and employed as instruments of prehension and of touch. In the power of executing an infinite variety of movements and of actions, requiring either strength, delicacy, or precision, the human arm and hand, considered in their mechanism alone, are structures of unrivalled excellence; and, when viewed in relation to the intellectual energies to which they are subservient, plainly reveal to us the divine source, from which have emanated this exquisite workmanship, and these admirable adjustments, so fitted to excite in our breasts the deepest veneration, and to fill us with never ceasing wonder.

To specify all the details of express contrivance in the mechanical conformation of the hand would alone fill a separate treatise: but I must refrain from pursuing this interesting subject, as, fortunately, the task has devolved upon one far more able than myself to do it justice.

Chapter X.

VERTEBRATA CAPABLE OF FLYING.

§ 1. *Vertebrata without Feathers, formed for flying.*

FEW problems in mechanic art present greater practical difficulties than that of raising from the ground, and of sustaining and moving rapidly through the air an animal body, composed as it must be of many ponderous organs, that are requisite for the performance of the higher functions of life: yet Nature has achieved all this, not only in endless tribes of the more diminutive invertebrate animals, but also in the more solid and massive organizations which are modelled on the vertebrate type. These objects have been accomplished, in all cases, without the employment of any other than the ordinary elements of those organizations; modified, indeed, to suit the particular purpose in view, but yet essentially the same, and regulated by the same laws of developement which prevail throughout the whole animal system. The adaptation of these elements to the construction of an apparatus of so refined a nature as that which is required for flying, implies the deepest foresight, the most extensive plan, and the most artificial combination of means. The foundations for these peculiar forms of mechanism are laid in the primeval constitution of the embryo; and a long and curious series of preparatory changes must take place before the completion of the finished structures. Of this we have already had a remarkable example in the metamorphoses of insects, which exhibit, in their last stage of developement, the highest degree of perfection compatible with the articulate type. Birds, in like manner, present us with the highest refinement of mechanical conformation which can be attained by the developement of a vertebrated structure.

The power of flying is derived altogether from the resistance which the air opposes to bodies moving through it, or acting upon it by mechanical impulse. In the ordinary movements of our own bodies, this resistance is scarcely sensible, and hardly ever attracts notice: but it increases in proportion to the surface which acts upon the air, and still more according to the velocity of the moving body; for the increase is not merely in the simple ratio of the velocity, but as its square, or perhaps even a higher power. In order that an animal may be able to fly, therefore, two principal conditions are required: there must, first, be a considerable extent of surface in the wings, or instruments which act upon the air; and there must, secondly, be sufficient muscular power to give these instruments a very great velocity. Both these advantages are found combined in the anterior extremities of birds, and no animals belonging to any other class possess them in the same perfection. No quadruped, except the bat, has sufficient muscular power in its limbs, however aided by an expansion of surface, to strike the air with the force requisite for flight. No refinement of mechanic ingenuity has ever placed the Dædalian art of flying within the reach of human power; for even if the lightest possible wings could be so artificially adapted to the body as to receive the full force of the actions of the limbs, however these actions might be combined, they would fall very far short of the exertion necessary for raising the body from the ground.

Examples, however, occur in every one of the classes of vertebrated animals, where an approach is made to this faculty. In the *Exocætus*, or flying-fish, the pectoral fins have been enormously expanded, evidently for the purpose of enabling the animal to leap out of the water, and support itself for a short interval in the air: but its utmost efforts are inadequate to sustain it beyond a few moments in that element, and it can never rise to more than five or six feet above the surface of the water.

A species of lizard, called the *Draco Volans*,

has a singularly constructed apparatus, which appears like two wings, affixed to the sides of the back, and quite independent of either the fore or the hind extremities. By the aid of these moveable flaps, the animal is able to descend from the tops of trees, or flutter lightly from branch to branch: but this is the utmost that it can accomplish by means of these imperfect organs. The construction of these anomalous members is highly curious in a physiological point of view; as showing how Nature, in effecting a new purpose, is inclined to resort to the modification of structures already established as constituent parts of the frame, in preference to creating new organs, or such as have no prototype in the model of its formation. Frequent proofs of this law, indeed, are afforded by the comparative examination of the anatomy of the organs of progressive motion. The ribs, in particular, are often the subject of these conversions to uses very different from their ordinary function, which is that of assisting in respiration. Thus we have seen that in the Tortoise they are expanded to form the carapace, uniting with corresponding dilatations of the sternum, and sterno-costal appendages, in composing a general osseous encasement to the body. In Serpents, again, the ribs are employed as organs of progressive motion; performing the functions of legs, and having affixed to their extremities the

FLYING LIZARD. 549

abdominal scuta, by way of feet. The cervical ribs of the *Cobra de Capello*, or hooded snake of the East Indies, are employed for the mechanical purpose of supporting an expansion of the skin of the neck, which forms a kind of hood, capable of being raised or depressed at the pleasure of the animal.* These ribs are entirely unconnected with the respiration of the serpent.

In the Draco volans, which was to be furnished with instruments for assisting it in its distant leaps through the air, it is again the ribs which are resorted to for furnishing the basis of such an apparatus. On each side of the dorsal vertebræ, as is seen in the skeleton of this animal (Fig. 222), the eight posterior ribs on each side, instead of having the usual curvature inwards, and instead of being continued round to encircle the body, are extended outwards and elongated, and are covered with a thin cuticle, derived from the common integuments. The ordinary muscles which move the ribs still remain, but with greatly increased power, and serve to flap these strangely formed wings at the pleasure of the animal, during its short aerial excursions.

Among the mammalia we meet with a few species, which have a broad membrane, formed of a duplicature of the skin, extended like a cloak from the fore to the hind extremities, and

* Phil. Trans. for 1804, p. 346.

enabling the animal to flutter in the air, and to break its fall during its descent from the

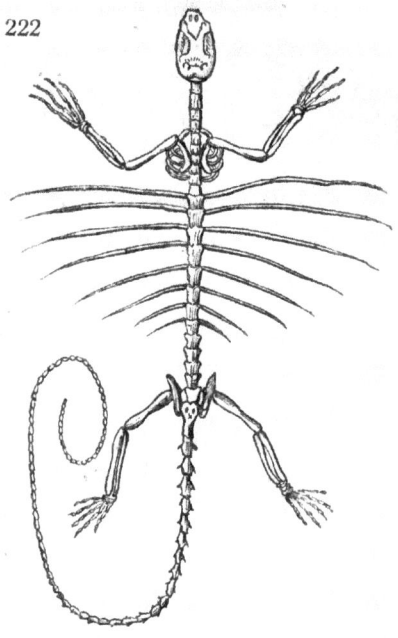

222

branches of trees. Structures of this kind are possessed by the *Sciurus volans*, or flying squirrel, and also by some other species of the same genus. They are seen on a still larger scale in the *Lemur volans*, or *Galeopithecus*. The resistance which these broad expansions of skin oppose to the air, when the limbs are spread out, enables the animal to descend in perfect safety through that medium from very considerable heights: but these appendages to the body are mere parachutes, not wings, and none of the animals which possess them can, by their means, and with the utmost efforts which their muscles are capable of exerting, ever rise from the ground, or even suspend themselves for a moment in the air.

The only quadruped that can properly be said to be endowed with the power of flying is the *Bat*. In this animal the portions of the skeleton (F, Fig. 223) which correspond to the pha-

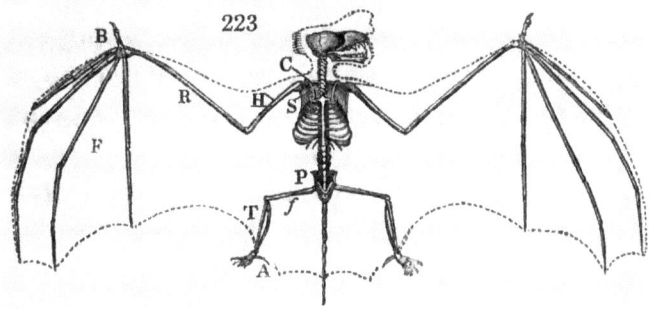

langes of the fingers are extended to an enormous length, and the pectoral muscles, which move the anterior extremities, are of extraordinary size and power. In the larger species, each wing is at least two feet in length. The fine membrane, which is spread between these lengthened fingers, has its origin in the sides of the neck, and reaches all along the body to the extremities of the hinder legs, which it encloses in its folds. Thus, not only is the surface, by which it acts upon the air, sufficiently extensive, but the muscular power, by which its motions are effected, is adequate to give it those quick and sudden impulses which are requisite for flying: and thus, although its structure is totally different from that of birds, it yet performs fully the office of a real wing. The bat flies with perfect ease, even while carrying along with it one or two of its young: it is not, however, fitted for very long flights.

The conformation of the skeleton is adapted to this new and important function. The chest is broad and capacious to admit of free respiration while the animal is flying, and to afford ample space for the attachment of the large muscles which have become necessary. The scapulæ (s) are large, and of a singular form, and they are kept at a considerable distance asunder by the expanded chest: their coracoid processes are also large, and extend in the direction of the sternum. The clavicles (c) are of enormous size and length, being larger than either the scapula or the sternum, and remarkably curved in their shape. The sternum is much developed, extending laterally, and having a projecting crest along the middle of its lower surface. The humerus (h) is strong, but short; apparently in order to avoid the danger of its being snapped asunder by the violent actions of the pectoral muscles, had it been longer. As the leading object of the structure is to give power to the wing, there was no necessity for the rotatory motion of the bones of the fore-arm; and accordingly we find them consolidated into one (R); or rather no part of the ulna is developed, except the process of the olecranon, or elbow, which has become soldered to the radius.

These advantages in the construction of the fore extremities are obtained at the expense of the hinder, which are too feeble to support the weight of the body in the upright position required for walking, in consequence of the centre of gravity being between the wings. On a level plane, indeed, the bat can advance only by a kind of crawling or hopping motion. The whole anterior half of the trunk is much more fully developed than the posterior half, which appears as if it had been checked in its growth. The pelvis (P) is of diminutive size, compared with the rest of the skeleton: the pubic bones are lengthened backwards, and are joined merely at a small point. The whole posterior limb is short, the femur (f) comparatively long, and the fibula is a very slender bone, yet quite distinct from the tibia (T). The slight degree of motion which is thus allowed between them is useful to the animal, in enabling the feet to lay hold of cornices or other projecting parts of the roofs of buildings, on which the animal fastens itself, and hangs with the head downwards. It is probably with the intention of facilitating this action that the toes are turned completely backwards; and that they are of a curved shape, and generally armed with sharp claws. A bony appendix (A) projects outwards from the heel, for the purpose of supporting the hinder prolongation of the membrane, which often extends between the hind feet, and is further sustained by the tail, in those species which have the spine prolonged to form one.

Bats are also provided with another instrument for suspending themselves to projecting objects, formed by the thumb (B), which is, apparently for this express purpose, detached from the fingers that support the wing, and is terminated by a strong claw, which projects, even when the wings are folded, and is useful in progression, serving as a point of support.

§ 2. *Birds.*

It is in Birds alone that we find the most perfect adaptation of structure to the purposes of rapid and extensive flight: in them the frame of the skeleton, the figure, position, and structure of the wings, the size of the muscles, the peculiar nature of their irritability, and even the outward form of the body have all a direct and beautiful relation to the properties of the element in which Nature has intended them to move.

In their formation a new, and in as far as relates to the organs of progressive motion, a more developed type is adopted; still preserving a conformity with the general plan of the vertebral organization, and with the general laws of its developement.

The skeleton of birds has the same constituent parts as that of other vertebrated classes: the bones of the anterior extremity, though destined exclusively to support the wing, retain the same divisions, and are composed of the usual elements: and the general form of the body is that best calculated to glide through the air with the least resistance. As birds swallow their food entire, there is no necessity for any part of the bulky apparatus of hard and solid teeth, large muscles and heavy jaws which are required by most quadrupeds: hence the head admits of being greatly reduced in its dimensions; and the form of the beak, which is drawn to a point, and cuts the opposing air, tends to facilitate the progress of the bird in its flight.

In the conformation of the body, also, every circumstance that could contribute to give it lightness has been sedulously studied. The general size of birds is considerably smaller than quadrupeds of corresponding habits. No where has Nature attempted to endow a huge ponderous animal, like the fabled Pegasus, with the power of flight. Great condensation has been given to the osseous substance,* in order that the greatest degree of strength might be procured with the same weight of solid materials; and the mechanical advantage derived from their being disposed in the circumference rather than in central masses, has been obtained to the utmost extent. The horny material, of which the stems of the feathers are constructed, are, in like manner, formed into hollow cylinders, which, compared with their weight, are exceedingly strong. A similar shape has been given to the cylindrical bones, which are fashioned into tubes with dense but thin sides: most of the other bones have likewise been made hollow, and instead of their cavities being filled with marrow, they contain only air.† Thus the whole skeleton is rendered remarkably light: that of the *Pelicanus onocrotalus*, for instance, or white Pelican, which is five feet in length, was found by the Parisian Academicians to weigh only twenty-three ounces, while the entire bird weighed nearly twenty-five pounds. The cavities in the bones communicate with large air cells, which are distributed in various parts of the body, and

* Ossification not only proceeds more rapidly, but is also carried to a greater extent in this class of animals than in any other; as a proof of which, the tendons, especially those of the muscles of the legs, are frequently ossified.

† In the bat there is no provision of this kind for lightening the bones, and we find them containing marrow, as in other mammalia, and not air.

which contribute still further to diminish its specific gravity: and by means of canals which open into the air passages of the lungs, this air finds a ready outlet when it becomes rarefied by the ascent of the bird into the higher regions of the atmosphere.*

The conditions in which a bird is placed with regard to the density of the surrounding medium, as well as their mode of progression, are so opposite to those of fishes, that we should expect to find great corresponding differences in their conformation. These two classes of vertebrata, accordingly, are remarkably contrasted

---

* This air, being contained in the interior of the body, which preserves a very elevated temperature, must be constantly in a state of greater rarefaction than the cooler external air; a condition which must contribute in some slight degree to render the whole body lighter than it would otherwise have been. It appears to me, however, that considerably greater importance has been attached to this circumstance than it really possesses. Many have gone so far as to represent the condition of a bird as approaching to that of a balloon filled with a lighter gas than atmospheric air: and have been lavish in their expressions of admiration at the beauty of the contrivance which thus converted a living structure into an aerostatic machine. A little sober consideration will suffice to show that the amount of the supposed advantages resulting to the bird from the diminution of weight, occasioned by the difference of temperature between the air included in its body and the external atmosphere, is perfectly insignificant. Any one who will take the trouble to calculate the real diminution of weight arising from this cause, under the most favourable circumstances, will find that, even in the case of the largest bird, it can never amount to more than a few grains.

with respect to the structure of their skeletons. In fishes we have seen that the chest and all the viscera are carried as far forwards as possible; the respiratory organs and the centre of circulation being close to the head, the neck having disappeared, and the trunk being continued into the lengthened tail, in which the chief bulk of the muscles are situated. In birds, on the contrary, the ribs, and the viscera which they protect, are placed as far back along the spinal column as possible; and a long and flexible neck extends from the trunk to the head, which is thus carried considerably forwards. These circumstances are very apparent in the skeleton of the swan, represented in Fig. 224. In the fish, progressive motion is effected principally by the movements of the tail, which impels the body alternately from side to side: in the bird, the only instruments of motion are the wings, which are affixed to the fore part of the trunk, and are moved by muscles situated in that region. In the fish, the spine is flexible nearly throughout its whole extent; in the bird, it is rigid and immoveable in the trunk, and is capable of extensive motion only in the neck.

In order that the body may be exactly balanced while the bird is flying, its centre of gravity must be brought precisely under the line connecting the articulations of the wings with the trunk, for it is at these points that the re-

BIRDS. 559

sistance of the air causes it to be supported by the wings. When the bird is resting upon its legs, the centre of gravity must, in like manner,

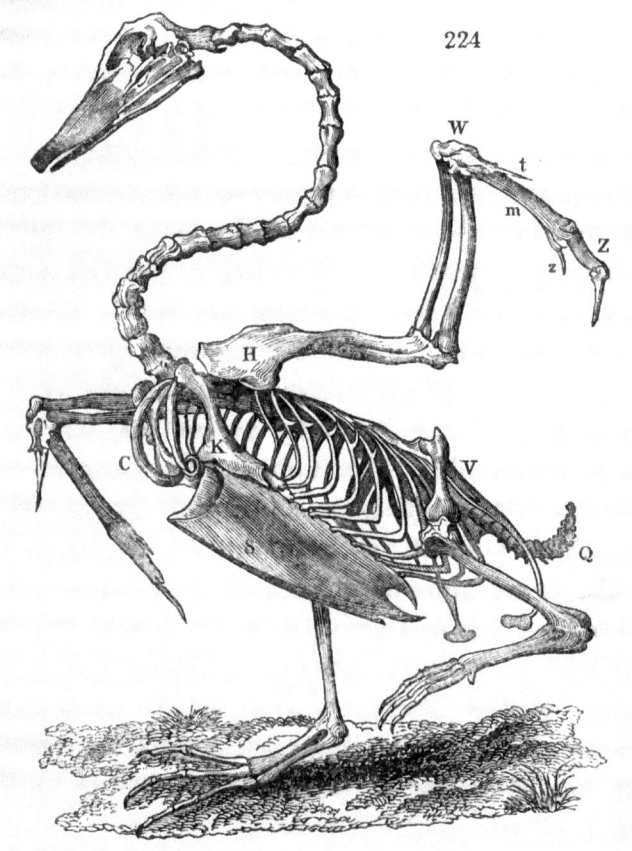

be brought immediately over the base of support formed by the toes: it becomes necessary, therefore, to provide means for shifting the centre of gravity from one place to another, according to circumstances, and to adjust its position with considerable nicety; otherwise there would be danger of the equilibrium being destroyed, and the body oversetting. The principal means of effecting these adjustments consist in the motions of the head and neck, which last is, for that purpose, rendered exceedingly long and flexible. The number of cervical vertebræ is generally very considerable; in the mammalia, as we have seen, there are always seven, but in many birds there are more than twice that number. In the swan (Fig. 224), there are twenty-three, and they are joined together by articulations, generally allowing free motion in all directions; that is, laterally, as well as forwards and backwards. This unusual degree of mobility is conferred by a peculiar mechanism, which is not met with in the other classes of vertebrated animals. A cartilage is interposed between each of the vertebræ, to the surfaces of which these cartilages are curiously adapted, being enclosed between folds of the membrane lining the joint: so that each joint is in reality double, consisting of two cavities, with an intervening cartilage.*

It is to be observed, however, that in consequence of the positions of the oblique processes,

* See Mr. H. Earle's paper on this subject in the Philosophical Transactions for 1823, p. 277.

the upper vertebræ of the neck bend with more facility forwards than backwards; while those in the lower half of the neck bend more readily backwards: hence, in a state of repose, the neck naturally assumes a double curvature, like that of the letter S, as is well seen in the graceful form of the swan's neck. By extending the neck in a straight line, the bird can, while flying, carry forwards the centre of gravity, so as to bring it under the wings; and when resting on its feet, or floating on the water, it can transfer that centre backwards, so as to bring it towards the middle of the body, by merely bending back the neck into the curved form which has just been described; and thus the equilibrium is, under all circumstances, preserved by movements remarkable for their elegance and grace.*

Another advantage arising from the length and mobility of the neck is, that it facilitates the application of the head to every part of the surface of the body. Birds require this power in order that they may be enabled to adjust their plumage, whenever it has by any accident become ruffled. In aquatic birds, it is necessary

* The great mobility of the neck enables the bird to employ its beak as an organ of prehension for taking its food: an object which was the more necessary, in consequence of the conversion of the fore extremities into wings, of which the structure is incompatible with any prehensile power, such as is often possessed by the anterior extremity of a quadruped.

that every feather should be constantly anointed with an oily secretion, which preserves it from being wetted, and which is copiously provided for that purpose by glands situated near the tail. The flexibility of the neck alone would have been insufficient for enabling the bird to bring its bill in contact with every feather, in order to distribute this fluid equally over them; and there is, accordingly, a farther provision made for the accomplishment of this object in the mode of articulation of the head with the neck. We have seen that, in fishes, and in most reptiles, this articulation consists of a ball and socket joint; a rounded tubercle of the occipital bone being received into a hemispherical depression in the first vertebra of the neck. In the mammalia the plan is changed, and there are two articular surfaces, one on each side of the spinal canal, formed on processes corresponding to the leaves of the first cranial vertebra, and assimilating it more to a hinge joint. In birds, however, where, as we have just seen, the most extensive lateral motions are required, the plan of the ball and socket joint is again resorted to; and the occipital bone is made to turn upon the atlas by a single pivot. So great is the freedom of motion in this joint, that the bird can readily turn its head completely back upon its neck, on either side.

As spinous or transverse processes of any length would have interfered with the flexions of the neck, we find scarcely a trace of these processes in the cervical vertebræ of birds. But another, and a still more important consideration was to be attended to in the construction of this part of the spine. It must be recollected that the spinal marrow passes down along the canal formed by the arches of the vertebræ, and that any pressure applied to its tender substance would instantly paralyze the whole body, and speedily put an end to life. Some extraordinary provision was therefore required to be made, in order to guard against the possibility of this accident occurring during the many violent contortions into which the column is liable to be thrown. This is accomplished in the simplest and most effectual manner by enlarging the diameter of the canal at the upper and lower part of each vertebra, while at the

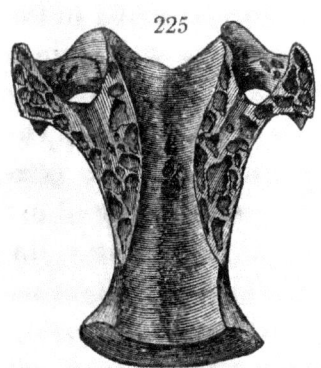

middle it remains of the usual size, so that the shape of the cavity, as is well seen in Fig. 225, which shows a vertical section of one of the cervical vertebræ of the ostrich, resembles that of an hour glass.* Thus a wide space is left at the junction of each successive vertebra, allowing

* For the specimen from which this engraving was made, I am indebted to the kindness of Mr. Owen.

of very considerable flexion, without reducing the diameter of the canal beyond that of the narrow portion, and therefore without producing compression of the spinal marrow. Mr. Earle found † that vertebræ united in this manner may be bent backwards to a right angle, and laterally to half a right angle, without injury to the enclosed nervous substance. The design of this structure is further evident from its not existing in the dorsal and lumbar portions of the spine, which admit of no motion whatever, and where there is no variation in the diameter of the spinal canal.

A plan entirely different is followed in the vertebræ of the back and loins. For the purpose of ensuring the proper actions of the wings, the great object here is to prevent motion, and to give all possible strength and security; and accordingly the whole of this portion of the spine, together with the sacrum, is consolidated into one piece. All the processes are largely developed, and pass obliquely from one vertebra to the next, mutually locking them together: and, in order most effectually to preclude the possibility of any flexion, the spinous processes, and sometimes even the bodies of the dorsal vertebræ are immoveably soldered together by ossific matter, so as to form one continuous bone.

The sacrum (v, Fig. 224) consists of the union of a great number of vertebræ, as many as twenty

† In the paper already quoted, p. 278.

being anchylosed together for this purpose; so that they form a bone of great length. The coccygeal vertebræ (q) are also numerous, but are compressed into a small space, and enjoy great latitude of motion, being subservient to the movements of the tail.

The ribs are numerous, and of considerable strength: they send out processes, which are directed backwards, passing over the next rib before they terminate, and giving very effectual support to the walls of the chest. The ribs are continued along the abdomen, and afford protection to the viscera in that cavity; and some arise even from the sacrum, and from the iliac bones. Those which are in front are united to the sternum (s) by means of sternal appendices, which are ossified, and appear as the continuations of the ribs, or as if the ribs were jointed in the middle.

The sternum is of enormous size, extending over a considerable part of the abdomen, and having a large perpendicular crest descending, like the keel of a ship, from its lower surface. The object of this great developement is to furnish extensive attachment to the large pectoral muscles employed to move the wings, and which, taken together, are generally heavier than the rest of the body. Considered with reference to all the other muscles, and to the weight of the body itself, these pectoral muscles are of enormous strength. The flap of a swan's wing is capable of breaking a man's leg; and a similar blow from an eagle has been known to be instantly fatal. The bat is the only instance, among the mammalia, where the sternum presents this peculiar *carinated*, or keel-like shape: and the purpose is evidently the same as in the bird.*

The scapula is generally a small and slender bone. The coracoid bone (K) is largely developed, and assumes much of the appearance of a clavicle.† But the real clavicles (c) are united below, where they join the fore part of the sternum, appearing as one bone, which, from its forked shape, has been denominated the *furcular bone*. In the fowl it is commonly known by the name of the *merry-thought*. This bone, placed at the origin of the wings, and stretching from the one to the other, is of great importance as constituting a firm basis for their support, and for securing their steadiness of action; and being, at the same time, very elastic, it tends to restore them to their proper situations, after they have been disturbed by any violent impulse.

---

* Notwithstanding the great modification the sternum has received in the bird, when compared with its form in the tortoise and the quadruped, we may still trace the same nine elements entering into its composition, though developed in very different proportions.

† Many have considered this bone as being the clavicle, and have regarded the furcular bone as a new bone, or supplementary clavicle: but all the analogies of position and of developement are in favour of the views stated in the text.

The wing of a bird does not, at first view, present much analogy with the fore extremity of a quadruped: but on a closer examination we find it to contain all the principal bones of the latter, though somewhat altered in shape, and still more changed in their functions. Yet still the same unity of plan, and perfect harmony of execution may be discerned in the mechanism of this refined instrument of a higher mode of progression.

The head of the humerus (H) has a compressed form; and in order to obtain great extent of motion, it is made to play by a very small cylindrical surface upon the scapula; thus admitting of the complete descent of the wing, unobstructed by any opposing process, but at the same time limiting its motion to one plane. It is connected below, by broad attachments, to the radius and ulna, forming with them a hinge joint. These latter bones are separate, and of great length, but so firmly united together by ligament as scarcely to have any motion on one another. The carpus (w), consists of two bones only, the one articulated with the radius, the other with the ulna. They move together as one piece; but, contrary to what takes place in quadrupeds, the movements are made from side to side, instead of their consisting of flexion and extension; this variation from the usual structure being for the purpose of folding down the joints of the wing, and bringing them close to the body. The metacarpus (m) consists originally of two bones, which soon become united into one at the upper part. On the radial side it has a process, derived perhaps from a third metacarpal bone, which is anchylosed at a still earlier period of ossification; and to this process a small pointed bone is connected, corresponding to a rudimental thumb (t). There are generally two fingers, of which the first exhibits traces of having been originally two bones: the inner finger consists of two or three long phalanges, and the outer one of a single phalanx: there is sometimes also a rudimental bone corresponding to a little finger. The degree of developement of these bones varies in different tribes of birds.

Feathers are attached to all these divisions of the limb, namely, to the humerus, the fore arm, the hand, and occasionally to the single phalanx of the thumb. The structure of feathers is calculated in an eminent degree to combine the qualities of lightness and of strength, which we elsewhere rarely find united. The horny materials of which the stem of the quill is made are tough, pliant, and elastic; and, as we have already seen, are disposed in the most advantageous manner for resisting flexion by being formed into a hollow cylinder. But the vane of the feather is still more artificially constructed; being composed of a number of flat threads, or filaments, so arranged as to oppose a much greater resistance to a force striking perpendicularly against their surface, than to one which is directed laterally; that is, in the plane of the stem. They derive this power of resistance from their flattened shape, which allows them to bend less easily in the direction of their flat surfaces than in any other; in the same way that a slip of card cannot easily be bent by a force acting in its own plane, though it easily yields to one at right angles to it. Now it is exactly in the direction in which they do not bend that the filaments of the feather have to encounter the resistance and impulse of the air. It is here that strength is wanted, and it is here that strength has been bestowed.

On examining the assemblage of these laminated filaments still more minutely, we find that they appear to adhere to one another. As we cannot perceive that they are united by any glutinous matter, it is evident that their connexion must be effected by some mechanism invisible to the unassisted eye. By the aid of the microscope the mystery is unravelled, and we discover the presence of a number of minute fibrils, arranged along the margin of the laminæ, and fitted to catch upon and clasp one another, whenever the laminæ are brought within a certain distance. The fibrils of a feather from the wing of a goose are represented magnified at a, a, b, b, Fig. 226, as they arise from the two sides of the edges of each lamina: they are exceedingly numerous, above a thousand being

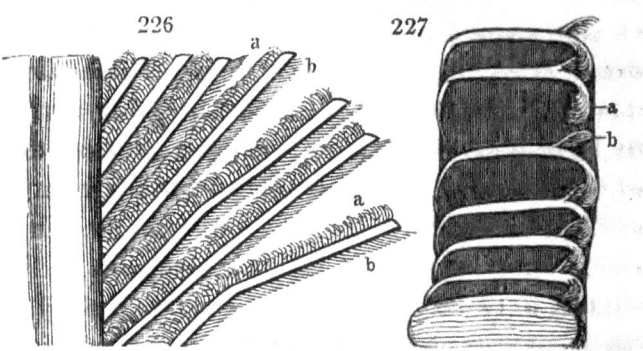

contained in the space of an inch; and they are of two kinds, each kind having a different form and curvature. Those marked a, a, which arise from the side next to the extremity of the feather are branched or tufted, and bend downwards, while those marked b, b, proceeding from the other side of the lamina, or that nearest the root of the feather, are shorter and firmer, and do not divide into branches, but are hooked at the extremities, and are directed upwards. When the two laminæ are brought close to one another, the long, curved fibrils of the one being carried over the short and straight fibrils of the other, both sets become entangled together; their crooked ends fastening into one another, just as the latch of a door falls into the cavity of the catch which is fixed in the door-post to receive it. The way in which this takes place will be readily perceived by making a section of the vane of a feather across the laminæ, and examining with a good microscope their cut edges, while they are gently separated from one another. The appearance they then present is exhibited in Fig. 227, which shows distinctly the form, direction, and relative positions of each set of fibrils, and the manner in which they lay hold of one another. This mechanism is repeated over every part of the feather, and constitutes a closely reticulated surface of great extent, admirably calculated to prevent the passage of the air through it, and to create by its motion that degree of resistance which it is intended the wing should encounter.* In feathers not intended for flight, as in those of the ostrich, the fibrils are altogether wanting: in those of the peacock's tail, the fibrils, though large, have not the construction which fits them for clasping those of the contiguous lamina; and in other instances they do so very imperfectly.

A construction so refined and artificial as the one I have been describing, and so perfectly

* A very clear account of the mechanism described in the text is given by Paley, in the 12th chapter of his " Natural Theology." Many of the minuter details I have supplied from my own observations with the microscope. The branched form of the upper fibrils, and the reticulated structure of the laminæ themselves, when viewed with a high magnifying power, are particularly beautiful microscopic objects.

adapted to the mechanical object which it is to answer, cannot be contemplated without the deepest feeling of admiration, and without the most eager curiosity to gain an insight into the elaborate processes, which, we cannot doubt, are employed by nature in the formation of a fabric so highly finished, and displaying such minute and curious workmanship. It is only very recently that we have been admitted to a close inspection of the complicated machinery, which is put in action in this branch of what may be called *organic architecture;* and certainly none is more fitted to call forth our profoundest wonder at the comprehensiveness of the vast scheme of divine providence, which extends its care equally to the perfect construction of the minutest and apparently most insignificant portions of the organized frame, whether it be the down of a thistle, the scales of a moth, or the fibrils of a feather, as well as to the completion of the larger and more important organs of vitality.

Every bird, on quitting the egg, is found to be covered on all parts, except the under side, with a kind of down, consisting of minute filaments, collected in tufts, and resembling in their arrangement the fibres of a camel-hair pencil. Each tuft contains about ten or twelve filaments, growing from the upper ends of bulbous roots implanted in the skin, and which are the rudiments of the organs that afterwards form the feathers, of which this down, serving the purpose of a first garment, hastily spread over the young bird, is but the precursor; for the tufts generally soon fall off and disappear, except in the rapacious tribes, as the eagle and the vulture, where they remain attached to the feathers for a considerable time.

While this temporary protection is given to the integument, extensive preparations are making underneath for furnishing a more effective raiment, adapted to the future wants of the bird. The apparatus by which the feathers are to be formed is gradually constructing; and its rudiments are receiving the necessary supply of nutrient juices, and of vessels for their circulation, together with their usual complement of nerves and absorbents. When first visible, this organ has the form of a very minute cone, attached by a filament proceeding from its base to one of the papillæ of the skin, and establishing its connexion with the living system. In the course of a few days, this cone has become elongated into a cylinder, with a pointed extremity, while its base is united to the skin by a more distinct bond of connexion formed by the enlarged vessels, which are supplying it with nourishment. It is in the interior of this cylinder that all the parts of the feather are constructed; their earliest rudiments being formed at the upper part, or apex of this organ; and the materials of the several parts of the feather being successively deposited and fashioned into their proper shapes in different places: for while the first laminæ are constructing in one portion of the cylinder, the next are only just beginning to be formed in another; and while the outer covering of the stem is growing from one membrane, the interior spongy tissue is deposited in other places, in various stages of softness or consolidation: so that the whole composes a system of operations, which may be said to resemble in its complication at least, although on a microscopic scale, an extensive manufactory. Hence will be readily understood how great must be the difficulty of tracing all the steps of these multifarious processes, which are carried on in so small a space: and this difficulty is much increased from the circumstance that the organ in which they take place is itself only developed as the work proceeds, its different parts being produced successively in proportion as they are wanted, and their form and structure undergoing frequent variation in the course of their developement.

The most elaborate, and apparently accurate researches on this intricate subject, are those lately undertaken by M. Frederick Cuvier, from whose memoir* I have selected the following abridged statement of the principal results of his

* Mémoires du Muséum, xiii. 327; and Annales des Sciences Naturelles, ix. 113.

FEATHERS OF BIRDS. 575

observations. It will be necessary in order to obtain a clear idea of the several steps of the process to be described, to advert to the structure of a feather in its finished state. For this purpose we need only examine a common feather, such as that represented in Fig. 228, where s is

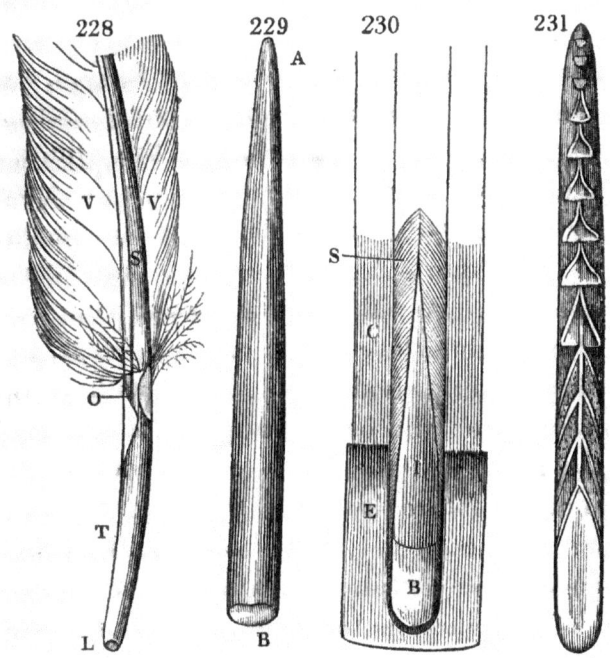

the posterior surface of the solid stem, which, it will be perceived, is divided into two parts by a longitudinal groove, and from either side of which proceed a series of laminæ, composing, with their fibrils, what is termed the vane of the feather (v). The lines from which these laminæ arise, approach one another at the lower part of the stem, till they meet at a point, where the longitudinal groove terminates, and where there is a small orifice (o), leading to the interior of the quill. From this part the transparent tubular portion of the quill (T) commences; and at its lower extremity (L) there exists a second, or lower orifice.

The entire organ which forms the feather, and which may be termed its *matrix*, is represented in Fig. 229, when it has attained the cylindric form already described; of which A is the apex, or conical part that rises above the cuticle, and B the base, by which it is attached to the corium, or true skin. A white line is seen running longitudinally the whole length of the cylinder, and another, exactly similar to it, is met with on the opposite side: the one corresponds in situation to the front, and the other to the back of the stem of the future feather. On laying open the matrix longitudinally, as is shown in Fig. 230, it is found to be composed of a sheath or capsule, and of a central pulpy mass, termed *the bulb*. The capsule consists of several membranous layers (c, E, s, I), which are more consolidated near the apex, and become gradually softer and more delicate, as we trace them towards the base of the matrix, where their formation is only beginning to take place.

The laminæ and their fibrils, the assemblage

of which constitutes the vane of the feather, are the parts which are first formed; and their construction is effected in the space between the outer capsule (c), and the central bulb (b), in a mode which is exceedingly remarkable, and different from that of the formation of any other organic product with which we are acquainted. Instead of growing from a base, like hairs, and other productions of the integuments, by successive depositions of layers, the materials which are to compose the laminæ are cast in moulds, where they harden and acquire the exact shape of the recipient cavities. The next object of our curiosity, then, is to learn the way in which these moulds are constructed; and on careful examination they appear to be formed by two striated membranes, the exterior one (e) enveloping the other (i), or interior membrane. These membranes are separated by a series of partitions, which commence at the edges of the longitudinal white band, seen in Fig. 229, and wind obliquely upwards till they reach the opposite longitudinal band already described, where they join a longitudinal partition which occupies a line answering to that posterior band. Thus they leave between them narrow spaces, which constitute so many compartments for the deposition, as in a mould, of the material of each lamina. The course of these channels, and their junction at the back of the matrix is seen at s, Fig. 230. It is exceedingly probable, though from the minuteness of the parts it is scarcely possible to obtain ocular demonstration of the fact, that the fibrils of the laminæ are formed in a similar manner, by being moulded in still more minute compartments, formed by transverse membranous partitions.

The proper office of the bulb, after it has supplied the materials for the formation of the laminæ, is to construct the stem of the feather, and unite the laminæ to its sides. For this purpose the anterior portion of the bulb deposits on its surface a plate of horny substance, while another plate is formed by the posterior part in the interior of the bulb. Thus the bulb becomes divided into two portions, one anterior and the other posterior. The former of these, after having finished the external plate, proceeds to form the spongy substance, which is to connect the two plates, and the posterior portion of the bulb embraces the inner plate, and gradually folds it inwards till its sides meet at the middle groove along the back of the stem. The anterior part of the bulb, during the process of filling up the stem, exhibits a series of conical shaped membranes, as is seen in the section, Fig. 231; the points of the cones being directed upwards, and their intervals being occupied by the spongy substance in different stages of consolidation, and more perfected in proportion as they are situated nearer the apex of the stem.

While the construction of the feather, in its different stages, is thus advancing from below, those parts which are completely formed, are rising above the surface of the skin, still enveloped in the capsule which originally protected them, but the upper portions of which, from the action of the air, and the obliteration of the vessels that nourished them, now decaying, shrivel and fall off in shreds, allowing the successive portions of the feather to come forth, and the laminæ to unfold themselves as they rise and assume their proper shapes. This successive evolution proceeds until the principal parts of the stem and of the vane are completed; and then a different kind of action takes place. The posterior part of the bulb now contracts itself, and bringing the edges of that surface of the stem closer together at length unites them at the superior orifice (o), Fig. 228; where the laminæ, which follow these lines, also terminate. Having thus performed the office assigned to it, it ceases to be nourished, and is incapable any longer of depositing a horny covering to the feather: all that remains of its substance is a thin membrane which adheres to the outside of the tubular part or barrel of the quill, and which must be scraped off before the latter can be used as a pen. The tubular part is the product of the anterior part of the bulb, which now ceases to deposit the spongy substance, but forms a transparent horny material over the whole of its external surface; but as it retires towards the root, it leaves a succession of very thin pellucid membranes, in the form of cones, which, when dried, form what is termed *the pith* of the quill. The last remnant of the bulb is seen in the slender ligament which passes through the lower orifice, and preserves the attachment of the feather to the skin. In process of time, this also decays, and the whole feather is cast off, preparatory to the formation of another, which in due season is to replace it. All the feathers are, in general, moulted annually, or even at shorter periods; and the same complicated process is again begun and completed by a new matrix produced for the occasion, every time a new feather is to be formed.

It is impossible, on reviewing these curious facts, not to be struck with the admirable art and foresight which are implied in all this long and complicated series of operations. While the bird was yet nourished by the fluids of the egg, the ground had already been prepared for its future plumage, and for the formation of instruments of flight. A temporary investment of down is in readiness to shelter the tender chicken from the rude impressions of the air, and an apparatus is preparing for the construction of the most refined instruments for clothing and for motion: first the scaffolding, as it may be called, is erected, by the help of which each portion is built up in succession, and in proper order. Nature's next care is to construct the vane, which is the part of the feather most essential to its office: and then to form the shaft, to which the vane is to be affixed, and from which it receives its support: lastly, she forms the barrel of the quill, which is prolonged for the purpose of converting it into a lever of sufficient length for the mechanical office it has to perform. In proportion as each structure is finished, she neglects not to remove the scaffolding which had been set up as a temporary structure; the membranes, with all their partitions, are carried away, the vascular pulp of the bulb is absorbed, and its place supplied by air, thus securing the utmost lightness, without any diminution of strength. Is it possible for any rational mind, after meditating upon these facts, to arrive at the persuasion that they are all the mere results of chance?

Several circumstances remain to be noticed respecting the structure and actions of the wings of birds. If we attend to the mode of their articulation with the scapula, we find it producing a motion oblique with regard to the axis of the body, so that the stroke which they give to the air is directed both downwards and backwards; and the bird, while moving forwards, is at the same time supported in opposition to the force of gravity. The different portions of the wing are likewise so disposed as to be contracted and folded together when the wing is drawn up, but fully expanded when it descends in order to strike the air. It is obvious that, without this provision, a great part of the motion acquired by the resistance of the air against the wing in its descent would have been lost by a counteracting resistance during its ascent. The disposition of the great feathers is such that they strike the air with their flat sides, but present only their edges in rising: what is called *feathering the oar* in rowing is a similar operation, performed with the same intention, and deriving its name from this resemblance.

As the inclination of the wing is chiefly backwards, the greatest part of the effect produced by its action is to move the body forwards. Birds of prey have a great obliquity of wing, and are consequently better formed for horizontal progressive motion, which is what they chiefly practise in pursuing their prey, than for a rapid perpendicular ascent. Those birds, on the contrary, which rise to great heights in a direction nearly vertical, such as the *Quail* and the *Lark*, have the wings so disposed as to strike directly downwards, without any obliquity whatsoever. For the same reason, birds rise better against the wind, which, acting upon the oblique surface presented by the wings during their flexion, contributes to the ascent of the body on the same principle that a kite is carried up into the air when retained in an oblique position. This circumstance is particularly observable in the ascent of birds of prey, whose wings have a great obliquity, and, when fully expanded, present a very large extent of surface.

The actions of the tail, which operates as a rudder, are useful chiefly in directing the flight. When the tail is short, this office is supplied by the legs, which are in that case generally very long; and being raised high and extended backwards in a straight line, are of considerable assistance in the steerage of the animal. In many birds, as in the wood-pecker, the tail is much employed as a support to the body in climbing trees. The caudal vertebræ are often numerous, but are short and compressed together; they are remarkable for the great developement of their transverse processes, and for having spinous processes both on their lower and upper sides. The last vertebra, instead of being cylindrical, has a broad carinated spine for the insertion of large feathers.

Birds could not, of course, be always on the wing; for a great expenditure of muscular power is constantly going on while they support themselves in the air. Occasional rest is necessary to them as well as to other animals, and means are accordingly provided by nature for their mechanical support and progressive motion while on land.

The anterior extremities having been exclusively appropriated to flight, and constructed with reference to the properties of the atmosphere, the offices of sustaining and of moving the body along the ground must be entrusted wholly to the hind limbs. The centre of gravity, before sustained by the wings, must now be brought over the new basis of support formed by the feet; or rather, as it is placed far forwards, the feet must be considerably advanced so as to be brought underneath that centre. But as the bones of the posterior extremity have their origin from the remote part of the pelvis, which is elongated backwards, at a considerable distance from the wings, it became necessary to lengthen some of their parts, and to bend their joints at very acute angles. We accordingly find that while nature, in the formation of the limb, has preserved an accordance with the vertebrated type, both as to the number of pieces which compose it, and as to their relative situations, she has deviated from the model of quadrupeds in giving much greater length to the division corresponding to the foot. At the same time that the foot is brought forwards, the toes are lengthened, and made to spread out so as to enclose a wide base, over which the centre of gravity is situated. The extent of this base is so considerable that a bird can, in general, support itself with ease upon a single foot, without danger of being overset by the unavoidable vacillations of its body.

The femur is short compared with the tibia, which is generally large, especially in the order of *Grallæ*, or wading birds: the fibula is exceedingly slender and always united, at its lower part, with the tibia; and there is a total deficiency of tarsal bones, except in the *Ostrich*, where rudiments of them may be traced. Already we have seen, in ruminant quadrupeds, that these bones have dwindled to a very small size: but here they have wholly disappeared. The long bone which succeeds to the tibia, though considered by some anatomists as the tarsus, is properly the metatarsal bone, and in the Grallæ is of great length. At its lower end it has three articulations, shaped like pullies, for the attachment of the three toes: there is besides, in almost all birds, a small rudiment of another metatarsal bone, on which is situated the fourth toe. The number of bones which compose each respective toe appears to be regulated by a uniform law. The innermost toe, which may be compared to a thumb, consists invariably of two bones: that which is next to it in the order of sequence has always three; that which follows has four; and the outermost toe has five bones: the claws in every case being affixed to the last joints, which have therefore been termed the *ungual bones*. This remarkable numercial relation among the several bones of the toes exists quite independently of their length.

There is one whole order of birds which are particularly fitted for climbing and perching upon trees, having the two middle toes parallel to each other, and the inner and outer toes turned back, so as to be opposed to them in their action. They are thus enabled to grasp objects with the greatest facility; having, in fact, two thumbs, which are opposable to the two fingers. They have been termed *Scansores*, or *Zygodactyli*. Almost all other birds have three toes before, and one behind.

From this enumeration it would appear as if Nature, in modifying the type of vertebrated animals to suit the purposes required in the bird, had purposely omitted one of the toes, which are usually five in number. But instances occur of birds, in which we may trace the rudiment of a fifth toe high upon the metatarsus, and upon its inner side. The spur of the cock may be regarded as having this origin. What confirms this view of the subject, is, that in those birds which have only three toes, namely, in the *Emu*, the *Cassowary*, and the *Rhea*, it is again the inner toe which disappears, leaving only the three outer toes, namely, those which have respectively three, four, and five phalanges. The

Ostrich has only two toes, one having four, and the other five phalanges; here, again, it is the innermost of the three former, that is, the one having three phalanges, which has been suppressed.*

A bird is capable of shifting the position of the centre of gravity of its body, according as circumstances require it, simply by advancing or drawing back its head. While flying, the neck is stretched forwards to the utmost, in order to bring the centre of gravity immediately under the origin of the wings, by which the body is then suspended. When birds stand upon their feet, they carry the head back as far as possible; so as to balance the body on the base of support. When preparing to sleep, they bring the centre of gravity still lower, by turning the head round and placing it under the wing. These motions of the head are again resorted to when the bird walks; and the centre of gravity is thus transferred alternately from one foot to the other: hence, in walking, the head of a bird is in constant motion; whilst the duck and other birds, whose legs are very short, have a waddling gait. It may be observed that the more perfectly predaceous birds are not the best formed

---

* The last bone of the outer toe of the ostrich is very small, and being usually lost in preparing the skeleton, has been overlooked by naturalists; but Dr. Grant has ascertained, by the careful dissection of a recent specimen, the existence of this fifth phalanx.

for walking; because, were they to use their feet for that purpose, their talons, which are required to be kept sharp for seizing and tearing their prey, would be blunted; and accordingly the eagle, when moving along the ground, supports itself partly by the motion of its wings.

In roosting, birds support themselves upon their perch by means of one leg only, the other being folded close to the body. They even maintain this attitude with greater ease and security than if they rested upon both feet. The true explanation of this curious fact was long ago given by Borelli. On tracing the tendons (T, T Fig. 233) of the muscles (M, M) which bend the claws, and enable them to grasp an object, we find them passing over the outer angles of each of the intervening joints, so that whenever these joints are bent, as shown in Fig. 234, those tendons are put upon the stretch, and mechanically, or without any action of the muscles, tend to close the foot. When the bird is on its perch, this effect is produced by the mere weight of the body, which, of course, tends to bend all the joints of the limb on which it rests; so that the greater that weight, the greater is the force with which the toes grasp the perch. All this takes place without muscular effort or volition on the part of the bird. It remains in this position with more security on one foot than it would have done by resting upon both; because in the latter case, the weight of the body, being divided between them, does not stretch the tendons sufficiently. In this position the bird not only sleeps in perfect security, but resists the impulse of the wind and the shaking of the bough.

The great length of the toes of birds enables them to stand steadily on one leg: and in this

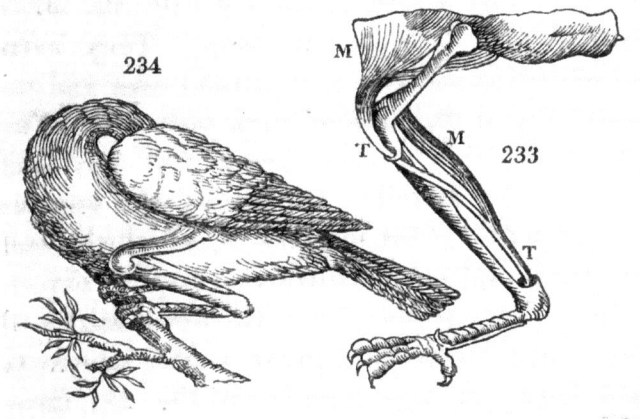

attitude many employ the other foot as a hand; especially parrots, whose head is too heavy to be readily brought to the ground. Some birds, which frequent the banks of rivers, are in the practice of holding a stone in one foot, while they rest upon the other: this contributes to increase their stability in two ways; first, it adds to the weight of the body, which is the force that stretches the tendons, and causes them to grasp the bough; and, secondly, it also lowers the centre of gravity.

The stork, and some other birds belonging to the same order, which sleep standing on one foot, have a curious mechanical contrivance for locking the joint of the tarsus, and preserving the leg in a state of extension without any muscular effort. The mechanism is such as to withstand the effect of the ordinary oscillations of the body, when the bird is reposing; but it is easily unlocked by a voluntary muscular exertion, when the limb is to be bent for progression. On these occasions the ball of the metatarsal bone is driven with some force into the socket of the tibia.*

I must content myself with this general view of the mechanism of birds; as it would exceed the limits within which I must confine myself, to enter more fully into the peculiarities which distinguish the different orders and families. Some of the more remarkable deviations from what may be considered as the standard conformation, may, however, for a moment arrest our attention.

The *Ostrich* is of all birds the one that presents the greatest number of exceptions to the general rules which appear to regulate the

* This mechanism is noticed by Dr. Macartney in the Transactions of the Royal Irish Academy, vol. xiii, p. 20, and is more fully described in Rees's Cyclopædia, Art. BIRD. He observes that both Cuvier and Duméril have committed an error in referring this peculiarity of structure to the knee instead of the tarsal joint.

conformation of birds, and in many of its peculiarities of structure it makes some approach to that which characterises the quadruped. Though this bird is provided with wings, it was evidently never intended that they should be used for the purposes of flight. Hence the chief muscular power has been bestowed on the legs, which are remarkably thick and strong, and well fitted for rapid progression. The sternum is flat and does not present the keel-like projection which is so remarkable in that of all other birds. The clavicles do not reach the sternum, nor even meet at the anterior part of the chest to form the furcular bone: for as the wings are not employed in flying, the usual office of that bone is not wanted. The form of the pelvis is different from the ordinary structure; for the pubic bones, which in all other birds are separated by an interval, here unite as they do in quadrupeds.

The feathers are unprovided with that elaborate apparatus of crotchets and fibres, which are universally met with in birds that fly. The filaments of the ostrich's feathers, in consequence of having none of these fibrils, hang loose and detached from one another, forming the fine hair or down, which, however ornamental as an article of dress, must be viewed, when considered physiologically, as a species of degeneracy in the structure of feathers.

The Penguin, in like manner, has a wing, which is, by its shortness, totally unfitted for raising the body in the air: it has, indeed, received a very different destination, being formed for swimming. In external form it resembles the anterior extremity of the turtle; but still we find it constructed on the model of the wings of birds; as if nature had bound herself by a law not to depart from the standard of organization, although the purpose of the structure is altogether changed. As penguins are intended for a maritime life, all their extremities are formed for swimming. Their legs are exceedingly short, and placed far backwards so that these birds are compelled, when resting on their feet on the shore, to raise their bodies in a perpendicular attitude in order to place the centre of gravity immediately above the base of support: a posture which gives them a strange and grotesque appearance.

I have already alluded to the lengthened legs and feet of the waders, the utility of which to birds frequenting marshy places, and shallow waters, is very obvious. Their legs are not covered with feathers, which would have been injured by continual exposure to wet. But birds of a truly aquatic nature, have their toes webbed, that is, united by a membrane, a mechanism which qualifies them to act as oars, and indeed gives them a great advantage over all artificial oars that have been constructed by human ingenuity; for as soon as the expanded foot has impelled the water behind it, the toes collapse, and while it is drawn forward it presents a very small surface to the opposing water. Their plumage is so constructed as to prevent the water from penetrating through it, and for the purpose of preserving it in this condition these birds are provided with an oily fluid, which they carefully spread over the whole surface of their bodies. The Swan, and many other water-fowls, employ their wings as sails, and are carried forwards on the water with considerable velocity, by the impulse of the wind.

Birds excel all other vertebrated animals in the energy of their muscular powers. The promptitude, the force, and the activity they display in all their movements, and the unwearied vigour with which they persevere for hours and days in the violent exertions required for flight, far exceed those of any quadruped, and implies a higher degree of irritability, dependent probably on the great extent of their respiratory functions, than is possessed by any other class of animals.

END OF VOL. I.

Milton Keynes UK
Ingram Content Group UK Ltd.
UKHW020847030424
440506UK00008B/1054